# Old West

*A Captivating Guide to the Wild West, Billy the Kid, Buffalo Bill, Seth Bullock, Davy Crockett, Annie Oakley, Jesse James, and Geronimo*

# Free Bonus from Captivating History
## (Available for a Limited time)

Hi History Lovers!

Now you have a chance to join our exclusive history list so you can get your first history ebook for free as well as discounts and a potential to get more history books for free! Simply visit the link below to join.

Captivatinghistory.com/ebook

Also, make sure to follow us on Facebook, Twitter and Youtube by searching for Captivating History.

# Contents

# Part 1: The Wild West

*A Captivating Guide to the American Old West, Including Stories of Famous Outlaws and Lawmen Such as Billy the Kid, Pat Garrett, Wyatt Earp, Wild Bill Hickok, and More*

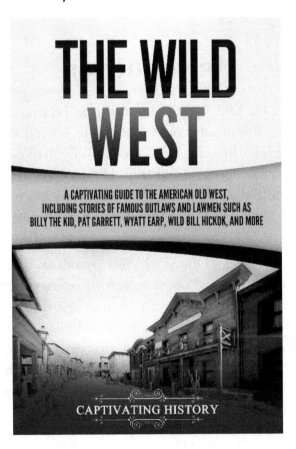

# Introduction

The story of the Old West is one that is as heartbreaking as it is exciting. It is a brilliantly colorful period in history, and its many icons have names that ring familiar even to modern ears: Billy the Kid, Lewis and Clark, Wild Bill Hickok, Wyatt Earp, Doc Holliday, and Buffalo Bill Cody. Yet, there is so much more to the tale of the Wild West than simply a pitched battle of outlaws versus lawmen.

In fact, the history of the Wild West extends far further into the past and encompasses so much more rich heritage than we might first expect. There is so much to learn, such as the Native Americans and what they were truly like and what they truly lost or how modern-day Texas and New Mexico were first explored and colonized by Spain. There were the mountain men who first explored the wilderness of the Northwest, gold rushes, buffalo hunters, and infamous outlaws who populated the American West 150 years ago.

It's a hard tale to hear at times and one that sometimes seems impossible to believe. There are times when the reality is even stranger than the tall tales. But the story of the Wild West holds vital importance for us today. We should not only enjoy the incredible and fascinating stories of the places and people that forged the United States into the country it is today but also relearn the hard lessons that our ancestors forgot. Lessons about true justice, human rights, and what it really means to be free.

The Wild West was a place where wilderness and freedom clashed. And its story is a breathtaking one.

# Chapter 1 – The Free West

*Illustration I: Plains people photographed in 1915*

Long before cowboys wielded six-shooters, bandanna-masked outlaws roamed the prairie, or courageous homesteaders eked out a living in some of the most inhospitable wilderness America had to offer, the West was a rich cultural tapestry, one that was all but destroyed by the arrival of European settlers.

For thousands of years, Americans lived, farmed, worshiped, played games, fell in love, built societies, and survived in the vast region known as the West. Their cultures, languages, and religions differed tremendously. Pre-Colombian America and the pre-frontier West teemed with human life.

Over 562 separate American tribes thrived throughout North America in pre-Colombian times; they spoke over 2,000 different languages and numbered some 60 million individuals. More languages were spoken in modern-day California alone than in the whole of Europe. These people built beautiful societies, practiced medicine, and had cultures and beliefs as elaborate and sophisticated as those of the Old World.

But they didn't have ships. And they didn't have gunpowder. And so, the Native Americans would be swept away in the face of colonization, leaving only a decimated handful of survivors. Entire tribes were wiped out by disease, while others were crushed by enslavement and war. Whole cultures, languages, and religions were simply wiped from the face of the earth.

Before that day, though, the West was filled with societies that built cities, made war, and created art. A long, long time before the West was ever known as being wild, it was free. This history focuses on the late 19th century, which was when this area of the United States was known as "the Wild West." But the late 19th century was also the time during which the native peoples were massacred. It would be remiss not to include a glimpse of what was lost in that lawless time.

### The Plains Culture

The vastness of the Great Plains, stretching from Canada to the Gulf of Mexico and from the Mississippi River to the Rockies, was almost unpopulated before the 18th century. In fact, the basis for the Native American stereotype that has been perpetuated in pop culture didn't even exist before European settlers came to North

America. There were no feather-dressed braves galloping bareback on horses as they hunted buffalo on the wild prairie back then.

Instead, the tiny, scattered handful of people who made the Great Plains their home were farmers and hunters who lived in quiet, lonely settlements and villages. There were far more fertile areas to be farmed in the vastness of North America, so the Plains were generally avoided. It was only when Europeans started pushing eastern natives out of the homelands they had lived in for generations that they started to wander westward, eventually ending up in the Plains. In fact, some of the most famously western tribes we know today didn't originate in the West at all. Tribes like the Sioux, Cheyenne, and Crow originated in the East and were forced to move to the Great Plains by the constant influx of European settlers.

Once on the Great Plains, many tribes attempted to carry on with their way of life, living in their quiet villages and tilling this far less fertile land. Hunting was a part of survival for them. Everything they killed was thoroughly utilized; every bit of skin, bone, meat, and hair would be used for food, clothing, equipment, or shelter. Many Plains tribes celebrated an annual Sun Dance during the summer solstice—a merry festival that is still celebrated today.

In fact, these people didn't have horses at all before their first encounters with Spanish traders in the 18$^{th}$ century. Despite the fact that the wild horse has become a symbol of the West and the frontier, these animals are actually not wild at all. Even the mustangs, which have been roaming the prairies for centuries, originated from domestic horses that escaped or were abandoned, making them feral, not wild. The Native Americans didn't capture their first horses from the wild; rather, they traded with the Spanish for them. And almost instantly, their lives and cultures were changed.

The horse changed transport for the people of that era as swiftly and surely as the invention of flight would do centuries later. Suddenly, the Plains cultures found their horizons broadened.

War and travel were revolutionized, and perhaps more than anything else, hunting changed completely. The Plains people had always venerated the buffalo as one of the most powerful and useful animals, but bringing down one of these enormous, swift beasts was all but impossible for a man on foot. On horseback, though, hunters could keep up not only with individual animals but also with the herds that migrated across the expanse of the Plains.

Over time, the buffalo became central to the Plains people's diet, lifestyle, and even religion. A single buffalo provided so much more than just its meat. Every single part of the buffalo could be utilized in some way, from its hide to its bones, and the Plains hunters revered this animal for its strength and usefulness. In fact, it soon became evident that hunting buffalo was much easier and more useful than attempting to farm the often-dry and infertile Plains. As a result, more and more Plains tribes abandoned their homes and quiet farms and began to live as nomads instead, wandering wherever the buffalo herds led them. Once, they had lived in small, cozy homes. Now, they had to resort to a lighter and more portable shelter to live in, and so, the teepee was born. It was constructed, of course, from buffalo hides.

By the time the West became a place that the Europeans wanted to invade and tame for themselves, the Plains cultures were unrecognizable compared to what they had been before the arrival of Europeans in North America. These people had been uprooted from their homes in the East, and then they even abandoned their villages on the Plains. Many trekked across the expanse of wilderness, following wherever the buffalo wherever led, and theirs was a life of total liberty.

Tragically, it would not remain that way for long.

### The Southwest Cultures

The people of the Southwest culture area lived mainly in an arid desert encompassing modern-day Arizona and New Mexico, but it also extended to Utah, Texas, Colorado, and even as far as Mexico itself. And despite the unforgiving desert sun, one of the Southwestern cultures became the very first farmers in America.

The Ancestral Puebloans, more correctly known as the Anasazi, were probably the first culture ever to attempt farming in the modern-day United States—and they were excellent at it. This tribe of former hunter-gatherers was the first culture to start growing corn, a crop that would become a staple all over the world in the centuries to come. In 2000 BCE, though, the Anasazi were the only people in North America growing anything at all, and corn became their staple diet for quite some time. In fact, this crop became so important to the Anasazi that it eventually featured in their creation myths. To them, corn was life.

It was also the only crop that would grow in the inhospitable conditions of the Southwest—that is, until another similar group of people developed one of the most sophisticated systems of pre-Colombian America. The Hohokam, too, farmed corn, but they had also grown used to the squash and beans that grew wild in some parts of the Southwest. However, these plants required far more water to grow than corn did. So, the Hohokam came up with a solution. They dug an incredibly intricate series of canals and formed an irrigation system that spanned thousands of miles, bringing life-giving water to the Southwest and creating fields where there had once been nothing but desert. This massive project, which reached its peak around 800 CE, must have been a huge undertaking. It would have required the cooperation of many different tribes, but the end result was breathtaking. Squash and beans brought some much-needed variety into the diet of the Hohokam, Anasazi, and Mogollon—collectively known as the Puebloans.

Soon, the Pueblo culture was built around farming. Instead of hunting, men tilled the fields. Whole villages would be involved in farming numerous fields, and soon, the villages began to grow. Since the Puebloans no longer needed to roam around the desert hunting and gathering, they began to dig in and build larger and larger towns. Using adobe and stone, they constructed the large buildings that would give them their name: "pueblo" is Spanish for "dwelling."

Eventually, Pueblo towns grew until they could hold thousands of occupants, and their buildings became large and intricate, with multiple stories and many different rooms. In fact, some Pueblo homes were as large as some modern-day apartment buildings. Each town would also have a central ceremonial building known as a kiva, which was a gathering place for rituals and other sacred festivals. The Puebloans evolved into different tribes, among them being the Hopi, Zuni, Yuma, and Yaqui.

These large towns traded extensively with one another, not only in basic necessities for survival but also in all kinds of trinkets and luxuries, like seashells or birds. A need arose for a trade center that could unify the tribes and make business easier. As a result, Chaco Canyon became a bustling hub for trade, with over four hundred miles of roads leading to the canyon from places as distant as California, Central America, and the Rocky Mountains.

However, around the early 12th century, disaster began to strike the Puebloans. This was an advanced and sophisticated people, but they had focused their attention on building towns, trade, and farms, not weapons. Even if they had weapons, the first disasters to befall them were natural. Drought shriveled their crops for decades in the 12th century, which was followed by a terrible flood that wiped away much of the Hohokams' life-giving irrigation system in the mid-14th century. Some canals survived—and can still be seen to this day—but it was the beginning of the end for the Puebloans.

As a result, when the Spanish arrived in the Southwest, most of the Anasazi and Hohokam had abandoned the area completely. The handful of Yaqui, Yuma, Hopi, and Zuni that remained could do little against the gun-wielding foreigners who decided that they were entitled to the land that the Puebloans had been farming for centuries, and they were overwhelmed and enslaved. Now, they discovered a very different type of farming. Entire communities once worked together to take care of the land, the crops, and one another. But the Spanish farmed on vast fields under the encomienda system. These enormous tracts of lands were owned by men who might never put their hands to the soil. These men lived in the lap of luxury in their mansions instead, and the Puebloans were forced to work on the fields. No one lasted long.

By the time Anglo-Americans began to arrive in the Southwest, the Puebloans had been all but exterminated by the Spanish; in fact, only a handful of Pueblo people remain in New Mexico today. The remaining cultures were very different from the sophisticated Puebloans. These were wild, warlike, and nomadic peoples: the Navajo and Apache.

Where the Puebloans had been farming the Southwest for over a thousand years before the area was known as part of the "Wild West," the Navajo and Apache had only arrived around the 13th century. Unlike the Puebloans, they had little interest in agriculture and didn't build permanent dwellings. Instead, they roamed around the Southwest, looking for prey to hunt, food to gather, and crops to steal. These nomadic tribes became a thorn in the side of the Puebloans since they raided their towns and made off with their crops.

The Navajo and Apache lived in mud and bark dwellings called hogans, which were always built to face toward the east and the rising sun. Perhaps because of their nomadic nature, they were able to escape the Spanish, and they still roamed warily around the Southwest by the time Americans arrived in the area in the 19th century.

### The West Culture

The rest of the West was populated by a diverse array of tribes, particularly in the rich and fertile Great Basin. In fact, modern-day California alone contained over one hundred individual tribes. These tribes would be unified by their beliefs and lifestyles, but they were further divided into tribelets, which were small groups of people who lived in close proximity.

Unlike the Puebloans, most cultures of the West were primarily hunter-gatherers; thus, they lived on a far healthier diet than their agriculturally-minded counterparts. While the Puebloans lived almost exclusively on three staple foods, the people of the West enjoyed the wonderful variety of an entirely natural diet. They gathered all kinds of wild plants and hunted many different kinds of animals, from the mighty buffalo down to snakes, lizards, and rodents.

In fact, one of the cornerstones of their diet was salmon, and as a result, the western tribes' population was most dense around rivers. Using traps, spears, or harpoons, as well as fishing from canoes, these people caught fresh salmon every season. As the buffalo was to the people of the Plains, so was the salmon to the people of the West—an almost sacred creature, part of the very lifeblood of civilization. It is a recurring theme in the beliefs of these pre-Colombian peoples that they venerated and revered— even worshiped—the creatures that gave them sustenance, which was in sharp contrast to the attitude of the average European of that era toward a pig or a cow.

Another important part of their diet was acorns. While most of a raw acorn is toxic, the interior can be hollowed out and ground into a flour that can be made into flat cakes or bread. Acorns were also used as currency, along with seashells, in the bustling trade that took place among these diverse and distinct tribes.

While almost none of these tribes practiced agriculture, many lived in areas that were so fertile that they could live in permanent villages even though they hunted and gathered instead of farming. Others were nomadic, going wherever they could find enough resources, and they lived in portable homes made of wood, bark, and other light materials. These dwellings were called wikiups or wigwams.

Regardless of whether they roamed or stayed, many of these tribes had a very intricate society, which included a strict hierarchy. These societies were so strict, in fact, that they may have practiced slavery long before Europeans shipped Africans across the Atlantic. The Chinook tribe, in particular, is known to have practiced slavery. While they didn't have fields to put their slaves to work in, they were adept hunters who would frequently bring down huge quarries such as the ubiquitous buffalo. Slaves were useful during buffalo season to process these enormous animals, so they were thoroughly utilized by the Chinook.

## The Great Dying

Prior to the 16th century, the United States was populated by a dizzying variety of people. But colonization changed all that.

Just a few centuries after the arrival of Christopher Columbus, fields would be turned into wastelands. Teepees, hogans, wikiups, and pueblos would be burned to the ground. Vibrant cultures and religions would be wiped from the earth. And where large towns of people had thrived, traded, and enjoyed their freedom, there would be nothing but silence.

It was known in that time as the Great Dying: the relentless and devastating epidemics brought on in waves by the introduction of European diseases into a world where there was no smallpox, plague, or even the flu. The European settlers flooding into the New World carried these illnesses without being sick, as they were immune to them. But the Native Americans' immune systems had no way of fighting these diseases, and the contagions spread at a horrifying pace among these people, wiping out entire villages and even whole tribes.

While war, slavery, and other cruelties committed by the colonists certainly contributed to the appalling rate at which Native Americans died as colonization began, disease was undoubtedly the main culprit. And the Great Dying was one of the most appalling events in human history. Ninety percent of the pre-

Colombian population was wiped out by the middle of the 17$^{th}$ century. The figure is absolutely staggering, almost incomprehensible. The Great Dying killed 10 percent of the global population—a figure so vast that it actually caused global cooling at the beginning of the 17$^{th}$ century, sparking harsh winters and famines that would have staggering repercussions in Europe and Asia.

In fact, the only known event in human history that killed more people is World War II. Eight million people died during that dark time, compared with the fifty-six million Native Americans that died during early colonization.

By the time colonists began to arrive in what we know as the Wild West, the greatest tragedy of all had already taken place. The vibrant cultures, bustling trade routes, adobe towns, and ancestral beliefs of the people who originally lived in the West had been reduced to almost nothing. The fields lay empty. The towns lay abandoned. And the West was no longer free.

But soon, it would become wild. And the Wild West would be one of the most iconic chapters in all of American history.

# Chapter 2 – Early Exploration and Spanish Settlement

As the Age of Exploration reached its peak, and the world became more and more connected, the West would ultimately become one of the last European frontiers. But before the East was even fully colonized, there were bands of intrepid—and occasionally greedy and opportunistic—explorers making their way into the beautiful wilderness of the West. One of the very first was Francisco Vázquez de Coronado.

### The Seven Golden Cities of Cíbola

Coronado had always been an opportunist.

It would seem, considering his early life, that he wouldn't have to be. He was born to a wealthy, noble Spanish family in 1510, and he grew up educated and well cared for. But Coronado had one stroke of bad luck: he wasn't the eldest son. As a result, none of the wealth and opulence that surrounded him growing up would ever belong to him, and so, Coronado had to find his own way in the world.

As for many other young European men of the time, the New World seemed to be the ideal place to seek a fortune. When Coronado's family connections led him to Antonio de Mendoza, who had just been appointed as viceroy over New Spain, he jumped at the chance to travel with Mendoza as his assistant and take his chances in Central America.

Mendoza and Coronado traveled to New Spain—modern-day Mexico—in 1535, and Coronado wasted no time in building himself a life there. He married well in 1537, inheriting a considerable chunk of wealth from his new bride; that same year, he was involved in dealing with a number of slave rebellions by the hapless African and Native American people who had been subjugated into slavery by the Spanish. Coronado was successful in quelling these uprisings. This won him Mendoza's respect, and by 1538, Coronado could have been very comfortable with his life. He had been made the governor of Nueva Galicia. He was well-off and respected, and things were going just fine for him in the New World.

But Coronado still wasn't satisfied. He wanted more—more wealth and more fame. So, when explorers and Native Americans started to come to Nueva Galicia with stories of mind-boggling wealth, Coronado was listening.

The stories all centered around that most coveted of the New World's natural resources: gold. Ironically, it was the one resource that most Native American tribes couldn't care less about. They said that there were entire cities flowing with gold up north, cities of unimaginable riches, ripe for the taking. They were called the Seven Golden Cities of Cíbola, and whoever discovered them would be rich beyond all imagination.

It didn't occur to Coronado or Mendoza that the Seven Golden Cities might rightfully belong to the people who lived in them. In their eyes, the New World's wealth was there for them to take. What was more, none of the myths suggested that the Golden Cities had been built by the native people who had been living there for so many centuries. Instead, they suggested that Spanish bishops fleeing Muslim invasions in the Middle Ages had somehow made their way to North America and built the Golden Cities.

Even after the terrible fall of the wealthy city of Tenochtitlán, the capital of the Aztec Empire, the Spanish still arrogantly believed that Native Americans were uneducated, uncultured, and incapable of building large cities or societies.

No matter how far-fetched the stories might have seemed, Coronado met with numerous people who seemed able to confirm the reports about the Golden Cities. Excited about the idea, he told Mendoza everything. This was an era when exploration was key to the future wealth of European nations. Mendoza was on board with launching an expedition to the north to look for the Seven Golden Cities, but he needed investors. Coronado was more than willing to chip in. He poured most of his wife's wealth into the expedition, and by February 1540, he was ready to go.

Coronado's expedition left Nueva Galicia with about 1,300 men; 300 of them were Spanish, while the rest were Native American—it is possible they were enslaved. Their guides led them northward into the desert of the modern-day Southwest. They traveled through the wilderness for days that turned into weeks that turned into months. But eventually, their guides told them that they were not far away. Soon, they would feast their eyes on cities composed of glimmering gold.

In June, four months after leaving home, the tired expedition had trekked over a thousand miles through the inhospitable desert. Their guides finally told them that they were approaching the first of the Golden Cities; its name was Hawikuh. Coronado and his men must have gained an extra spring in their step, a little hope now that they believed they were so close to their goal. Surely all the exhaustion, thirst, and suffering of the past four months would be worth it once they found the unimaginable wealth of a golden city.

But when Hawikuh finally came into view through the shimmering desert mirage, it was nothing like what Coronado had expected.

There was no gold in Hawikuh. The walls, instead, were made of adobe. There were no jewels; just laughter, food, and verdant farmland stretching in every direction. There was no silver, no diamonds, no rubies. This was no golden city—it was a Zuni city, home to a Pueblo tribe. The treasures held in the city of Hawikuh were very different than the gemstones and precious metals that Coronado desired. Hawikuh contained a close-knit community, thriving farms, a unique culture, and happy families. Perhaps one could argue that the treasures the city contained were beyond the value of mere metals or jewels.

But to Coronado, the sight of the tall adobe buildings towering against the desert sun was bitterly disappointing. He had spent his entire life chasing money, and Hawikuh held none.

Still, even if the streets of Hawikuh were not paved with gold, Coronado still wanted it for his own; he still wanted to have something to show for his efforts. Accordingly, he wasted no time in attacking the town. The Zunis were farmers, not warriors, and when Coronado's hundreds of men swept down upon the town with their firearms and bayonets, they put up only a brief fight. The Zuni had hardly any weapons to speak of; for a short while, they fought with what they had, throwing stones at the attacking colonists. One of these struck Coronado himself, wounding him, but the attack was far from dissuaded by this eventuality. The Zunis fled into the inhospitable desert, and the colonists claimed Hawikuh for their own, capturing and enslaving as many of the Zunis as they could.

Coronado never did find the fabled Golden Cities because they never existed. Instead, he spent the rest of the summer in Hawikuh recovering from his injuries, and his men explored parts of New Mexico and Colorado, going as far as the Grand Canyon itself. By winter, he decided that Hawikuh hadn't been worth it after all. His men lacked the knowledge to thrive here as the Zunis had done for generations. They moved to a new base on the Rio Grande for the winter, did a little more exploring in modern-day Texas when the winter was over, and eventually returned to Nueva Galicia in 1542.

Mendoza was bitterly disappointed in Coronado's efforts. Coronado returned with no news of fabulous natural resources, riches, or fame. In fact, he would only hold his position as governor until 1544, when Mendoza removed him from the position.

Ultimately, Coronado's expedition was considered a dismal failure since it didn't bring in any money for the Spanish government. However, he was the first European to explore much of modern-day New Mexico, along with parts of Texas, Kansas, and Colorado. One of his men became the first European to ever lay eyes on the Grand Canyon itself. As far as we know, Coronado was the first European to explore the American West.

### Francis Drake and San Francisco

If Coronado was a failure in regards to exploration, Francis Drake was a golden child.

His origins were improbable for a man who would become one of the most influential explorers in human history. Drake grew up as a commoner, the son of a farmer, preacher, and possibly petty criminal. His Protestant family was forced to move from his birthplace in Devon, possibly because of their religion or because of his father's nefarious ways. They ended up living in Kent in—of all things—an old, abandoned ship.

While there is little doubt that Drake's mother must have hated raising her twelve sons in the belly of an unseaworthy vessel, for young Francis, the ship was an utterly enchanting thing. He fell in love with everything about it, from bows to rigging to bowsprit to stern, and it wasn't long before he took an apprenticeship with a sailor. By the time he was twenty years old—sometime in the 1560s or early 1570s—Drake inherited a ship from his master. And so, his life on the open seas began.

Drake would eventually be hired by Queen Elizabeth I, a generally peaceable monarch who avoided conflict where possible, but she still wanted to cash in on the New World's treasures and make her mark in the Age of Exploration. While she had long been avoiding open war with the Spanish (the Anglo-Spanish War had been simmering between the two nations for decades), she was certainly not above plundering their ships for New World treasures. Accordingly, the queen hired Drake as a buccaneer, and he began to voyage the open seas and raid Spanish ships and trade ports at every possible opportunity.

In 1577, Drake was sent out with an entire fleet of ships: five, to be exact, including the most famous of them all, the *Golden Hind*. He headed for the Pacific side of South America, determined to plunder the wealthy Spaniards there. Two of his ships had to remain there, but Drake made his way north up the Strait of Magellan with the other three, raiding and pirating merrily as he went.

While it wasn't long before Drake's ships were filled with gold, silver, and other treasures, storms began to batter the *Golden Hind* and her companions. It wasn't long before one ship had no choice but to turn back, and it would eventually limp back across the sea to England, badly damaged. The other was not so lucky. In one of the chaotic storms, she was wrecked, and the ship, her treasures, and many of her crew were lost to the devastating force of the American seas.

Only the *Golden Hind* was left, but Drake was undaunted, butting his way beyond Spanish territories and into the waters along the western coast of North America. He was seeking the fabled Northeast Passage, the very same thing that Christopher Columbus had been looking for when he stumbled upon the New World nearly a century before. But there was none to be found. Drake didn't know yet the vastness of the continent that lay between him and Asia, but he did try to map much of it. Decades later, Drake's maps of this coastline would assist the Pilgrims in their search for

Plymouth Harbor. In fact, in 1580, Drake even explored Plymouth Harbor itself, nearly forty years before the *Mayflower* would ever anchor there.

Before finding Plymouth Harbor, though, Drake would explore many other lands, and one of those turned out to be the first western state to be claimed by an Englishman. He had sailed all the way around South America and headed up the western side of North America, becoming one of the first explorers ever to do so. In fact, Drake sailed all the way up to modern-day Washington State before he decided to turn around. On his way back, in 1579, the *Golden Hind* was desperate for some repairs. He sought a suitable bay to anchor in while he put his ship back together, eventually sailing into a little harbor that would eventually be part of modern-day California.

Together with his crew, which included an African woman who was most likely a slave, Drake became the first Englishman to set foot in the American West, and he was likely the first European ever to walk on the soil of modern-day California. The harbor was located near the spot where the city of San Francisco would eventually be founded. For now, it was a beautiful, pristine wilderness populated by a glorious abundance of Native American cultures.

Luckily for them, Drake didn't intend to conquer anything inland. He was bent on getting back to his ship, as he was forever called by the open sea. Instead, he merely staked England's claim on this part of the New World, naming it Nova Albion, and then sailed off again.

Drake's voyage would ultimately take him all the way around the Cape of Good Hope before he returned back to London, becoming the second person in history (after the Portuguese explorer Ferdinand Magellan) to circumnavigate the globe. The *Golden Hind* made her way into home waters in 1580, and the following year, Drake was knighted for his feats of navigation and exploration.

## Nuevo México

While the English would focus their colonial efforts on what is now the eastern United States, pouring their effort and energy into settlements like Jamestown and Plymouth, the Spanish were the first to establish a European colony in what would become the Wild West. The growth and role of Hispanic culture in the Old West have been much neglected in favor of the stereotypical American cowboy, but in reality, the Spanish were subjugating the West long before the California Gold Rush.

After the doomed expedition of Francisco Coronado, a slow trickle of Spanish colonists nonetheless began to move northward from modern-day Mexico. The ever-expanding population was always seeking somewhere to go, and while kings and governments were focused on finding untold wealth and riches on the frontier, most of the people moving northward were just ordinary families looking for a bit of fertile land to farm. Following the Rio Grande's abundant banks, knots of settlers began to eke out a living for themselves wherever they could. They were encouraged to do so by the government, but they were not particularly supported in a military capacity.

Still, this was all just a disorganized trickle before the arrival of one of the Old West's first dreadful villains: Juan de Oñate.

Oñate had been born in Mexico, then known as New Spain, to noble Spanish parents, and accordingly, he was both wealthy and well-trained in warfare. This made him the ideal candidate to become the first governor of the territory that Coronado had explored. It was time for the Spanish to marshal their people's efforts to subdue the Native Americans and take over their lands, and the ruthless Oñate would lead these efforts.

With a large band of missionaries, soldiers, and settlers, Oñate left New Spain in 1598 for the territory that had been dubbed Nuevo México. If the native people of the land were worried by the sight of real soldiers with armor and weapons flooding toward them, they had a right to be. Oñate would prove to be both greedy and cruel, even by the standards of colonial America.

After conquering the hapless Pueblo town of Ohkay Owingeh, Oñate established Nuevo México's first capital there and renamed it San Juan de los Caballeros. The Hispanic population there rapidly began to grow. People flooded into this new land, driven by hope for more natural resources and wealth, as well as by a hope to Christianize the Native Americans of the area. But as it turned out, Oñate's men would be far from peaceful missionaries spreading the word. Instead, Oñate actively encouraged his settlers to mistreat the Puebloans. He wanted them to oppress these native people and demand tribute from them, and it wasn't long before opportunistic settlers took full advantage of this.

Oñate's soldiers were particularly brutal. They physically mistreated and even killed Puebloans at will, with Oñate's encouragement always driving them on. Eventually, this resulted in the Acoma Massacre in the fall of 1598.

This was still early on in the development of Oñate's colony of Nuevo México, and there was no way that the Spanish could survive without the help of the Puebloans. Often, this meant simply enslaving them, but the Spanish also engaged in trade with some of the tribes. This trade was seldom ever a good thing, as was made abundantly clear to the Acoma Puebloans when a group of Oñate's men visited their town wanting to buy stored food for the winter. Adept farmers though the Acoma were, they had only stored enough food for their own people, so they declined to trade with the Spanish. When the Spanish grew angry and violent, the Acoma retaliated, capturing and killing twelve Spaniards, including Oñate's nephew.

Of course, Oñate did not take kindly to this act of violence. In January 1599, when the worst of the winter was over, he declared that the Acoma had been acting in rebellion and that the insurrection needed to be stopped immediately. He sent his soldiers to attack the Acoma, and the event that ensued was no battle. It was a slaughter. The Acoma had been able to stand up to the small band of unsuspecting Spanish who had come to take their food, but this was more than any of them could stand against. Blood flowed, staining the desert sand, and when it was over, around one thousand Acoma were dead. It was the first massacre of Native Americans by colonists in the Old West, and horrifically, it would not be the last. The surviving Acoma were enslaved, and the adult men had their toes brutally amputated in an attempt to disgrace them and break their spirits.

Today, Acoma Puebloans still live in New Mexico, with their population now numbering around five thousand.

The Puebloans, however, were not the only people to suffer at Oñate's hands. He was cruel and oppressive to his colonists as well. When the harsh conditions of Nuevo México forced some colonists to abandon San Juan de los Caballeros and head back to New Spain instead, Oñate reacted violently. He sent his soldiers after these people, labeling them as deserters, and had them beheaded.

As a result, when King Philip II of Spain got wind of Oñate's butcher of the Puebloans and colonists alike in 1606, Oñate found himself on trial for his cruelty. While he would continue in his position as governor until 1610, his days were numbered.

During the twelve years of his rule in Nuevo México, Oñate established the Province of Santa Fé de Nuevo México, with its capital numbering around two hundred colonists by 1610. In the later years of his governorship, Oñate led a small expedition eastward in the hopes of discovering another fabled golden city. These explorers made it all the way to the Great Plains, exploring parts of modern-day Oklahoma, Texas, and Kansas, but they never did find any golden cities. Eventually, attacks by wary natives of the region forced them to turn back. In 1605, Oñate launched another expedition and followed the Colorado River all the way to the Gulf of California. This was land that had already been claimed by the

British Crown, even though there were no colonists living there at that point.

Ultimately, Oñate's cruelties eventually caught up with him. His position as governor was taken away from him in 1610, and he was entirely exiled from Nuevo México. Although he was forced to return to New Spain, Oñate nonetheless still managed to gain positions of power back in the Old World.

That left Nuevo México without a governor. While Oñate had requested that the governorship be given to his son, the Spanish viceroy had had more than enough of Oñate and his troubles. He firmly informed Oñate that another replacement had already been found. This was a Spanish-born noble named Don Pedro de Peralta, and he was already on his way to San Juan de los Caballeros by the time Oñate was getting ready to leave.

Peralta was well aware that Oñate had caused chaos and division with his tyrannical ways in Nuevo México, and he would have his work cut out for him if he wanted to unify the colony and help it thrive. Accordingly, Peralta made an effort to be more diplomatic than his predecessor. He arrived in the capital with only twenty men accompanying him: twelve soldiers and eight Franciscan monks. Peralta desired prosperity for the Spanish colony, but he was willing to gain it peacefully.

As a result, Peralta proved far more successful than Oñate. His first decision was that the capital at San Juan de los Caballeros was situated in a terrible position. The soil was dry and infertile there, and colonists were struggling to scratch out an existence in the desert even though there was an expanse of beautiful, fertile land just thirty miles away, the perfect place to establish a new capital. Oñate had recognized this fact, too, and drew up plans for building another city in this better, more prosperous position.

While some colonists would remain at San Juan de los Caballeros, which today exists once again as Ohkay Owingeh, Peralta wasted no time in building a new capital. By the end of

1610, he had already made a good start on building a new city. The center of the city was a church, a sturdy adobe building named the San Miguel Church, which still stands today more than four hundred years later as the oldest church in the United States, predating the King James Bible. Peralta had also started building his Palace of the Governors, which was completed in 1612; today, it remains the oldest US government building still in use.

The city itself was named La Villa Real de Santa Fé de San Francisco de Asís (the Royal Town of the Holy Faith of Saint Francis of Assisi), and it is known today as Santa Fe. It is the third oldest town in the entire United States of America, with only St. Augustine, Florida, and Jamestown, Virginia, predating it by a few years. Santa Fe is also the oldest state capital in the United States. Peralta made it the state capital of Nuevo México during his time as governor, and it is still the capital of New Mexico today.

Peralta himself would eventually be accused of cruelty to the Native Americans just as Oñate had been. He spent a year in prison because of this, but he was ultimately found to be innocent. He would spend many years governing Nuevo México, only resigning in 1654 when he was very old. His governorship ushered in a time of comparative peace in Nuevo México, where colonists thrived and violence toward the Puebloans was generally low. However, Puebloans were still stripped of their rights and had many of their possessions taken from them. A few decades after Peralta left Nuevo México for good, these tensions inevitably bubbled over into open revolt.

### The Pueblo Revolt

Known as the "first American revolution," the Pueblo Revolt of 1680 started with Spanish conquistadors' determination to stamp out any vestige of the Puebloans' ancestral religion.

Po'Pay, a holy man and war captain from Ohkay Owingeh, was a victim of this religious persecution. He had always been determined to cling to the old ways and preserve the culture of his people, but the Spanish were bent on Christianization. Sometime in the late 1670s, Juan Francisco Treviño, the governor of Nuevo México at the time, ordered that all Pueblo holy men be captured and executed. Po'Pay was one of them. While he was not killed, he was brutally beaten in front of all his people. They could only watch in horrified silence as one of their most respected community members was struck again and again with a whip.

The experience only fueled Po'Pay's rising resentment toward the Spanish, a resentment shared by other Puebloans for obvious reasons. Along with his tireless campaign to preserve the ancestral Pueblo beliefs, Po'Pay also started reaching out to like-minded people—people who might even remember a time before the Spanish culture began to take over the Puebloans' world. People who wanted things to go back to the way they used to be, before the conquistadors came. And Po'Pay was the leader who wanted to make that happen.

Setting up a base in Taos Pueblo near Santa Fe, Po'Pay started meeting with more and more people, even involving some leaders from the Apache and Navajo tribes who had been the Puebloans' enemies. While the Apache and Navajo did not see their towns captured and used by the Spanish as the Puebloans did, their way of life was being threatened too, and they did not take kindly to the Spanish presence. They were willing to unite with the Puebloans, no matter their differences if it meant they could get rid of the Spanish.

Po'Pay told his followers that if they succeeded in driving the Spanish and Christianity out of their homeland, it would bring an end to the drought that had been plaguing Nuevo México for several years by that point. The powers of the Pueblo religion, he told them, would reward them for returning to the old ways by sending rain on their lands again. This was a powerful factor that convinced many Puebloans to join the rebellion. The drought would have made life difficult enough, even without the oppressive Spanish regime, as the Puebloans were expected to produce food for the Spanish as well as for themselves, and they were often punished if they failed to meet the expectations of the Spanish.

After the long, dry summer of 1680, with a meager harvest on the horizon, Po'Pay started planning the final stages of the rebellion. Several men were selected to carry a secret message throughout Santa Fe and the surrounding settlements. Each carried a knotted cord in full view, and every day, one knot was undone. When there were no more knots in the cord, the rebellion would begin.

That day was August 11ᵗʰ, 1680. Santa Fe was running very low on food; the harvest had not yet begun. That was when the Puebloans struck. They laid siege to Santa Fe, determined to starve out the Spanish inside the city, and launched raids on the settlements outside the city, where they were aided by the experienced Apache and Navajo. Over four hundred Spaniards were killed that day, many of them innocent families and children, and Santa Fe was locked in the siege for nine long days. Food had been scarce enough even before the siege; now, people were actively starving to death.

After the Spanish executed a desperate attack on the Puebloans, breaking through their ranks just enough to open a way to flee, the entire Spanish population of Santa Fe—then numbering around two thousand—bolted south along the Rio Grande, heading back toward the safety of New Spain. To their surprise, the Puebloans did not pursue them. They only followed them until they had left northern Nuevo México behind. Po'Pay's objective was not to massacre the Spanish. He just wanted his people's towns and lands back.

And at first, it seemed as though Po'Pay had been successful. The Spanish of Santa Fe resettled in other parts of Nuevo México, and for twelve years, Puebloans once again enjoyed their city as free people. They burned down the churches, slaughtered all the European livestock, and even cut down the fruit trees that the Spanish had planted. Po'Pay was determined to return life to the way it had been before the Spanish had ever come to the land of the Puebloans.

Po'Pay himself, however, would not remain in command of the Puebloans for those full twelve years. One year after the rebellion, the people had grown discontent with him as their leader. The greatest issue was that the rains Po'Pay had promised never did come. The sky remained shut up, as empty and hard as stone, and the continued drought increased the people's hunger. The Spanish were gone, but the Puebloans were still starving. Accordingly, the fickle Apache and Navajo, who had assisted in the rebellion, returned to their old ways of raiding and stealing from the Puebloans. Po'Pay was deposed, and the Puebloans tried to scrape together a life for themselves once again, despite the drought.

It was not to be. In 1692, when the Puebloans were struggling with hunger and enemies, the Spanish decided that the time was right to take back Santa Fe. Diego de Vargas rode into Santa Fe in September 1692, hoping to take back the city with minimal bloodshed. After lengthy negotiations, the Puebloans realized that they couldn't fight both the Spanish and the weather. They signed a peace treaty on September 14th, and Vargas retook control over Santa Fe. Spanish settlers streamed back inside, ready to rebuild their churches. San Miguel was one of the few that had more or less survived the onslaught.

By December 1693, the Puebloans were regretting their decision to let the Spanish return. They attempted another uprising, and this time, Vargas was not interested in a peaceful resolution. He suppressed it harshly, buying an uneasy peace that lasted only three years. In 1696, still frustrated by their lack of religious freedom and the exploitation of their land and people, the Puebloans attacked and murdered five innocent missionaries. This act appalled the Spanish; the missionaries had not been soldiers, so their deaths were incredibly shocking. Vargas reacted harshly. He started a bloodthirsty campaign to suppress the Puebloans once and for all, and he traveled from town to town in Nuevo México, shedding blood in every pueblo and cutting the entire tribe down to their knees. It was a devastating conquest, and the Puebloans would not rise again.

In one way, Po'Pay's rebellion had achieved its aim: it preserved Pueblo religion and culture for generations to come. While Christianization continued and the Pueblo culture did meld with the Spanish culture to some extent, their way of life and beliefs were not completely wiped out the way they might have been without Po'Pay's efforts. Today, around sixty thousand Puebloans still live in New Mexico, many of them along the Rio Grande, including in Taos Pueblo itself.

The Pueblo Revolt was the first major conflict between Native Americans and colonizers in the American West, but tragically, it would not be the last.

### The Battle of the Twin Villages

By the mid-18th century, European forces were stretching farther and farther across the West. Despite Sir Francis Drake's arrival in California in the 1670s, the British had not yet made any substantial claims on the West at this time. The Spanish, however, continued to spread farther and farther across Nuevo México, which included modern-day New Mexico and also parts of other southwestern states. Small missions began to crop up across Nuevo México. Their first town in modern-day Texas was established around 1718 when the Misión San Antonio de Valero was founded. This would later become known as the Alamo Mission.

However, the Spanish were not the only European power colonizing the Southwest. France extensively explored Canada and parts of the northern United States. Most of their expeditions concentrated on the eastern part of the US, but some explorers made it as far as the Dakotas, claiming this area for France. From Louisiana, the French also made their way west across Arkansas and Alabama. In fact, parts of these states were included in "Lower

Louisiana"; France's Louisiana Territory was considerably larger than modern-day Louisiana State.

As a rule, the French were peaceful in their interactions with Native Americans across most of their colonies. Arkansas, Alabama, and eventually Oklahoma were no exception to this rule. France was interested in trading with Native Americans, and most of their settlements were established as trading posts in or near Native American towns. In modern-day Oklahoma, the French traded and became allies with the Wichita and Comanche tribes to the point where they were welcomed into some of the strongest Wichita towns as friends and partners against the Wichitas' own enemies.

It would soon turn out that some of those enemies would be the Spanish. While the Wichita had no beef with the Spanish directly, they were actively at war with the Apache, which forced the luckless Apache deeper and deeper into Spanish Texas.

Unable to maintain a war with both the Wichita and the Spanish, the Apache agreed to peace with the Spanish by the 1750s. They submitted to Christianization and cooperated with the missions that were being built all over Texas, even living with the Spanish in small communities. Perhaps European culture was more attractive to the Apache because they had not established stable towns and agriculture like the Puebloans had; they had something to gain from learning skills from the Spanish, such as growing and producing their own food instead of having to raid it from the Puebloans.

The war with the Wichita, however, was going very badly. The Spanish refused to sell weapons to the Apache, particularly after the last Pueblo rebellion in 1696, which the Puebloans had conducted using weapons they'd bought from the Spaniards themselves. The Wichita and Comanche, on the other hand, had plenty of weapons from their French allies, which allowed them to slaughter the Apache in conflict after conflict.

It was inevitable that the Spanish would become collateral damage in this war between the two Native American tribes. That finally happened in late 1758 when a group of Wichita and Comanche attacked a small mission at San Sabá in modern-day Texas. Several Apache were killed in the attack, and so were two innocent Spanish missionaries.

The Spanish were incensed by this attack, and they refused to become collateral damage in the Apaches' war. They considered the killing of missionaries to be an inexcusable act, and the Spanish had the full support of the Apache in this matter. They wanted revenge on the Wichita—no matter how much blood had to be shed to get it.

In 1759, that quest for revenge was led by Colonel Diego Ortiz Parrilla, a Spanish officer who had seen plenty of combat against Native Americans in New Spain. With a mixed group of native and Spanish troops numbering around five hundred men, Ortiz Parrilla headed for the ruins of San Sabá. Riding through the blackened buildings only fueled his anger. He headed out of Apache territory, beyond modern-day Texas, and into modern-day Oklahoma in search of a Wichita town he could attack.

After putting a small group of Yojuanes to flight, Ortiz Parrilla reached what he had expected to be a little settlement of uneducated barbarians on the banks of the Red River. Instead, he came across a strong fortress with high walls—and French flags flying over the rooftops. This place was called the Twin Villages, and while the French had left in a bid to avoid war with the Spanish, there were still many Wichita warriors inside, possibly even thousands of them. They were well-armed as well, and they were ready to fight.

Outnumbered, Ortiz Parrilla nonetheless prepared for battle. He tried to intimidate the Wichita with his two cannons, but this was a dismal failure. The Wichita laughed at him and mocked the Spaniards, then poured fire down from the walls upon them. The Spanish strove to fight back, and for hours, a bloody battle raged.

But try as he might, Ortiz Parrilla could not break down those walls.

When the Wichita started bursting out of the fortress on horseback at intervals, launching lightning-swift attacks on the flanks of Ortiz Parrilla's troops and causing chaos among them, the hearts of the men began to fail. They started to desert, fleeing off into the wilderness in a bid to escape what they presumed to be certain death. With his lines crumbling and his men dying, Ortiz Parrilla decided that he had no choice. He pulled back, fleeing from the Twin Villages. The Wichita did not pursue, but their haunting songs of victory followed Ortiz Parrilla as he fled in ignominy.

Spanish egos were badly wounded by this defeat, and about nineteen Spaniards died in the battle. The Spanish would later claim that the Wichita casualties numbered around one hundred. Either way, the Spanish never did subjugate this proud and powerful people. It was smallpox that brought them to their knees nearly twenty years later in an epidemic that claimed around one-third of the tribe. Eventually, after conflicts with American settlers in the 19th century, the Wichita were forced onto a reservation in Oklahoma.

Soon after the Battle of the Twin Villages, France lost its grip on the American West, giving its territory to the Spanish near the end of the French and Indian War in 1762. The Louisiana Territory would be returned to the French in the era of Napoleon Bonaparte, who ultimately sold it to the United States of America in 1803.

Another bloody Native American war would take place shortly after the Battle of the Twin Villages, and this time, the Native Americans would be on the losing side.

## "Dangerous Man"

When Juan Bautista de Anza saw the chief riding toward him across the desert, he knew that the man he was about to face in battle considered himself to be immortal.

Tavibo Naritgant, whose name means "Dangerous Man" in the Comanche language, was better known to the Spanish as Cuerno Verde: "Greenhorn." It was easy for de Anza to see why. The chief's most striking feature was his headdress. Far from the elaborately feathered headdresses of the Plains Indians, Tavibo Naritgant wore bison horns that rose in two great curves from his forehead. They were tinted faintly green, and they were a sign of honor, of a pair of shoulders strong enough to hold up the mighty horns of the bison. Only the boldest of Comanche warriors wore the green horns, and Tavibo had inherited that honor from his father, a man who went by the same name.

The original Tavibo Naritgant had been killed eleven years earlier, in 1768. For decades, the Comanche had been conducting regular raids on the Spanish in the area encompassing modern-day Colorado. As in Texas, Spanish missions had been popping up all over the region, and the Comanche were far from welcoming. They had been making war on the Apache for decades, and they were fearless of the Spanish and well-armed by the French. They weren't about to let their lands go without a fight.

The elder Tavibo Naritgant had raided many Spanish people in his day, but he had been overly ambitious in attacking Ojo Caliente. This Spanish settlement, located near some hot springs in modern-day New Mexico, had been well guarded at the time, and Tavibo Naritgant fell there in battle, killed by the Spanish. The warriors brought his headdress back to his firstborn son, who took the headdress and his father's name. He was determined to carry on his father's crusade against the Spanish.

As the raids increased, the viceroy of New Spain appointed a warlike governor to Nuevo México: Juan Bautista de Anza. De Anza had been born in New Spain and grew up on the frontier, which came with consequences suffered by many a Spanish boy at that time: he lost both his father and his grandfather to Apache raiders. Bitter and grieving, de Anza took revenge on the Apache by fighting against them numerous times in his decorated military career. He was chosen as governor of Nuevo México specifically to subdue the Native Americans in that area.

Now, it was 1779, and de Anza had been chasing Tavibo Naritgant for months through the hostile landscape of untamed Colorado. The Comanche raids on Spanish settlements continued, and de Anza was determined to catch the man he knew as Greenhorn and kill him. In his eyes, Tavibo Naritgant was just another murderer, just like the Apache who had killed his father. His accounts depict the Comanche chief as being unbearably cruel, a "scourge" in de Anza's own words.

Whether cruelty was part of Tavibo's psyche or not, it would appear that pride most certainly was. When de Anza and Tavibo Naritgant finally came face to face on September 3rd, 1779, the Comanche chief had a force of only about fifty men behind him. De Anza, by contrast, had around six hundred men with him.

Still, when Tavibo Naritgant rode toward the Spanish on his plunging, rearing horse, he was fearless. All his life, he'd been accompanied wherever he went by a Comanche holy man who had persuaded him that he was sacred somehow and could never die. What could de Anza do to him if the spiritual powers of his religion were on his side? Tavibo was a terrifying sight as he approached the Spanish. He wore his very long, black hair in two braids, with his scalp brightly painted and another single, slender braid hanging down his back with a feather at the end of it. He was the picture of a warlike Comanche chief. And the green horns only enhanced his frightening appearance.

But Tavibo Naritgant wasn't immortal. He was just a man, and when his fifty Comanche clashed with the six hundred Spanish, they were outnumbered more than ten to one. The battle was a devastating one. Tavibo Naritgant was slaughtered in the chaos, and his men were put to flight. They were allowed to flee by de Anza so that they could tell everyone that their great chief lay dead at the hands of a Spaniard.

### Further British and Spanish Exploration

By the end of the 18th century, many parts of the American West were still completely unknown to the European world. The Spanish, however, had made a mighty effort to explore and colonize this vast area, and they had met with some success.

Apart from their growing colony in Nuevo México, the Spanish had also ventured northward by ship, reaching and settling the area that Sir Francis Drake had called "Nova Albion." The English had made no further attempt to claim this area for themselves, so the Spanish soon began to build missions along the coast. They gave this area the name it still bears today: Las Californias.

There are rumors that conquistador Hernán Cortés made it as far as California on his expeditions, but the first colonies built there would only come to life in the 18th century. At first, these were concentrated around the southernmost parts of modern California, with no one venturing farther than Baja California. But in 1763, when the brutal Seven Years' War in Europe had finally come to an end after millions of deaths and years of terrible suffering, the Old World powers were able to turn their attention once more to the New World. Spain started to push for heavier colonization, and California became an important focus of this effort.

Interestingly enough, while Nuevo México had largely been explored by military men in the late 16th century and early 17th centuries, it was men of the cloth, particularly Franciscan friars, who led most of the expeditions of the 18th century. This era of colonization, therefore, was significantly more peaceful than the brutal conquest of Nuevo México.

One such father, Junípero Serra, made the daring bid to venture toward northern California. Under Serra's leadership, an expedition pushed as far north as 170 miles from Baja California, then built a mission there for the local people. They called it San Diego. Shortly afterward, they continued more and more northward, building mission after mission, and these would eventually blossom into some of California's largest cities: Santa Barbara, San Francisco, and Monterey. Later, San José became the first secular settlement to be built in northern California. By the end of the century, there were over twenty Spanish missions in the area.

While most of these Spanish friars had peaceful relations with the native people of the region, they nonetheless caused the deaths of thousands upon thousands of Californians. There was peace in their hearts but death in their bodies. Old World diseases, to which these Spaniards were immune, devastated the Native Americans of the area. In a brief period, one-third of the Native American population of California was wiped out by disease. All of those verdant tribes and diverse languages were destroyed by the European scourge.

A few years later, now that there were established Spanish settlements in California, the people of Nuevo México began to hope that there might be a way for them to travel north and find their Californian counterparts overland. At the time, some scholars actually believed that California could be an island—there had been so little exploration in the West that no one really knew. Two more Franciscan friars decided that there was only one way to find out. In 1776, Atanasio Domínguez and Silvestre Vélez de Escalante set out from Santa Fe with a tiny group of men and livestock, hoping to find a road to Monterey, California. This was a distance of over one thousand miles, an almost unthinkable trek even for experienced explorers, let alone a little group of holy men with almost no weapons to speak of. Domínguez and Escalante took no soldiers and almost no weapons with them. They hoped that they would be able to make peace with any Native Americans they encountered and that the locals might even help them to find Monterey.

At first, the Franciscan fathers' hopes were realized. Having left Santa Fe in the summer of 1776, they traveled north and west through modern-day Colorado. Although they had taken a major risk by traveling in such a small and poorly armed group, they met with no resistance. Soon, they discovered a tribe that had had little contact with Europeans at this point: the Ute. The Ute were friendly and received the expedition with kindness, even sending two of their people along with the Spanish as guides. Their real names are lost to history, so we know them only by the Spanish names that Domínguez and Escalante gave them: Silvestre, named after Escalante, and Joaquin. Joaquin was just a boy of twelve, but he was already well versed in the landscape that was his home.

With the help of these two guides, the Domínguez-Escalante expedition continued all the way through Colorado and into what is now Utah. Everywhere they went, the expedition was impressed by the fertility of the landscape and how suitable it would be for settlement. Their Ute guides appeared only too happy to cooperate and led them all the way into the Uinta Basin itself, making them the first Europeans ever to set foot there. Once in the basin, they met up with more friendly Ute. While their original guides opted to stay with their tribe members, another guide was provided for the expedition, who led them deeper into Utah Valley.

It was here that the expedition paused. They didn't know it yet, but though they had traveled almost six hundred miles, they were less than two hundred miles nearer to Monterey than they had been when they left Santa Fe. They had been heading too far to the north. Now, Domínguez and Escalante decided that a better course of action would be to build a mission and settle in Utah Valley.

However, it was not to be. They needed their guide to take them deeper into the valley, but when one of the native servants that the Spanish had in their retinue erred in some way, his Spanish master (it is unclear who exactly this was) punished him severely. The hapless servant was likely beaten, and their Ute guide was appalled by the sight. He melted into the landscape, returning to his home village, never to be seen by the Spanish again.

As a result, the Domínguez-Escalante expedition was forced to turn back and limp home to Santa Fe, struggling through parts of Utah, Arizona, and Colorado before they finally found their way back to Nuevo México. Even their return would have been impossible if not for the kindness and assistance of several Native American tribes they encountered along the way. And while this expedition, like that of Francisco Coronado, ultimately failed in its main objective, Domínguez and Escalante did keep a meticulously detailed journal about their explorations. This information would be invaluable to the explorers who would later follow in their footsteps in exploring and colonizing the American West.

It was only in 1792 that any English explorers would reach the West again, more than a hundred years after Sir Francis Drake landed in California. This time, it was Captain George Vancouver, a decorated English explorer, who would map huge tracts of the Pacific from Canada to the United States to Hawaii. While he did very little inland exploration, he did visit parts of Spanish California and met with both colonists and natives there. He was also the first European to explore the coastlines of two western states: Oregon and Washington.

With the 19th century looming, the American West was already a very different place than it had been in the pristine days of the pre-Columbian era. Now, colonists were fighting natives and each other as they sought to take hold of more and more of the West. And the story of the Wild West that we know—the era of sheriffs and cowboys, outlaws and gunslingers—was only just beginning.

# Chapter 3 – American Exploration and Settlement of the West

*Illustration II: A map of the Lewis and Clark expedition*

After the Louisiana Purchase of 1803, the newly minted United States of America first started to take an interest in the western part of the country. While much of what we know as the American West was still under Spanish control at the time, all that was soon about to change. The first major American exploration of the West was the famous Lewis and Clark expedition, and it was an incredible feat that would pave the way for westward expansion in the years to come.

### The Lewis and Clark Expedition

Perhaps one of the most daring and incredible feats of exploration in American history, the Lewis and Clark expedition was arranged shortly after the Louisiana Purchase. Although the American government had paid $15 million for this territory—over $350 billion in today's money—the majority of the land was unexplored.

While the Spanish, French, and English had been exploring the American West for centuries, the Americans themselves had hardly set foot in any part of it at this point in history. All that was about to change.

Like the Domínguez-Escalante expedition, the Lewis and Clark expedition was meant to find an overland route to the Pacific Ocean. The other objective of the expedition was to map the vast Louisiana Territory, over 800,000 square miles of largely untouched wilderness. President Thomas Jefferson considered Meriwether Lewis to be the perfect person for the job. Lewis had served as a captain in the US Army, and he now worked for Jefferson as a secretary. He was considered both tough and trustworthy.

Lewis himself was well aware that the undertaking that Jefferson had proposed was a tremendous one. He knew he would need a courageous and capable person to help him command the expedition, and for this role, he chose William Clark. Clark had been his superior in the army, and he trusted him deeply.

After almost a year spent training, equipping, and preparing their expedition, Lewis and Clark set off up the Missouri River on a keelboat on May 14th, 1804. Their expedition was not a particularly large one, numbering only forty-five men. With the exception of Clark's slave, York, this group was made up of well-trained hunters and soldiers that the commanders had handpicked. They were well-armed, too, with blunderbusses and muskets, and they were ready to face whatever came their way. While their goal was to interact peacefully with whatever Native American tribes they met, these were no unarmed Franciscan friars but military men bent on achieving their aim.

While Lewis and Clark both treated their own men very harshly, punishing them by beating them for the smallest infraction, they were mostly diplomatic in their dealings with Native Americans. Jefferson had given them peace medals to hand out to Native American chiefs, and they had also brought along plenty of gifts, such as face paint, beads, mirrors, and colored ribbon. Some tribes met them, eager to trade; they had heard stories of the white men and the treasures they brought from their southern and northern neighbors. Others were hostile and tried to avoid Lewis and Clark as much as they could. But for the time being, there was no open conflict.

Peace was better than fighting, yet it's still clear that Lewis and Clark did not treat the Native Americans with any real respect. These people had been living on American soil for thousands of years, yet when the explorers reached them, they simply stated that the United States of America now owned the land on which the natives lived. The Native Americans had absolutely no part or say in the fact that their land was now suddenly the possession of an entirely foreign nation.

It was during this early phase of the expedition that Lewis and Clark suffered their first and only casualty. One of their soldiers contracted a gastrointestinal disease and died as they were sailing up the Missouri.

In an attempt to foster better relations with the Native Americans, Lewis and Clark held several large meetings with numerous tribes in August of 1804. By this time, they had reached Iowa and South Dakota, becoming the first Anglo-Americans to set foot there. Reaching North Dakota that fall, they were over one thousand miles away from their homes in St. Louis, Missouri. With winter looming, they would have to dig in and wait out the coldest months of the year. They built Fort Mandan near modern-day Washburn, North Dakota, and settled there for five months.

This brought Lewis and Clark close to the border of Canada—then a British colony—and while in Fort Mandan, they encountered one of its citizens. Toussaint Charbonneau was Canadian-born and of French descent and had been trapping animals for the fur trade at that point, but he became an interpreter for the expedition.

However, Charbonneau would not prove to be essential to the success of the expedition. It was his wife, Sacagawea. She was a proud Shoshone, but she had been taken by a rival tribe when she was only a girl. Charbonneau had set her free from her captors - or possibly bought her against her will - and married her, and by the time they joined up with Lewis and Clark, Sacagawea was heavily pregnant. She had faced plenty of tribulation in her young life, and she was more than ready to embark on a dangerous expedition—one which would take them through the territory of her own people. She hoped she might be able to see her family and friends again.

It is almost incomprehensible that this girl of sixteen would undertake one of the longest expeditions in American history while breastfeeding a baby who was only two months old when the journey began. But Sacagawea was made of strong stuff, and she tackled the journey with vigor.

When summer came, the expedition headed west and north across what was then the Louisiana Purchase territory. They left North Dakota behind and headed into Montana, crossing the vast state and meeting with the Native American tribes there. Sacagawea was instrumental in forming good relations with these tribes. Soon, they reached her own people, the Shoshone. These were Plains people with herds of strong and tough horses, and Lewis and Clark needed horses more than anything to enable them to finish their long journey. For Sacagawea, however, meeting up with the Shoshone was deeply important for a far more personal reason. She was finally able to see her brother again for the first time since she had been kidnapped.

Perhaps it was tempting for Sacagawea to stay with her own people, but instead, with her baby son Jean Baptiste in her arms, she decided to continue on with the expedition. She facilitated the purchase of several horses from the Shoshone, and along with some guides, the expedition headed toward Idaho, following the brutal Lolo Trail. Here, cold, hunger, and disease plagued the expedition. It must have been intolerable for everyone, especially the young mother and baby. Without their horses and Shoshone guides, it is unlikely that the expedition would ever have made it down that trail. Ultimately, however, they did, and they did so without losing a single person.

The Lolo Trail brought the exhausted, starving, and sickly expedition into Idaho, where they met yet another Native American tribe, the Nez Perce. They welcomed the suffering travelers with open arms and nursed them back to health after the trials of the Lolo Trail.

After spending some time with the Nez Perce, the expedition continued west, crossing through part of Washington before they reached Oregon. In November 1805, with fall slipping quickly past them, Lewis, Clark, Sacagawea, her little boy (who had been fondly nicknamed Pompey), and the rest of the expedition finally saw the glorious, glimmering expanse of the Pacific Ocean. On November 5th, 1805, they reached the sea.

The Lewis and Clark expedition still had a very long winter to spend by the wild sea, not to mention the equally long journey back to St. Louis, but they had achieved something that had never been done before: they had crossed North America. Their expedition remains one of the most ambitious successes ever recorded in exploration.

After wintering in Fort Clatsop, which they built near the ocean, the expedition would return home via Montana and North Dakota. It was on the journey home that the only Native American casualties were recorded when Lewis and his men fired on a group of Blackfeet who were attempting to steal their horses, which were vital to their survival. But on September 23rd, 1806, having left Sacagawea and her family in Mandan, they returned to St. Louis at last.

### Further Exploration and Colonization

The United States of America was growing as a global power during the first decades of the 19th century, with the War of 1812 establishing it as a formidable military opponent. It was no longer considered a mere group of colonial rebels but a country in its own right. Accordingly, the US was working hard to establish its power on its frontier and to secure its borders with its neighbors.

Of course, Native Americans suffered as the US strove to claim their lands. The Osage Nation, which was part of the Southern Sioux, was one of the first Native American tribes of the West to fall to the US in open battle. The Osage were still no match for the US Army, and they were forced to sign the Treaty of Fort Clark in 1808, which left the US in possession of all of their lands in parts of modern-day Missouri and Arkansas.

New Spain won its independence from Spain after a bloody eleven-year struggle in 1821, becoming Mexico. Most of California became a territory of Mexico, but Russia had control over Alaska at the time, and Russian Americans built forts as far south as Fort Ross in modern-day California (then known as Russian America). California would only become an American territory in 1848, but Russia's claims to modern-day California were transferred to the United States by the Russo-American Treaty of 1824.

Russians weren't the only other Europeans to move to the modern United States either. A group of Scottish and Irish people was the first to build a permanent European fort in North Dakota.

In 1811, Fort Astoria in modern-day Oregon was built very near to where Lewis and Clark had reached the Pacific Ocean. Many more forts were built in the following decades in western states such as Arkansas (which became a territory in 1819), Nebraska, Oklahoma, Kansas, Wyoming, and Idaho. With forts cropping up all over the West and colonists trickling to them, the first western states were admitted. In 1812, Louisiana became the eighteenth state and the first to have any western territory; Missouri would follow in 1821 and then Arkansas in 1836.

The US also solidified its boundaries in the West early in the 19th century, with numerous treaties confirming its borders with Canada and Mexico.

It was also at this time that two more important American expeditions took place. While Lewis and Clark were exploring the northern parts of the Louisiana Purchase, Lieutenant Zebulon Pike was conducting another expedition to explore the Southwest, leading to run-ins with Nuevo México. Later, in 1812, Robert Stuart would lead a desperate mission across the Continental Divide and into modern-day Wyoming, blazing a trail across the South Pass for hundreds of thousands of settlers later that century.

The expedition led by Stephen H. Long, which took place in 1820, was a very different type of exploration. Long had been involved with building the first fort in present-day Nebraska in 1819, but now, he sought not to subdue the landscape of the American West but to study it. Using a paddleboat steamer, he took a group of artists, naturalists, and scientists into the wild to document the breathtaking wilderness and its many species. They traveled along the Rocky Mountains up the Platte River, becoming the first scientists in the American West, and they scaled Pikes Peak as well as explored the Canadian and Arkansas Rivers. It was the first scientific documentation of the Great Plains, and Long would return to the East with awed depictions of the wilderness, beauty, and barrenness of that area.

The year 1820 also brought another change, one that had tremendous political importance. While the American Civil War would only begin in 1861, tensions were already building between slave and free states in the United States. There was a roughly equal number of slave and free states at the time, maintaining a tenuous balance in a country so thoroughly divided on the issue of slavery. That changed when Missouri tried to join the US as a slave state. This would disrupt the balance, and tensions escalated violently. As westward expansion gained momentum, these divided states were particularly concerned over what would happen as more and more western states were admitted. Would the US become predominantly free, or would the western states, too, be filled with slaves?

The government's resolution to this conflict was the ill-conceived Missouri Compromise, which maintained a tenuous peace for a period of around forty years before the American Civil War began.

The Missouri Compromise admitted Missouri as a slave state, but it also made Maine, which had previously been part of Massachusetts, a new free state. It also decreed that the US would literally be divided along a latitude line—known as the Mason-Dixon line—which split the country into the free North and the Southern slave states.

As a result, of the western states, modern-day Alabama, Arkansas, and Missouri were made slave states. The great, vast territory of the northern Louisiana Purchase, which was still largely unexplored, was temporarily free. This included modern-day Nebraska, Idaho, Wyoming, and the Dakotas. The Oregon Country (including modern-day Oregon and Washington) would be free too.

The Missouri Compromise would ultimately have devastating repercussions in the East when the Civil War broke out, but it also affected the West. But that was all in the future. For now, settlers were heading west with renewed hope and vigor, ready to claim the land they believed to be their own.

### Ashley's Hundred

Although many imagine the first Western settlers to have been quiet colonial families desperate to eke out a living in this hostile wilderness, the first few people to live permanently in the West were very different. They were the original mountain men, and they would become the stuff of legend.

Jedediah Smith was perhaps the most legendary mountain man of all. While he was born in modern-day Bainbridge, New York, in 1799, "Jed" Smith grew up dreaming of a wilder place. He loved venturing into the rich woods of the East and became an adept hunter and trapper in his youth. Trapping was a reliable stream of income at that time. This was before the fur trade had practically annihilated hundreds of American species and endangered others such as the beaver and otter. The fur of beavers and otters, as well as others, was coveted, particularly in Europe, to make hats, coats, and other fashionable items. Trapping and killing these animals to sell their pelts was a lucrative business for any enterprising young man.

However, it was more than just money that Smith sought. The wilderness called to him, and when he read the journals of the Lewis and Clark expedition as a boy, it poured fuel on the flame that was driving him to the frontier.

By 1822, Smith was a young man living in Ohio with his poverty-stricken family. He tried to support them as well as he could, but he needed a better opportunity, one that would bring in more money and allow him to fulfill his frontier dreams. That opportunity came in the form of a newspaper advertisement. Its first line immediately caught his eye: "To enterprising young men..."

As Smith read, he grew more and more excited about what he was seeing. The advertisement was asking for around a hundred men who would be willing to explore the Missouri River, with the goal being to find its source and tap into its natural resources. The contract would last up to three years, and Smith knew that the money would be good. He couldn't pass it up. He responded to the advertisement, packed up his meager possessions, and set off for St. Louis.

Once there, Smith met up with William Henry Ashley. An adventurer and businessman, Ashley had reached the rank of brigadier general during the brutal War of 1812, and now he was practically bankrupt and growing desperate. There was nothing left for him in the East, and he had no choice but to head west and claim the riches to be found there. Together with Andrew Henry, he formed the Rocky Mountain Fur Company in 1822, and they decided to find one hundred capable young men who would travel up the Missouri River and trap animals for the insatiable European market.

That was how Smith ended up finding Ashley's advertisement in the paper, and in a few short months, he was traveling up the Missouri alongside ninety-nine other young men who were ready to seek their fortunes in the wilderness. They would become known as Ashley's Hundred, and they were some of the very first Anglo-Americans ever to live permanently in the American West. They were no homesteaders, though; there were no ranches, growing families, or little houses on the prairie. These were mountain men, and they were as rugged and fierce as the predators that roamed the wilds. They lived a life of utter loneliness and also absolute freedom.

Smith took to that life effortlessly. Ashley's Hundred started out by exploring around the Yellowstone and Missouri Rivers, eventually following the Cheyenne all the way to its mouth through modern-day Wyoming and South Dakota. Ultimately, however, Ashley decided to concentrate his efforts on the Rocky Mountains.

As a mountain man, Smith, like the other members of Ashley's Hundred, would spend many months all alone in the wilderness, hunting and trapping. There was absolutely no contact with the rest of the world; the mountain men had to rely on their wits and ability to read the landscape. They also had to survive almost entirely on whatever they could hunt or scavenge in the woods, relying on their survival skills for food, water, warmth, and protection from both the elements and predators. Smith himself would find out, painfully and brutally, just how dangerous those predators could be. During his time in the Rocky Mountains, he was attacked and mauled by one of America's most powerful predators—a grizzly bear. If he had been alone at the time, he likely wouldn't have survived. Luckily for Smith, he was with a small party of other mountain men, and he talked one of them into stitching his ripped scalp back together. He would be scarred for the rest of his short life, and he wore his hair long to hide this fact until his dying day.

Most of the time, though, Smith and his counterparts were alone. They only had contact with the East during set times when they would rendezvous with Ashley and others to trade their furs and receive money and supplies. These gatherings would become enormous, attracting large numbers of friendly Native Americans who wanted to trade, as well as the growing number of mountain men in the region.

In a matter of a few years, there were hundreds of mountain men exploring the Rocky Mountains, and not all of them were hunters and trappers. Many were land surveyors or army scouts and men who had journeyed to the wilderness simply to explore and map the land. They would become known as the "generation after Lewis and Clark." The land that the famed expedition had once crossed would now be thoroughly mapped and explored by the mountain men.

By 1826, Smith had made enough money that he could not only assist his destitute family in Ohio but also—with two other mountain men—purchase the Rocky Mountain Fur Company from

Ashley. By that point, Smith had been in the wilderness for four years. He had experienced some terrible trials, most notably the attack by the grizzly bear, as well as multiple attacks from hostile Native Americans such as the Arikara, Blackfeet, and Assiniboine. However, he was still bent on exploring the West. In fact, now that he owned the company and no longer had to spend all his time trapping, Smith could start to explore the West in earnest.

In just a few short years, Smith explored and recorded a truly amazing amount of the western landscape. Not only did he follow the Pacific Coast all the way along the Oregon Country and California, but he also found the South Pass that Robert Stuart had first discovered and then attempted to keep secret. Smith also crossed the Mojave Desert and explored enormous tracts of South Dakota and Wyoming.

Ultimately, however, even Smith grew tired of the rough and dangerous life of the mountain man. By the time he reached his early thirties, he had made a comfortable fortune off the profits of the company. In 1830, he sold the company, which allowed him to give his family enough money to buy a farm and a house, as well as two slaves.

He returned to St. Louis shortly after selling the company and started to seek what he might have considered to be a safer means of making a living. Smith couldn't put himself behind a desk, however. He decided on trading with Santa Fe, by then a major city in Mexico-controlled Texas, and set off along the Santa Fe Trail with a handful of men.

Smith had survived in the mountains on his own for so long, yet now, at the age of thirty-two, he would finally meet his match. Ever the wanderer, he left his party behind to scout ahead and never returned. He was most likely slain by a band of Comanche, as his belongings were later found in their possession. It was a tragic end to a wild explorer who was finally seeking a little peace, but at least Jed Smith died as he had lived—in freedom.

He would leave behind a lasting legacy for the colonists who would follow in his footsteps. While Lewis and Clark had established the existence of the American West, it was the mountain men who would make it feasible for colonization. Their maps made westward expansion possible, and not only were they the first Anglo-American residents of the West, but they also paved the way for the families that would follow.

## The Old Three Hundred

Stephen F. Austin was a man with a vision, and that vision included carrying on his father's legacy.

Considering what Austin's early childhood was like, it is almost surprising that he would be so dedicated to a cause his father, Moses Austin, had first conceived. Born in modern-day Austinville, Virginia, Stephen's family moved to Ste. Genevieve, Missouri, when he was a very small child. In 1804, he was sent away at the tender age of eleven to go to school all the way in Connecticut— more than one thousand miles away. Perhaps it would have been easy for young Austin to feel abandoned by his father, whom he would hardly see for years to come. It was only in 1810, having been well educated in the East, that he finally returned to Ste. Genevieve to join his father's business. Moses owned a lead mine and needed help managing the growing business, but even this involved sending young Stephen away at regular intervals to handle lead shipments. One of these landed Stephen in New Orleans, where he contracted malaria. He would remain sickly for the rest of his life, but it does not appear to have affected his vigor and determination.

Moses's fortunes in lead mining would ultimately turn, leading him to uproot his life and start traveling through Texas. At the time, Texas was under Spanish control, although their grip on their colonists was growing more and more tenuous. Neither the Spanish Crown nor its Mexican residents had any beef with the United States, however, and so, Moses was able to explore the wild and barren beauty of this western state. Spain had colonized parts of it, but much of it was rich, empty, untouched land. To the 19th-century American psyche, this made it ripe for the picking.

Moses conceived the thought of getting permits from the Spanish government to settle Anglo-American colonists on their soil, and with the help of a high-up friend, he managed to secure these permits in 1821. But Moses himself would never see colonists arrive in what would eventually become the Lone Star State. He died that same year, leaving all of his possessions to Stephen—including the permits and the dream of colonizing Texas.

Stephen F. Austin unhesitatingly decided to carry on his father's legacy, even though he was part of Missouri's territorial legislature at the time. Upon starting to live out his father's dream, he almost immediately ran into what would seem to be an insurmountable obstacle. After a brutal war, which lasted more than a decade, Mexico finally succeeded in winning its independence from Spain. The Treaty of Córdoba was signed on August 24th, 1821, and "New Spain" became Mexico. "Nuevo México" became a Mexican territory, which included Texas.

Luckily for Austin, however, the Mexicans had no quarrel with the Americans, and he was able to renegotiate his permits and gain permission to settle three hundred families in Texas.

Austin quickly began to advertise his offer in the United States. It was an attractive one in many ways. Settlers would be given an allotment of land that they would legally own. For farmers, it was just under 200 acres; for ranchers, it was just under 4,500 acres. This was good land around the Brazos, Colorado, and San Bernard Rivers, with fertile soil and plenty of water. With the eastern US getting more and more crowded as the population boomed, there was a constant hunger for farming and ranching land, and this opportunity to colonize a whole new area was a good one.

However, there were disadvantages. Chief among them was the fact that this land that Austin and the Mexican government were happily giving away as "untouched" had actually been populated for thousands of years. Tribes like the Comanche were not welcoming of colonists who suddenly believed they owned the land that these people had been living on for generations.

Another caveat was that these new landowners couldn't sit on their hands once they were given the land. Within two years, they had to have settled there and also "improved" the land by utilizing it for some form of agriculture. There wasn't time to mess around, so Austin was looking for hard workers.

Still, there was no shortage of people willing to take this opportunity. By 1824, Austin had issued 307 permits to new settlers. Some of these settlers had taken two permits per family, and as a result, there were 297 families moving to Texas that year. They are known as the "Old Three Hundred": the first farmers and ranchers of the American Old West. Despite the presence of Native Americans, they were quick to put down roots and build a small town, and only 7 of the 297 families failed to improve the land within two short years.

These "families" didn't always consist of a conventional set of parents and children, however. When young, single men wanted to apply for this opportunity, they were simply grouped together in twos and threes to form legal families.

On the surface, the story of the Old Three Hundred is a familiar one with a tagline we know all too well. Courageous and enterprising Anglo-American settlers set out to tame a hostile wilderness and succeed by their sheer grit and gumption. However, there is a dark side to their story, one that is little told. The Old Three Hundred families were far from desperate Easterners, stricken by poverty, who had to struggle to scratch out a living in this hostile territory. In fact, most of these people were literate, upper class, and already fairly wealthy before they moved to Texas. While they nominated themselves as livestock ranchers in a bid to get the larger allotments of land, most of them were more interested in farming crops.

And of the 297 families, 69 were slave owners.

As a result, the Old Three Hundred would eventually develop vast slave-holding plantations, which would ultimately contribute to the chaos of the American Civil War. These were Texas's first settlers, to be sure, but they would also become the first plantations in the American West.

What was more, the presence of the Old Three Hundred and their almost immediate success would soon encourage more colonists to stream to Texas. While many of these gained legal permits from Austin, who continued to act as an agent for Mexico in selling them, some were squatters who simply moved onto open land and started farming it. As a result, the Anglo-American population of Texas boomed. By 1835, it numbered as many as twenty thousand, and this was just eleven years after the Old Three Hundred had moved there.

As for Stephen F. Austin, his contribution to history was far from over. Tensions were brewing between Mexico and its Texan territory. And those tensions would eventually erupt into a little-known period when Texas was part of neither the United States nor Mexico.

Texas was about to become a country all its own.

# Chapter 4 – Anglo-Americans Go to War for the West

AGE 82   ELIZABETH (BROWN) STEPHENS   TAKEN 1903

*Illustration III: Elizabeth Brown, a survivor of the Trail of Tears*

By the early 1830s, many parts of the American West had been explored. While much of those lands were still wild and free and would remain so for decades, the explorers and mountain men had mapped most of them. Early settlements, often beginning as forts or small trading posts, were popping up all over the West. Native Americans everywhere were starting to realize that Anglo-American encroachment was not far away, and the Mexican government of Texas was beginning to feel threatened by the insatiable Anglo-American thirst for western land. Westward expansion had begun in earnest.

Much of this expansion was driven by the idea of manifest destiny. While the term would be used for the first time as late as 1845, manifest destiny was an idea as old as America itself—something akin to the thought process that had driven the Pilgrims to Plymouth in the 17th century. The majority of Anglo-Americans held the firm belief that they were divinely destined to control and colonize the whole of North America. They considered this to be inevitable. This drove much of their confidence as they swept aside entire nations in their unstoppable expansion toward the Pacific.

As a result, the United States was more than willing to make war on anyone who would dare to stand in its way. Its conflicts with the Native Americans are fairly well known, and rightfully so; this was a cruel and bloody chapter of American history, one that caused deep and lasting pain. However, the native tribes were not the only people who would go to war with the United States for their land. Mexico was another combatant, as well as Texas as an independent republic.

First, however, President Andrew Jackson would sign the Indian Removal Act, causing terrible suffering to tens of thousands of people.

## The Indian Removal Act

Conflicts with Native Americans were starting to flare up all over the Old West by 1830. While the first open war by Anglo-Americans on Native Americans in the West would only begin in 1838, skirmishes, small conflicts, and the raiding and plundering of entire towns were common by this time. The buzzword of the day was the "Indian problem." To much of the United States, Native Americans were an inconvenience. They were in the way.

President George Washington had even come up with ways to deal with the "Indian problem" during his time as the first president. His idea was slightly more peaceful; he considered it a necessity to "civilize" Native Americans, practically forcing them to give up their cultures and start behaving like Anglo-Americans. Of course, they would never be considered equal, but Washington hoped to assimilate them into the greater Anglo-American culture by having them Christianized, giving them English names, and educating them in English. Many eastern tribes realized that their options were civilization or death, so they chose civilization, most notably the Chickasaw, Cherokee, Choctaw, Seminole, and Creek. All five of these tribes—known as the Five Civilized Tribes—had had conflicts with the United States before and knew that if they failed to comply, they would be massacred.

But try as they might to give up their cultures and blend in, these Native American tribes just couldn't seem to please the Anglo-Americans. President Andrew Jackson was the driving force behind the thought that civilization would never work when it came to Native Americans. He had fought against the Creek during his time in the US Army as a major general, and by the time he became president, the country was rapidly expanding into areas like Alabama, Mississippi, Missouri, Oregon, and beyond. He was tired of fighting the Native Americans, and he simply wanted them gone—all 125,000 of them living in the Southeastern states at the time.

His solution was the Indian Removal Act. Under this act, Native Americans could be moved off their land and onto the "Indian Territory," which was originally a large tract of disorganized territory in the West, encompassing states like Wyoming and the Dakotas. The act stipulated that Native Americans had to move voluntarily and could not be forced and that the US government was obliged to provide them with food, supplies, money, and transport for the journey. What was more, it also guaranteed to Native Americans that the "Indian Territory" would be their undisputed possession for all time. None of these stipulations were met. The act was passed on May 28th, 1830.

The first tribe to sign over their ancestral land in Alabama and Mississippi was the Choctaw. Once they signed over their land, they voluntarily began the long migration to modern-day Oklahoma in 1831. Their journey took them over five thousand miles across nine states, and it would take them months to complete. What was more, the financial assistance promised by the United States was not forthcoming. Some of them were even bound and chained on the journey by the US Army and forced to march. Women, children, young men, the sick and elderly—they all had to go. They left behind a heartbreaking document by one of their leaders, dutifully named George W. Harkins in accordance with "civilization," titled "Farewell Letter to the American People." It included the line "we as Choctaws rather choose to suffer and be free." Suffering was a terrible reality for them; freedom never would be. Over the four years after the signing of the Indian Removal Act, 12,500 Choctaw would leave their homes and journey west. Only around 8,500 would reach their destination. The rest were dead and buried along the trail, which quickly earned its name as the Trail of Tears.

### The Trail of Tears

The Creek were the next to be removed. Leaving in 1836, 15,000 Creek took on the deadly trail, losing 3,500 of their people along the way.

Having seen what had happened to their Creek and Choctaw counterparts, the Cherokee were far less willing to make the long journey west. Many were adamant that it would be better and safer to stay and fight, even though they had seen an unrecorded number of their Seminole neighbors killed during the First Seminole War. It didn't matter whether they fought or fled; people were going to die either way. Some of the Cherokee reasoned it was better to die fighting.

However, a small number of Cherokee believed that it would be far less risky to take on the Trail of Tears and move. Maybe they would find peace and freedom in the Indian Territory, after all, even though there were Native American tribes already living there that might not be so welcoming of their new neighbors. A small group of people in this camp decided to represent their entire tribe by negotiating the Treaty of New Echota in 1835. Their actual chief, John Ross, was not involved in the negotiation of this treaty—a fact that Jackson conveniently ignored.

It would appear that the majority of Cherokee were deeply reluctant to take on the Trail of Tears. While two thousand Cherokee moved voluntarily in 1838—a well-planned journey that took less than a month and resulted in under twenty-five casualties—John Ross instead wrote a petition that protested the fact that the majority of Cherokee were not represented or involved in the signing of the treaty. Sixteen thousand Cherokee signed his petition. It was thoroughly ignored. The treaty was ratified, and the Cherokees' land was officially no longer their property.

Meanwhile, in northeast Texas, other Cherokee tribelets had decided to go to war with the Anglo-American settlers of the area. The war would continue until 1839, killing hundreds of Cherokee and members of other tribes and ultimately resulting in their removal. Many Anglo-American and Spanish soldiers also died during this time, as well as an untold number of settlers who were murdered during Native American raids. The Cherokee would journey north to join what was left of the Choctaw after they themselves had traversed the Trail of Tears. Known as the Cherokee War, this was only a tiny part of an enormous conflict collectively known as the Texas-Indian wars, which would continue throughout the 19th century—just as war with Native Americans continued all over the Wild West.

Back in the East, John Ross and the other Cherokee were running out of time. When they had still refused to move by the summer of 1838, President Martin van Buren—Jackson's successor—decided that it was time to deal with them violently. Seven thousand US Army soldiers were sent to get rid of the Cherokee, whether they liked it or not.

The Cherokee had been living in their homeland, which encompassed parts of Alabama, North Carolina, Tennessee, and Georgia, for thousands of years. They spoke an Iroquoian language and had inhabited the Appalachians since around 1000 BCE. As a Woodland culture, they were a sedentary people, living in organized towns and villages and practicing agriculture. In their religion, every daily experience was spiritual, from the growing of the crops that sustained them—corn, squash, and beans—to cooking, cleaning, hunting, dancing, singing, and maintaining the fire in the central council house of each town.

It had been a long time since the Cherokee had been allowed to live the way their ancestors had done for hundreds of years before the Anglo-Americans came, and now, they were hardly being allowed to live at all.

The scene that unfolded throughout the Cherokees' homeland was a horrifying one for everyone who had to survive it. One moment, a young man might be outside in his fields, tending squash, beans, or corn the way his people had been doing for over two thousand years. The next, a contingent of well-armed soldiers would be charging down upon him, trampling his crops with the hooves of their horses. With guns and bayonets aimed at him, our hypothetical young man would have no choice but to stumble back toward his town. He would be informed that he was under arrested and that he would be removed from his land.

Once the young Cherokee reached his town, he would come upon a scene of absolute terror. The shrieks of frightened people being chased with bayonets into stockades, like cattle, would echo through the air. Soldiers were everywhere, and they were not only harassing the people but also freely looting their homes, taking everything that they owned. The Cherokee had been told that they would be given money in exchange for their land and that they would be supported on their journey to the Indian Territory. Instead, they were literally robbed, and they were powerless to stop the soldiers.

The Cherokee would spend several nights imprisoned in the stockades. Their comfortable homes were hollowed out and empty, and they were allowed none of their possessions. They slept on the ground, with families huddling together under the open sky, regardless of the weather.

With guns trained upon them, the Cherokee were then forced to start walking. No matter how old or young or sick or lame they were, they had to walk to the nearest river with soldiers surrounding them as if they were driving "hogs," in the words of Reverend Daniel Butrick. Butrick was a missionary who had been living and working among the Cherokee for decades; they were his congregation, and he was heartbroken to see what was being done to them. He joined them on their journey, as did 1,500 Africans, some as slaves and some as freemen.

The camps were appalling. With no shelter or sanitation, disease was absolutely rife, and hundreds of Cherokees were killed in the first two weeks. Dysentery, whooping cough, and measles were the main culprits; the camps echoed with the moans of the dying. The US Army made no effort to help tend to the sick, hurrying the living along instead. Many were left to die or hastily buried in shallow graves.

Eventually, the Cherokee would reach the nearest river and find themselves shoved onto cramped, airless, and crowded boats. More disease would spread as they continued their journey on the water, with the stifling heat and filth making the holds reek of sweat and excrement. If our hypothetical young man was still alive by this point, he would be weakened and sick and have witnessed the deaths of his people—of people he knew.

In the fall, the Cherokee would continue their journey overland. There was still eight hundred miles to go before they reached the Indian Territory, but they were able to ask the commanding officer if they would be allowed to oversee the journey themselves from this point onward. The US Army was well aware that their main objective had been achieved: they had removed the Cherokee from their homes. The officer agreed, and the Cherokee would suffer less harassment for the rest of their journey, although the army still accompanied them to prevent any revolts.

Conditions barely improved. The Cherokee were still largely starving and had to rely on rations of flour and salt pork—a plain and tasteless diet that also left them intensely malnourished. Disease continued to spread, and at the pace they were moving, they were unable to reach the Indian Territory before the winter. Instead, the winter was unusually cruel, and the Cherokee had to break the ice on streams or pools in order to get water for themselves and the horses.

Perhaps our hypothetical young man was one of the lucky ones who was still able to walk. He would be burdened with supplies and plodding through great drifts of snow; there were no roads to the Indian Territory back then. Or if he was sick or hurt, he might be able to hitch a ride in one of the wagons. However, twenty people would be crammed into a single wagon, and they sat shoulder to shoulder with the sick and dying as they bumped along the trail.

The scene was so appalling that, in later years, a soldier who had witnessed both the Trail of Tears and the brutal American Civil War would claim that the Trail of Tears was by far the worst.

Some of the Cherokee groups took as many as four months to reach the Indian Territory. One unlucky group covered only sixty-five miles in three months, having to stop continually to bury the dead and rest the sick. It was only in March 1839 that all the Cherokee finally reached their new homes. However, they would only be able to stay there for about twenty years before more settlers would push them farther and farther west until all that remained of the once-vast Indian Territory was a tiny piece of Oklahoma. By 1907, there was no Indian Territory anymore. Today, most Cherokee live on a reservation in Oklahoma—a far cry from the vast, free lands that they were promised.

The story of the Cherokee is by no means a unique one. All over the West, Native American tribes were forced from their lands. Conflicts with Native Americans would continue to rage throughout the history of the Old West until most tribes had been forced onto small, infertile reservations. The Trail of Tears remains a particularly tragic chapter of the long, heartbreaking story of the Native Americans.

However, the Native Americans weren't the only people against whom the Anglo-Americans went to war. Another nation had control over vast tracts of the American West, and that nation was the newly minted independent Mexico.

### The Birth of the Texas Rangers

One of the most enduring symbols of the Wild West remains the Texas Rangers. And while this group of men would serve in many different capacities in their effort to keep Texans safe, the roots of the Texas Rangers are tightly intertwined with the Texas Revolution and the Mexican-American War.

Stephen F. Austin's attempt to settle American families into Texas had been a resounding success. However, those families faced significant trouble in the form of Native American tribes who wanted them off their land. What was more, Anglo-American and Mexican thieves had teamed up with the Native Americans in conducting raids on the growing farms and homesteads. Mexico, whose government was in total chaos directly after the revolution, was not particularly interested in protecting some immigrant families in one of its more far-flung territories. What was more, the people living in Texas were true settlers, not mountain men who could defend themselves against these threats.

Austin's solution was to form a group of Texan men who wanted to protect their fellow settlers. He would have to pay for this himself, so he could only afford ten. But he wanted ten of the very best, men who could hunt, track, ride, shoot, and fight. The original force of ten proved so effective that Austin ultimately would hire many more, and volunteers would join the force too. They came from a variety of different backgrounds; many were Anglo-Americans, but there were some Mexicans and Native Americans who had befriended the Anglo-American settlers and wanted to help protect them or get back at the thieves who had stolen from them.

Lack of protection wasn't the only problem that Austin and the settlers had with the Mexican government either. Mexico was being governed by a line of power-grabbing despots at the time, as corrupt men took advantage of the post-revolution chaos. Chief among them was Antonio López de Santa Anna. His tyranny drove many powerful people out of Mexico itself and into Texas, which became a hotbed for Santa Anna's enemies.

Santa Anna's corruption affected even the far-flung settlers of Texas. They faced the pressure of tremendous taxation, particularly very high customs on goods being imported and exported from the United States. Smuggling grew rife, and the Mexican government's crackdown on smugglers was far more organized than any attempt to protect the settlers from thieves or raiders. As a result, the settlers grew deeply dissatisfied. They complained to Austin, who resolved to travel to Mexico City and speak to Santa Anna himself.

By the time Austin made his trip in 1833, tensions were high between Texas and Mexico. The Mexican residents of Texas were dissatisfied too, and skirmishes between government forces and smugglers were growing more and more common. The Crises of Anahuac, culminating in the Battle of Velasco, had already seen Mexicans and Texans fighting bloody battles against one another. While Mexico had tried to solve the problem by dismissing the Mexican commander whose ire had sparked the conflict, things were far from peaceful in Texas. In fact, many residents had been talking with Austin—a well-respected leader throughout Texas— about seceding from Mexico and perhaps becoming a part of the United States instead.

Austin was on his way to Mexico City when Santa Anna got wind of these discussions. When Austin arrived, Santa Anna promptly had him thrown into prison for eighteen long months. Austin was never given a trial or even told what he had done to earn his imprisonment, but he was left to languish there anyway. And a Mexican prison in the 19th century was a miserable experience.

Austin's imprisonment was the straw that broke the camel's back for the people of Texas, particularly the Anglo-Americans. There were more Anglos in eastern Texas than Mexicans by that point, and many of them were powerful people. Chief among these was a man who would become nothing less than a legend: David Crockett.

### Davy Crockett, King of the Wild Frontier

Born in Tennessee in the summer of 1786, Davy Crockett had an inauspicious start for a man who would ultimately sit in Congress. His father sent him off to work as a hired hand when he was only twelve. His task was to drive a herd of cattle on horseback, and he became a cowboy long before that term had officially been coined. When his new employer tried to kidnap him after his contract was over, young Davy simply ran away, covering seven miles in two hours through snowdrifts. This was just the beginning of his career as an outdoorsman, one which would even outshine his prowess as a politician.

Crockett's family, like thousands of others in America at the time, was quick to take advantage of the opportunities presented by western expansion. They constantly moved west, always seeking the next great opportunity. Crockett avoided school passionately and even disappeared for long periods of time, making his own way in the world, but he ultimately managed to get a little education.

The War of 1812 and the Creek War of 1813 gave him his first taste of blood, and after that, Crockett felt ready for anything. He was willing to go to war, but he preferred exploring and hunting. He gained a reputation for being an adept shooter.

His status as a legend truly began in 1827 when he was campaigning to be elected to Congress. Newspapers started to publish tall tales and yarns about him, singing his praises as an outdoorsman. The yarns were wildly popular, some of them enduring to this day. These fun, outrageous stories only served to grow his reputation. Some of them told how Davy Crockett was born weighing two hundred pounds and dancing. A particularly entertaining version tells of how Davy Crockett and his mythical wife, Sally Ann Thunder Ann Whirlwind, were being kept up by the sound of alligators dancing on the roof of their cabin. Both Davy and Sally Ann climbed onto the roof of the cabin, seized the alligators by their tails, swung them over their heads lasso-style, and launched them all the way across Tennessee and into the Mississippi.

The yarns were always told in the drawn-out style of the old frontier, and they gave birth to the tall tale that would characterize so much of American mythology.

While this makes it difficult to separate fact from fiction when it comes to Crockett's real life, it is very clear that he earned the title "King of the Wild Frontier." And the yarns made him hugely popular. He was elected to Congress for the state of Tennessee that year and enjoyed a brief but successful career in politics.

Originally, Crockett supported President Andrew Jackson. However, when Jackson turned fickle and favored Crockett's opponent in another election to Congress, Crockett quickly became anti-Jackson and won his seat back in 1833. Jackson's political opponents, the Whigs (this was long before the Republicans), were even grooming him for president, but Crockett lost his seat for the last time in 1835.

Tired of politics and ready for a new adventure, Crockett moved back to the one place that had always been home: the frontier. This time, he chose Texas, just as tensions were boiling over. He arrived there while Austin was still in jail and while trouble was brewing all over the state. Ready to go back to war, Crockett quickly became an important figure to the Texan militia that was gathering to attack Mexico.

### The Texas Revolution

It was in 1835, shortly after Crockett had arrived, that the revolution truly began. Releasing Stephen F. Austin from prison did little to appease the Texans, especially when Austin returned to Texas feeling thoroughly anti-Mexican.

Aware that the Texans were growing out of control, a Mexican force approached Gonzales, Texas, to seize the cannon stationed there, which was under Texan control. A battle broke out, commanded by members of the Old Three Hundred, and the Texans fought a hard victory. The Texas Revolution was under way.

Shortly after this, Texans declared their independence, forming the Republic of Texas, and chose Samuel Houston to become their general. Open war between Texas and Mexico had begun, and it would be a hard and bitter fight.

One of the most brutal battles of the Texas Revolution was the Battle of the Alamo. It had been over a hundred years since the Alamo Mission had been established by the Spanish, and it now acted as an important fort near San Antonio. Capturing it was an important early foothold for the Texans. General Houston, however, decided it should be abandoned, and he promptly did so. The volunteers inside the Alamo ignored him. John Bowie and Davy Crockett were among those who decided they would defend it to their last breath.

It was an ill-conceived plan at the start, and this became obvious when thousands of Mexicans attacked. If this had been one of Davy Crockett's yarns, he would have conquered them single-handedly with nothing more than a bit of rope and a toothpick. But this was no yarn. It was reality, and when the battle began on February 23rd, 1836, the odds were weighed heavily against the Texans.

Somehow, though, for thirteen long days, the Texans held out, all the while pleading for reinforcements. Houston never responded. There was only one group of people who came, courageous figures who would later become the stuff of legend: the Texas Rangers. They were mostly volunteers at that time, and they rode boldly to assist the Alamo despite the ridiculous odds.

Yet this tall tale had a tragic end. Ultimately, despite the unrelenting courage of the two hundred men inside the Alamo, the Mexicans prevailed. The Texan casualties were devastating, with Davy Crockett himself dying in the fight. He lived as the King of the Wild Frontier, and he died defending it.

His death was only fuel for the Texas Revolution. Davy Crockett had been one of the most adored folk heroes of his time, and his death outraged his fellow Texans.

The Mexican Army felt unstoppable after defeating the Alamo, and they swept east toward the US border, terrifying the colonists who lived there. Houston was forced to withdraw his forces all the way to the San Jacinto River. Here, again, the Texas Rangers played an integral role. They fully conformed to their original mission—to protect the colonists—and helped thousands of families to safely escape the Mexicans by protecting them and harrying Mexican troops to slow them down so that Texans could flee.

Eventually, having pursued the Texans hard for miles and fighting a brief victory against them near the San Jacinto River, the Mexicans came to a halt on April 20th, 1836. The Texas Rangers, who had been acting as scouts and spying on the Mexican Army since the start of the revolution, were quick to bring Houston the information that Mexico had set up camp and that their guard was down. Thanks to their intelligence, Houston was able to strike, and he struck both fast and hard. While it had taken the Mexicans 13 days to overwhelm 200 men inside the Alamo, Houston's Texan army, which numbered 910 men, defeated the 1,360 strong Mexicans in only 18 minutes. The Mexicans were annihilated; the entire army was killed or captured by the end of those fateful few minutes.

The Battle of San Jacinto brought the Texas Revolution to an end, ushering in the nine years during which Texas would be a country of its own. Ultimately, however, Texas negotiated its annexation by the United States of America and became a state in 1845. The US was forced to defend its right to Texas in the Mexican-American War of 1846–1848, but this was a decisive victory for the US and fought almost entirely on Mexican soil. By the time it was all over, the American West had grown considerably. Mexico ceded many territories to the United States, including modern-day Utah, New Mexico, Texas, California, Nevada, and Arizona.

During the Mexican-American War, the Texas Rangers truly began to make their mark in history. They were actually known as the "Texas Devils" during the war. Ultimately, they would be known for bringing together the best of all the different places that had influenced Texan history, shooting Spanish pistols and Tennessee rifles as they rode Mexican ponies and wielded Bowie knives. They became a symbol of Texas's proud freedom and tough tenacity, and they continue to serve as Texas's state investigative bureau to this day.

Another symbol of the Wild West that had its roots in the Mexican-American War was the Colt revolver—the six-shooter championed by outlaws and lawmen alike later in the history of the West. Samuel Colt patented his revolving gun, the first handgun to be able to fire multiple shots between reloads, in 1836; however, it was during the war that the Colt revolver was popularized. Later, the Colt revolver's successor, the Colt Single Action Army revolver, would be widely used in wars with Native Americans in the West. It became known as the "gun that won the West."

The Texas Rangers, of course, were quick to adopt the six-shooters, and so, the Texas Ranger adored by legend was born.

With that, the American West as we know it belonged to the United States of America. And the US was quick to tap into its riches, particularly its mineral wealth. This would lead to one of the greatest migrations westward in history: the California Gold Rush.

# Chapter 5 – A Different Kind of Wildness

*Illustration IV: A photograph of Belle Starr, the Bandit Queen*

With the Western frontier now thoroughly explored and mostly conquered, colonists were streaming into the West. At first, many of them were simply seeking land they could ranch or farm; after all, the richest natural resource of all was space. Soon, however, Easterners would realize that the West held more than just land. There was mineral wealth there—great untapped lodes of precious metals—and if there was anything a colonist valued more than land, it was gold.

## The California Gold Rush

By the time California became a United States territory in 1848, it was still largely untouched by colonists. Only about 6,500 Hispanic people were living there, mostly missionaries and farmers. The Native American population still controlled most of the land. Only around seven hundred European Americans had made California their home.

One of them was John Sutter, and he wasn't even looking for gold on a cool winter's day early in 1848. He just wanted to have a waterwheel built. Sutter, a Swiss immigrant, had come to California from the Old World looking to start a new settlement. He named it Nueva Helvetia, and his first idea was to make money out of the vast forests that stretched throughout California. These giant forests were breathtaking, as they were filled with pine trees and species that have since all but vanished. All that changed with the arrival of the Europeans, and Sutter was chief among them; he even enslaved hundreds of Native Americans to work his lands. But the greatest change of all was still to come, and it wouldn't be caused by lumber.

Sutter wanted to have a sawmill built to process timber for Nueva Helvetia, and he enlisted the help of one of his colonists, a carpenter named James Wilson Marshall, who hailed from the East. Marshall was meant to build a waterwheel that would be powered by the steady flow of the American River.

Marshall was splashing around in the river, preparing to build the mill, when something glittering caught his eye. When he bent down, he saw them: little flakes of brilliance peppering the pebbly bottom of the river, sparkling like bits of sunshine made solid. According to Marshall himself, his breath instantly caught in his chest, his heart pounding as he bent down to lift one of those tiny flakes from the river. It sparkled on his fingers, and he immediately knew what it was. It was gold.

When Marshall took the discovery to Sutter, the two men immediately agreed that they should keep their discovery as quiet as possible. They wanted to keep the gold to themselves. And as they explored more of the American River and its tributary, Sutter's Creek, they realized that both waterways were flowing with millions of dollars in gold. Quietly, they began to pan for gold, extracting it cheaply and easily and then taking it to the nearest town to sell. That town happened to be San Francisco, which was about ninety miles away.

But despite Marshall's and Sutter's best efforts, it was inevitable that people would begin to talk. After all, someone had to be receiving, refining, and reselling that gold. Word got out, and it rapidly spread around San Francisco. In the age of tall tales, the story was largely ignored at first; after all, just months ago, these people had been reading about how Davy Crockett fell into a crack in the earth and subsequently became best friends with a bear named Death Hug.

Their incredulity changed a few weeks after the discovery of the gold. By then, the United States had signed the Treaty of Guadalupe Hidalgo, which ended the Mexican-American War, and California had become a US territory. San Francisco was still a quiet little port town, but it certainly woke up when a shopkeeper paraded down the streets, holding something in his hand that glittered like a fallen sun. It was a vial of pure gold from Sutter's Creek—its value unimaginable to the people of the sleepy settlement—and he was saying that there was more. In fact, the American River was flowing with gold at Nueva Helvetia, and it was ripe for the picking.

The response was immediate. Men started to flow toward Nueva Helvetia, and with every lucky miner who panned gold from Sutter's Creek, its fame grew out of control. That summer, San Francisco was practically abandoned. Who would want to run a trade port or a shop when they could be picking gold right out of the river? There were four thousand miners in Nueva Helvetia by the end of that summer, and that was only the beginning.

Sutter's Creek wasn't the only place where gold was to be found. As more and more people were attracted to California, arriving via steamboat at San Francisco or overland from the East, surveyors were finding gold everywhere. People started to flow to various spots throughout the territory, and not all of them were from the eastern United States. News of the gold at Sutter's Creek spread all over the world; soon, people were arriving from as far away as Chile and China.

The Gold Rush really gathered momentum, however, after President James K. Polk mentioned the discovery of gold in an address in December 1848. When he confirmed the rumors that had been spreading across the globe, it set the eastern United States alight. Polk had had the matter investigated by one of his military officers, and the man had come back with reports of an almost fantastical amount of gold. Best of all, the gold was easily found; no expensive mining tools were required. Sometimes, men could just dig chunks of gold right out of the rocks with their pocket knives. At worst, all they needed was a pick and shovel. They would dig up handfuls of gold-rich gravel and take it down to the nearest running water to pan it, letting the water wash away the larger fragments of soil or rocks and leave behind nuggets and flakes of gold.

"Gold fever" ripped through the US, igniting thousands of men to rush west in search of their fortune. In many men, the thought of finding gold and making a fortune in the West inspired in them a kind of frenzy. Even early on in the Gold Rush, there were reports of entire towns being left abandoned, crops left to rot in the fields, and livestock wandering all over the landscape on their own. In the East, men would sell or mortgage everything they owned for passage to California, either overland or by steamboat. These became known as the forty-niners: men who uprooted their entire lives to go searching for gold in 1849.

The Gold Rush itself would last for three more years, and at its peak, it drew around 125,000 people to California. The territory's European population was eighteen times larger by the end of the Gold Rush. This was terrible news for the Native Americans living there, of course, as they were driven off the land. Gold was something they had never had any real use for, yet Europeans were violently driving them away or even, at times, enslaving them to get their hands on it. The increasing population and concentration of people in California also meant an increased opportunity for the spread of disease. What was more, gold-fevered men sometimes thought nothing of it to murder their Native American counterparts. Famine, too, spread rapidly among these people, as their crop-growing lands were ripped to shreds in the insatiable search for inedible gold. The death toll of the Gold Rush was practically equal to the number of people it drew to California: 120,000 Native Americans perished during this time. They were not the only ones to suffer, though. Chinese miners faced constant hatred, from dreadful mass lynchings to a Foreign Miners' Tax that cost Chinese citizens a high price each month. Hispanics suffered as well, and Anglo-Americans, of course, were not exempt from the terrible trials of the Gold Rush either. Casualties were high regardless of ethnicity.

For the rest of California, it meant that mining towns were appearing all over its landscape. These towns were chaotic jumbles of huts, tents, and ramshackle buildings slapped together to accommodate the rough and wild men who went to live there.

Despite the news of gold, hundreds of thousands of men who poured into California would often find themselves disappointed. While some men were lucky enough to strike it rich and make their fortunes, countless more would have ruined their families and finances to discover that not every square inch of soil was rich with gold. In the unhygienic, crowded conditions of the mining camps, disease spread swiftly. Even the lucky ones, the ones who found gold at all, would spend their time in California suffering in poor shelters with limited access to supplies or services. The unlucky ones would die there, alone and poor with nothing to show for it.

The relentless greed of gold fever ultimately led to the destruction of much of California's landscape. Forests were felled to build mining equipment and towns, while fields were torn up. Eventually, the surface gold ran out. The Gold Rush went from being an opportunity for any lucky individual to strike it rich to becoming another battle between titans, as mining companies sought to dig mines and turn a profit. Many of the desperate and disillusioned miners who had flooded to California in a bid to bring home buckets of gold now had no choice but to turn to these companies and go to work in the mines for them, digging chunks of gold from dark mineshafts in exchange for pitiful wages and poor living conditions.

It was the mining companies who made the most money. The Gold Rush peaked in 1852 when the deeper mines were flourishing. A staggering $81 million worth of gold was extracted from this territory in a single year, which equates to almost $3 trillion in today's money. After that, the gold began to run out. Mines would still operate there for centuries, but the Gold Rush itself was over.

It left California deeply changed. Its native population had been decimated, the landscape was torn open, and forests had been hacked down. California was now dotted with mining towns. San Francisco had gone from a little port to a bustling city. Los Angeles was incorporated, and Nueva Helvetia became the city of Sacramento. One of the world's largest and most enduring companies, Levi's, had its roots in the Gold Rush when Levi Strauss opened his first store in San Francisco. It catered to miners and produced all sorts of supplies at first; his blue jeans would be patented by 1873, just in time for the cowboys of the Old West to popularize them.

California's population reached 380,000 by 1860. Most of these people, especially during the Gold Rush itself, were fortune-seeking men living in ramshackle mining towns.

These mining towns would be the beginning of the most well-known era of the Old West: the time we know best from Western films and American legend. For it was during the Gold Rush that the first towns filled with disreputable characters would be born. The mining towns were built around a population of young, lonely men, and it showed. Saloons and brothels were more common than churches or general stores; prostitution, drunkenness, and gambling were the most common forms of entertainment for tired forty-niners after a long day of mining. As people grew more and more desperate, crime became rampant. Law enforcement was practically nonexistent, though. Westward expansion was happening so quickly that the government simply couldn't keep up. In fact, it was during the Gold Rush that the phrase "Go West, young man" was coined by a journalist, and young men were responding to that call in droves.

This ushered in a whole new era for the West, a time when lawlessness was absolutely rife all across the area. The California Gold Rush was not the only one of its kind either; more gold and silver rushes would take place all over the West, rapidly populating it with desperate men who would turn to stealing as easily as to mining.

The West was once known as the "Wild" West because of its true wilderness, its vast landscapes of empty space, its teeming wildlife, its free tribes, and its untamed beauty. After the arrival of Anglo-Americans, the West would still be wild but in a very different way.

An era of outlaws and lawmen was about to be ushered in, one as violent as it was iconic. While many of the names to follow will ring with familiarity, the story to follow has often been lost to history. And despite being one of the most unbelievable tales history has to offer, it is entirely true.

## Two Colt Revolvers and a Bowie Knife

Captain Jonathan R. Davis had had enough of violence, and that was before he killed eleven men in a matter of minutes.

Davis had served in the Mexican-American War, and while he had earned the rank of captain, he was quick to get out of the army as soon as the war was over. That had been five years earlier. Leaving behind the army life, Davis remained in California once the Gold Rush began, and he was one of the thousands who joined the stream to the Sierra Nevada Mountains looking for gold.

It was on a cold winter's day in December 1854 that Davis would be confronted with the worst odds of his life, and he wasn't even looking for a fight at the time. Instead, he was simply climbing a trail through the mountains, hoping to find some gold and make a fortune, just like the thousands of other young men in California at that time. He was accompanied by two friends, Dr. Bolivar Sparks and James McDonald, and they were just prospecting for gold and minding their own business.

They were doing this with a wary eye on the landscape, however. Reports had reached them that the Sydney Ducks, a gang of bloodthirsty Australian outlaws, had gone on a devastating killing spree earlier that week. Ten prospectors had already been murdered, and hundreds of dollars in money and gold had been stolen. No one in those days wandered the West unarmed; Davis himself had taken the added precaution of carrying two of the Wild West's most iconic weapons, the Colt revolver. He also had a Bowie knife at his hip, a twelve-inch-long blade with a razor-sharp point designed for self-defense and responsible for hundreds—if not thousands—of deaths by this point. Having been trained in fencing at university, Davis knew how to use it too.

And in just moments, he would need to use it more skillfully than ever before.

The three men were advancing innocently up the trail, their hearts full of thoughts of gold, when suddenly the landscape around them exploded with gunfire. In a matter of seconds, McDonald and Sparks had both dropped to the ground, their blood pooling into the snow around them. Davis's revolvers were in his hands as the shots rang out, zipping through his clothes, the zing of tearing cotton in his ears as they broke through his hat and slashed two flesh wounds into his body. His war-trained eyes picked out the flashes of movement in the heavy brush, and without hesitation, Davis fired back. His revolvers whirred and cracked. Twelve shots rang out in rapid succession, and when the guns were both empty, seven men lay dead.

But there were seven more. Out of ammunition, they stalked from the bushes, armed with short swords and Bowie knives of their own. McDonald lay dead, and Sparks was barely breathing. Davis was alone, and the seven outlaws believed that finishing him would be easy now that his revolvers were both empty.

Davis wasn't done yet. Perhaps he could have fled, but Sparks was still alive, and he wouldn't abandon him. Drawing his Bowie knife, Davis turned to face all seven attackers at once. They came at him, and with quick, flashing strokes of the knife, he killed four more men in a matter of seconds.

With his enemies dying at his feet, Davis faced the remaining three outlaws. Three against one: the best odds he'd had all day. These outlaws, however, were well aware that facing this man was like facing a thousand. They turned and fled, and Davis dropped to the ground, ripping off his shirt and slicing it into shreds to form bandages and tourniquets for Sparks.

There was a clatter of feet while Davis was tending to Sparks's wounds, and Davis lunged to snatch McDonald's weapon where it still lay in his holster—he hadn't even had time to draw it. But the three men who ran up the trail were fellow prospectors; they had seen the lone gunman facing the fourteen outlaws, and they'd come to help.

Their help, however, was not needed. All they did was to help Davis bandage up Sparks and rifle through the pockets of the outlaws, where they discovered over $500 in stolen cash, watches, and gold—over $16,000 worth in today's money. Then Davis lifted Sparks onto his back and carried the wounded man back to the nearest town, where Sparks would sadly die a week later. Davis donated all of his bounty to Sparks's family.

While much of the Wild West as we know it today is composed of tales as tall as Davy Crockett's, the story of Jonathan R. Davis and the fourteen outlaws is true. It was contested in its day, and Davis and three witnesses described the event in court, proving its truth. Why this incredible fight is often unknown is a mystery; however, in recent years, it has been commemorated with a sculpture by Michael Trcic. The sculpture was fittingly entitled with a phrase that summarizes this event: "One Man With Courage is a Majority."

In these early years of the Wild West, stories of heroes of law and order are few and far between. Instead, we hear many tales of wild outlaws, and one of the earliest was Jim Reynolds.

### The Civil War in the West

The story of the American Civil War in the West is often untold, but the American West suffered under the burden of this bloody conflict just as the East did. And it all started with the Gold Rush itself.

By 1850, California's population was so large that it applied to be admitted as a state. This caused immediate trouble, adding fuel to the already fiery situation in American politics at the time. In 1845, after being annexed by the US, Texas became the twenty-eighth state, and it was admitted as a slave state. This tipped the balance of power toward the slave states of the South, upsetting the free North despite the Missouri Compromise. The South was quite comfortable with this state of affairs until California petitioned to become a free state.

Once again, America's leaders were left to scramble for a solution to prevent the all-out war that had been brewing for decades. Senator Henry Clay came up with the Compromise of 1850. It would admit California as a free state, define a border between Texas and New Mexico, establish the Fugitive Slave Act, which allowed slave-catchers to drag escaped slaves back to their masters even if they made it to a free state, and abolish the slave trade in Washington, DC. All of this was an attempt to appease both sides slightly, but it brought only a stay of execution.

The uneasy peace was ready to fracture once again in 1854 when Kansas (which encompassed modern-day Colorado) and Nebraska were attempting to become US territories. The United States was very motivated to admit these two territories, as it would allow the government to distribute land to homesteaders and continue the all-important westward expansion, but both of these lay north of the Mason Dixon Line, which would make them free states. The balance of power would be even more skewed toward the North, and balance was key to peace in this period of United States history.

As a result, the Kansas-Nebraska Act would be passed. This was yet another attempt at compromise, but this time, it would fail. The act repealed the Missouri Compromise and allowed the Territory of Kansas (now Kansas and Colorado) and the Nebraska Territory (modern-day Nebraska, Montana, and the Dakotas) to vote on the issue of whether they would be slave or free states.

The North was immediately incensed by this development. As for Kansas and Nebraska, absolute chaos broke out in these states. Intense violence took place between pro-slavery and anti-slavery groups, particularly in the Territory of Kansas, leading to multiple massacres, shootouts, fires, and riots in a spate of violence known as Bleeding Kansas, which claimed fifty-five lives.

Trouble brewed all over America, and by 1861, peace was no longer an option. The American Civil War began, and bloody battles were fought all over the country, including the Old West.

The bloodiest of all would be the Battle of Westport in 1864, which was fought near Kansas City. It was known as the Gettysburg of the West, and it was a resounding Union victory. The battle brought an end to Confederate power in Kansas, at least for the most part. The Battle of Palmito Ranch, which took place in Texas in 1865, is thought to be the last Civil War battle.

In the midst of all this, however, the story of the Old West outlaw was just beginning. One of the first and most legendary men to be labeled an outlaw in the West would turn out not to be an outlaw at all but a Confederate soldier whose illegal execution would change the way history has viewed him for centuries.

### The Treasure and Tragedy of the Reynolds Gang

Jim Reynolds would go down in history as one of the West's worst outlaws, but newer evidence suggests that he was no criminal but a soldier.

In 1861, James "Jim" Reynolds and his brother, John, were captured in New Mexico and brought to Denver—the modern-day capital of Colorado but then a city in the Territory of Kansas. They were Confederate soldiers who had been captured by Union forces during the Battle of Mace's Hole, and they were brought there to be kept as prisoners of war. Yet little did their captors know that the jailer was himself a secret Confederate. In the night, he smuggled the men out of prison and set them free into the Wild West.

The Reynolds brothers had to lay low for some time, but over the next three years, they drummed up support in Kansas for the Confederate cause. There was no shortage of pro-slavery elements in Kansas at the time, as had become abundantly obvious during Bleeding Kansas. Soon the Reynolds brothers had put together a force of over twenty men. This group would become known as the Reynolds Gang; it would go down in history as a group of raping, pillaging outlaws. In reality, though, it was an official Confederate force; they were members of Company A of Wells's Battalion, Third Texas Cavalry.

The men began to make their way along the Santa Fe Trail through the West, hoping to stay behind Union lines and cause as much chaos as they could. There was plenty of trouble to be found there; in fact, they were forced to fight Apache more often than Union soldiers.

It's unclear exactly when the Reynolds Gang started robbing and raiding in Union territory, but by 1864, they had a solid purpose. With orders from their Confederate leaders to disrupt stagecoaches and ranches as much as possible, they would rustle cattle, burn ranch houses, and rob stagecoaches. Even though railroad surveyors had been looking for a way to build the first transcontinental railroad since the 1850s, it would only become a reality in 1869, and the stagecoach remained the fastest and most reliable way to transport goods and people from the East to the West.

One such stagecoach traveled through Buckskin Joe—modern-day Laurette, Colorado—and stopped at a vast cattle ranch known as the McLaughlin Ranch. It was here that Jim Reynolds first encountered the man who would later murder him: Abner Williamson. Williamson was a Union cavalryman who had been appointed to escort the stagecoach, and when the Reynolds Gang ambushed the coach at McLaughlin Ranch, he was utterly unprepared to fight them. The highwaymen quickly overpowered him and ordered the passengers out of the coach in a classic stick-up. Reynolds broke open the coach's safe, stole about $4,000 in gold dust, robbed the passengers, and then took an ax to the coach, utterly destroying it before making his escape.

There's little doubt that Williamson faced derision and perhaps even punishment for allowing the Reynolds Gang to take the coach, and his bitterness brewed with every new report of violence wrought by the gang. Ranches and towns were being pillaged, and panic quickly spread among the people of the area. It seemed as though the gang was everywhere. Reports of their violence grew out of proportion and probably beyond what was actually true. People were hearing that the Reynolds brothers were rapists and murderers, that they would butcher everyone in their path and worked only as wanton criminals who were more interested in their own wealth than in supporting the Confederate cause. This last thought may actually be true; by the summer of 1864, the Reynolds Gang had amassed around $40,000, and they seemed pretty comfortable with the idea of keeping it.

Still, the people of Colorado were unwilling to allow the Reynolds Gang to pillage their lands. Groups of soldiers and citizens started to gather to defend their homes. By July 1864, the Reynolds brothers were wanted men, and Union forces were tracking them down.

Aware that they were being hunted, John and Jim decided that steps had to be taken to protect their vast treasure, which would be worth around $70,000 today. They gave each of their gang members (which had dwindled to about fifteen men) some of it, and Jim hid the rest somewhere in South Park.

They were finally cornered near modern-day Grant, Colorado, on July 31ª, 1864. The resultant shootout killed one of the gang members—Owen Singletary—and scattered the rest. Most of them would be captured in the following days, including Jim Reynolds. John and one of his men, Jack Stowe, were the only ones to escape. In triumph, the Colorado men who had killed Owen Singletary preserved his head in a jar of alcohol and paraded it around local towns as a token of victory.

After Jim and the others were tried by the Union court in Denver, things grew ugly. The court failed to find them guilty of either rape or murder, but the robbery charges stuck, and they were sent to Fort Lyon for sentencing. One of the guards in charge of bringing them safely to Fort Lyon was Abner Williamson. His heart still burned with anger over the stagecoach they had stolen and destroyed right out from under him, and he was about to take bloody revenge. He may have been part of convincing his commanding officer, Sergeant Alston Shaw, to enact the terrible scene that unfolded next.

Only a few miles outside of Denver, Shaw ordered the prisoners to be blindfolded. They were bound to one another and to a solid tree, and then Shaw ordered his men to execute them—judge and jury notwithstanding. Most of his men flatly refused. Despite what the papers had been publishing about the "Reynolds Gang," these were Union soldiers, and they recognized Jim and the others for what they were: Confederate soldiers and prisoners of war. Shaw insisted, however, so Williamson drew his weapon and killed them all, one by one. Together, Shaw and Williamson cooked up a story about how the devious Reynolds Gang had tried to escape and how the Union soldiers had been forced to kill them in the chaos. The press at the time, of course, ate it all up. And before Shaw's death, he had all his records destroyed. His version of the story was popularized for centuries, making Jim Reynolds one of the most terrible villains of the West in popular culture.

John Reynolds would have a similarly sad ending. He was killed in a shootout in 1871 but not before drawing a map to where his brother's treasure lay. To this day, the fate of that treasure—and even its existence—remains completely unknown.

Jim Reynolds might be one of the Old West's most notorious outlaws, yet it turns out that he might have been nothing more than a soldier on the wrong side of history. However, one man whose status as a true Wild West bad guy remains undisputed; that man is Robert "Clay" Allison.

### The "Shootist"

Robert Clay Allison was riding down the street of Hemphill wearing nothing but what he considered to be absolutely essential: a gun belt, with his two revolvers—either Colt or, by that time, Smith & Wesson—in their holsters. And this was far from the weirdest or even most anti-social thing he had ever done.

Women panicked. The sheriff was called, and he tried to get Allison to get down from his horse and put on a pair of Levi's or anything, for that matter. Allison was having none of it. He drew his gun on the sheriff and marched the helpless lawman into the nearest saloon, where he instructed him to drink until he fell over.

This is just one of many colorful anecdotes surrounding the chaotic life of Robert Andrew "Clay" Allison, a Tennessee-born Civil War veteran who would become a cowboy, outlaw, vigilante, and rancher rolled into one. Born in 1840 on a plantation in Tennessee, Allison fought on the Confederate side during the Civil War from the age of twenty-one, but he was given a medical discharge in 1862 thanks to the fact that he tried to kill his commanders for refusing to let him pursue Union troops in retreat. The reason for his medical discharge was given as mania related to a head injury as a child, which might explain some of his greatly erratic behavior, which would only worsen as he grew older and ventured into the West.

His wild violence made him a valued member of the Ku Klux Klan (a hate group that targets minorities) in the area, but even the KKK couldn't get along with him. By 1866, Allison was heading west to make his fortune there. He journeyed toward New Mexico, causing chaos as he went. When a hapless ferryman had the audacity to overcharge him, Allison beat him to a pulp and left him for dead.

Once in New Mexico, Allison found that he was considered far less disreputable here than he had been back in civilized Tennessee. New Mexico was still very much a frontier at the time, although numerous advances in cattle ranching had changed its barren landscape into mile after mile of enormous ranches. Barbed wire had been invented in 1867, allowing for vast areas of the prairie to be enclosed for tough beef cattle to roam; a single ranch could manage a herd thousands strong. That meant that the ranchers needed men who could wrangle the cattle from horseback. They would have to be tough, skilled riders who could rope, brand, and herd with the best of them. The true era of the cowboy had begun. New Mexico was filled with Levi's-wearing, Colt-toting, lariat-wielding men who worked and rode long hours.

It was as a cowboy that Allison first found employment with a New Mexican rancher, and he would partake in yet another truly classic chapter of Wild West history: cattle drives. Before the transcontinental railroad made it possible for cattle to be moved long distances via train, ranchers from the West, which had become the nation's main beef producer, had to drive their cattle vast distances over the open prairie. Cowboys had to do more than just drive the cattle; cattle rustling had become one of the most lucrative crimes in the West, popularized by villainous outlaws like "Hurricane Bill" Martin. Allison's first task was to help on one of these drives. He rode a horse for mile upon mile alongside a vast herd of cattle, dust rising into the air and the thunder of hooves a constant accompaniment. He was instantly smitten with the West. The openness, the wilderness—it was all he wanted.

At the end of his cowboy career, Allison was rewarded with three hundred head of cattle and enough money that he was able to start his own ranch near modern-day Springer, New Mexico. This turned out to be a highly profitable venture, and Allison chose to spend his money on binge-drinking at the local saloons. The drunker he became, the angrier he got, and Allison soon gained a reputation as a fighter who wouldn't think twice about drawing a gun and killing a man in one of his rages.

It was during his time ranching in New Mexico that some of Allison's most famous escapades took place. One involved the brother of the ferryman he had beaten senseless on his journey to the West. Chunk Colbert had earned himself something of a reputation as a gunslinger, and he swaggered into Cimarron— Allison's hometown—looking for nothing but trouble. He certainly found it. Inviting Allison to dinner at a nearby inn, Colbert tried to shoot his rival from under the table. The shot ricocheted, missing

Allison by far. But when Allison drew his own revolver and shot Colbert point-blank in the head, he didn't miss.

He was also drinking and gambling at a Cimarron saloon when the panicking wife of a Ute man, who had been murdering people and hiding their bodies in his cabin for months (possibly even holding his poor wife hostage; she was covered in blood), came running in. Allison tracked down her husband, tortured him to death, and then dragged his body over some rocks for good measure. His eccentricity was balanced only by his absolute brutality, and the humorous side of his stories turns chilling at the thought of how much he appeared to take pleasure in pain and violence.

One of the few times that Allison was on the right side of history was during the Colfax County War. During the lawless era of the Wild West, bloody feuds were common. Sometimes these would take place between families if one encroached on the ranching land of the other or perhaps killed a member in one of the fatal brawls that were all too common in Old West saloons. The Colfax County War, however, was the common man's stand against bureaucracy. Ranchers and other business owners in Colfax County found their land sold right out from under them to a group of investors associated with the Santa Fe Ring: a crime ring composed as much of corrupt lawmen as of outlaws. Allison founded and led the Colfax County Ring, which opposed the Santa Fe Ring, and attacked his enemies with his trademark ferocity. His fierceness only intensified after the Santa Fe Ring shot a friend of his, Pastor Franklin Toby, in the back, killing him.

Despite Allison's strenuous efforts, however, the Santa Fe Ring ultimately prevailed. He was forced off his land and moved briefly to Texas, where he rode through the streets naked in the above anecdote, only to return to New Mexico in 1883. Marriage and the birth of his first daughter, Pattie, seemed to mellow Allison somewhat; he didn't kill anyone for some time, even though he did yank a few molars out of a dentist whose services he found unsatisfactory.

It would almost be expected that Allison would eventually die in violence, but in the end, it was a freak accident that killed him. In 1887, he was moving some supplies by wagon when the wheels hit a rock and jolted, panicking the horses and throwing him right into the path of the wheels. The wheel ran right over his head and neck, killing him almost instantly, and Allison would live on only as an emblem of the wildest days of the West.

### Jesse James, The First American Bank Robber

In 2019, almost 2,500 bank robberies took place in the US. And while robbery has grown less dramatic since the chaotic time of the Wild West, it remains an enduring problem in the United States, and it is one that has its roots in an Old West outlaw whose name has become legendary.

Considering that Jesse James would become one of the most infamous outlaws of the Wild West, his upbringing was surprisingly calm and stable. Born in 1847 to a Baptist minister and his wife who owned a farm in Missouri, James and his brother Frank grew up with a stable family and a solid education. The Civil War changed all that, of course. When James was only sixteen years old, Union troops invaded Tennessee and began to burn and pillage everything in their path, especially slave owners' farms and fields. The fields burned to the ground, and James could do nothing but watch. The experience was devastatingly traumatic. James would never forget it.

He wasted no time in enlisting directly after this attack and was sent to the West to fight in the gruesome guerrilla war that was ongoing there. His commanding officer, Captain William Anderson, was none other than "Bloody Bill": the man responsible for dozens of terrifying atrocities during Bleeding Kansas and the Civil War itself, including the Lawrence massacre, which resulted in the death of nearly two hundred people. Bloody Bill was a vicious enemy, but he was well-loved by his loyal men, who were known as Quantrill's Raiders. Jesse, Frank, and the rest of the Raiders were bushwhackers—guerrilla fighters who became adept horsemen and soldiers during the chaos of the Civil War in the West.

James looked up to Bloody Bill, and their relationship became one of trust and respect between a commanding officer who believed passionately—if brutally—in his cause and a subordinate who was willing to die for what he believed in. Perhaps, having left his family at such a young age, James looked to Bloody Bill as a kind of father figure.

This made it all the more traumatic for young James when, at the age of seventeen, he witnessed the violent end of a violent man. Quantrill's Raiders were cornered by Union troops in Missouri, and in the battle that followed, Bloody Bill received a bullet to the brain. He died as he had lived, in violence, and the two James brothers were left feeling lost and bitter without their beloved captain. The name of the lieutenant colonel who had led the Union assault on Bloody Bill, Samuel Cox, was emblazoned deep on James's heart. Revenge brewed within him, and his bloodthirst slowly grew.

When the Civil War was over, James, like so many other unsatisfied Confederates, found himself having to find a way to survive in a Union-ruled South. James had been raised to believe that slavery was the divine order of things and that the Union had it all wrong. The paradigm shift to abolition was one that James was unable to make. After all, he had been ready to die for the Confederate cause; he had even seen Bloody Bill killed for that cause. He couldn't let it go, and as a result, he started to draw nearer and nearer to his bushwhacker brothers.

Missouri's Reconstruction proved too much for James and his peers. They believed that the Union should be stopped, that somehow the Confederacy could still rally, and so, they decided to launch attacks on Union institutions in some desperate, crazy bid to weaken the Union. Somewhere during the planning, however, James and his gang lost sight of their original objective to fight against the Union. They left the war behind and strayed instead to simple lawlessness, deciding that they wouldn't attack their target—they would simply rob it.

On the day before Valentine's Day of 1866, Jesse and Frank James, along with the four Younger brothers who had joined their gang (Bob, Cole, John, and Jim), strolled into the Clay County Savings Association with drawn weapons. It was broad daylight. The cashiers had no idea what to do when the gang aimed their guns at them and told them to open the safes and unlock the doors. They didn't know how a stick-up worked because there had never before been a bank robbery in the history of the United States. Ultimately, they complied, and the James-Younger Gang helped themselves to the bounty inside the bank. This was so much more lucrative than robbing a stagecoach; they made off with around $60,000 or around $1 million today. As they rushed out of the bank with their new wealth, some courageous or foolish soul tried to fire on them. The gang returned fire, claiming their first murder victim: a bystander who was only seventeen years old.

This was the start of one of the most famous and lucrative criminal careers of the entire Wild West. Jesse James and the rest of the gang would rob as many as twelve banks during the course of their career, and it quickly became obvious that while upholding the Confederacy might have been his outspoken cause, Jesse was mostly interested in making tons and tons of money. In this goal, he succeeded outright. During the next decade or so, the James-Younger Gang would steal around $200,000—about $3.5 million in today's money. Bank robberies, once unprecedented, became commonplace throughout the Wild West as other outlaws started to emulate trailblazer Jesse James.

For three years, James and his gang would continue to rob banks at will, sometimes murdering people in the process, sometimes not. In 1869, James committed his first murder in cold blood, and with that, the gang became notorious throughout the Old West. James and his gang were robbing a bank in Gallatin, Missouri, when he looked over the counter into the eyes of a cashier who seemed familiar. With adrenaline flowing through his veins, James suddenly and firmly believed that this cashier was none other than Samuel Cox, the man who had killed Bloody Bill. Without a second thought, he drew his weapon and shot the cashier in the chest. The bullet obliterated his heart, killing him instantly, and James finished robbing the bank and left.

Newspapers all over the West blew up with wild accounts of this brutal act, and as a result, James and his crew became wanted men. And there was a pretty price on their heads too.

Banks weren't the only victims that James and his gang chose either. Just a few months after the James-Younger Gang robbed their first bank, two brothers named Simeon and John Reno made history by becoming the first train robbers of the Wild West. Things had been stolen from trains before this, of course. Transcontinental trains were simply too tempting to leave alone. All that gold and silver from places like California and South Dakota had to reach the East somehow, and much of it crossed the Old West by train, meaning that while most trains carried some passengers, many were absolutely laden with spectacular riches. Stealing from a train at the station was risky, though, as there were guards and soldiers everywhere.

The Reno brothers realized that a train in motion was largely unguarded and that if it could be stopped in an isolated area—like any of the many, many uninhabited miles of the Old West in those days—it was easy pickings for an enterprising outlaw. The Reno brothers looted around $13,000, a small fortune at the time.

By 1873, the James-Younger Gang turned to train robberies too. Jesse James has become a well-loved figure in popular culture: the gun-toting, bandanna-wearing cowboy with a cocky attitude and a rebellious nature, fighting against the government and the institution. What we often forget today is that the institution he was rebelling against was abolition. James and his gang wore KKK masks on their train robberies to draw the attention of the engineer and distract him from his task. On their first robbery, this worked so well that they were able to pull part of the track aside and derail the train, killing the engineer instantly and stealing thousands of dollars.

Jesse James would never be caught by the law. He came very close during a bank robbery in Minnesota during the fall of 1876, however. While the gang was inside holding up the cashier, townsfolk attacked from outside, scattering the James-Younger Gang and defeating them for the first time since they had started robbing banks ten years before. Two of James's gang members were killed. The James and Younger brothers themselves narrowly escaped, but the Youngers would soon be caught and sentenced. All but Bob would die in prison.

James wasn't sure what to do. Frank seemed content to give up the outlaw life, settling down with a wife, a family, and his vast stolen fortune. Jesse, while he was married with children and appeared to have been very fond of his kids, was unable to give up his wild ways. He formed a second gang, the James Gang, in 1879 and started robbing anything that he could. This time, however, James wasn't surrounded by his Confederate brethren who had fought alongside him in the brutality of the Civil War. His new gang members were out to make money, and when a $10,000 bounty was placed on James's head, their loyalties were quick to change. One of them, Bob Ford, shot James in the head during a quiet afternoon at home in 1882. The outlaw died immediately at the age of thirty-five.

Frank James was far luckier. While he was arrested and tried, there was never enough evidence to convict him, and he would live out the rest of his years in the peace that Jesse never got to experience after the horrors he had witnessed during the Civil War.

## Belle Starr, The Bandit Queen

Jesse James may have been one of the Wild West's most legendary outlaws, but he was easily equaled by a woman who obliterated societal constructs and headbutted her way through life with fearlessness and brutality: Belle Starr.

Born Myra Maybelle Shirley in Carthage, Missouri, Belle grew up as exactly that—a Southern belle. She was educated in one of the lady's academies of the day, as the men in her life considered her brain too delicate for mathematics or science and had her learn music and languages instead. While Belle loved playing piano and became an adept musician, what her teachers at the academy didn't know was that their pet student had a wild side. Belle had four brothers and no sisters, and she particularly adored her oldest brother, Bud. Bud never seemed to see her as a sister; he treated her just the same as he treated his other younger siblings even though they were male. He taught her how to ride a horse and shoot a gun with the best of them. Belle took to shooting and riding—sitting sidesaddle and slinging any weapon you care to name—with as much ease as she made elegant conversation and delicate music.

Belle's life fell apart, however, in 1864. She had been born during the Mexican-American War of 1848-1849, and she was only a teenager when her best friend, Bud, was torn away from her. He joined Quantrill's Raiders during Bleeding Kansas, becoming a scarred veteran by the time the James and Younger brothers joined during the Civil War itself.

Bud's absence was not the only disaster to befall the Shirley family by this time. Belle's father ran a livery stable, and in the chaos of the war, the business fell apart. When Bud was killed in 1864, it was the last straw. The Shirley family had to get out of Missouri with all its hard memories and the heat they were feeling as sworn Confederates. They headed west instead, settling in Texas and hoping for a little peace and quiet. The grieving Belle's education ended, and for a few years, she was at a loose end.

Her first encounter with lawlessness would come in 1866. Right after committing their first bank robbery, the James-Younger Gang was roaming the West, seeking refuge. They knew the Shirleys because they had fought alongside Bud, and when the Youngers heard that the Shirleys were in Texas, they headed there for shelter. The Shirleys hid them without question. Belle, then eighteen, was immediately struck with the romantic and lawless idea of the outlaw, particularly the very handsome Cole Younger. He may have been her first conquest—and she had many.

If Belle had a relationship with Cole, it didn't last long. Later that same year, Belle married another Quantrill's Raider named Jim Reed, who was then just an ordinary farmer and homesteader. In 1869, however, he would be convicted of murder. Fleeing Missouri, Jim took Belle and their two children—Rosie Lee "Pearl" and James Edwin—to hide out in California.

It was during this time in California that Belle's own life of crime started. Now that he was a wanted man, Jim abandoned his efforts to be a normal member of society and started robbing and pillaging wherever he went. Unlike most outlaws' wives, Belle was not content to wait at home for his return. Instead, she rode right alongside him, effortlessly keeping pace and proving to be a useful ally in a gunfight. In one particularly brutal instance, she and Jim attacked an aging member of the Creek tribe who was rumored to know the location of thousands of dollars' worth of treasure. They savagely forced him to tell them where it was, then rode over and stole it.

Despite the ethnicity of this hapless victim, it appears that Belle was not particularly racist. When Jim's own posse picked a gunfight with Jim and killed him, Belle quickly moved on and began seeing a Cherokee outlaw known only as Blue Duck. Her first remarriage, however, was to another Cherokee named Sam Starr. In an age of glorious aliases like Hurricane Bill or Butch Cassidy, the romantically ringing "Belle Starr" was actually this outlaw's real name.

Belle and Sam put together an outlaw posse of their own, but this time, Belle was no sidekick. Instead, she was the leader of the gang, even though Sam might have argued with this assertion. She masterminded countless crimes such as horse theft, cattle rustling, and bootlegging whiskey. And despite numerous arrests, she was only ever convicted once. She would spend six months in jail for her crimes in 1882/83. The rest of the times that Belle and other members of the posse were arrested, she would charm their freedom out of the local lawmen, adding seduction to her long list of skills.

Even during her life, Belle became a legend and an icon. There was something irresistibly Wild Western about her, even though she was one of a kind. She wore a long dress and a feathered hat and rode sidesaddle like any proper Southern lady. Yet instead of choosing a quiet old hack, her horse was a fleet-footed red mare named Venus, which was as fiery and headstrong as the woman who rode her. She had left her children with her mother when her life of crime truly began, and her "baby" was her .45 Colt, which was always at her hip. Belle was deadly, unstoppable, and—to the stifled women of the Victorian world—perhaps an object of both horror and envy.

Ultimately, as with most outlaws of the Wild West era, Belle would succumb to her own wild ways. Sam was shot and killed in 1886, and Belle remarried badly. Her young new husband, Jim July, was nothing but trouble. There were many fights between them, and less than a year after they were married, Belle was ambushed and shot dead at the age of forty-one. To this day, no one knows who killed her, but Jim July is a prime suspect.

Belle's beloved daughter, Pearl, had a headstone erected over her mother's grave that featured a sculpture of her swift, treasured Venus at the top. The poem engraved upon it closed with the lines, "'Tis but the casket that lies here/The gem that fills it sparkles yet." And, indeed, Belle Starr would be immortalized as one of the most romantic and colorful figures in the entire Wild West.

The age of the Old West outlaw is one that lends itself well to stories, but ultimately, it was a time of difficulty and terror for the many law-abiding citizens of the Old West who were simply trying to make an honest living. The wanton violence that burned down entire towns or embroiled whole counties in crazy blood feuds would ultimately have to come to an end if the ever-growing society was to survive in the American West. And as the frontier slowly disappeared and as the West officially joined the United States, something would have to be done about the outlaws.

The era of the outlaws would soon be ended by a group of history's most questionable heroes: the lawmen of the Wild West.

# Chapter 6 – The Men Who Tamed the West

*Illustration V: The steely-eyed stare that made Seth Bullock a legend*

The lawmen of the Old West were often barely any different to the outlaws themselves. Old West sheriffs and deputies often had criminal records of their own and sometimes abused their positions of power. Nonetheless, the West was ultimately tamed, and the bank and train robbers who had controlled the landscape for years would eventually lose their power.

Some of the earliest Old West lawmen would have their roots in a particularly gruesome chapter of Wild West history: the great buffalo hunts.

### From 60 Million to 300 in 50 Years

During the time that the Plains Indians could enjoy their freedom, their lifestyles and even religions often revolved around one of North America's largest land animals: the American buffalo. These tremendous beasts numbered in the tens of millions by 1850, roaming across the plains in herds so vast that they made the ground tremble. While they served as food for the Plains people for centuries, there was a natural balance between the human population and the healthy buffalo herds. What was more, the Plains people practically worshiped these animals. They were something sacred, and to take one of their lives was considered a blessing and a necessity for survival. To waste any part of the buffalo's body would be considered heartless disrespect for the life of that great animal, and so, the buffalo herds remained huge and strong despite centuries or even millennia of hunting by Native Americans.

Even when Anglo-American trappers decimated the beaver and otter populations and turned to hunting buffalo for their pelts, there just weren't enough trappers in the West to make a dent in the vast numbers of these creatures. However, this state of affairs would not last long. These trappers-turned-hunters had already all but destroyed several other species. And the American buffalo would become yet another conquest.

When the transcontinental railroad was completed in 1869, it sounded a death knell for the buffalo herds. The American Indian Wars were drawing to a close; the Civil War was over. Violent men with a penchant for killing found themselves with nothing to do, so they turned to hunting for sport. This had long been a favorite hobby with rich and idle folk from all over the world throughout all human civilization, and the buffalo would simply become another target for wanton killing.

Soon, dignitaries from all over the globe were coming to America to hunt buffalo for sport, and out-of-work soldiers were only too happy to be employed as guides and hunters themselves. The result was an absolutely abhorrent scene that most likely fills the modern-day reader with appalled horror. As eastern hunters swept across the newly conquered Great Plains, they left a trail of dead buffalo in their wake and in unimaginable numbers. Entire herds could be destroyed in a single day, and hunters left the landscape littered with naked carcasses that were stripped of their hides and left to rot in the baking sun. One hunter killed six thousand of these creatures all on his own. Often, the transcontinental trains would slow down if a buffalo herd was spotted and allow passengers to open fire on these creatures from the safety of their cars. To the Native Americans, who were already rapidly losing their land, it was a horrifying sight akin to the burning of a church. To kill so many and to leave their valuable meat to decompose and fill with flies and maggots was more than just horrible. It was desecration and blasphemy in their eyes.

In fact, the killing of the buffalo herds sped up the final conquest of the Native Americans. Without the buffalo, many tribes were stripped of their lifeblood. They were left to move onto small reservations within the vast territories that had once been all their own.

By the end of the century, only three hundred buffalo were still alive on the Plains. In fact, the species was perilously near to being entirely extinct. It was only thanks to the efforts of early conservationists like Theodore Roosevelt and the first national parks, such as Yellowstone, that the buffalo survived at all. Today, their numbers are recovering, but at 200,000, they are still a long way from being the vast herds of the early 19$^{th}$ century.

### Buffalo Bill Cody

One of the most iconic people of the Old West earned his fame during the great and terrible buffalo hunts. In fact, the buffalo lent him the moniker by which we know him best today: Buffalo Bill.

Born in 1846, William Cody wasted no time in getting to the West. By the age of twelve, he was in Wyoming, helping out with a wagon train that was taking settlers to the ever-shrinking frontier. When gold was found in Colorado, Cody was there, chasing down those elusive nuggets of wealth. He was an adventurer to the core, a nomad, and a free spirit who always seemed ready for another great escapade.

During the American Indian Wars, Cody served as a scout, doing so with the kind of courage that earned him a Medal of Honor. Later in life, he would earn a reputation as an advocate for "fair" treatment of Native Americans.

Back in the 1870s, Cody was on the Great Plains, hunting buffalo. His time as a US Army scout had made him adept at reading the landscape and tracking both people and animals, and he was often employed by Asian or European royalty to take them to the buffalo. He became so good at this and was such an excellent shot that he was soon known as Buffalo Bill, a moniker that he defended during a legendary rivalry with yet another of the Old West's almost mythical "Bills": Medicine Bill Comstock. These two great buffalo hunters squared off in an eight-hour contest to see who could kill the most buffalo in that period. Buffalo Bill defended his title and won the match, but he found Medicine Bill to be a worthy opponent. Medicine Bill, himself an intriguing and colorful character, would become almost forgotten in the face of Cody's fame.

However, it was Buffalo Bill's Wild West Show that truly made Cody famous. While he did a little acting in his earlier years, in 1883, Cody would start his own show. Buffalo Bill's Wild West was a kind of traveling circus of the West, showing off feats of horsemanship and shooting, as well as reenacting battle scenes from the American Indian Wars.

Buffalo Bill's Wild West Show proved wildly popular. Buffalo Bill became an icon of the West and one of its most well-known figures, and while his show was all fake, Cody himself truly was a frontiersman. He was as fearsome and controversial as the era he embodied.

Cody also brought fame and fortune to some of the Wild West's other icons, such as Wild Bill Hickok and another of the strong and fascinating women that became legends of the West: Phoebe Ann Moses, better known by her stage name of Annie Oakley.

### Annie Oakley

Born in the summer of 1860 in the backwoods of Ohio, Phoebe Ann Moses was immediately plunged into a difficult childhood—one that would shape one of the West's most well-known heroines.

Phoebe Ann, who went by "Annie" from an early age, lost her father when she was only six years old. Despite being one of the youngest girls, Annie scorned the gentler playthings her sisters enjoyed and quickly began to take on responsibility for the household. Her mother remarried and bore a baby to her new husband, but Annie's stepfather passed away when she was still very young. Annie decided that if there was no man of the house, she would take charge.

She shot a rifle for the first time when her family had grown hungry and desperate. After spotting a fat squirrel sitting on the fence in the front yard, Annie loaded her father's old rifle. She thrusted the ammunition into the front of the muzzle—the weapon was practically an antique even then—and fired off a single shot. It struck the squirrel's head, killing it instantly. For the next seven years, although she was often shipped off to live with other families in a desperate bid to have fewer mouths to feed, Annie would continue to hunt game at every opportunity. She sold it to a local grocer, eventually paying off the mortgage on her mother's house as a result. Her hunting perhaps served as an escape at times. One couple with whom Annie lived was extremely abusive to the point of putting her outside barefoot in the snow as a punishment. She would never reveal their real names, calling them only "the wolves." She ran away from them when she turned twelve.

By the time Annie was fifteen, she had become something of a local legend. So much so, in fact, that when competitive sharpshooter Frank Butler came to town, the locals encouraged her to compete against him. Annie was more than willing to oblige. Butler was, at first, amused by the idea of competing against a fifteen-year-old girl. The challenge was to hit twenty-five targets, and when Butler hit twenty-four of them, he was smugly satisfied. That was until Annie hit all twenty-five. He was awed by her. Just a few months later, the two were married.

This launched Annie into a whole new life. Butler made a good living as a sharpshooter, and he traveled all over the country, taking Annie out of Ohio for the very first time. She even became a part of his shows. But despite her obviously superior shooting prowess, Butler made her his assistant at first. In 1882, when Annie was twenty-two years old, his partner suddenly took ill. Butler was desperate for a replacement. Annie filled in and became an enormous hit. At this point, she took a stage name: Annie Oakley, supposedly after the town the two lived in after getting married.

Three years later, Buffalo Bill Cody had an opening for a sharpshooting act in his Wild West Show. He decided to hire the sensational couple. Butler quickly faded into obscurity, as the crowd absolutely loved Annie Oakley.

For sixteen years, Annie lived a life she could never have imagined as an impoverished child desperately hunting in Ohio's woods to pay off her mother's mortgage. They not only traveled all over the Wild West and the rest of the United States but also all the way to Europe and beyond. Annie was a sensation.

Annie met many fascinating figures during this time, but perhaps the most iconic was Lakota Chief Sitting Bull, the warrior chief who had put General George Custer to shame at the Battle of the Little Bighorn. Sitting Bull had a brief stint with the Wild West Show himself, many years after being forced onto the reservation, and he was so taken with Annie that he adopted her as his daughter. She was named "Little Sure Shot," and she would think of Sitting Bull as a close friend for the rest of his life.

She would perform in Buffalo Bill's show for sixteen years, only retiring in 1901 after a back injury sustained during a train accident.

Retirement was by no means the end of Annie Oakley's tale. When the First World War broke out in 1917, Annie wrote to President Woodrow Wilson with two offers that were considered absolutely preposterous at the time. Firstly, she was happy to put together a whole regiment of self-funded woman sharpshooters to go to the war. And secondly, she offered her services as a shooting instructor for male soldiers. Appallingly, despite her obvious prowess, both offers were turned down.

Five years later, Annie toured again but only for a short time. By 1925, the legend was ailing. She died in 1926, and Frank Butler, who had remained stoutly by her side, passed away less than a month later after half a century of marriage.

## Pat Garrett and Billy the Kid

Another Old West icon who found his origins in the buffalo hunts of the 1870s was Pat Garrett. Alabama-born and Louisiana-raised, Garrett ventured west shortly after the transcontinental railroad was laid. He worked as a cowboy in Texas for some time, getting to know the range and the wild men who worked it.

Frontier life suited him, and he became desensitized to the violence of the era. He grew used to fending off cattle rustlers and drunken confrontations in chaotic saloons.

When buffalo hunting opened up a whole new economic opportunity, Garrett was quick to capitalize on it. In the 1870s, he joined the droves of men who headed to the Great Plains not to hunt for sport but for hides. Buffalo robes were all the rage back East and in Europe and Asia, and there was plenty of money to be made on them. The buffalo herds became yet another natural resource plundered by greed.

It was greed that motivated Garrett to kill his first man in 1878. As a group of hunters was skinning the fallen buffalo, leaving their bleeding carcasses on the dusty prairie, Garrett and another hunter started to argue over the ownership of some of the hides. The argument grew heated, and a reckless rage came over Garrett. He drew a gun, believing that he was in the right, and killed the other hunter. This made him a murderer, but he would still become a respected lawman in the years to come.

Perhaps because of this altercation, Garrett tired of buffalo hunting; not to mention, the industry was beginning to cause its own demise by that time. He moved to New Mexico and opened a saloon of his own, where he was well-liked by the locals and earned the nickname of "Big John" for his tall, slender height. While he was managing his saloon, he first ran into one of the unluckiest and yet most-loved outlaws of the Wild West: Henry McCarty, who was then operating under the alias of William H. Bonney. But readers perhaps best know him as Billy the Kid.

"The Kid" was a fitting suffix for this outlaw. He was only around seventeen or eighteen when he first met Garrett, but he had already killed his first man and would kill eight more. Although he would never attain the notoriety of a man like Jesse James, Billy the Kid had started young, driven to a life of crime by the sheer brutality of his childhood. He'd grown up in the Irish slums of New York, lost his father and mother at a young age, and was so abused by his stepfather that he ultimately ran away. He'd quickly fallen into petty theft, then killed a man who had been belligerent and threatening toward him during his time working at an army post in New Mexico.

By the time Billy the Kid found himself in Garrett's saloon, he was already a notable outlaw. However, Garrett had no qualms about serving him booze. Of course, in those days, there was no national minimum drinking age. Thus, the Kid could knock back as much booze as he wanted, and Garrett was all too willing to sell to whoever was buying. Back then, Billy was a well-liked youngster with an affable demeanor offset only by his willingness to kill.

Two years later, however, everything changed between Garrett and Billy. Garrett had been active in local politics, and when the Lincoln County War prompted the local sheriff to resign, he was elected to become the new Lincoln County sheriff.

Garrett became the sheriff after one of the most violent chapters in Lincoln County's history. Rival posses had been clashing over the cold-blooded killing of John Tunstall, one of Billy the Kid's closest friends and one of the few men who had ever been a stable figure in his life. On one side was the Lincoln County Regulators, led by Dick Brewer and whose members included Billy the Kid, who was fighting against a monopoly on dry goods and cattle in the area held by a general store named The House. The House had local law enforcement in their pockets; the Regulators were a group of hired guns who had grown loyal to Tunstall and sought to avenge his death. Blood was inevitable.

The war would bring about years of brutal conflict that threatened to tear small towns apart. In fact, the Battle of Lincoln had done exactly that back in 1878. Multiple buildings in the small town of Lincoln were burned down, and seven people died, including the non-violent Alexander McSween—another friend of Billy's.

Billy the Kid had murdered several people during the Lincoln County War, some of them in cold blood, and he was a wanted man for his involvement in the war when Garrett became the sheriff. Billy had been jailed for a brief period of time; in fact, he was promised a pardon if he testified against his opponents in the Lincoln County War. However, he escaped when the pardon never materialized. Now, he was on the run, and it was Garrett's mission to bring him to justice. There was a $500 bounty for his capture, after all—a tidy sum in those days.

In the winter of 1880, Garrett finally tracked down Billy the Kid and two of his best friends, Charlie Bowdre and Tom O'Folliard. In a desperate firefight, Garrett shot and killed both Charlie and Tom, and Billy narrowly escaped with his life. Garrett captured the young outlaw and took him back to the nearest jailhouse to be held for trial. But Billy the Kid had had quite enough of the local justice system. He escaped just months later, murdering one of the guards in the process, which only made Garrett angrier.

That summer, Garrett searched relentlessly for the young murderer, who had just turned twenty-one. Eventually, he tracked Billy down at Pedro Maxwell's house in Fort Sumner. Maxwell was a friend of Billy's, but he couldn't resist Garrett's insistence that he be allowed into the house. It was very dark, and Billy the Kid was asleep when Garrett entered and hid in the kitchen. Sure enough, deep in the night, Billy the Kid came down into the kitchen looking for a snack. Garrett would later swear that the young outlaw was armed, but no weapon was ever found with his body. In Spanish, Billy the Kid asked, "Who is it?" In response, Garrett shot him dead. Billy the Kid was given no chance to surrender.

Pat Garrett hoped that killing Billy the Kid would earn him a reputation as an excellent lawman. To an extent, it did, at least for a brief period of time; he was appointed as a lawman a few times after this. However, when word got out of exactly how Billy the Kid died, Garrett became a pariah. Despite a brief friendship with President Theodore Roosevelt, who had himself been a lawman who had captured outlaws—a friendship that ended when Garrett directly embarrassed the president through his association with a well-known good-for-nothing gambler—Garrett never did find favor in the public eye again. He had a book ghostwritten in which he greatly exaggerated Billy the Kid's cruelty and gave his own version of how the young outlaw had died, but it never took off.

In the end, Garrett began to drink and gamble, spending all his money on these pursuits instead of paying his taxes. He ultimately had to hire out some of his lands in an effort to pay these taxes. On February 28th, 1908, when he got into a violent argument with the lessor and allegedly reached for his shotgun during the fight, he was shot and killed.

### The Gunfight at O.K. Corral

The same year that Billy the Kid was killed, one of the most notorious gunfights in Wild West history took place hundreds of miles away in Tombstone, Arizona.

The years leading up to those thirty seconds of violence had shaped the stone-cold killers who would be the combatants of that brief but brutal fight. Their names ring with familiarity; Doc Holliday and the Earp brothers have been immortalized time and time again in popular culture as heroes upholding the letter of the law. In reality, though, like so many lawmen of the Old West, they were little different from the men they fought.

The most famous among these was Wyatt Earp; he was one of four brothers who were all acting as law enforcement in Tombstone at the time. The Earps had grown up in the Midwest, moving west during the American Civil War, where they worked together at various different occupations in California, Missouri, Texas, and eventually Arizona. Despite being known today as a great lawman, Wyatt was definitely the wild child. Even as a kid, he'd tried to run away from home and join the Union Army, only to be dragged back home by his annoyed father—who was a justice of the peace as well as a bootlegger. Virgil was the one with a cooler head on his shoulders. Five years Wyatt's senior, he had fought in the American Civil War and lost everything when he was reported dead and returned home only to find that his wife had grieved him and then remarried. With his family torn away from him, Virgil decided to go west with Wyatt and his other two brothers, Morgan and James.

Things seemed to be stabilizing for Wyatt by 1870 when he became a local constable in Lamar, Missouri. Virgil was also working as a sawmill manager and earning a steady living. But Wyatt quickly shot himself in the foot; he mishandled public funds and got himself fired in 1871, at which point he headed for greener pastures by becoming a horse thief in Oklahoma for some time. He also hunted buffalo, like most young men, during the 1870s.

By 1874, when Virgil had become a deputy marshal in Tucson, Arizona, Wyatt seemed to have come to his senses again. It was not difficult to escape any kind of criminal charge in those days— one simply had to get away from whichever town held their warrant. Despite his earlier accusations, Wyatt was able to become a lawman in Wichita, Kansas, but he just kept on causing trouble for himself. He beat some luckless fool to a near pulp in a bare-handed fight during his time as a lawman there and fled under scrutiny from local authorities.

That led him to Dodge City, Kansas, in 1875. At the time, Dodge City was known as the "wickedest little city in the West." Dodge City was a boomtown teeming with cattle ranchers and everyone else involved in that industry, and it was growing too quickly for authorities to maintain control over it. Due to that fact, it had become a den of violence and vice. It was here that Wyatt was appointed as assistant marshal, and he appears to have conducted his duties well enough. None of them prevented him from moonlighting as a professional gambler, however. And it was here that he met one of his closest friends and a man who would stick with the Earps throughout their lives: John Henry Holliday, "Doc" to his friends.

Holliday had a difficult childhood, but not for the same reasons as many of the outlaws and lawmen featured in this book. In fact, Holliday's mother had been relentlessly loving and determined to give her boy a good life, despite the fact that Holliday had been born with a cleft palate. She spent endless hours working through his speech impediment with him. To his dying day, Holliday had a gentle mannerism about him that he had learned from her. Tragically, his mother died from tuberculosis in 1866, but her love still drove him on, and he graduated as a trained dentist in 1872. Intending to practice in his hometown in Georgia, Holliday's plans were harshly derailed when his own physician broke some very bad news to him: he had tuberculosis too. And if he didn't move away from the wet climate of the South, he would likely meet the same ending as his mother had.

Panicking, Holliday fled to Dallas, Texas, where he tried to set up a practice. But without his mother to keep him on the straight and narrow, he soon fell into drinking and gambling in the Wild West. Drinking led to fighting, and fighting led to a murder charge. Holliday fled Dallas as a wanted man in 1878.

The only place he could think to go was Dodge City, where he could lay low around other outlaws. However, when he met the lawman Wyatt Earp while gambling there, Holliday found that he had nothing to fear from the local law enforcement. The two men hit it off immediately, and the lonely Holliday practically clung to Wyatt.

Virgil was still doing well for himself in Arizona, so Wyatt decided to move there around 1880, with Holliday loyally following him. At this point, Virgil had been made the city marshal of Tombstone, Arizona, and he had his hands full. Not only was he facing off with a group of cowboys, known as the Clanton-McLaury Gang, who supplemented their income by rustling cattle and stealing horses, but he was also struggling with the local sheriff, John Behan. Behan was well aware that Virgil wanted nothing more than to be elected sheriff in Behan's stead, so the sheriff was failing to back him up against the Clanton-McLaury Gang.

As a result, Virgil turned to four men whom he knew would have his back in any kind of fight: his three brothers and their best friend, Doc Holliday. They were made deputy marshals of Tombstone, where violence with the Clanton-McLaury Gang was about to get ugly.

Behan knew that the younger Earps and Holliday were trouble the moment he saw them. He arrested Holliday for the suspected murder of a stagecoach driver. The charges never stuck, though, and Holliday would go free.

Still, although evidence suggests that Holliday really was innocent, Behan wasn't wrong that these men were out to cause trouble. Tensions escalated in Tombstone throughout 1881, and by the fall, they were ready to boil over.

On an October day in 1881, Ike Clanton and Tom McLaury were looking for trouble. They sauntered into town and stopped by the local saloon, where Doc Holliday was drinking. Fired up, Holliday demanded that Ike draw his weapon and have it out with him, there and then. But Ike incensed him by walking away, prompting Holliday to run to Virgil with his complaint. Virgil arrested Ike and Tom for carrying weapons inside the city, which was illegal at the time. Still, there wasn't much he could do to them. He just disarmed them and sent them on their way.

Irate, Ike and Frank knew that Virgil and Holliday were both looking for trouble. The next day—October 26th, 1881—they met up with some of their cohorts at the edge of town, including Billy Clanton and Frank McLaury. Soon, a group of Clanton-McLaury members was gathering just outside the back gate of the O.K. Corral, a livery stable on Fremont Street. These were all outlaws, and their intentions were unmistakable.

Once again, Sheriff Behan saw trouble coming. He rode over and begged the outlaws to get out of town or hand their weapons over to him. The gang responded by demanding he disarm the Earps and Holliday instead of them. Behan rode back only to find that the four Earps and Holliday were already on their way to the O.K. Corral, and when he tried to stop them, they had none of it. They wanted a fight. And in seconds, they would have one.

When the Earps and Holliday reached the Clanton-McLaury Gang, Virgil didn't mince any words. "I want your guns," he said.

It's uncertain how exactly the fight began. Some reports say that Billy Clanton fired on Virgil Earp; others say that Virgil simply shot Billy right in the chest. Either way, Doc Holliday responded by emptying a shotgun into Tom McLaury, who died instantly. Wyatt, too, was shooting his gun, sending a bullet into Frank McLaury's stomach; the outlaw fired as he died, drawing blood. Thirty shots went off in total—thirty shots in thirty seconds. By the end of those breathless few seconds, Billy Clanton and the McLaurys were dead. Ike and his companions had fled into the hills, and Virgil, Morgan, and Holliday were wounded.

Incensed by the way the Earps ignored his demands, Sheriff Behan had them arrested for murder. However, they would all be pardoned by the local judge, and Virgil would be reinstated as town marshal. After an attempt on his life by the remaining Clantons, Virgil once again made Wyatt his deputy, and the bloody feud would continue with the Clantons that led to the death of Morgan in 1882.

Ultimately, the Earp brothers regained control of Tombstone after some brutal murders of local cowboys, but they would never quite recover from the death of Morgan. Their reputation in tatters, they left Arizona for California, where Virgil opened a gambling hall, and Wyatt trained racehorses and refereed boxing fights. Doc Holliday left the Earps after the killings in Arizona. He moved to Colorado, where tuberculosis caught up with him just a few short years later, in 1887. Virgil, Wyatt, and Holliday would be some of the few early lawmen of the West to die peacefully.

## Wild Bill Hickok

One of the most famous cowboys and lawmen of the American West would also precipitate the career of a less famous sheriff who was nonetheless one of the rare true heroes of the Wild West.

He didn't know it, though, and he never would. On the last day of his life—August 2$^{nd}$, 1877—Wild Bill Hickok was sitting quietly in Nuttal & Mann's, a saloon in Deadwood, South Dakota. His back was to the door; he was partially blind by them, even though he was just forty years old. Still, he could vaguely see the cards in his hands. Two black aces, two black eights. Soon, it would be known as the dead man's hand. But right now, Wild Bill just wanted to get a drink, play some cards, and forget his hardships.

He had had many hardships in his life. James Butler Hickok was born in Illinois in 1837. Even as a boy, he worked hard to become an excellent shooter. The allure of the West was irresistible, and as soon as he turned eighteen, he headed for Kansas—right as Bleeding Kansas was erupting into chaos. While he'd gone to Kansas to farm the rich land, Hickok joined one of the forces that were fighting for abolition during Bleeding Kansas, and he would serve it well. Just a few years later, he had earned enough respect to be appointed as the constable of Monticello Township.

In 1861, he earned the nickname of "Wild Bill" when he shot and killed three men in self-defense despite being wounded himself. The incident would be called the McCanles massacre, and it was just the start of his reputation as one of the West's finest gunslingers.

Even the American Civil War seemed to go well for Hickok. He served as a teamster, scout, provost marshal, and, according to some accounts, as a spy for the Union Army. By the end of the war, Wild Bill was cocksure and absolutely confident in his capabilities as a gunman. This was on full display in 1865 when one of the most legendary gunfights of the Old West took place: the duel between Wild Bill Hickok and his once-friend Davis Tutt.

Hickok and Tutt had been friends once, but rivalries had driven them apart. By the time they met again in Springfield, Missouri, they were solid enemies. Gambling and drinking only sparked old fights between them, and finally, they challenged one another to an old-fashioned duel. They would face one another across the town square of Springfield, and whoever survived would be the winner.

The two men stood shoulder to shoulder, seventy-five yards apart across the town square. After a few moments of tense, steely-eyed staring, Tutt lunged for his weapon. But Hickok was quicker. Before Tutt could draw his gun, Hickok had shot him stone dead.

The duel became legend, and the story of Wild Bill spread all over the West, with people singing his praises as a legendary gunman. When he returned to Kansas shortly after the duel in Springfield, Wild Bill was quickly elected sheriff of Hays City, Kansas. The town was absolutely chaotic when he arrived, but between his reputation and his brutality, Hickok restored order to the town in just a few short years. He did the same in Abilene, Kansas. The city was the center of chaos, gambling, prostitution, drunkenness, and robbery, but Hickok whipped the residents into shape. His methods were questionable, but there was no doubting that the man was effective.

However, his trigger-happy ways and willingness to dole out barbaric frontier justice would eventually catch up to him. In 1871, while engaged in a shootout with a saloon owner, Hickok spotted movement and whirled around, firing straight at it. He had thought that another enemy was approaching him. Instead, he shot and killed his own deputy, Mike Williams, without even meaning to. Hickok had killed plenty of men by that time, but the death of Mike Williams shook him to the very core. When an inquest into the matter exposed Hickok's brutal frontier justice and got him fired, he was a broken man. He never aimed a gun at another human being again.

Instead, Hickok joined Buffalo Bill's Wild West Show, where he entertained scores of crowds with his feats of marksmanship. For a few years, it seemed as though Hickok had found his place in the world once more, even if he would never again be a lawman. Even after he suffered from glaucoma and started to lose his sight, Wild Bill fell in love with a circus owner named Agnes Thatcher and married her. He wasn't a young man anymore, but it seemed as though he was ready for a new start.

That was what had brought him to Deadwood in the first place. Two years before, gold had been discovered in the Black Hills of South Dakota, leading to a gold rush that saw mining towns cropping up all over the territory. Deadwood was one of them, and it was a lawless place, filled with brothels and saloons and packed with desperate miners. Many of them, including Wild Bill, failed to find any fortune at all. They turned to gambling instead, just as Wild Bill was doing on that afternoon in August 1876. He was just hoping to win a little money and get back to his lovely wife. But he would never rise from his chair.

The day before, Wild Bill had been playing poker with a prospector named Jack McCall. McCall had had terrible luck and lost a significant amount of money; Hickok had taken pity on him and given him a little cash for food. This seemed to be a gesture of kindness, but to McCall, it was disgusting slight.

McCall, drunk, swaggered into the saloon on that fateful afternoon and immediately spotted Hickok sitting with his back to the door. McCall gave no warning. He simply drew his gun and shot Hickok in the back, killing him instantly.

McCall would flee and escape from any kind of justice for months. Even though he was captured by a group of miners and dragged back to Deadwood, there was no official court to try him, and he was eventually released. While the law eventually caught up with him—he was tried and hanged in March 1877—Hickok's murder was a shocking wake-up call to the authorities of the time. If Jack McCall could kill an ex-lawman and a beloved public figure so blatantly, then Deadwood truly was out of control.

### Seth Bullock Tames the West

Luckily for the local government, the solution to their problems had come riding into town just one day before Hickok was murdered. His name was Seth Bullock, and he was the one lawman who truly held himself to the highest moral standards.

This American legend was Canadian-born, but after a troubled childhood, during which Bullock practically had to raise his siblings himself, he had come to Helena, Montana, at the age of eighteen in 1867. He had a passion for the wilderness, and while the likes of Wyatt Earp and Pat Garrett were hunting buffalo to extinction, Seth Bullock was working hard at establishing Yellowstone National Park, which would ultimately be a huge part of saving the species. Bullock's father had also had a brief and very corrupt career in politics, and so, when Bullock was elected to the Territorial Legislature in 1871, he took his duties seriously. For two years, he was an exemplary leader.

As a result, Bullock had no trouble being elected as the sheriff of Lewis and Clark County in 1873. Unlike other lawmen of his era, Bullock had zero interest in frontier justice. He believed in the criminal justice system of the time, firmly refusing to shoot and kill outlaws.

Still, during his time as sheriff in Montana, he killed his first and only victim. Clell Watson, a horse thief, was fool enough to fire on Seth Bullock while he was busy stealing a horse. The two men traded bullets, and Bullock suffered a mild injury before taking Watson down—without killing him. He was sentenced to execution for shooting at the sheriff, but when Watson was to be hanged, an angry mob surrounded the platform, demanding that he be pardoned. The executioner fled, but Bullock put a shotgun on his shoulder and kept the crowd at bay while he pulled the lever. He would never kill another man in his life.

By the time Bullock's term as sheriff ended, he had gone into business with a close Jewish friend, Solomon "Sol" Star. The two men were trying to open a hardware store in Montana, but after the gold rush in South Dakota, they relocated their operation there. It was on August 1ˢᵗ, 1876—the day Jack McCall was losing money to Wild Bill Hickok—that Bullock and Star arrived. And after Hickok's death, the territorial government was quick to search for a sheriff who could tame Deadwood. They needed someone upright and honest, someone with a cool head and integrity. Seth Bullock was the obvious choice.

While Bullock only served as sheriff of Deadwood for a few months, he was unquestionably the single most important factor in turning the town around, and he never had to kill anyone to do it. "He could stare down a mad cobra," his son would later say of him, and his steely-eyed gaze seemed to be enough to marshal even the rowdiest elements of Deadwood into order. In fact, just a few short years after Bullock's arrival—he continued to serve as Deputy US Marshal long after his time as sheriff had ended—he felt that Deadwood was so safe that he could bring his wife and children there to live with him.

Bullock was more than a lawman, but unlike the Earps and Pat Garrett, he made his living as honestly as possible. Together with Sol Star, he built a huge cattle ranch, founded the town of Belle Fourche, and built the Bullock Hotel, one of the most luxurious establishments of the entire Old West. In fact, it is still in operation today. He was also a good friend of Theodore Roosevelt, and unlike Garrett, he never fell out of favor with the president. In fact, Theodore Roosevelt called him "the finest type of frontiersman." History is inclined to agree.

Seth Bullock would be one of the Wild West's last legends. By 1890, just a few years after the era of the O.K. Corral, Billy the Kid, and the chaos of Deadwood, the American frontier had officially come to an end. Bullock himself would pass away in 1919, dying peacefully of cancer.

The Wild West era we know and love—the time of cowboys and outlaws—only lasted a few decades. Yet it remains one of the most iconic eras of them all, with its gray areas of morality, its fascinating stories, and its characters that loomed so much larger than life.

# Conclusion

The end of the Western frontier was by no means the end of crime in the American West. Crime legends like Butch Cassidy, the Sundance Kid, the Dalton Gang, and Pearl Hart were still to come. Nor did the American Civil War or the Treaty of Fort Laramie, which ushered in the modern-day reservation system, bring an end to racial violence in the West. The American Indian Wars continued to be fought all over this area for decades more. Massacres were commonplace, with Native American tribes murdering and scalping whole families of colonists and with US troops butchering whole tribes of Native Americans. The cycle of violence would continue for many decades to come.

The days of the wild frontier, however, ended in 1890. Westward migration had finally slowed to a trickle as the population began to spread itself more evenly around the United States of America. By that time, almost all of the western states we know had been admitted to the Union. Utah, Oklahoma, New Mexico, and Arizona would all be admitted by 1912, and that was the end of the wild territories of the West. In fact, it would be forty years before the last two states—Alaska and Hawaii—would be admitted.

The story of the Wild West is one we all know very well. Yet our romanticized ideas about gunslinger cowboys who "tamed" the wilderness are far amiss. In reality, the West was more lost than won. Most lawmen of the era were as corrupt as the outlaws they pursued. And the natural resources of the West would be horrendously depleted by the turn of the century.

Still, the Wild West holds more than just entertaining stories for us. It holds hard lessons about the way we treat one another and the environment all around us. With every step we take into the future, we can be better. And perhaps the true heroes of the Old West—people like Seth Bullock—have blazed that trail for us, just like Lewis and Clark blazed the trail all the way from Missouri to the glittering waters of the Pacific Ocean itself.

# Part 2: Billy the Kid

*A Captivating Guide to a Notorious Gunfighter of the American Old West and His Feud with Pat Garrett*

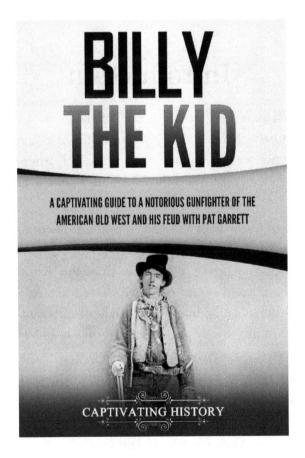

# Introduction

Billy the Kid may have become one of the most legendary and deadly criminals of the Old West, but a life of crime was a path that he did not actively pursue at first. In fact, when he was still fourteen or fifteen years old, the Kid didn't choose crime. Crime chose him.

Many of us know Billy the Kid as a notorious outlaw, a legend of the Wild West. Indeed, sometimes it can be hard to separate fact from fiction when it comes to Billy the Kid. He himself claimed to have killed twenty-one men, "one for each year that I've been alive." In reality, he likely killed eight or nine, and only two of those were on his own. The rest died in shootings with other outlaws involved.

Nonetheless, the Kid was certainly a deadly criminal, yet looking into his life offers a glimpse into a tragic past. We all know that Billy the Kid was an Old West murderer, but did you know that he grew up in a New York City slum? Did you know that his deadbeat dad walked out on him right before his beloved mother died? Did you know that most of his murders followed the day that his mentor and friend, John Henry Tunstall, was killed in cold blood right in front of his eyes?

Billy the Kid is an emblem of a piece of history as problematic, complicated, and yet charismatic as he was: the American Old West. Just like the Wild West, the Kid has become legendary. And just like the West, he endured terrible suffering, made terrible choices, and bore the awful consequences.

And this is his story.

# Chapter 1 – The Orphan Thief

Billy the Kid would ultimately become a legend of the Wild West, but he was born a nobody, a poor boy in some of the darkest slums in New York City.

Both of his parents—Catherine and Patrick McCarty—were from one of the most downtrodden and oppressed minorities across the globe during that era: the Irish. It was the 1850s, just a handful of years after Ireland had found itself in an indescribable crisis during the Great Potato Famine of 1845, which killed around one million Irish people. They fled in droves to England and to the New World, but wherever the Irish went, they were met with derision and hatred. The United States of America was no exception. This profoundly Protestant nation looked with great disfavor upon the Irish, who were mostly Catholic, and treated them as being less than human.

New York City was one of the most appalling places to live as an Irish person during the late 19th century. While the majority of the city was already a sprawling mass of poor tenement buildings, many Irish were denied access even to the moderately better tenements where living conditions were vaguely humane. Instead, they were crammed into the worst slums of the Lower East Side. Some accounts describe utterly chilling living conditions, almost unimaginable to most readers: single rooms housing as many as five families, with one or two families to a bed and no access to running water or any kind of basic sanitation, with corners of the same room where people slept and ate being used as lavatories. Filth upon filth piled up in these slums. There were few opportunities for the Irish, and in desperation, many turned to all kinds of crimes.

History is vague on the subject of Catherine and Patrick McCarty, but it would appear that Catherine, at least, was just a normal woman who was trying to eke out an honest living and a tolerable existence for herself and her family. There is very little information on her husband, Patrick, except that he fathered both of Catherine's children. The first was born on a disputed date in 1859, possibly September 28th. This was a little boy, whom she named Henry. It was Henry who would later become a scourge of the Old West. But at his birth, he was just another malnourished little baby, crying his nights away in the chaos of the Lower East Side.

Catherine's second child was born in 1863, and she named him Joseph McCarty, giving Henry a little brother. The little family of four continued trying to scratch out a living in their unsanitary home, but soon, things would change drastically.

Little Henry was somewhere between four and ten years old when he suffered the first of numerous awful losses that would pepper his short life. His father, Patrick, either died or left his family (sources differ) sometime during the 1860s. Catherine was left completely alone with two little boys and very few opportunities to make an honest living. As an Irish Catholic widow, she had almost no rights and practically no future. Still, she was determined to raise Henry and Joseph, and she held on to them fiercely. She decided to make a bold and radical move. She was going to move them from the slums of New York to find greener pastures in Indianapolis, Indiana, some seven hundred miles away.

How Catherine raised the funds for the journey and tackled it alone as a single woman with two very small boys, no one knows. In fact, we don't even know how old Henry was when his mother undertook the trip; he was younger than eleven at least, and little Joseph couldn't have been much more than a toddler. Indianapolis was not particularly welcoming to this Irish widow with her two little boys, but Catherine did find one piece of solace: William Henry Harrison Antrim.

As with much of Henry's early life, very little is known about what William was really like as a man and as Catherine's boyfriend, but he would certainly prove to be a disreputable character later in Henry's life. But for a time, Catherine seemed to be in love with him, and she soon began a steady relationship with him.

By 1870, Catherine and William were living together, and they decided to leave Indiana behind and embark on a journey that would take them even farther west and into a region that had recently been torn apart by the American Civil War: Kansas. With the boys in tow, Catherine and William arrived in Wichita, Kansas, another seven hundred miles from Indianapolis, sometime in 1870. Henry was around eleven years old by then, and little Joseph was seven, and they were about to step into what might have been the only happy period of Henry McCarty's life.

Wichita was good to Catherine and the rest of her little family. It's unclear what William did to occupy his time, but Catherine proved to be a hardworking and resourceful woman, certainly one not content with simply sitting back and allowing destiny to do to her as it would. She had an entrepreneurial spirit and started several small businesses in town, including laundry services and working in property sales. Irish or not, Catholic or not, female or not, Catherine was not going to let anything get in the way of her future with her children and William.

Henry and Joseph likely spent their days like any other kid in Wichita. They went to school, where Henry proved to be a good, quiet, courteous, and charming little student who loved to read. In the afternoons, they would play with their friends all over town, little Joseph forever tagging along as Henry and the big boys played cowboys and Indians or cops and robbers. Little did young Henry know then that his childhood games of cat and mouse eventually would bleed into his real life with real-life stakes.

For now, though, Henry enjoyed long, happy days of playing with his friends and brother, days of just being a normal kid. For three years, the boy who would become Billy the Kid was able to actually be a kid. But trouble loomed on the horizon. Trouble that would ultimately lead to a bloodthirsty life of crime.

\* \* \* \*

Henry was fourteen years old when Catherine's doctor gave her some absolutely devastating news: she had consumption.

Catherine had achieved more in her life than most American women could dream of at the time. She'd taken her children from a New York slum to a carefree life in a Western boomtown. She owned businesses and made her own way in the world instead of waiting for a man to do it for her. And now her doctor was telling her that she didn't have much time left to live.

Consumption was, back then, a death knell for thousands of people all over the world. It was a vivid description of a disease that seemed to eat its victims alive, known today as tuberculosis. While tuberculosis is nearly unheard-of in developed countries today, and its incidence across the globe continues to fall steadily, it is still a deadly illness that preys upon the immunocompromised.

In 1873, however, tuberculosis was still a global threat and a silent killer that stalked all humanity. This was before antibiotics or even a thorough understanding of modern disease theories, and so, people with tuberculosis almost invariably died. For Catherine, it must have been like a diagnosis of cancer.

The doctor's recommendation was a common one for the time: to move south, away from the ravaging winters that would make Catherine's fragile lungs even more vulnerable. And so, with

William and the boys in tow, Catherine was forced to leave the one place where she had been truly happy.

Teenage Henry must have felt that his whole world was about to change. His blissful existence in Wichita with his academics, his books, his friends, and his brother was being stripped away from him, and the next thing he knew, his mother was moving them six hundred miles south to Santa Fe, New Mexico. Another major change took place shortly after they arrived in Santa Fe. Catherine and William had been together for a minimum of four years or so by this point yet had never married. But spurred on by the hovering specter of her own death—and possibly trying to secure a future for Henry and Joseph after she was gone—Catherine decided it was time that they were officially married. The ceremony was performed in a church in Santa Fe, and fourteen-year-old Henry and ten-year-old Joseph were the witnesses for the marriage.

Henry's life had gotten suddenly very complicated. While little is known about his relationship with William at that point, Henry must have had a little trouble accepting that William was now officially his stepfather. It would be an adjustment for any child, let alone a child whose mother had been given a devastating diagnosis and who had just moved across the country from his friends. Nonetheless, both Henry and Joseph would take William Antrim's last name, and Henry McCarty became Henry Antrim.

Their stay in Santa Fe didn't last long. Soon, William and Catherine moved their little family three hundred miles south to Silver City, New Mexico. This new environment would soon prove instrumental in shaping the person that young Henry was to become. Silver City was a town in its infancy, having existed for only around three years when the Antrim family moved there; much of it still consisted of tents instead of buildings. As the name indicated, it had exploded into existence after silver was discovered in the nearby landscape, with prospectors flooding into the town. It was silver that had brought the Antrims there too. The journey from Wichita had sapped all but the very last of Catherine's strength, and the bustling, resourceful, industrious mother that Henry had once known was reduced to a pale skeleton of her former self. She was unable to work, and so, perhaps for the first time, William became the sole breadwinner. Prospecting was the only way he could think of to earn a living.

Silver was abundant in Silver City, but it also came at a high price. The Apache tribe still controlled large tracts of New Mexico, and they weren't about to surrender their ancestral lands to the influx of white settlers without a fight. In fact, the founder of Silver City himself had been killed just a year after the town was built, dying in an Apache raid. The threat of attack hung heavy over the town, and while it's hard to blame the Apache for defending their home, their ominous presence must have had an effect on Henry.

More than that, Silver City was completely lawless at the time. The hundreds of miners living there were not governed by any sheriff, and crime was rampant as poverty rose. For every prospector who succeeded in finding silver, there were many who were reduced to starving beggars.

This was a fate that would soon face the Antrim family. Catherine had always been the heart and soul of the family and the only reason for its continued financial survival. Now that she was bedridden, William completely failed to pick up the slack. They had moved to Silver City so that he could work in the mines; instead, William mostly gambled, losing more than he won, as gamblers often do. Henry and Joseph went from having a happy, carefree childhood, with friends and playtime and an education, to being two hungry children with a dying mother. The sicker Catherine became, the more William withdrew into himself and his gambling. It seems the thought of losing her was more than he could even imagine.

By 1874, Catherine's condition was critical. Fifteen-year-old Henry and eleven-year-old Joseph were faced with the terrible prospect of losing the woman who had been their anchor and pillar all their lives, but before they would be dealt that devastating blow, another tragedy quickly befell them. If Catherine had married William in the hopes that he would care for the boys when she died, she had overestimated William's commitment to their marriage and family. With Catherine on her deathbed, instead of supporting the boys, William simply left, disappearing from Silver City and from the lives of the boys.

Henry was left with a dying mother and with a little brother who could now only look to Henry for help and safety. The responsibility must have been crushing; the fear, even more so. It is unknown how Henry and Joseph survived for the next few months, but it must have been terrifying.

Tuberculosis was doing exactly what it always did: it was consuming Catherine, piece by piece. Her toiling lungs grew less and less capable of sustaining her body as she was reduced to little more than a skeleton wrapped in blue-tinged skin. There was nothing anyone could do for her, not in the 1870s. Slowly, agonizingly, she continued to fade in front of Henry's eyes as he struggled to care for his mother and little brother all on his own. She breathed her last on September 16th, 1874.

Catherine's death was a terrible trauma and must have plunged the boys into inexpressible grief, but Henry didn't have time to grieve; there were even more pressing concerns in his life. His parents were dead, his stepfather had disappeared, and he had a little brother to care for. Silver City was no place for an orphan, and Henry and Joseph may very well have faced an uncertain fate—and Billy the Kid may have lived an even shorter life—if it weren't for a few kind families in the city who decided to take them in. The boys were separated, and Henry found himself completely alone and dependent on the kindness of strangers.

For whatever reason, Henry never managed to stay with any of his foster homes for very long. Perhaps most families simply didn't have the resources to feed another mouth long-term; perhaps grief and anger had made Henry difficult to deal with, although most accounts suggest that Catherine's death did not change him on the surface and that he was still the sweet, funny, polite boy he had been back in Wichita.

Either way, by 1875, the troubled youngster was considered old enough to earn his keep, if not any wages. He was sent to live and work in the Star Hotel in Silver City, owned and managed by one Sarah Brown. He was something of a general worker, washing dishes and waiting on guests. It is unclear whether Henry was paid anything at all for his work, even though he was fast approaching sixteen, but he was given a roof over his head and presumably some food. Clearly, however, Henry's circumstances were not ideal. Perhaps Brown was abusive, as so many people were of their employees in those days. Beatings may have become a part of Henry's life; he was fed barely enough to survive, and so, Henry began to grow more and more desperate.

Every bit of stability that Henry had ever known was gone. He was fending for himself now, and he knew he had to do whatever it took to survive. Soon, he would be faced with a choice that would send him down a slippery slope to a violent life and an early death.

That choice had to do, prosaically, with butter. In the Star Hotel's dealings, plenty of merchandise came through the doors, and one day, Henry found himself alone with several pounds of a rancher's fresh butter. It was a fairly expensive and luxurious commodity in Silver City at the time, and Henry knew he could capitalize on it. He stole the butter, sold it quickly to another merchant, and finally had some money for the first time since his mother had died.

But the boy was not yet the seasoned criminal that he would later become. It wasn't long before Sarah Brown found out what he had done, and she was quick to call for Silver City's brand-new sheriff, Harvey Whitehill. Sheriff Whitehill was a formidable figure in his late thirties; a veteran of the Apache Wars, Whitehill had been chosen to bring order to the wilderness of Silver City for a reason, and Henry must have been terrified when he found out that Sheriff Whitehill was going to handle his case.

The moment that Sheriff Whitehill set eyes on Henry, however, he knew that this was no hardened criminal. Henry had always been a small, skinny boy with youthful features and great, sad, brilliantly blue eyes, and he looked more pitiful than ever now, a ragged little orphan who was completely alone in the world. Sheriff Whitehill couldn't bring himself to punish the boy. He simply gave Henry a stern talking-to and allowed him to return to the Star Hotel and continue with his life in peace.

Perhaps this reprieve would have convinced some boys to stay forever on the right side of the law after that. But Henry's encounter with Sheriff Whitehill seemed to have exactly the opposite effect.

It wouldn't be long before the sheriff would have no choice but to clap young Henry in irons.

# Chapter 2 – First Blood

*Illustration I: A photograph of Billy the Kid by Ben Wittick*

After the theft of the butter and his encounter with Sheriff Whitehill, young Henry continued to live and work in the Star Hotel, but his life was by no means easy. Apart from the hard work and the lack of good food, Henry was also deeply deprived of something he constantly missed: a family. William had been imperfect, and like all siblings, Henry and Joseph must have squabbled. Even Catherine could hardly have been all sunshine and roses. But all his life, even in the ugly slums of New York, even through the many moves across the country, Henry had had the stability of a family unit.

Now even that was gone. And having been in Silver City for only about two years, most of those years spent caring for his bedridden mother and little Joseph or bouncing around foster homes, Henry didn't have many friends at all.

The only person he counted as being a friend was a man named George Schaefer, also known as Sombrero Jack. Like a vast number of the men in Silver City at the time, Jack was bad news. He drank constantly and gambled even more so, possibly even in the hotel, if Sarah Brown was in the habit of serving drinks to anyone who would pay for them. Whether Henry knew it or not, Jack was also a thief. But perhaps it didn't matter to Henry even if he did know since Jack was the only person in his world who treated him with kindness.

It's unclear what Jack's motivations really were for being the only kind face that Henry ever saw. Perhaps Jack's heart was touched by the plight of this sweet young orphan, with his gentle voice and big, mournful eyes. Given how this part of Henry's story ends, however, it's far more likely that Jack knew an opportunity when he saw it. Jack more than likely knew that Henry would be an easy target, someone easy to manipulate and easy to use whenever and however he saw fit.

One day in 1875, Jack knew it was time to use his young friend for his intended purpose. He had just robbed the laundry down the street, which, like most laundries of the time, was staffed almost entirely by overworked Chinese men. Jack had stolen a large bundle of clothes from the laundry, as well as two guns, and he needed somewhere to hide it. With Sheriff Whitehill rapidly cleaning up Silver City, Jack was running out of hiding spaces.

He went over to the Star Hotel and got the attention of young Henry. Pointing out to Henry that he was wearing little more than rags, Jack offered him the bundle of clothes. It would appear that Henry was aware that the clothes had been stolen. Nonetheless, the boy was desperate. He took the bundle and hurried to hide it in his room, where Mrs. Brown discovered it in a trunk a short while later. She knew immediately that the clothes had been stolen.

Once again, Mrs. Brown was quick to call on Sheriff Whitehill, and this time, the sheriff knew that his stern talking-to had had no effect on Henry's choices when it came to crime. He decided that he was going to scare the boy straight, and he arrested him and dragged him to the Silver City jailhouse.

Henry would be held for a short while before he would be required to appear in court. It seems, however, that Sheriff Whitehill was not particularly interested in prosecuting the boy. He just wanted to make it clear that a life of crime would not be tolerated in Silver City and to hopefully influence Henry to make better choices. Accordingly, Sheriff Whitehill didn't leave young Henry locked up in the cells with the real criminals. Instead, he let him stay in the hallway outside the cells, giving him a little more freedom to move about. By all accounts, Sheriff Whitehill treated Henry with respect, trying to be kind to him. Perhaps, if Henry had only reached out, if he had only seen that Sheriff Whitehill's tough love held far more kindness than Sombrero Jack's empty promises and smooth words, his life might have been a very different one.

But Henry saw Sheriff Whitehill as the enemy; the star on his chest made him evil in Henry's eyes, and while he was civil and courteous to the sheriff the way he was to everyone at that point in his life, Henry knew he had to escape. He was locked in the hallway; Sheriff Whitehill knew that Henry wasn't a seasoned enough criminal to pick a lock. But the sheriff had underestimated Henry's slenderness and agility. His thin frame had often been the subject of ridicule by other boys, but now, it was his ticket to freedom. After just two days in custody, Henry climbed into the fireplace, reached into the chimney, and shimmied right out onto the jailhouse roof. From there, it was just a hop, a skip, and a jump to freedom.

The moment Henry's feet hit the ground outside the jailhouse, he knew immediately that his life had changed. He had been abused, starved, and overworked before; he had always been just an orphan, just a kid. Suddenly, although the moniker of "the Kid" would follow him for the rest of his brief years, Henry had to start thinking like a man. Child or not, he was an escapee now. He was a fugitive from the law.

Mrs. Brown was his erstwhile guardian, but she had proven twice that she couldn't be trusted in Henry's eyes by turning him in to the sheriff. Sombrero Jack had betrayed him and had since disappeared completely from Silver City. Now, Henry turned to the only people he could think of, a couple named the Truesdells, who lived nearby and had been among the people to foster him after his mother died. They were horrified when Henry turned up at their door. A story had been printed in the *Grant County Herald* shortly before Henry's escape, and while its wording was generally sympathetic to Henry, calling him "the tool of Sombrero Jack," it had made it clear that Henry had been arrested. The Truesdells knew at once that Henry was a fugitive from the law.

However, instead of turning him in to face the wrath of Sheriff Whitehill, they decided that it was high time his stepfather stepped up to the plate. They knew that William Antrim had gone to Clifton, Arizona, ostensibly for prospecting (although it would appear that William did about as much prospecting in Clifton as he did in Silver City). So, they bought a ticket and loaded the young Henry on a stagecoach to Clifton, hoping that William would be able to get some sense into him.

The stagecoach journey must have been a frightening one for Henry. Given all the traveling that he had done with his family in earlier years, he must have traveled by stagecoach before but never alone. Now, he found himself being jostled from one stage to the other, always swapping drivers, switching passengers, surrounded by strangers. He had just run from the law, and every other person he saw must have looked like a sheriff to him.

It was a wide-eyed and scared teenager who found himself on the doorstep of his stepfather's home in Clifton. Henry was frightened and desperate, and at first glance, William must have been able to tell how much hardship the boy had endured since William had walked out on him. He was clothed in rags, half-starved, and filthy, the kind of condition that Catherine would never have allowed.

If Henry had hoped that the sight of him would inspire some kind of paternal warmth in his stepfather, his hopes were entirely in vain. William allowed him to come inside and stay with him, but his stay was very brief—perhaps only a few days. It would appear that William was still mostly interested in gambling and generally being a deadbeat, but he was very quick to judge Henry based on the boy's own mistakes.

It didn't take long for William to pry the truth out of Henry about what had happened back in Silver City. As soon as William heard that Henry had been arrested for theft, he lost his temper, telling him that he was unworthy of staying in his house and ordering him to get out. The moment William's back was turned, Henry did just that but not before helping himself to some of William's supplies.

It had been made abundantly obvious to Henry that he had absolutely no one left in the world. His little brother Joseph had been passed on to a foster family back in New Mexico, nearly a hundred miles away, an impassable distance for a lonely boy on foot. Besides, his foster families hadn't wanted him, Mrs. Brown had betrayed him, and even Sombrero Jack had chosen to use him and then disappear. Perhaps, ironically, the only person left in Silver City who might have helped him was the sheriff. But in Henry's eyes, Sheriff Whitehall was his greatest enemy.

He was on his own. And his youthful heart, hopelessly scarred by the grief, abuse, desperation, and lack he had endured, had grown hard and cold. He thought nothing of taking clothes from William's closet and helping himself to some of William's supply of guns before walking out into the wilderness of Arizona.

\* \* \* \*

It was a very different person who left William Antrim's home for good. Henry was no longer the wide-eyed innocent who had been a teacher's pet that liked to read. Hardship had toughened him, and despite the fact that his cheeks were still smooth and his frame still puny, Henry felt that he was a little boy no longer. In conduct, he thought himself a man.

The truth was, as he headed southeast deeper into the Territory of Arizona, Henry was still just fifteen or sixteen years old. But he had no choice. All the people he depended on had failed him. He could only trust himself now.

It was this hardened youth who found a job working as a ranch hand in Arizona. Though his wages couldn't have been much, they were all his, and it was better than living with Sarah Brown. Still, Henry had no idea what to really do with money, and he was surrounded by the rough cowboys of the Wild West. They were bad influences on him, and he turned to gambling just like his stepfather, squandering his wages at the poker table. His job at that ranch didn't last very long, but his career as a ranch hand continued in 1876 when he went to work for businessman and rancher Henry Hooker. Hooker was a skilled businessman and an upright citizen—in fact, he was a friend of one of the Old West's most famous lawmen, Wyatt Earp. He was also the employer of one of its most infamous criminals—Billy the Kid.

Having grown rich on a single wild scheme involving herding five hundred turkeys over the Sierra River, Hooker now owned a prosperous ranch called Sierra Bonita, and it was here that young Henry Antrim worked. Perhaps Hooker could have taught Henry a thing or two, but instead, Henry was attracted to another man who tended to hang around the ranch: John R. Mackie. Mackie was about as disreputable as one could get. The Scotsman had been in the US Army in past years, but war had made him harsh and bitter, and the bloody realities of what he had witnessed had failed to build in his spirit the kind of loyal camaraderie that they inspired in so many other soldiers. Instead, Mackie cared only for himself.

He had been stationed at Camp Grant, a fort near the Sierra Bonita Ranch, and he still tended to hang around the outskirts of the army camp. His intentions, however, were by no means sentimental or nostalgic. Camp Grant was filled with cavalrymen and their fast, fit horses. In Arizona Territory at the time, horses were not simply a means of transport; they were a means of survival. A man on horseback could cross hundreds of miles of desert, whereas a man on foot would starve. Horses made it possible to transport goods, flee from enemies, and survive. And, of course, they were priced accordingly.

While horse theft carried a heavy penalty—hanging—it was still a business in which many criminals were interested thanks to its lucrative nature. John R. Mackie was no exception. Stealing horses from the US Army was so much easier than actually serving in it. It wasn't long before he introduced Henry to this lucrative business, and the two men started stealing and smuggling horses out of Camp Grant regularly.

It was around this time in 1877, as Henry's notoriety began to grow, that he needed an alias, which was a common practice in the Old West. Back then, the West was populated by people with nicknames like Wild Bill, Crazy Steve, and Calamity Jane. For Henry, it was easy to choose one. Among the grizzled veterans of the criminal world surrounding him, he stood out like a sore thumb: a scrawny, weak-jawed figure, with not even a trace of a beard, his youthfulness obvious in every line of his face and body. It wasn't long before he was becoming known as "Kid Antrim" or just "the Kid," a nickname that would stay with him for the few years he had left to live.

In a matter of two years, the Kid had escalated from getting a sheriff's scolding for stealing some butter to committing a capital crime by stealing horses from an Army camp. And it wasn't long before he sank even deeper into crime. He was taking horses now, but soon, he would take a human life.

\* \* \* \*

After his stint working as a ranch hand for Henry Hooker, Kid Antrim found a new job closer to the scene of most of his crimes. In fact, this new position was right in the middle of Camp Grant, and it even led him to work with the very animals he was stealing from the army camp.

Stealing so many horses had given the Kid a way with them, and he proved himself to be a capable horseman. Along with his youth and agility, this made him an ideal candidate to work as a teamster. His task was to hitch two enormous draft horses to logs that had been hewed in the woods just down the hill from Camp Grant and then juggle the horses and the log as the mighty animals hauled it up the hill. It was a tricky task, but the Kid took to it well, and it made it even easier for him and Mackie to steal horses.

In his role, the Kid would encounter a man who became a terrible thorn in his side. This was Frank Cahill, nicknamed Windy. Windy was a blacksmith, and he and the Kid met each other often as he trimmed and shod the draft horses' feet. What was more, they both frequented the same saloon in the nearby village of Bonita. Windy was a huge, angry, sharp-tongued figure who instantly resented the Kid's popularity. Despite the fact that he was now a seasoned thief, the Kid was still the same nice young man whose teachers had liked him back in Wichita and Silver City. Everyone liked him. Everyone but Windy.

Whenever the Kid was in the saloon, he just wanted to relax. It was the place where all the men gathered, and while the Kid was still a few weeks from his eighteenth birthday, he had long since stopped thinking of himself as a boy. He just wanted to drink, gamble, and hang out in peace. But Windy made that impossible. He loved to sling insults at the Kid after a few drinks, and sometimes, it went further than just insults. It started when he would simply ruffle the Kid's unruly dark hair, but soon, he started to shove him around, shouting and spitting in his face, pushing him to the floor. And most of the time, the Kid was his usual polite self, never allowing the confrontation to escalate—until one fateful evening.

August 17th, 1877, was the day that the Kid's life changed forever. He wasn't looking for trouble at the time. Why would he? He had a lucrative criminal career and plenty of friends; all he wanted to do was spend some of his stolen earnings on booze. But when Windy shouted at him as usual, calling him a "pimp," something snapped inside the Kid. He wheeled around and shouted at Windy that he was a "son of a b***."

Windy let out a roar of anger and lunged across the saloon. Like any blacksmith, he was a massive, powerful, heavily built man, easily twice the weight of the Kid, and he was an imposing figure as he attacked. The Kid was thrown to the ground, and Windy was on top, straddling the Kid's thin body. Blows rained down on the Kid's face as Windy's meaty fists pounded into his delicate features.

The Kid panicked. But instead of waiting for his friends to come to his aid, he reached for the pistol that always rested in his holster. He had never yet used it to draw human blood, but tonight, all that would change. He wrestled it out of the holster. It's unclear whether he actually meant to pull the trigger, but either way, there was a terrible, deafening crack, and blood bloomed across Windy's abdomen. The blacksmith collapsed, and the panicking Kid slithered out from under him. His clothes were stained with Windy's blood.

Windy was still breathing, but the blood was spreading in a massive pool around the fallen blacksmith. The Kid knew that Windy wouldn't survive and that he had just killed a man in the middle of a crowded saloon. Panic seized him, and he rushed out of the building. The patrons' horses were standing tied outside, and his eyes rested immediately on a long-limbed animal with strong muscles and wide nostrils—a racehorse. The Kid yanked its reins free, vaulted into the saddle, and spurred it away into the desert.

The swift horse carried the Kid away into the night but not away from the reality of what he had done or the fact that he had no idea what he was going to do next. He hid in the desert for a few days, long enough that he realized that there were countless angry Apache out there and that there was little water or food. He couldn't survive, he had no one to turn to, and he didn't know what to do. So, he returned to Camp Grant, which was a terrible mistake.

After the Kid had fled from the area, Windy died, bleeding out painfully and slowly through the bullet hole in his abdomen. The justice of the peace in the area— Miles Wood—was out for blood: the Kid's blood. It seems that once again, the Kid's friends had all abandoned him. He was arrested a few days after Windy's death, and Wood took him to the Camp Grant guardhouse, where he could be kept under lock and key until the sheriff could come and take him away.

The Kid was terrified. He knew that this time, he was facing a far greater threat than Sheriff Whitehill and his tough love. It had already been decided that the shooting was unjustifiable. The Kid had committed murder, and he knew he would hang for it. His only hope of survival was to escape. And escaping from Camp Grant would be far harder than shimmying up the chimney of the jailhouse in Silver City, for this time, the Kid had been placed in iron shackles and was kept inside a real cell.

The Kid was in luck, however. There was a dance going on in the nearby village that evening, and the guards believed that the Kid wasn't going anywhere, seeing as he was shackled and behind bars. They went off to attend the dance, and when they returned, the cell and the shackles were empty. It's not clear how he did it, but Kid Antrim had escaped again.

Once again, the Kid stole a horse and rode off into the night, but this time, he knew there could be no going back to his cushy life in Camp Grant. Instead, he decided that he would have to flee right across territorial lines. He only knew the way to one place: Silver City. It was the only place he could think of to go. Alone and in darkness, the Kid rode toward New Mexico as fast as his horse could carry him.

But traveling alone was a terrifying and dangerous undertaking, even for a murderer. The Kid was armed, but he was also heavily outnumbered when a band of Apache attacked. It's not clear whether the Apache saw him as an enemy or simply as an opportunity. Possibly, they were just raiders or thieves because they could have easily killed the Kid if they so chose. Instead, they simply threw him to the ground, stole his horse, and disappeared into the desert.

The Kid now found himself in as much mortal peril as he had been back in that guardhouse. Alone in the desert, with no food, no water, no horse, and no weapons, he was a dead man walking. If predators or Apache didn't kill him, starvation or thirst certainly would. But there was no turning back now. All he could do was continue stumbling onward through the desert, with its jagged red peaks and its endless sagebrush, and hope that he would eventually find his way home.

The Kid didn't quite make it to Silver City, but he did find his way to an old friend: an outlaw named John Jones. Jones lived in Dona Ana County, New Mexico, and somehow, the Kid dragged himself half-dead to Jones's door. He had trekked two hundred miles across the desert with practically no resources, and it was astonishing that he was alive at all. He was starving, his always-bony frame reduced to a pale skeleton, his great blue eyes filled with suffering. There was hardly any strength left in him, and he was at the brink of collapse when he met John Jones.

Jones quickly scooped up his young friend and carried him to his mother's home. It's unclear whether Barbara Jones was particularly supportive of her son's illegal endeavors, but even though the Kid was a murderer and a fugitive, she couldn't just let him die. Painstakingly, Barbara nursed him back to life, proving to be one of the Kid's few allies who was actually there for him when he needed it.

As soon as the Kid was well again, he knew he had to move on. He was a wanted man now, and not just for the theft of some clothes or horses but for killing Frank Cahill. Still, he was closer to Silver City than he had been in years, and he couldn't resist the pull of home. He rode to Silver City and visited there for a short while, spending time with some of the foster families that had taken him in after Catherine's death, including the Truesdells, who had first put him on that stagecoach to Arizona.

Still, the Kid couldn't stay long. Even though it felt like decades, it had been just three years since he'd fled Silver City, and he would be easily recognized. He began to wander across New Mexico, ultimately finding himself near Apache Tejo, a tiny settlement in Lincoln County.

There, the Kid accepted that ordinary work would never again be his lot in life. Instead, he joined a gang known simply as "the Boys," where his skill in stealing horses could be put to good use. The Boys were cattle rustlers, and Lincoln County was rich in abundant herds just ripe for the picking.

Little did the Kid know that some of those herds belonged to a man whose death would trigger one of the bloodiest feuds in the Old West. A feud that would catapult the Kid's name from notorious thief to enduring legend.

# Chapter 3 – The Lincoln County War

*Illustration II: John Henry Tunstall photographed in 1872*

During his stint as a cattle rustler, the Kid continually grew in notoriety among his peers. Something about his sweet manners, innocent appearance, and deadly reputation quickly made him the stuff of legend, and rumors about him began to spread. It was perhaps because of this that the Kid finally stopped using his real name of Henry Antrim. Even "Kid Antrim" was no longer safe. Instead, he adopted an entirely new moniker: William Henry Bonney. It is possibly ironic that he chose to use his stepfather's first names, considering that William's abandonment was the event that had set Henry's life on this tragic trajectory in the first place. Either way, it wasn't long before he never heard the name Henry anymore, as he went by Billy instead. Thus was born one of the most famous aliases ever heard in the Old West: Billy the Kid.

\* \* \* \*

While Billy the Kid was growing in notoriety as a cattle rustler in Lincoln County, he was only a very small part of John Henry Tunstall's problems.

John Henry had been born in England, a young man from a wealthy middle-class family who had excellent prospects and was an eligible bachelor for many a twittering young Victorian-era socialite. All of this disgusted him. John Henry was hungry for one thing alone—adventure—and marriage did not fit into his plans. He moved to British Columbia, Canada, in the early 1870s to join his father's business (a general store in the town of Victoria). Canada was still a few years away from becoming a British colony, and it all felt terribly tame to John Henry. There were still girls who wanted to marry him and boring, ordinary business to conduct. He wanted more, and when a friend tried to persuade him to take up sheep ranching in California, John Henry was all too quick to accept.

He moved in February 1876, but ranching there quickly proved to be unsuccessful. Still, California had proved one thing to John Henry: the West was the place that he wanted to be. It was a wild area, filled with crime and danger, steeped in vice, but for a young man seeking adventure, there was no better place to be. John Henry moved to Lincoln County, New Mexico, in 1876.

By the time Billy the Kid arrived in Lincoln County, John Henry had finally found success, not only as an adventurer but also, finally, as a businessman. He owned a general store in the town of Lincoln itself, and his vast herds of horses and cattle roamed contentedly across the slopes of his nearby ranch. They were beautiful, fat, healthy animals—exactly the kind that the Boys loved to steal.

Deep in the winter of 1877, the Kid did what he could do best: he stole a handful of John Henry's horses. The rancher was outraged, and the sheriff was called in. He arrested the Kid quickly, charging him with theft. Instead of having the young man hanged, however, John Henry seemed to recognize a kindred spirit in young Billy's eyes. He was only six years older than Billy, and the young man's charming personality quickly won him over. Instead of pressing charges, John Henry gave the Kid a job as a cowboy and gunman on his ranch.

What the Kid might not have known was that his theft of John Henry's horses wasn't simply a crime of opportunity. In fact, the Boys, led by toughened outlaw Jesse Evans, had possibly been contracted to rustle John Henry's stock. This was all thanks to a deeply rooted feud that was being waged all over Lincoln County.

Before John Henry had come to Lincoln and gone into business with attorney Alexander McSween, two Irish-born businessmen had had almost complete control over the county's economy. These men were Lawrence Murphy and his protégé, James Dolan. Dolan, himself a veteran of the American Civil War, had had a harsh life until Murphy took him under his wing. Murphy was a visionary businessman, and he capitalized on every opportunity until his general store, the House, had a monopoly on the beef business in Lincoln. He made Dolan his business partner, which led to an easy and wealthy existence for Dolan until John Henry Tunstall showed up.

John Henry discovered that the House had made it nearly impossible for other cattle businesses to survive in Lincoln, and he decided that it was unjust for one business to control everything. He decided to set up a rival business, knowing that many cattle ranchers were unhappy with the state of affairs and hoping to make a fortune for himself.

By this time, Lawrence Murphy was lying in a hospital in Lincoln, sick and dying from cancer. Dolan was already losing the man who served as a father figure for him, and now, he was in danger of losing his very business to this young upstart. To make matters worse, enmity still simmered between the Irish and English everywhere. Dolan started to grow angrier as John Henry's business continued to grow. He had possibly hired the Boys to steal John Henry's cattle, and he also wasted no opportunity to threaten and insult John Henry.

All this meant that John Henry knew he needed armed support, both at his general store and on his ranch, and the Kid worked on the latter. He was all too happy to leave the Boys behind. Even though the Kid was officially a murderer, he was a long way from being a toughened gang member. They also treated him poorly, considering him to be nothing but a child, even throwing him out of the camp at times. The Kid hadn't known where else to go; John Henry's offer must have felt like a reprieve. In reality, it would drag him far deeper into the world of death and murder.

The Kid spent a few blissful winter months working as a cowboy and guard on John Henry Tunstall's ranch, but things grew steadily worse for everyone on the Tunstall side of the growing feud. Alexander McSween was jailed for embezzlement charges that were almost certainly false. Later, Dolan threatened John Henry directly, even going as far as drawing his pistol.

John Henry appears to have taken these threats seriously, although not seriously enough to get out of the business. The men who worked for him were always armed; in fact, he gave the Kid a Winchester rifle. The Kid appears to have loved the structure and stability that his life as John Henry's cowboy gave him. He worked with men who, while tough, were more interested in business than crime. They also took an instant liking to the charming young boy, and they appear to have readily accepted him despite his involvement with the Boys. The foreman, Dick Brewer, became someone that the Kid looked up to and admired.

But just as it seemed that the Kid might be on a more reputable path, disaster struck. A court order was issued to John Henry, claiming that the cattle on his ranch had to be seized in connection with McSween's ongoing court battle to prove his innocence. John Henry knew he couldn't save all of his livestock from being taken, but he had just won back his horses from Billy the Kid and the rest of the Boys, and he wasn't about to let them go once more.

Sheriff William Brady, who supported Dolan and the House, knew that John Henry wasn't going to let his horses go without a fight. He gathered a posse that included Jesse Evans—the Kid's erstwhile boss in the Boys—and sent it to John Henry's ranch on February 18th, 1878. When the posse leader, William Morton, got there, the horses and John Henry were gone. He had driven them toward Lincoln, hoping to hide them in a nearby canyon.

John Henry was riding at the head of his herd, accompanied by Dick Brewer and Deputy US Marshal Robert Widenmann. The Kid and another ranch hand, John Middleton, were riding along behind the herd, doing what was called "riding drag." Their job was to keep the horses moving smartly along as they fled from the posse. It was unpleasant work, hot and dusty and frightening, but the Kid was doing his best.

A sudden flutter of wings startled some of the horses. When the Kid looked up, he saw some wild turkeys fluttering among the sagebrush nearby. Wild turkeys were good eating, and they were much prized in the Old West. Anticipating that they might overnight out in the desert, the two men riding with John Henry rode after the turkeys, wanting to shoot them for dinner.

That was when the Kid spotted it: dust rising like a rooster's tail on the horizon. It was a familiar pattern, one that he had seen all too often. He knew that the dust had been kicked up by the hooves of galloping horses. The posse was coming, and the Kid panicked.

John Middleton set spurs to his horse, riding to warn John Henry. The Kid rode toward Dick and Robert, trying wildly to get their attention. It was too late. The posse was upon them. John Henry was alone. There was an awful crack, and the Kid remembered the way the sound rang through the saloon in Bonita, felt once again the slick warmth of Windy Cahill's blood. Only this time, the Kid was not the killer. Jesse Evans was, and he had shot John Henry in the head at point-blank range with no warning. Bill Morton had also shot John Henry, likely in the chest.

John Henry fell out of the saddle, dead, and with him fell the Kid's last hope of living a normal life. His world was shattered once again.

Seeking retribution, the following day, Dick and the Kid approached the local justice of the peace and testified to him that John Henry's killing had been cold-blooded murder. The justice of the peace, already disgruntled with the fact that Sheriff Brady had composed almost his entire posse from known outlaws, was quick to make them both his deputies and told them to go and arrest Jesse Evans and the other Boys who had been in the posse. But when Dick and the Kid approached the building where the posse was hiding with Sheriff Brady, the sheriff took the law into his own hands. He captured the two grieving men, ostensibly arresting them. They were released two days later, on February 22nd, 1878, when Marshal Widenmann arrested Brady's jailers and set Dick and the Kid free.

Even though the Kid had only known John Henry for a matter of months, he was deeply bereaved after the rancher's death, and he struggled to come to terms with what he had lost. In the harsh language of the frontier, he could think of only one answer to grief: revenge.

Dick Brewer was thinking along the same lines, and seeing that the local government was either turning a blind eye or siding with Sheriff Brady, he decided that the only thing he could do was to form a group of vigilantes in a bid to overthrow the House, support Alexander McSween, and avenge John Henry Tunstall's tragic young death. The Kid, who was approaching nineteen, was one of the first men to join the group, which became known as the Lincoln County Regulators.

The Regulators were quick to spring into action. On March 9th, 1878, Dick, the Kid, and others bloodied their hands as Regulators for the first time. They captured two of the men who had been involved in John Henry's killing: Frank Baker and, most importantly, Bill Morton, the leader of Sheriff Brady's posse and one of the men who had killed John Henry. Later, they would say that Baker and Morton were killed when they fought back in an attempt to escape the Regulators' clutches. However, it's far more likely that the two men were executed. The Regulators had decided that they were a law unto themselves. Frontier justice was brutally served, and the Kid, warped by grief, was all for it.

For several weeks, the Regulators were less active, and it almost seemed as though the Lincoln County War might be over. Then they struck again on April 1st, 1878, this time even more violently. Sheriff Brady and two of his cronies, George Hindman and Bill Matthews, were walking down Lincoln's main street when Regulators suddenly erupted from all around them in a devastating ambush. The Kid was focused on one thing: vengeance. While the other Regulators wanted to take down Sheriff Brady, as he was perceived as the leader of the House's supporters, the Kid blamed Bill Matthews most for John Henry's death. He fired at him wildly, and Matthews ducked under cover. It was evident now that the Kid was no longer the frightened boy who had accidentally shot Windy Cahill. He was ready to kill.

Meanwhile, Dick and the others killed Hindman and Brady. The bullets went quiet, and the Kid noticed something lying on the ground beside Brady: the Winchester rifle that John Henry had given him. He hurried over to the dead man to retrieve his gun, and Bill Matthews appeared from behind cover and fired. The bullet slashed through the Kid's hip with blinding pain. It was frightening and excruciating, but when the smoke had cleared, his friends assured him that he was all right—the wound was merely a graze.

So it was that the Kid, still nursing the minor injury, was with Dick, John Middleton, and the other Regulators three days later when they all trooped over to a little restaurant in a tiny nearby village known as Blazer's Mill. It consisted of little more than a post office, a tiny store, a mill, and a few houses, but it had hot food. The Regulators were all fugitives now, having murdered Brady and Hindman, and they had fled the Lincoln area to lie low in Blazer's Mill. But they found far more than a peaceful meal there.

Andrew "Buckshot" Roberts was also headed for Blazer's Mill on that tragic day. A grizzled old veteran of the West, Buckshot was a buffalo hunter and rancher. He had been a supporter of the House at one point, but after John Henry's death, he foresaw trouble. In fact, he had just sold his ranch in the area and came to Blazer's Mill to get payment from the buyer. Instead, he found a deadly battle.

When Buckshot arrived, the Regulators quickly realized that this was an opportunity to take down one of their enemies. One of them went outside to talk with Buckshot in a bid to get him to surrender. Knowing how Baker and Morton had died, Buckshot refused. Minutes later, Dick sent three of his men outside to dispose of the old hunter.

Outnumbered though he was, Buckshot proved to be a deadly opponent in a gunfight. No sooner had the armed men walked out of the restaurant than Buckshot was pouring bullets at them, wounding three men in quick succession. One of them, Charlie Bowdre, managed to get off a shot and wounded Buckshot badly in the chest, but the old cowboy still had life in him and went on shooting until his gun ran empty.

The Kid had been staying under cover in the restaurant while the bullets flew, but when he heard the metallic click of an empty weapon, he made his move. Rushing out of the restaurant, he charged at the bleeding and unarmed Buckshot. Wounded Regulators lay everywhere; John Middleton, who had been riding alongside the Kid the day John Henry died, was badly injured and bleeding from his chest. Perhaps it was seeing John that made the Kid hesitate to use his regained Winchester. Either way, before he could attack, Buckshot reversed the pistol in his hand and dealt a ringing blow to the Kid's temple. For Billy the Kid, everything went black.

He awoke to a devastating scene. The gunfight had been a brutal one. Wounded though he was, Buckshot crawled into a nearby house. The other Regulators all rushed to care for their wounded, but Dick Brewer was irate and blinded with grief and vengeance. He recklessly put himself in Buckshot's line of fire, and the old hunter shot him dead. Buckshot himself died shortly afterward.

This brutal killing was by no means the end of the Lincoln County War. It would grow even bloodier as time went on, and with every tragic attack and killing, the Kid only grew more desensitized to the violence, more accustomed to fighting and to murder.

The Regulators lay low for a few weeks after the death of Buckshot Roberts, but on April 29th, a new sheriff came to town to replace the murdered Brady: Sheriff George Peppin. Peppin was decidedly pro-House, and he was determined not to bring justice to Lincoln but to wipe out the Regulators. He quickly allied with Jesse Evans, and the two of them attacked and killed two Regulators on a local ranch. The Regulators realized that fighting once more was inevitable, and they prepared for battle, many of them gathering in Lincoln at Alexander McSween's house.

With Dick and John Henry both dead, Alexander McSween—whom the Kid knew as "Alex"—was the only leader that the Regulators had left. Fearing for Alex's life, George Coe, a Regulator who had his trigger finger shot off in the fight with Buckshot, decided to sit up on Alex's roof and defend his home. From this position, he famously shot and wounded one of the House's men at 350 yards.

The Kid himself next saw action on May 15th. With a group of Regulators, led by a sheriff's deputy who was on their side, he tracked, ambushed, and murdered one of the House's men.

By this point, it was clear to Alex that an all-out battle was brewing, and the Regulators' ranks had been badly thinned by the fighting. He left Lincoln in search of reinforcements, returning in mid-July 1878, accompanied by forty-one men.

Alex's return was a rallying call for the rest of the Regulators. They knew that they were going to have to take a stand, and they hastened to his side. Many of them were scattered around town in various hotels and homes, but ten stayed at Alex's house, and the Kid was among them. He had proven himself to be one of the most trusted Regulators, and Alex wanted him close by his side.

On July 15th, George Peppin rode into town, leading a posse alongside Jesse Evans—the Kid's nemesis. Evans had treated him brutally during his time as one of the Boys and had been involved in many gunfights since, and the Kid was ready to do battle against him. Immediately, fighting broke out. The innocent citizens of Lincoln could only lay low and hope for the best as the feud raged around them, bullets hissing and whining through the air, the crack of guns and the cries of the wounded filling the little frontier town.

The first casualty was one of Peppin's men. Shocked by the loss, Peppin briefly withdrew, realizing that the Regulators were more than he'd bargained for. He sent word to a nearby Army post at Fort Stanton, begging for help. The Army initially refused, and the battle dragged on day after day. Several Regulators fell, and so did another of Peppin's men. But the Regulators were gaining the upper hand.

That changed on July 18th. The thunder of hooves filled the air, drowning out even the gunfire, as the US Army came charging into Lincoln. Lieutenant Colonel Nathan Dudley was at the head of a troop of Buffalo Soldiers, which was the name given to this unit of African American men, so named by the Native Americans for the texture of their hair. They had come to Peppin's aid after all, and their strength and numbers made quick work of most of the Regulators. By the following day, only the handful of men who stayed at Alex's house were still fighting. The rest had all been captured.

The Kid knew that disaster was upon them, but he was determined to hold out, and Alex was in no frame of mind to surrender. They continued to defend Alex's adobe house as the US Army closed in on July 19th. Unable to get the Regulators to surrender, the Army decided to drive them out of the house by force. The next thing the Kid knew, the house was on fire. Thick smoke choked the rooms; Alex's home was engulfed in flames, and the Regulators could do nothing to stop it. Panic filled the air. In the chaos, many of the Regulators broke cover and dashed out into the street, where they fell like flies from the guns of the Army.

It wasn't a soldier but a House supporter named Robert Beckwith who rushed into the smoke and saw a figure coming toward him. Without looking, Beckwith fired, and the figure crumpled to the ground only for him to see that he had killed Alex McSween, who was unarmed. The Kid was appalled to see Alex fall. His next action came naturally; after all, killing was easy for him by now.

He raised his weapon, and he shot Robert Beckwith dead.

* * * *

It was the Kid who ultimately saved most of the Regulators that day. Rallying them in the single room that was not yet on fire, he led them out of Lincoln and to the comparative safety of the surrounding wilderness, becoming in one day both a killer and a hero. But it was a terrible, terrible moment for the Kid. He had just lost so many men who were important to him: Alex, John Henry, and Dick, just to name a few. And it was abundantly clear that, although spats would continue into the mid-1880s, the Lincoln County War was over. The Regulators had lost.

Now, the Kid found himself once again alone and desperate in a country filled with his enemies. He was swiftly indicted for the murder of Sheriff Brady, among others, and warrants were issued for his arrest.

Billy the Kid was a wanted man and an outlaw. And he would die for his crimes.

# Chapter 4 – Dying Young

*Illustration III: The gravestone that Billy the Kid shares with two of his friends*

By the time a year had passed since John Henry's killing, the Kid had grown arrogant.

Hardened by the trauma of the Lincoln County War, the Kid had given up any hope of a normal life and had thrown himself into living as an outlaw. For him, that meant doing whatever he wanted: rustling horses, womanizing, drinking, gambling—he had thrown all thought of normality to the wind. He had escaped Lincoln with his life, after all, and with every month of freedom that passed, the Kid felt more and more invincible.

After the so-called Battle of Lincoln in July 1878, the Kid, along with several other Regulators, fled a hundred miles north to the village of Fort Sumner. Here, for months, the law failed to find him, and the Kid did as he pleased with his Regulator friends. There was one instance of violence when some of the Kid's new Mexican cronies clashed with the Mescalero Apache over the theft of some horses; an accountant who lived nearby, Morris Bernstein, rode into the chaos and was shot and killed by one of the Mexicans. Because the Kid was nearby, however, he was indicted for the murder.

Nonetheless, the Kid continued to evade the law and grow rich on the proceeds of horse theft. He even returned to Lincoln to steal horses from Fritz Ranch, the very same ranch where two Regulators had died in 1878. He sold them in Tascosa, Texas, and settled there for some time, continuing to live the outlaw life.

His bliss could not last long. Things were shifting and changing in Lincoln. A new governor had been appointed named Lew Wallace, who had served as a general during the American Civil War. Wallace was determined to whip New Mexico Territory into shape, starting with notorious Lincoln. His job was not made easy. Jesse Evans and the Boys were still rustling and causing trouble in Lincoln, and a new gang led by John Selman had taken it a step further, adding gang rape and the murder of children to Wallace's list of worries.

The Lincoln County War and its aftermath were a headache that Wallace just didn't need. Accordingly, he granted amnesty to all of the combatants in the war, except for those who already had indictments. The Kid didn't get to benefit from the amnesty, but he did feel as though Wallace's action was a step toward putting the feud behind him. Knowing he couldn't escape the law, the Kid hoped to escape at least the threat of being killed by the Boys, and he wrote to Jesse Evans asking if they could parley and hopefully make peace.

In the meantime, Alex McSween's widow, Susan, was seeking justice for the senseless murder of her husband. She had approached a mild-mannered attorney named Huston Chapman to assist her. He had been representing Susan for some time, and he was in Lincoln the day that the Regulators and the Boys met, February 18th, 1878, exactly one year after John Henry's death.

Surprisingly enough, the parley managed to proceed without any violence. The Boys and the Regulators agreed to put an end to their feud. The Kid shook hands with Jesse Evans, and then in true outlaw fashion, they all proceeded to the nearby saloons and became utterly intoxicated.

While the men were sitting around the street, all in an advanced state of inebriation, Huston Chapman came walking down the main street of Lincoln, where Sheriff Brady and his deputies had been killed just months earlier. Jesse Evans immediately began to mock the attorney, asking him where he was going and telling him to dance. One of his men, an excitable youngster named Billy Campbell, joined in the mocking. James Dolan, the owner of the House, was also present, and he was also drunk.

As the mocking grew worse and Chapman continued to try to get away, the Kid realized trouble was coming. He tried to leave, but Evans pointed his pistol at him and ordered him to stay.

Chapman was growing more and more tired of this tomfoolery. Eventually, he lost his patience, realizing that he was speaking with his enemies, the very men whom he wanted to bring to justice for Alex's sake. He demanded to know if he was speaking to Dolan, and Evans responded instead, saying that he was a friend of Dolan's. At that point, unprovoked, Dolan drew his weapon. He and Billy Campbell both fired, and Chapman dropped dead.

Next, Evans ordered the Kid to draw Chapman's weapon from his holster and place it in his hand so that the sheriff would think Chapman had fired first. The Kid crept nearer to the body, but instead of doing as he was told, he bolted, just managing to escape with his life.

The tragic end to what the Kid had hoped would be a treaty had broken his heart. He knew now that there was no trusting Jesse Evans and no hope for peace. To make matters worse, he feared that he would be indicted for Chapman's murder too. On top of that, the Kid had hoped that Chapman would be able to get justice for Alex. Now, he wanted to bring Chapman's killers to justice, and he could think of just one way to do that.

The Kid wrote to Wallace shortly after Chapman's death with a staggering offer: he would testify about Chapman's murder if Wallace could guarantee his safety and treat him with lenience. Wallace was quick to agree—perhaps a little too quick. Yet, the Kid, for all his killings, still had his soulful blue eyes, his smooth baby face, and the naivete to go along with it. He trusted Wallace, and on March 21ˢᵗ, 1879, the Kid allowed himself to be arrested and taken to Lincoln's jailhouse.

The Kid held up his end of the deal. He testified truthfully about Chapman's murder, seeing the trial through to the end, and was then returned to the jailhouse in Lincoln. Wallace, however, had no intention of honoring his promises. He ignored the Kid completely thenceforth, and the local district attorney refused to let the Kid go.

For nearly three months, the Kid languished in jail, waiting for his freedom. By June, it had become evident to him that he was never going to be set free. He was reluctant to return to the life of a wanted fugitive, but he had been left no choice. With a heavy heart, the Kid planned yet another jailbreak, escaping on June 17th, 1879.

The Kid fled straight back to Fort Sumner, where he continued to live his outlaw life, drinking, carousing, and stealing as he pleased. He had given himself over to the reality that he was a murderer and that peace would never again be possible. Killing had become almost casual to him. This was made evident on a cold evening in January 1880 when the Kid was drinking and gambling as usual with some friends in a saloon in Fort Sumner. Joe Grant, a large, loud-mouthed man, had come into the saloon just looking for trouble. He was pushing other patrons around and spoiling for a fight, and the Kid was ready to give it to him. Grant reminded him of Windy Cahill, and what was more, it is possible that Grant was planning to kill the Kid and that someone had told him this.

The Kid went up to Grant and commented on the beautiful six-shooter pistol that the man was carrying. Looming over the scrawny figure of the Kid, who was then only twenty years old, Grant handed over the pistol with drunken laughter. The Kid realized that there were less than six bullets in the cylinder. He spun it quietly to present an empty chamber to the barrel, returned the gun to Grant, and walked away.

Minutes later, Grant pulled out his pistol and fired it at the Kid. The pistol clicked on its empty chamber, and the Kid coolly returned fire, killing Grant immediately.

It was in 1880 that the Kid also befriended a rancher near Fort Sumner named Jim Greathouse. Greathouse was a wealthy and useful ally, a fact that became abundantly obvious the following November. The Kid had just turned twenty-one and was heading into another winter of stealing horses and drinking when a local sheriff's deputy decided that it was time to bring the Kid to justice. James Carlysle gathered a posse and rode to corner the Kid and some of his friends in Fort Sumner. The Kid narrowly evaded them and rode straight for Greathouse's ranch, hoping to seek shelter with his friend. Greathouse welcomed him into his home, and when James Carlysle arrived, the rancher told Carlysle that he was being held hostage. It's unclear whether this was actually the case or whether Greathouse was simply playing along.

Either way, Carlysle boldly offered to exchange himself for Greathouse as a hostage. Not only was he trying to protect the civilian, but he also wanted the opportunity to negotiate with the Kid. Greathouse agreed, and Carlysle entered the house, starting to talk to the Kid. By this time, it was obvious to the Kid that he could trust no one, especially not a lawman. Tensions escalated within the house, and Carlysle rushed for a nearby window on the second floor, breaking it open and leaping out.

He was still alive when he hit the ground, but immediately, bullets began to fly. It would appear that Carlysle's posse panicked and began randomly shooting everything that moved. Some accounts say that they even killed Carlysle themselves; others say that the Kid leaned out of the window, looked Carlysle in the eye, and shot him dead. Either way, the Kid and his friends escaped in the chaos, but it was evident to the Kid that his time was running out. The law was drawing the noose tighter and tighter around him.

The man pulling that noose was the new sheriff of Lincoln County, Pat Garrett. Strangely enough, Garrett's varied career—from a barman to a ranch hand to the county sheriff—had actually brought him into contact with the Kid during previous years. Before the Lincoln County War, Garrett and the Kid had been drinking buddies. But now, Garrett saw the Kid as his ticket to fame. He had become the stuff of legend, a bogeyman of New Mexico. Bringing him to justice would be a highlight of any lawman's career. And Pat Garrett had just been elected a few weeks before the Greathouse incident.

It didn't take long for Garrett to learn that Fort Sumner was the Kid's favorite hideout. Just weeks after the Greathouse incident, Garrett summoned a posse of his own and rode quietly into Fort Sumner to lay a trap for the Kid. The Kid was hiding out on another ranch at the time, but Garrett craftily had a note written and sent to the Kid, telling him that the lawmen had left. Delighted to be able to return to Fort Sumner and get back to his wayward life, the Kid gathered his friends—among them Tom O'Folliard, with whom he had become very close since the Lincoln County War—and rode back into Fort Sumner. Tom was riding in the front, and the first warning the Kid had of Garrett's presence was a terrible crack of gunfire. Tom slumped dead in the saddle, and Garrett and his men erupted from behind their cover.

The Kid wheeled his horse around and rode off into the fog as quickly as he could, but Garrett was close behind. Along with his remaining friends, Billy the Kid barricaded himself in a nearby ranch house. A miserable stand-off ensued the next day, December 19th, 1880. The outlaws did their best to outlast the lawmen, but where gunfire had failed, starvation and cold succeeded. The Kid gave himself up. Garrett dragged him into Fort Sumner, where the local blacksmith fitted him with heavy iron shackles on his arms and legs. Garrett wasn't going to let him escape this time.

For some months, it appeared that Garrett had succeeded. The Kid was still struggling to escape, but the jailhouse in Santa Fe proved to be far more difficult to get out of than the many cells that the Kid had previously escaped. He tried digging through the floor and ended up chained to the wall. This time, there would be no slipping away. Attorneys had little interest in representing him; in desperation, he even wrote to Wallace, who flatly ignored him. In his eyes, seeing the Kid hang would get rid of a considerable nuisance, deal or no deal.

Late in March, the Kid was moved to nearby Mesilla, where he stood trial. Ironically, it has been debated whether the two murders for which he was tried were among the many murders he actually committed. He was tried for killing Sheriff Brady, who was killed by the other Regulators during an ambush, and Buckshot Roberts, who was killed by Charlie Bowdre. However, he was found guilty on April 15th, 1881, and was sentenced to hang on May 13th, 1881.

Before the hanging, he was moved back to Lincoln, where he was confined next to Garrett's own office in the two-story courthouse. One of his guards was Bill Matthews, the very man who had given him his first gunshot wound at the very beginning of the Lincoln County War. The Kid was kept handcuffed, chained, and under twenty-four-hour guard, and it seemed that he would live out the rest of his brief and miserable days under constant scrutiny.

Perhaps this gave Garrett a false sense of security; perhaps he felt he had already won, that the Billy the Kid debacle was over even before the Kid was hanged. Either way, he left town on a tax-collecting expedition, and the Kid was left with two guards: Bob Olinger and James Bell.

On April 28th, Olinger left the room to feed the other prisoners by taking them across the street to a nearby hotel for lunch. The Kid was allowed no such luxury, but when he asked Bell to take him to the outhouse, the guard complied. The Kid was still handcuffed and shackled, but he shuffled out of the back of the courthouse with a plan in mind. He had grown very used to the handcuffs, and he knew that they were just a little big for his tiny, boyish hands. They had been the subject of ridicule before, but they served him well now. He slipped one of them out of the cuffs, whirled around, yanked Bell's weapon from his holster, and struck him over the head with it. Bell stumbled away, panicked, and bolted. The Kid coolly shot him dead in the back.

He left the dead lawman and ran back into the courthouse, looking for an ax with which to get rid of his shackles. Instead, he came across Olinger's shotgun in one of the second-story rooms. Leaning out of the window with the shotgun, he spotted Olinger hurrying back across the street.

"Look out, old boy," he called out, "and see what you get."

Olinger looked up, and he got both barrels in the chest, killing him instantly.

The Kid escaped yet again, fleeing into the desert and dodging his execution. And while he never would face the hangman's noose, his death would nonetheless be quick and violent.

\* \* \* \*

Sheriff Garrett returned to Lincoln to find Billy the Kid gone and two of his deputies killed. In response, Wallace placed a $500 bounty on the Kid's head (about $12,000 in today's money). Garrett needed little motivation to go hunting after the Kid. His gut told him to go back to Fort Sumner, and unbelievably, that was exactly where the Kid had gone. With all of the Old West before him and so many different places to flee to, the Kid was unable to resist the pull of the village that had become his home.

Questioning several people in the town, Garrett found out that the Kid was staying with an old friend named Pete Maxwell. That evening, he went to Maxwell's home. Maxwell was shocked and frightened to see Garrett, and he quickly led him up to his own bedroom, hoping to keep him away from the Kid, who was asleep in a different room. Garrett sat down and started to interrogate Maxwell, desperate to find out where the Kid was but reluctant to be violent with the apparently innocent Maxwell. Maxwell talked in circles, trying not to tell Garrett anything, but the nervous pitch of his voice woke the Kid.

It was very dark, and when the Kid entered Maxwell's room, neither he nor Garrett recognized one another at first. Still, the Kid had heard Garrett's voice, and he knew there was a stranger inside. He drew his weapon, asking Maxwell, "Who is it? Who is it?" in Spanish.

Those would be his last words. The moment he spoke, Garrett knew his voice. He pulled out his gun and fired twice into the darkness. There was a terrible thud. The Kid had collapsed to the floor with a bullet in his chest, and he died there on that floor in a pool of his own blood.

# Conclusion

The proverb that those who live by the sword die by the sword has never been so apt as when applied to the life of Henry McCarty, better known as Billy the Kid. Yet it seems as though the Kid's choices, while appalling, were often driven by awful circumstances.

Starting from the slums of New York City, the Kid's life was never easy. His father died when he was young, he lost his mother just a few years later, and his stepfather walked out on him. After that, the few friends he had that did not betray him were killed in front of him. Anytime a semblance of peace or structure came into his life, it was cruelly torn away from him.

Nonetheless, it is certain that the Kid, folk hero though he has become, was a cold-blooded killer. He may have been pressured by circumstances, but at the end of the day, he alone made the choice to pull the trigger time and time again.

# Part 3: Buffalo Bill

*A Captivating Guide to a Cowboy Who Served in the American Civil War and Is Known for the Wild West Shows*

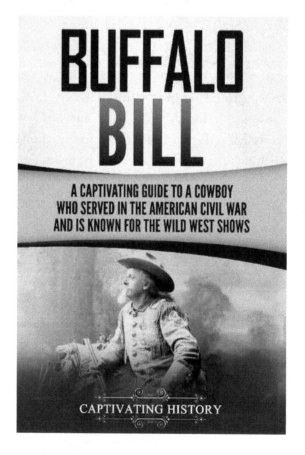

# Introduction: How He Made a Name for Himself

William Frederick Cody, better known as Buffalo Bill, was born on February 26th, 1846. His parents, Isaac and Mary Ann Cody, resided on the outskirts of what was then the small outpost of Le Claire, Iowa. Isaac was originally from Canada, and just a year after Bill's birth, the family decided to move up to Ontario, where they had their young son formally baptized as William Cody. The family would remain in Ontario, where they farmed their land, until 1853. They decided to pack up and move to the settlement of Fort Leavenworth in what was then the Territory of Kansas.

In those days, the people of Kansas were horribly divided over the issue of slavery. Kansas was on the verge of statehood, but it was caught between those who wished for the state to remain so-called "free soil" and those who wished to introduce slavery to the region. Outright violent altercations often erupted between those who were against the practice and those who supported it. Such turmoil gave rise to the region's nickname of "Bleeding Kansas."

Isaac was one of the residents who were against the institution of slavery. He was quite vocal in his views and would often meet with local men who shared his beliefs. The fact that he was against the expansion of slavery soon put him at odds with many of his pro-slavery neighbors. On one occasion, Isaac gave an impromptu speech against slavery, which provoked the wrath of some pro-slavery men who were present, one of whom actually lunged at Isaac and stabbed him twice with a knife.

Bill's father was seriously injured by the assault, and at least one of the knife blows pierced his lungs, but his friends managed to get him to the doctor so that he could be treated and recover from his wounds. Bill's father would sadly pass away just a few years later, in March of 1857, due to a respiratory infection that was exacerbated by the lasting damage of the knife attack. Bill was only eleven years old when his father passed, yet from this day forward—for all intents and purposes—he became a man.

It was now on his young shoulders to find a means to support not only himself but the rest of his family, which, at that time, included four sisters—Helen, Eliza, Julia, and Martha. After his father's passing, Bill's first gig was working for a neighbor, who had him drive his oxen for some "fifty cents a day." Such odd jobs were helpful, but Bill needed something more dependable. His major breakthrough came when he was hired to deliver parcels for a local company. This line of work would later lead to his efforts with the famed Pony Express.

Just prior to signing on with the Pony Express, fourteen-year-old Bill traveled west to investigate claims of the new gold rush in California. During this trip, he met a representative of the Pony Express, and Bill signed a contract with him to be a part of the team in 1860. It was also around this time that Bill Cody met the notorious frontiersman Wild Bill Hickok. His real name was James Butler Hickok, but he was better known by his nickname, which he earned due to his incredible fighting ability and his penchant for getting both into and out of wild situations. As he was ten years older than Bill, Hickok was already an experienced scout when Bill Cody was just beginning to learn the ropes.

The Pony Express was tasked with delivering mail from the state of Missouri to California in the early 1860s. The Pony Express utilized several relay stations that stretched from east to west. The rider would race from one station to another, switch horses, secure his bundle of packages, and ride off to the next station, only to repeat the process until the mail reached the final station from whence it would be delivered.

It was not only a tiresome task, but it was also a dangerous one. The riders risked being attacked by bandits, getting lost, or even freezing to death while en route to their next station. Bill himself was once allegedly ambushed while making a delivery. He allegedly outsmarted a bandit by pretending to be "scared and harmless" before using the heavy hooves of his pony to knock the man down. As Bill would later relate, "As I was galloping around a curve on a hillside trail one day, I rode flush up to a leveled pistol. The man behind it told me to throw up my hands. I obeyed. There is no use arguing with a leveled pistol. Frontiersmen in those days shot to kill. The road agent dismounted and walked up to me to take my saddle-bags. I tried to look scared and harmless. He lowered his revolver as he reached for the bags. Just then I whirled my pony around. The little horse's plunge knocked the man off his feet, and a stray kick from one of the iron-shod hoofs grazed the fellow's head, knocking him senseless. Having no further interest in him I was glad enough to make my escape, and rode in safety in time to the next station."

Once the Civil War broke out, Bill left his position with the Pony Express to render his services for the Union Army. Initially, he did not enlist as a regular soldier due to his young age. He also allegedly swore to his mother that he would not "enlist while she lived." Incidentally enough, shortly after his mom passed away, Bill ended up joining Union Company H, 7th Kansas Cavalry, in 1863. With this Kansas-based militia, Bill was able to carry out a revenge of sorts against the Missourian "border ruffians" who had encouraged the persecution of his father.

Bill later claimed that he was pressured to join by folks he used to know back in Kansas. And his colorful portrayal of their campaign to get him to join up is about as entertaining as they get. Bill would later explain, "I met quite a number of my old comrades and neighbors, who tried to induce me to enlist and go south with them. I had no idea of doing anything of the kind; but one day, after having been under the influence of bad whisky, I awoke to find myself a soldier in the Seventh Kansas. I did not remember how or when I had enlisted, but I saw I was in for it, and that it would not do for me to endeavor to back out."

Bill was apparently a jack of all trades while in the army. He rustled cattle, fought in battles, and, at one point, even worked as a spy. Bill also found time for romance. While he was on leave in 1865, he met the woman who would become his wife: Louisa Frederici. Bill asked her if she would marry him if he came "back after the war was over." Louisa agreed. So, after Bill had been discharged, he returned to her in the spring of 1866, and the two were married. This union would eventually produce four children.

In the early days of his marriage, Bill was a busy man and was often away from home. He worked intermittently as a scout and was basically on call for whenever his services were required. Nevertheless, on December 16th, 1866, he made sure he was at his wife's side, for it was on that day, his daughter Arta was born. During the winter, demand for scouts usually slowed down due to the inclement weather, but Bill was back on the trail by the spring of 1867.

At this point in time, Bill had already done much in his career, but when he was hired on by the Kansas Pacific Railroad, Bill would quite literally make a new name for himself. When the railroad company concocted a scheme to requisition buffalo meat as food for its many employees, Bill signed on to help hunt the wild animal down. It's said that from 1867 to 1868, he took out some 4,280 buffalos.

He wasn't the only one given this task. Bill found a major competitor in the form of a man named William Comstock. At the end of the day, though, Comstock was no match for the buffalo hunting prowess of Buffalo Bill Cody. As mentioned, Buffalo Bill managed to single-handedly kill around 4,280 Buffalo. Due to this feat, folks began to call him Buffalo Bill.

# Chapter 1 – Reaping the Rewards He Was Given

*"Harness mules and oxen, but give a horse a chance to run."*

*-Wild Bill Hickok*

Buffalo Bill was a well-known scout, hunter, and frontiersmen, and he managed to eke out a decent living for himself and his family. Although he had various employers, his most reliable paycheck usually came from scouting for the US government. As such, in 1868, when prospects began to dry up elsewhere, Buffalo Bill once again signed on with the US armed services, joining up with the 5th Cavalry Regiment. There, he worked as a dispatch carrier, and Bill is famous for the astonishing feat of covering some 350 miles over dangerous terrain in under 58 hours.

Due to this incredible feat, he was given several pay raises until he maxed out at the "highest level of pay for scouting," along with an additional $100 bonus, which was officially sanctioned by none other than the secretary of war. Bill was also promoted by General Philip Sheridan, who placed him as the chief of scouts for the 5th Cavalry Regiment. Although it was not exactly an official military ranking, by designating Bill the chief of scouts, the US Army was basically making Bill their number one man when it came to seeking advice on how scouting should be approached.

In the fall of 1868, Buffalo Bill and his fellow men of the 5ᵗʰ Cavalry saw action against "a band of Cheyenne Dog Men." This group was led by the famed chief of the so-called Dog Men, "Tall Bull." These fighters were known as "Dog Men" because of their peculiar habit of having their elite warriors tie themselves to a leash made of buffalo hide, which was attached to a stake in the ground, known as a "dog rope." These Dog Men absolutely refused to retreat, and the fact that they were on a leash proved it. The only ways they could leave the battlefield were if the enemy was vanquished or another Dog Man came along, picked up the stake, and "whipped him like a dog" in order to "drive him from battle."

After an engagement with the Dog Men, Bill was called upon to pursue the fleeing Dog Men, who had apparently decided to pick up their stakes and run away. Bill and his colleagues engaged in several skirmishes with the Dog Men across Kansas and well north of the border into Nebraska.

Tall Bull and his warriors managed to leave a trail of terror wherever they went, and by the summer of 1869, they had provoked the wrath of US authorities, as word was received that they had taken two female settlers captive. Bill's 5ᵗʰ Cavalry was tasked with taking on the bandits and freeing the hostages. Since Buffalo Bill was a veteran scout, he was given a front-row seat to the carnage, as he was the one to lead the 5ᵗʰ Cavalry to where Tall Bull and his men were holed up in Summit Springs, Colorado. Once the 5ᵗʰ Cavalry descended upon Tall Bull's camp, all hell broke loose.

In the desperate battle that ensued, it is said that fifty of Tall Bull's fighters were killed—with Tall Bull being among that number. It has never been verified just who killed Tall Bull, but Buffalo Bill was later lionized for being the one who pulled the trigger. Buffalo Bill himself eventually accepted this narrative, although his wife, Louisa, had her doubts. She later claimed that

Bill never really believed that he had been the one who had taken down Tall Bull and that he even thought it humorous that everyone assumed that he was the one to do it. Louisa later explained, "Many times afterward he laughed at the historical account of the killing—one out of the many heroic things with which he is credited that he did not accomplish."

In late 1869, at Nebraska's Fort McPherson, the wily scout once again met up with his wife Louisa and their daughter Arta. As wild as Bill was in those days, seeing his family helped to calm his temperament and remind him of what family life was like. It was also around this time that a guy named Ned Buntline showed up at the fort, looking for someone exciting to write about. Ned—whose real name was actually Edward Zane Carroll Judson Sr.—was a writer from New York who worked for several publishers and specialized in romantic tales of the West.

In his efforts to find a new Western hero to write about, Buntline made the acquaintance of Buffalo Bill. Bill made quite an impression on Buntline, and from their brief time together, Buntline crafted the first fictionalized account of the scout, which he called *Buffalo Bill, the King of the Border Men*. This romanticized telling of Buffalo Bill's exploits appeared in *New York Weekly* in December of 1869. In the 1870s, as his fame was beginning to grow in the East, Bill continued to carry out his rough and tumble life as he had been accustomed to doing in the West.

Buffalo Bill was a vital asset whether he served with the US military, freight companies, or rugged frontiersmen. But perhaps his most interesting feat during this period was when he was tasked to serve as a guide for a visiting Russian delegation led by the Russian grand duke, Alexei Alexandrovich. In January of 1872, Bill led the grand duke on a hunt across the American plains. Ironically enough, Alexei Alexandrovich had just spent the Christmas of 1871 in Buffalo, New York, and he was ready for Buffalo Bill to show him what the Wild West was all about.

The grand duke arrived by train on January 13th, 1872, and was immediately met by excited onlookers, who were being shepherded by an exuberant Buffalo Bill. Bill and a buddy of his, known as Texas Jack Omohundro (real name John Baker Omohundro), then led Alexei and his Russian entourage to the designated hunting grounds shortly thereafter. During this excursion, Alexei traveled by open carriage while Bill led in front, with several wagons of supplies behind them.

During the ride out to the hunting grounds, they would cover some fifty miles of terrain over the course of several hours. Once they had arrived at their destination, the group set up large tents where the duke and his company could relax and have their meals in between hunting. One of the highlights of the trip was when the duke met Spotted Tail, the chief of the Brulé Lakota. Buffalo Bill was on friendly terms with the chief and had explained that he had a "great chief [Alexei Alexandrovich] from across the water [from Russia] was coming there to visit him."

In all, it was said that some "600 warriors of different Sioux tribes, led by Spotted Tail," presented themselves at the hunting grounds. In what was essentially a precursor to the material Bill would use in his later Wild West shows, these Native American tribesmen proceeded to entertain their Russian guests by showing off their skills on horseback, by shooting their bows, and even engaging in a pretend battle, which was followed by a "grand war dance."

These were just the preliminary festivities, as the grand hunt itself took place on Alexei's twenty-second birthday, on January 14th, 1872. During the hunt, Alexei had the honor of riding on Buffalo Bill's own steed, the celebrated horse called "Buckskin Joe." This horse had been specifically trained in the art of hunting buffalo, and he was able to run at full speed with the beasts so that the hunter on his back could unload on the buffalo while in "full gallop."

Even so, Alexei had difficulty in bagging any game until Buffalo Bill rode up to him and demonstrated how it was done. Bill taught Alexei to only shoot once "he was on the flank of the buffalo." Alexei took Bill's advice to heart and was then able to finally take out a buffalo on his own. This animal was then gathered up and prepared for the duke so that he could take back the buffalo hide as a memento from his hunting trip in the American West.

Buffalo Bill was quite a showman, and his hunting trip with the Russian duke was perhaps the first time that he had fully put all of his skills as both scout and tour guide to use—skills that would prove invaluable when he made the transition from army scout to full-time Wild West showman. The US Army, meanwhile, was pleased with how things went with the duke, and for his efforts, Bill would earn himself the Congressional Medal of Honor. Of course, the medal wasn't just for the hunt; it was considered a reward for his entire history of work with the army.

While Bill was riding high on these accolades in the spring of 1872, Ned Buntline reached out to him again, extending a personal invitation for him to come out to New York. Bill consulted with his handlers in the army, and they must have been pleased with how things went with the duke since they readily granted him leave.

One of the main draws of Bill's visit was the opportunity to see the theatrical version of *The King of the Border Men*. Buffalo Bill was intrigued by the idea, and he reportedly remarked that he was "curious to see how [he] would look when represented by someone else." That someone else was a professional stage actor by the name of J. B. Studley. Studley worked hard to imitate Buffalo Bill, but as soon as the patrons of the theater realized that the actual man was in their presence, he quickly outshined the imitation. In fact, they invited him to get on stage to play himself. Swept up in their enthusiasm, Bill felt that he had no choice but to oblige. As Bill would later recall of that moment, "I felt very much embarrassed—never more so in my life—and I know not what to say. I made a desperate effort, and a few words escaped me, but what they were I could not tell, nor could anyone else in the house." Nevertheless, the manager of the theater was sufficiently impressed enough to offer Bill $500 a week simply to "play himself."

Bill initially resisted the idea. Even after he returned to the West, Buntline simply wouldn't let it go. After a flurry of letters, in which Buntline attempted to persuade Bill to consider the idea, Bill slowly came around to the notion. But what pushed him toward it more than anything else was his old buddy, Texas Jack, voicing his support to make a go of it. Ned Buntline had also guaranteed a big payout, so they figured they might as well give it a shot. So, in December of 1872, Bill made his way to Chicago to begin work with his fellow cowboy and partner, Texas Jack Omohundro, for Buntline's latest production.

Soon after meeting up with Buntline, Bill and Texas Jack were taken to meet Jim. Nixon—the owner of the amphitheater where the production would take place. According to the deal Buntline had arranged with the theater owner, Nixon was to provide the stage and orchestral arrangements, as well as furnish all local printing, while Buntline was to provide the acting company, the scripted dialogue, and the pictorial printing.

Nixon was distressed to find out that Buntline had yet to actually draft the script. This led to threats from Nixon, who said that he was going to cancel the whole thing, but after Buntline promised that he would have the final draft together soon, as well as personally laying out some $600 for that week's rent, Nixon begrudgingly agreed to continue with the efforts.

With no time to waste, Buntline got to work on the script. Taking most of his inspiration from his previous book, *Buffalo Bill, the King of the Border Men,* he hammered out the dialogue for the play. As Buntline later recalled of his mad dash to put words to the page, "After I begin I push ahead as fast as I can write, never blotting out anything I have once written and never making a correction or modification." And some four hours later, his clerks were making the final copies of his draft, which became the basis of the play, *Scouts of the Prairie*.

The next step was to hand the scripts over to Buffalo Bill and Texas Jack. As Bill later recalled, seeing all of the lines that they had to memorize was intimidating. Bill described it, "I looked at my part and then at Jack; and Jack looked at his part and then at me. Then we looked at each other, and then at Buntline. We did not know what to make of the man."

Since they didn't know what to make of Buntline or his script, they feared it would take them several months just to remember what they were supposed to say on stage. While Bill and Jack struggled to memorize their lines, Buntline got all of the extras together and requisitioned the costumes that they would wear. Texas Jack and Buffalo Bill Cody wouldn't need any special change of dress since they would only have to wear their regular everyday wilderness outfit.

As their debut neared, Buntline had Bill and Jack rehearse their lines in front of him. He was amazed to hear the two actors voice their cues and the action lines in the script. He heard Bill utter dialogue followed by "exit stage right" and "step to the footlights." No doubt Buntline was amazed by this, but he didn't have much time to ponder on it, as they were so close to showtime. The show must go on, and Buntline made sure that it did. By the time the curtain came up, he had made sure that Buffalo Bill and Texas Jack knew the difference between their cues and the dialogue.

When the curtain rose, the audience sat in rapt attention. The first few moments of the play depicted a Western landscape in which a trapper named Cale Durg—who was actually performed by Buntline himself—paced around on stage, pretending to examine his traps. Durg is upset since he believes that local tribal marauders have come along and stolen game right out of his traps. It was at this point that Buffalo Bill was cued to step onto the stage.

According to the later recollection of Buffalo Bill's sister, who was in attendance, Bill was incredibly nervous at the prospect of performing in front of a live audience and was overwhelmed with terrible stage fright. He recovered his wits soon enough, but he was unable to recall the rehearsed script he had been given, so he proceeded to adlib. He started talking about a humorous hunt he had led recently, and although it was not part of the script, the audience seemed to take it well enough.

The rest of the act went smoothly since it was mainly action sequences that did not require any lines. From this point forward, Buffalo Bill would learn to act much like he hunted buffalo, without much thought but with a whole lot of instinct. The first few rounds of this play went fairly well, and it brought in a lot of money for those involved. However, the critics were not always so kind, with some suggesting that the whole affair had been slapped together in a haphazard manner, which was basically true. Nevertheless, the audience loved it, and that was all that mattered.

After their first successful showing, Bill and his partners moved on from Chicago to showings in St. Louis. While he was on stage in St. Louis at DeBar's Opera House, he happened to look over and notice his wife in the crowd. He called out to her, "Honest, Mamma, does this look as awful out there as it feels up here?" The audience, realizing who Bill was talking to, encouraged her to go up and join her husband on the stage.

As the audience cheered and watched husband and wife reunite under the glare of the floodlights, Louisa shook with anxiety. It was at this point that Bill quietly remarked, "Now you can understand how hard your poor old husband has to work to make a living." Overcome with stage fright, Louisa made her way off stage and supposedly "sat in the darkest corner of the house."

After finishing up in St. Louis, the acting company then made their way to Pike's Opera House in Cincinnati. The price for admission was "seventy-five cents for a stall and twenty-five cents for the gallery," which was a pretty competitive rate at the time.

Buffalo Bill wasn't sure if acting was his future, but in the meantime, he was content to reap the rewards he was given.

# Chapter 2 – Buffalo Bill Answers the Call

*"When the war closed, I buried the hatchet, and I won't fight now unless I'm put upon."*

*-Wild Bill Hickok*

After his first touring season came to a close, Buffalo Bill was approached by a British man named Medley, who requested Buffalo Bill serve as his own personal scout during a hunting excursion in the West. It's not clear how well Bill viewed the idea of going back to his old stomping grounds as a scout once he had achieved fame on the stage, but the price was right enough. The man offered to pay him $1,000 in one go for his trouble. This was certainly a good chunk of cash in those days, and Bill gladly accepted the offer.

The following winter, Bill and company were back on stage. In the next few years, it would become a well-worn routine of his to scout in the warmer months and then make money with acting shows on the road during the winter. When he was off the stage and back on the trail in the West, his exploits were every bit as exciting as anything portrayed on stage.

For example, in May of 1872, Bill was sent to lead a group of men tasked with confronting "a band of marauding Indians," which had been engaged in local depredations. They followed the renegades to Missouri's Fort Sully, which was, at the time, located in the Territory of Dakota. They then doubled back to Fort Randall before heading back to Fort McPherson in Nebraska—a trip that had the group covering some 900 miles.

In late 1873, Bill was back on stage again. But there were some minor changes to the lineup. On August 31st, 1873, Texas Jack decided to marry one of the main leading ladies, an Italian actress named Giuseppina Morlacchi, who is notable for introducing the can-can to America. Texas Jack would eventually return to the cast, but it was decided that founding cast member Ned Buntline would take on more of a background role rather than sharing the spotlight with Buffalo Bill.

Along with these adjustments, there was a powerful new addition to the cast in the form of Buffalo Bill Cody's old partner, Wild Bill Hickok, who decided to join forces with him in the theater. Buffalo Bill had to do a bit of detective work to find his old friend since they had lost contact in the intervening years. After a bit of digging, he found that the old scout was currently "living in Missouri, eking out a living as a gambler."

From what Buffalo Bill Cody could gather, Hickok didn't seem to have much going for him at the time, and Bill believed Hickok would jump at the chance to be able to make a reliable income. But Buffalo Bill Cody didn't realize that Wild Bill had sworn off acting long ago due to a previous attempt Wild Bill himself had made as a showman in the late 1860s.

Wild Bill had tried to stage a "Grand Buffalo Hunt" for the public, which was similar in scope to what Buffalo Bill ended up doing with the Russian duke in 1872. However, Hickok's effort turned into a disaster when the buffalo and other wild animals he was using as living props decided to stampede the crowd. The audience had to literally run for their lives. After that debacle, Wild

Bill Hickok wasn't thrilled about further attempts at theatrical productions.

But once Buffalo Bill got into correspondence with Hickok, he managed to override his friend's concerns by promising him a hefty paycheck for his efforts. In the end, Hickok's fears proved to be overblown, and the show was a success. During the second season, crowds were routinely wowed by a combination of Texas Jack's "lasso tricks," Wild Bill's "fancy shooting," and Buffalo Bill's charismatic stage presence. For it was Buffalo Bill's ability to size up the audience—what pleased them and what didn't—that allowed for the continued success of the group.

In one instance, for example, Buffalo Bill Cody, Texas Jack, and Wild Bill Hickok were seated around a fake campfire, pretending to be drinking and swapping stories about life on the range. Wild Bill took a swig of what he thought was whisky only to violently spit the beverage from his mouth. He then broke out of character and shouted, "Cold tea don't count—either I get real whisky or I ain't tellin' no story!"

Initially, Cody was upset that Wild Bill would cause a disturbance right in the middle of a show, but when he saw the look of sheer delight on the faces of audience members, he realized that his antics were comic gold. This led him to oblige Wild Bill with all the alcohol he wanted, making his impromptu fits a part of the act. By the time the new lineup reached Indiana later that year, the reviews were generally quite good.

A review from the *Indianapolis Journal* declared, "They have made a study of their new chosen profession, and everywhere the press and public are loud in praise of their marked improvement." The *Indianapolis Journal* then commended the group for their "quick agile movements, earnestness of manner and rapid gesture."

The group most certainly had a lot of fans, but not everyone was an admirer. In fact, during a stop in Titusville, Pennsylvania, they managed to run into a group of hooligans who were intent upon causing a major disruption simply because they heard that the group had arrived in town. Buffalo Bill and company were staying at a local hotel, getting ready to take the stage at the Parshall Opera House, when a group of tough guys decided to surround the place, demanding to see them.

The hotel staff informed the cast of what was happening and advised them to slip out through a side door. Wild Bill Hickok didn't like this arrangement, however, and instead declared that he would "fight the whole mob" himself. Buffalo Bill Cody tried to stop him, but Hickok refused to listen. Instead, Wild Bill waltzed right into the hotel lobby where the cretins were waiting for the cast to come out.

Although the creeps saw Hickok, they confused him with Buffalo Bill. One of the guys greeted him, "Hello, Buffalo Bill! We have been looking for you all day!" Hickok, of course, told them that he wasn't Buffalo Bill, which caused the ruffian to accuse him of lying. As one might expect, Hickok did not appreciate being called a liar. One thing led to another, and soon enough, Wild Bill was getting into a physical altercation with this guy, as well as with several others.

The men learned pretty quickly why Hickok was called Wild Bill Hickok, as this one-man fighting machine turned his antagonists every which way but loose. The next thing Cody and the rest of the cast knew, Wild Bill came up to the room, "whistling a lively tune." Apparently quite happy and content with the outcome of his confrontation, Wild Bill then declared, "I have been interviewing that party who wanted to clean us out. I got lost among the cannons and then I ran in among the hostiles. But it is all right now. They won't bother us anymore."

Shortly after this incident, another writer, Hiram Robbins, hammered out a new play, which he called *Scouts of the Plains*. Due to its similar title to Buntline's *Scouts of the Prairie*, it was often confused with the previous production. It made its debut in—

of all places—Buffalo, New York, on November 13ᵗʰ, 1873, and the play was a real crowd-pleaser.

The narrative of this new play revolved around Buffalo Bill hearing about a trapper called Jim Daws, who had abducted his friend's daughter. Upon hearing of these developments, Buffalo Bill's character then swears to "take his [the abductor's] life's blood, or die in the attempt." The renegade trapper then predictably becomes Bill's archnemesis, and at one point, he even hooks up with a violent band of Comanche, who kill the abducted girl's parents before snatching up the family's two remaining daughters.

Much of the ensuring drama revolved around the back and forth of hostilities between Buffalo Bill's company and the renegade trapper and his Comanches. Although the plot was generally felt to be lacking, the crowd enjoyed the show that Cody and his associates put on. A review from the *Erie Morning Dispatch* described the drama as being "scarce the shadow of a plot and is like an animated dime novel with the Indian-killing multiplied by ten but—the bloodier the tragedy the broader was the comedy."

The group continued to do well, but before the season was out, Wild Bill decided to abruptly call it quits. Texas Jack had also become more and more sporadic with his appearances as he settled down into his married life. For Buffalo Bill, marriage and children didn't slow him down one bit, and he even brought his wife and children on tour with him whenever it was possible.

Buffalo Bill's world would be rocked by tragedy when his son, Kit Carson Cody, passed away from scarlet fever. The son, whom he had nicknamed "Kitty," ended up dying in Bill's own arms. As Buffalo Bill himself later recalled, "I found my little boy unable to speak but he seemed to recognize me and putting his little arms around my neck he tried to kiss me. We did everything in our power to save him, but my beloved little Kit died in my arms."

It was right around this time that war had broken out in the West between the US Army and the Sioux. General George Crook, who was overseeing the melee, extended an invitation to Buffalo Bill to join the fray. Bill, who was still mourning the loss of his son, initially declined, but after he finished up his last theater gig for the 1876 season, he announced, on stage, that he would indeed heed the call. A short time later, on June 9th, 1876, Buffalo Bill made his way to Cheyenne, Wyoming, in an attempt to tamp down what had become a major Sioux uprising.

# Chapter 3 – Just a Matter of Interpretation

*"The defeat of Custer was not a massacre. The Indians were being pursued by skilled fighters with orders to kill. For centuries they had been hounded from the Atlantic to the Pacific and back again. They had their wives and little ones to protect and they were fighting for their existence. In nine times out of ten, when there is trouble between white men and Indians, it will be found that the white man is responsible. Indians expect a man to keep his word. They can't understand how men can lie. Most of them would as soon cut off a leg as tell a lie."*

*-Buffalo Bill Cody*

The Great Sioux War of 1876 was essentially the result of a breakdown in talks between the US government and Lakota Sioux, as well as Northern Cheyenne tribal groups. Certain lands in a region known as the Black Hills had been allotted to Native Americans. The US attempted to reclaim part of these lands after gold had been discovered. In July of 1874, General George Armstrong Custer sent out an "expedition of twelve hundred men" through the Black Hills to make sure that the reports were true. The expedition confirmed what was already suspected. There was indeed gold in those hills. And gold prospectors, of course, couldn't resist the idea of prospecting this gold.

Knowing that an influx of miners would spark conflict, the US government tried to avoid trouble by negotiating new land deals with Native American leaders. The talks failed, and the tribal leaders were infuriated that the United States would try to go back on their original agreements. This led to the first of the conflicts of what would become known as the Great Sioux War, also known as the Black Hills War.

While these tensions were building, Buffalo Bill was finishing up his latest rounds with Wild West plays. At this point, the lineup had changed considerably. Both Wild Bill Hickok and Texas Jack were out of the picture, but Bill had gained an able new cast of supporting actors to help him carry on. Theater life was going well enough, and new scripts and storylines had been written, but since the outbreak of war in the West seemed all but inevitable, Buffalo Bill couldn't resist the call.

In order to shore up support for the US troops, Buffalo Bill arrived in Cheyenne, Wyoming, on June 9th, 1876. Upon arriving at the Union Pacific Depot to report for duty, Bill was greeted by Charles King, who was the first lieutenant. Bill was eventually escorted to Camp Robinson in Nebraska. Little did Buffalo Bill know that the resurgent resistance of the Sioux and Cheyenne would soon turn out to be much more than the United States Army had bargained for.

The first signs of the ill-prepared nature of the US response occurred on June 17th during the Battle of the Rosebud, in which a strong showing of Native American combatants fought US troops to a standstill. However, the worst was yet to come, doing so in the form of the Battle of the Little Bighorn, which took place in late June 1876. In this conflict, Hunkpapa Lakota Chief Sitting Bull was able to lead his fighters in the successful annihilation of an entire battalion, which resulted in George Armstrong Custer's famous "last stand."

Buffalo Bill was camped out with the troops on July 7th when he heard the news. Bill relayed the tragic setback to Lieutenant Charles King, with a look of deep concern on his face. As King later recalled, "His handsome face wore a look of deep trouble, and he brought us to a halt in stunned, awe-stricken silence with the announcement, 'Custer and five companies of the Seventh wiped out of existence. It's no rumor—General Merritt's got the official dispatch.'"

The troops at the camp had been talking about early reports that things hadn't gone well, and Bill gravely clarified that the reports were "no rumor." The old scout now knew that navigating a successful outcome was not going to be as easy as he made it seem on stage. Now that Custer's 7th Cavalry Regiment had been wiped out, the 5th Cavalry Regiment, to which Buffalo Bill was attached, was called forth to intercept the marauders.

They were informed that some "eight hundred Northern Cheyenne" were on the march, and Buffalo Bill and his compatriots were going to be sent to confront them. On July 16th, the 5th and its seven companies of troops initiated a "fifty-mile march" to meet their foes. Cody led the pack, and it was said that he was the first to engage the enemy when the leader of the Native American band came into view.

Christian Madsen, an army signalman, was supposedly watching Buffalo Bill "through his telescope" from a distance and saw what happened when the confrontation took place. According to Madsen, "The instant they were face to face their guns fired. It seemed almost like one shot. They met by accident and fired the moment they faced each other."

Christian Madsen claimed Buffalo Bill and the Native American warrior had basically stumbled right into each other and almost immediately reached for their weapons and fired at each other. Buffalo Bill's shot apparently hit the warrior in the leg, causing him to leap from his horse, whereas the warrior's own shot missed its mark entirely. Buffalo Bill's horse, meanwhile, had stepped into a "gopher dog hole" and lost its footing, forcing Bill to dismount as well.

After both Bill and the warrior got their bearings, they both opened fire on each other, almost simultaneously. The injured warrior missed once again, whereas Buffalo Bill managed to shoot his opponent right in the head. The man whom Buffalo Bill killed would later be identified as "a warrior named Yellow Hair," who would also later be "frequently mistranslated as Yellow Hand."

What allegedly happened next seems pretty brutal on Buffalo Bill's part, but it was not too uncommon during these violent conflicts. It has been said that Bill actually scalped Yellow Hair after he died. The practice of cutting off the scalp of a fallen enemy was actually a practice that Westerners had learned from Native American warriors. But no matter who was doing it—or where the practice came from—it's safe to say that such horrid exercises are appalling to modern sensibilities.

Along with the fallen warrior's scalp, it's said that Bill also took his bridle, whip, shield, and weapons as further souvenirs. While Buffalo Bill was preoccupied with this, the rest of his compatriots surged forward and began to drive back the rest of the Native Americans. There were a few more casualties, but most of the warriors apparently decided that they were no match for the US troops that had confronted them. They decided to turn themselves into the local Indian Agency that handled their affairs.

Buffalo Bill's "duel" with Yellow Hair would grow in fame and eventually become serialized in a novel before appearing in theatrical reenactments on stage. However, this entire incident was later called into question. For example, one author from Nebraska, Mari Sandoz, recorded an alternative telling of events that depicted Buffalo Bill as not being the killer of Yellow Hair. Sandoz "claimed that Yellow Hair taunted the troopers until one angered trooper fired and killed the Indian; that same trooper then scalped him."

Yellow Hair would be the last supposed kill of Buffalo Bill, and it would remain his most controversial. Nevertheless, it was this moment, superimposed upon the greater Battle of the Little Bighorn and Custer's Last Stand, that would soon be immortalized on stage for all to see and draw their own interpretations.

# Chapter 4 – The Gentleman Farmer

*"After traveling through fourteen foreign countries and appearing before all the royalty and nobility I have only one wish today. That is that when my eyes are closed in death that they will bury me back in that quiet little farm land where I was born."*

*-Annie Oakley*

By the late 1870s, what had originally been a way for Bill to pass his downtime of life as a military scout had become his main vocation. In January of 1877, Buffalo Bill was regularly performing in two main productions, one based on his service in the Great Sioux War, which was called *The Red Right Hand*, while the other drama was entitled *Life on the Border*. During these live-action shows, Buffalo Bill perfected the use of blank cartridges, stunning the crowds with the flash and bang caused by shooting blanks. At one show, the delivery was apparently so realistic that a young man by the name of Frank Helvey ran outside and shouted that Buffalo Bill "was massacring the whole audience."

Just because they were shooting blanks didn't mean that the weapons they wielded could not injure someone. One actor named Jack Crawford figured this out the hard way when during one dramatic scene in which he was supposed to quickly draw and fire his weapon, it "snagged and discharged" inside the man's holster, causing a mini-explosion to strike the poor fellow right in his groin. The actor was actually bleeding from the injury, but from a distance, the crowd could not tell, and due to the actor's realistic acting, the actors and the crowd did not believe that anything was amiss. But as soon as Crawford got off the stage, a doctor was immediately summoned to take stock of the injury. The doctor determined that the injured portion of the man's groin was "painful, but not necessarily dangerous."

Crawford recovered, but his relationship with Buffalo Bill was strained forever afterward. Whether it was the injury or artistic disagreements, he decided to part company shortly thereafter. Despite Crawford's departure from the show, the production of *Life on the Border* was performed with much anticipation in Virginia City, Nevada, on June 25th, 1877. The show went well enough, but Bill felt like he needed a change.

In July of 1877, while in Omaha, Nebraska, Buffalo Bill decided to disband his regular lineup for good. It was an emotional scene, and Bill personally said farewell to his fellow actors and actresses. It was noted that he was particularly passionate in the way he said goodbye to the actresses. He apparently kissed them, which was done right in front of his wife. Bill claimed that it was like kissing family, but his wife long suspected that he was cheating on her, and she would never forget the embarrassment this ordeal caused her.

At any rate, the rest of that summer would be a somewhat boring one for Bill. He was no longer acting, and he wasn't doing much scouting. Most of his time was spent trying to start a cattle ranch in Nebraska. By the fall, he was already considering getting the acting troupe back together.

He even reached out to Jack Crawford, but he did not get the answer he was looking for. Angry that Crawford wanted to branch out on his own, Buffalo Bill fired off a stinging rebuke to his former protégé, which read, in part, "My dear Jack...People have flattered you until you think as many others have done that you are a great man Jack go ahead. You will find out that all that glitters is not gold...I wish you success and will never do a thing to hurt you...I am very sorry the accident occurred and you know it was not my fault as I never wanted to put the horses on the stage. But had the accident not occurred I think you had made up your mind to start out for your self. So good luck."

Bill was quite defensive about how he parted ways with Crawford, and even though he adamantly denied being responsible for the accident, the mere fact that he was still addressing it seems to indicate some small modicum of guilt on Bill's part. Nevertheless, Bill moved forward and put together a brand-new theater troupe. This entailed him paying a visit to the Red Cloud Agency in Nebraska, where he recruited several Native Americans to join his acting tour.

With his new lineup arranged, Buffalo Bill then took his act east to New York. Despite her previous misgivings (or perhaps even because of them), Buffalo Bill's wife, Louisa, decided to tag along. Their daughter Arta was a student in Rochester at the time, and their other child, Orra, was in tow.

Buffalo Bill's new group made their debut at New York City's Bowery Theatre on September 3rd, 1877, with a piece called "May Cody; or, Lost and Won," which was written by Captain Andrew S. Burt, a veteran of the Civil War. Along with the new script, the act also made sure to create lively action on the side, which included a routine of sharpshooters known as the "Austin Brothers," who wowed the audience by shooting potatoes off each other's heads as well as snuffing out candles and cigars from other actors' hands.

After wrapping things up in New York, the group then hopped on a train and went over to Baltimore, Maryland. Shortly after their arrival, a reporter from the *American & Commercial Advertiser* interviewed a few of the Native American members of the group. One of the more memorable interviews came from a warrior named Man That Carries the Sword, who had actually fought against General Custer. He expressed that he was content with his newfound acting career and did not hold any grudges against the European Americans.

It is quite incredible that Buffalo Bill managed to cobble together a cast of costars who, just a few years prior, would have been his bitterest of enemies on the battlefield. Yet now, they were apparently the best of friends on stage. This latest season of acting went well for Cody, but toward the end, he began dropping hints that he wanted to give it all up and "retire to his ranch as a cattle dealer and gentleman farmer."

By this point, Buffalo Bill certainly had accumulated enough money to retire, but by November of 1877, Bill's own business manager, Josh Ogden, made it clear that Bill would not be retiring after all. It remains unclear if Bill had changed his mind or if the whole thing was just a slick ploy to generate more interest.

Lending credence to the idea that Bill was serious was the fact that he and an old army buddy of his, Frank North, made arrangements for what would become the Cody-North partnership. On behalf of this partnership, Frank North checked out land in Nebraska near "the headwaters of South Fork of the Dismal River, about sixty-five miles north of North Platte." North and Buffalo Bill Cody ended up acquiring a ranch in the region.

However, Buffalo Bill was not too eager to do much work while on the ranch, usually leaving that to hired hands, hence the reference to "gentlemen farmer." He mostly used the ranch as a place to relax and host get-togethers with his friends, although according to the man who later bought the ranch, John Bratt, some of these hangers-on could have been grifters who overstayed their welcome.

Bratt would later recall, "Some of the cowboys would take advantage of the Colonel's hospitality by going to his wagon and helping themselves to his cigars and sampling his liquors that had been brought along as an antidote against snake bites and other accidents." At any rate, by January of 1878, Bill had left the ranch and was back out on the road with his group, touring in Chicago. Buffalo Bill was a scout, an actor, a scholar, and a gentleman farmer all rolled into one.

# Chapter 5 – A One-Man Production Company

*"My debut upon the world's stage occurred on February 26ᵗʰ, 1845, in the State of Iowa."*

*-Buffalo Bill Cody*

By January of 1878, Buffalo Bill had left the comforts of his ranch behind and was back on the road with his acting group, touring in Chicago. Buffalo Bill took the stage at Chicago's Haverly's Theatre on January 7ᵗʰ to perform in front of a packed house. The *Chicago Tribune* had plenty of kind words for his performance. The publication mused that Buffalo Bill and company had "dashed off—in a kind of frolic by a careless genius."

When the group tried the same performance in Louisville, Kentucky, however, they were not greeted so warmly. One local paper complained that it was "a folly to tone down a wild Western sensational drama." For them, the dramatic sequences of the script in no way did justice to the real-life drama of the West. Nevertheless, this latest "theatrical season" was a lucrative one for Buffalo Bill, and after it was over, he was able to head back to his ranch in Nebraska with his saddlebags loaded with cash.

This time around, Bill's partner, Frank North, apparently put Bill to work. And rather than just being a "gentleman farmer" who directed others, he got into the thick of it all. Bill Cody later recalled how he had seriously reflected, "where the fun came in," as he had "to be in the saddle all day, and standing guard over the cattle at night, rain or shine." Buffalo Bill soon got into the swing of things and became quite used to the grueling schedule of a rancher.

Time went by fast with all of the work he was engaged in on the range, and before he knew it, it was time for the next season of theater work. In the fall of 1878, Bill was performing for large and expectant crowds in Baltimore, Maryland. Along with the main production, Buffalo Bill and his company also took a stab at feats of archery, rifle shooting, and war dances.

One of the real crowd-pleasers was a routine in which a potato was shot off the head of a female costar. It was an act that was repeated without a hitch just about every night. But as it grew in popularity, others began to emulate it, and tragically, in at least one instance, the attempt to imitate this feat led to death. Such things caused bad press for Bill Cody, leading locals to clamor for something to be done about his wild ways.

Matters would get even worse when Cody was shooting blanks at his opponents on stage during a show. Somehow, a loaded cartridge had accidentally been inserted into his gun. The bullet left his gun and actually hit a child in the audience. The bullet pierced the boy's lungs, and even after receiving treatment, he was just barely clinging to life. Buffalo Bill was understandably horrified at what had happened, and he pledged to pay for the child's treatment. Fortunately for all involved, the child recovered, and Buffalo Bill maintained contact with him afterward, even extending an invitation for him to come down to his ranch in person.

Despite the tragedy, Buffalo Bill's figure had really grown throughout the nation. Before, he was just a frontier scout; now, he was a community figure who had great responsibility for his fans. Shortly after this episode, Buffalo Bill headed out to Washington,

DC, where he had an appointment with the Bureau of Indian Affairs.

The Bureau of Indian Affairs wanted to question Buffalo Bill about his use of Native Americans in his shows. The director he spoke to—Secretary Carl Schurz—was particularly concerned about a group of "Pawnee Indians" with whom Bill had been traveling around. Schurz informed Bill that the Pawnee were "wards of the government, were off the reservation without leave, and...ordered them to return immediately."

Buffalo Bill pleaded with the secretary, explaining that he would suffer a severe financial loss if he had to send them back to the reservation, as it would disrupt his whole touring season. He also argued that getting out and seeing the world was good for his charges, and they were happier on the road with him than they would have been cooped up on the reservation. The secretary finally relented but only on the stipulation that Buffalo Bill be made an official "Indian agent" and that he "pledge to return them safely to their reservation."

Shortly after these developments, Buffalo Bill Cody was back on the road once again. This time around, he had a new act called *Knight of the Plains*. In this piece, as one might imagine, Buffalo Bill was cast as the Wild West's version of a chivalrous knight in shining armor—or in Bill's case, buckskin. This play, although it was dressed up and packaged differently, used the same basic formula as the others. Bill was the hero who went up against a group of local baddies, who he was supposed to straighten out. And somewhere along the way, there would be a damsel in distress that Bill was tasked with rescuing.

What's interesting about *Knight of the Plains* is not so much the watered-down plotline but the fact that Bill actually played four different characters. He played the main Buffalo Bill character, but he also wore disguises and played three other characters at different points throughout the play. Most of the praise for the production was good, but some were eager to criticize the different getups that Cody wore.

One critic criticized Buffalo Bill for wearing what he called "the habiliments of Eastern civilization." Another remarked that Buffalo Bill was basically the "whole show in himself," which could be viewed as either praise for Bill, in particular, or criticism of the whole production in general. Another critic seconded that view shortly thereafter, chiming in, "The play is too much of a one-man production to suit the public. He does not allow his support to make any hits, which is to be regretted." By the late 1870s, Buffalo Bill was indeed a one-man production company, taking the tales of his life and legend everywhere he went.

# Chapter 6 – A Time of Reflection

*"I felt only as a man can feel who is roaming over the prairies of the far West, well-armed, and mounted on a fleet and gallant steed."*

*-Buffalo Bill Cody*

By the late 1870s, Buffalo Bill had begun to reflect on his life as both an actor and a frontiersman of the Wild West. In doing so, he couldn't help but come to sympathize with the plight of the Native Americans that he had both fought and befriended. As he grew older, he began to empathize with the loss of their homeland more and more. While his act was on tour in Cleveland, Ohio, in February of 1879, he voiced these evolving views to a local reporter.

[It] is a mistaken idea to think the Indians are a treacherous race; they are peaceable and true if let alone, but they know that in fighting with white men they are outnumbered and therefore they seize any advantage they can. The fact is, the Indians have not been treated rightly by the American Government: they have had promises made them that were never fulfilled, and this has angered them. The Indians should not even be blamed for these cattle and horse raids we hear so much about, because they are merely retaliating. Although I have had many a tough fight with the red man, my sympathy is with him entirely, because he has been ill-used and trampled on by those whose duty it was to protect him.

Although Bill acknowledged the current skirmishes on the range that involved Native Americans committing depredations against settlers, such as stealing cattle, he still couldn't bring himself to condemn them, as he truly felt sorry for them. He knew that it was the Native Americans whose land and freedom had been infringed upon in the first place. While he was in this reflective mood, he wrote his first autobiography, which was also published in 1879.

There has been much debate over just how accurate his autobiography is, but regardless of the veracity of the claims made, it is certainly an entertaining read. The work covers his exploits from when he rode for the Pony Express, spied during the Civil War, and worked as a fearless scout on the range. The narratives are riveting, and Bill made sure to promote his book at the end of just about every performance.

After rapid rounds of touring in the early 1880s, which included a brief stint in Canada, Bill eventually made his way back home to his ranch in North Platte. In 1882, it was suggested of him to help the town celebrate its Independence Day activities. Bill was apparently at a local store chatting with a former mayor and other "prominent citizens" when the subject came up. Bill was amazed that the townspeople didn't usually do too much to celebrate the occasion, which he considered "unpatriotic." It was apparently at this point that Bill was talked into bringing the patriotic celebration to town.

The show began at 10:30 in the morning on July 4th, and there were thousands of locals in attendance. First, a parade was held on the main street in town. This apparently included a band, veterans, and regular townspeople, who all marched down the street. The festivities found their way to the town's race track, where Bill demonstrated buffalo hunting. The locals were then able to try their hand at riding, shooting, and "bronco busting," all of which were rewarded with prizes provided by local businesses.

This occasion was called the "Old Glory Blow-Out," and it was a real circus environment. It was a worthy precursor to the real Wild West circuses that Bill would soon cobble together for regular public consumption. Indeed, the very next year, Cody would debut his very first showing of what would be dubbed Buffalo Bill's Wild West.

However, just as Bill was getting back into the groove as a showman, his family life would start to weigh heavily on him. He and his wife Louisa were growing distant, and the more they squabbled, the more Bill drank, stayed out late, and further alienated their relationship. Yet in the midst of this, they still managed to produce another child, with Louisa giving birth to a daughter named Irma in February of 1883. This milestone would be overshadowed when their eleven-year-old daughter Orra died in October of that same year. It's always a horrible thing for parents to have to outlive their children, and Bill would ultimately outlive all but one of his kids before all was said and done.

The success of his Wild West shows and the massive influx of cash it brought served to offset all of these personal problems Bill was experiencing. It was probably in an effort to both try to forget about the sadness of the past and to get a fresh start in the present that Bill had what was left of his family pick up and move to a newly built ranch home in 1886. He named this new dwelling Scout's Rest Ranch, and as the name implies, it was the place he hoped would be his future retirement home.

The large barn at the ranch even had the words Scout's Rest Ranch emblazoned on the side of it. Seen from miles away, this site would become an icon of the community for many years to come, and one can still visit it today. Interestingly enough, Louisa would often stay on the old ranch property while Buffalo Bill entertained guests at Scout's Rest Ranch. Their marriage seemed to be on the rocks, and in the intervening years, it would only get rockier.

# Chapter 7 – Later Years of Loss and Personal Strain

*"I often feel sorry for her. She is a strange woman but I don't mind her—remember she is my wife—and let it go at that. If she gets cranky, just laugh at it, she can't help it."*

*-Buffalo Bill Cody*

Buffalo Bill essentially retired from the stage in the late 1880s. But although he was hanging up his hat when it came to theatrical performances, he was not yet done as a performer. Now instead of gracing the stage inside theaters, he would try his luck hosting massive live events outdoors, which he would call his Wild West shows. These grand extravaganzas are said to have boasted a large cadre of "cowboys, cowgirls, and genuine greasers, besides a hundred and fifty Indians of various tribes in full fig and feather."

In addition, the shows typically utilized countless horses, donkeys, elk, buffalo, deer, and other animals. These shows practically harkened back to the days of the Roman Coliseum, with its grand spectacle of live fighters and roving beasts. The American public ate it up, as they had never seen anything quite like it. One of Bill's greatest publicity stunts came in 1885 when he recruited

Native American Chief Sitting Bull to make appearances at the show.

Sitting Bull was, of course, famous for his role in the Battle of the Little Bighorn, which had led to Custer's Last Stand. Sitting Bull, along with twenty or so Native American men, appeared in several reenactments. Being able to see a former foe of the US Army as a fellow performer next to Cody, a former scout, was quite a turnaround, and it was a stunt that Buffalo Bill was quite proud of. He touted the phenomenon as "Foes in '76– Friends in '85" (1876 was the year of the Great Sioux War).

But with tensions in the West increasing in light of fresh settler encroachments and Native American unrest, Sitting Bull would not be able to remain a friend for long. Before the decade was out, a fervor of resistance, known as the Ghost Dance, swept the tribal groups of the West. This movement was started by a "Paiute Indian" by the name of Wovoka, whose teachings claimed that certain dances, chants, charms, and other rituals could raise slain warriors, bring back the buffalo, and make the living impervious to bullets, among other things.

It's unclear how many tribal members actually believed these things, but more important than these supernatural musings was the spirit of resistance that the Ghost Dance represented. And it soon caught on like wildfire among several tribes. This did not bode well with the US Army, and soon, they were trying to prevent a major uprising from taking root.

Of particular concern was Chief Sitting Bull, who was holed up at Standing Rock Agency. The US Army feared he was about to leave the reservation and take part in the impending hostilities; a man with his stature and leadership abilities would attract people in no time. This led to Indian agents attempting to take preventative measures, and they decided to strike first by arresting Sitting Bull. The agents arrived at his home in the early morning hours of December 15th, 1890.

Sitting Bull was led outside, but he began to argue with the agent. This drew the attention of others, and soon, there was a whole crowd of angry reservation residents wondering why their chief was being accosted. As the agents tried to force Sitting Bull onto a horse, one of the warriors opened fire and shot one of the agents. After being hit, the agent immediately pulled the trigger of his own weapon and shot Sitting Bull in the chest. Another agent then shot Sitting Bull in the head, thus ending the life of the great chief and the former friend of Buffalo Bill.

Bill, who had considered trying to serve as an intermediary between Sitting Bull and the army, was tremendously saddened to hear the news. Nevertheless, as was always the case with Buffalo Bill Cody, the show had to go on, and in the intervening years, it most certainly did. Bill took the show overseas, first going to England and then expanding his act to continental Europe. These tours were received with great fanfare by Europeans and established Buffalo Bill as a hero of international fame.

But despite the acclaim of his professional life, his personal life was rapidly unraveling at the seams. His wife had long suspected that Buffalo Bill had been unfaithful, and arguments about his fidelity were routine. They also frequently argued about how to spend money, with Cody accusing his wife of being too extravagant with her expenditures.

With the situation becoming more and more volatile, Buffalo Bill felt his hands were tied, and he delivered Louisa divorce papers in 1904. Divorce was not an easy thing to come by in those days, and if one's spouse didn't approve of the decision, they could make moving forward with the process extremely difficult. And that's precisely what Buffalo Bill's wife did.

Louisa made it clear that she did not want the divorce. Sadly enough, as Bill and his wife battled it out in court, their daughter, Arta, abruptly passed away, leaving the bickering couple with only one living child left between them. It was largely this unexpected sadness that compelled both parties to reconcile and shelve the idea of divorce. Despite their problems, Bill and Louisa would remain married for the rest of their days.

# Conclusion: The King of the West

The man the world had come to know as Buffalo Bill passed away on January 10th, 1917, at the age of seventy. He had thrilled audiences far and wide with his Wild West shows, and he had shown the world that the characters they read about in dime novels and magazines were real flesh and blood people.

Despite his fame, by the time of his demise, Bill's finances were in doubt, and it's reported that he had merely $100,000 to his name. This was certainly a respectable amount of money in the early 20th century, but considering how much money had slipped through Bill's fingers in the last few decades of his life, it's not very shocking that he did not have a higher net worth at the time of his demise. But money, of course, is not the only way one can measure the worth of an important figure like Buffalo Bill.

For many, Buffalo Bill had become the embodiment of the wild frontier, and both his legacy and his spirit would continue to live on. Buffalo Bill's place of burial was on Lookout Mountain in Golden, Colorado, just outside of Denver. In the ensuing years, it has become a kind of shrine, and to this very day, visitors and well-wishers arrive at Bill's gravesite to pay their respects to the King of the West.

# Part 4: Seth Bullock

*A Captivating Guide to Deadwood's First Sheriff Who Tamed This Wild West Town and Was Later Appointed US Marshal by Theodore Roosevelt*

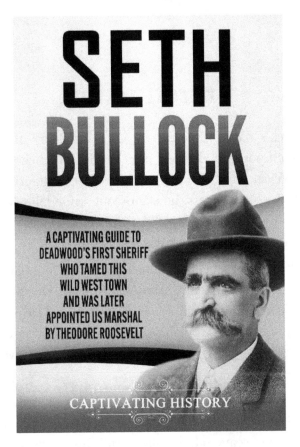

# Introduction

Seth Bullock's name is perhaps not so legendary as that of his many contemporaries. Names like Wild Bill Hickok, Calamity Jane, and Wyatt Earp have a more fabled ring to them than simple Seth Bullock. Nonetheless, he stands out among the characters of the Old West for one simple reason: if the Wild West was a mighty predator, Seth Bullock was a lion tamer.

Bullock's life has been fictionalized in the popular television series *Deadwood*. The namesake of the show, Deadwood, South Dakota, was a lawless mining camp in the late 19th century that desperately needed a strong-hearted lawman to bring order to its rowdy streets. Bullock was its first sheriff, and he achieved law and order without killing a single enemy.

This is Bullock's most famous exploit, but he was more than just an Old West sheriff. His life was always lived to the fullest, with his seventy-one years utterly filled with his many interests and achievements. Although he became an emblem of the American West, Seth was actually born in Canada as the son of a British major. Before moving to Deadwood, he was part of the Montana Territorial Legislature, even helping to found one of the world's most famous (and earliest) national parks.

Seth was also an adept businessman, building a hotel that still stands today, founding a town, and introducing one of South Dakota's key crops. His story is filled with fascinating people, from Wild Bill Hickok to Theodore Roosevelt to his treasured friend and business partner, Solomon Star.

These names may have the ring of fiction to them, but Seth Bullock's story of integrity and dedication to the letter of the law is one that rings deeply true. It is one that served as an inspiration in a time of great lawlessness, and it is one that can serve the same purpose today.

# Chapter 1 – The Birth of a Legend

Among the warmth and lushness of a Canadian midsummer, Anna Findley Bullock's screams rang through the quiet air of Amherstburg, Canada West (modern-day Ontario).

This was not her first time giving birth. Anna was a hardened Scot, and her hoarse accent rang out in her cries; like most women of the 19th century, she was well practiced in pushing out healthy babies in the most unlikely of conditions. Her marriage to a British sergeant major and an important figure in the local community had ensured that she had nothing but the best, yet at the time, the best was what would be considered almost inhumane today. Attended by an untrained midwife, sprawled in her own bed, Anna Findley Bullock was bringing her child into the world with no drugs, no sterile equipment, and no pain relief.

But as she had done before—and would do a total of at least eight times during her life—Anna made do. She brought forth a little son on July 23rd, 1849. He was born into a glorious summer and also into a life that promised brutality.

Anna knew that all too well.

\* \* \* \*

The little boy, soon named Seth, was one of eight children born to Anna and her husband, Sergeant Major George Bullock. At a time when Canada was still deep in the powerful grip of British occupation, a military man like George wielded considerable power. Native-born Canadians—both the indigenous peoples and those who descended from French and British colonists of earlier centuries—strived to loosen the terrible grasp of the British. Numerous bloody wars had been fought between the motherland and its colonists, and George had been hailed as a hero thanks to them.

In the home, however, George quickly proved to be anything but a hero to his wife and young family. While little is known about Seth Bullock's early life in Amherstburg and later Sandwich (modern-day Windsor) is that he suffered. His father was prosperous and well respected in his social circles, so Seth had no need to fear cold or hunger. There would always be books from which to learn, food on the table, and clothes on his back.

The deficiency from which young Seth suffered was a deficiency of compassion.

George was a violent man, given to fits of temper, and was deeply selfish. He was well used to power; in addition to his military accomplishments, he was elected as county treasurer in the 1850s. And he held that power over his family in a reign of pure terror. All of his children feared him. Perhaps even his wife as well, although she faded quickly from Seth's world when he was still very young. Anna's staunch Scottish blood had stood her in good stead through eight children, her marriage to the violent George, and many a Canadian winter. But it failed her at last sometime before 1860, leaving Seth alone with his siblings and his father.

One can only imagine that little Seth must have lived in fear. Even the tiniest of mistakes could spark an outburst of rage. In an age when the odd spanking was the norm, Seth suffered more than most. George was unafraid of heartily beating his children, and

Seth was no exception. Each time he made the smallest error, Seth felt his father's wrath physically.

George grew abusive enough that in 1858, when Seth was nine, he decided that he could no longer tolerate living with his cruel father. He fled from the home, but his runaway attempt didn't last for very long. Seth had nowhere else to go. And while freedom certainly appealed to him, the Canadian wilderness then surrounding Sandwich was no place for a nine-year-old boy to survive alone. He returned, dejected. This was the first of many times that Seth ran away from home. For the next five years, he would continue to run away any time the opportunity presented itself.

In 1860, however, Seth was suddenly and dramatically liberated from his father's iron fist—and, at the same time, catapulted into a world of total uncertainty. George had been enjoying his stint as county treasurer a little more than he should have. In fact, evidence was found that funds were missing from the treasury, causing George's superiors to become immediately suspicious that he was feathering his own nest at the county's expense. He was fired from his position as treasurer.

Instead of facing what he'd done, George showed his true colors shortly afterward. Like most cruel bullies, George was a total coward. Despite the fact that he still had many children at home—a few of Seth's older siblings had gotten married by this point—George regarded his own freedom and safety to be more important than his children's welfare. He simply disappeared from Sandwich, leaving his children all alone, and fled to Detroit, Michigan.

While Detroit was just a few miles away from Sandwich (now Windsor), George may as well have been living in another world. The United States of America had been an independent country for decades, and while George wasn't physically distant from the children, he had practically disappeared from their lives completely.

Eleven-year-old Seth and the others were left to fend for themselves. While this meant that Seth was finally free from the iron fist of his father, it also meant that he had to find some way to survive. Just a few years after George disappeared, it all became too much for Seth. His older sister, Agnes, was getting ready to go and live in Montana by then, and even though it was more than a thousand miles away, the teenage Seth made the trek to live with her. It was his first taste of the West, and it was love at first sight.

By the time Seth was fourteen years old, his childhood home had been sold off to the highest bidder. George had abandoned his children to the extent that he didn't even bother to continue paying the mortgage on the home that housed them. The house was claimed by the bank and auctioned, and nothing was left of the unhappy Bullock family that had once been so prominent in Sandwich.

For Seth Bullock, however, this was just the beginning. Despite his rebellious escapes as a child, Seth was nonetheless developing a keen sense of justice and a keen desire to avoid unnecessary violence. His father had inspired him to become someone important and respected in the community but also someone who could rule with a moderate hand. And in the future, that was the destiny Seth Bullock would fulfill.

\* \* \* \*

While the teenage Seth Bullock was growing familiar with the wild landscapes of the West, an all-too-familiar conflict was spreading farther and farther into the wilderness of South Dakota—a wilderness whose fate was inextricably linked to Seth's.

The stark yet lovely Black Hills of South Dakota had been the ancestral home of many different Native American tribes for untold centuries. While the word "hills" might conjure visions of a gently rolling landscape clothed in green, the Black Hills were a harsh landscape. With steep, rocky cliffs, deep gulches, and wild mountain streams, they were a gloriously pristine wilderness that was home to a vast array of wildlife, including great herds of buffalo.

These buffalo shaped the diet, culture, and even religion of one of the most prominent local tribes: the Lakota, also known as the Teton Sioux. Before the 19th century, the Lakota had been in sole control of a vast tract of land populated by the buffalo herds that provided them with food and leather. This nomadic tribe would roam across the Black Hills freely, hunting and fishing as they willed, loving and worshiping as their culture decreed.

But the Black Hills were rich in something other than buffalo. The streams there ran pure, clean, and cold—and they were speckled with gold. There was gold in the dirt, too, and the white man's incessant hunger for this metal would eventually bring him onto the doorstep of the Lakota.

This was a tragedy for the Lakota tribe. Not only did the Black Hills provide them with resources essential to their survival, but the hills were also sacred in their religion. To them, the colonists might as well have been pillaging a church building. Spats broke out between the colonists and the Lakota, and with the colonists vastly outnumbered by their Native American counterparts, a bloody war broke out in the 1860s.

In 1868, the US government finally decided to put an end to the fighting. The Treaty of Fort Laramie was signed, giving full possession of the Black Hills to the Lakota tribe. It seemed peace would come at last. But the Lakota had no use for the gold that ran so richly in their hills and streams, and the colonists cared little who the land belonged to: all they wanted was gold.

By 1870, hundreds of miners had set up their hovels on Lakota territory, trespassing, squatting, and then pillaging the sacred land for gold. Tensions began to rise. Trouble was on the way.

# Chapter 2 – First Blood

*Illustration I: Seth Bullock, photographed in 1893. This photograph now hangs in Theodore Roosevelt's birthplace, a National Historic Site.*

Agnes Bullock, one of Seth's three sisters, had fallen in love with an explorer: Lieutenant Frederick F. Kislingbury.

Frederick was only two years older than Seth, but he was far more traveled. Born in England, Frederick had moved to the US as a child and served during the American Civil War at the tender age of seventeen. By the time he married Agnes, he was only around twenty-one years old, but he was already a veteran of America's bloodiest war.

He was also a resident of Helena, Montana, which was about 1,700 miles from the town where Seth had grown up. Still, this didn't seem to be a problem for either Agnes or Seth. They likely wanted to put as much space as possible between them and their abusive past, so when Agnes married Frederick, Seth was only too eager to come right along and leave his life in Canada behind.

Seth's older sister, Agnes, was used to caring for him. Their father had disappeared seven years earlier, and their mother had died so long ago; Agnes was the only real parent Seth had left. Bringing him to Helena with her was a logical choice in her mind. And it was a choice that would change the path of Seth's life forever, as well as the history of a small but notorious South Dakota town. However, Agnes herself would not live to see most of Seth's fame. She died in 1878, after which Frederick married her younger sister, Jessie. Jessie would become a widow in 1884 when Frederick tragically died (and was probably cannibalized by his own starving, dying comrades) during an expedition to the Arctic Circle.

After the long journey to Montana, which was likely traveled by steam train the majority of the way, Seth was introduced to a whole new world. The long rocky beaches and verdant maples of Sandwich were replaced by the wild prairies and blue mountainsides of the West, and Seth had never known such freedom. While he found that he had a knack for business, quickly settling into becoming a tradesman and auctioneer in Helena, Seth's passion lay with the nearby wilderness.

The young man took to exploring the vast tracts of mountains, prairies, lakes, and rivers surrounding Helena, and he had a love for nature that was very different from most young men who moved out West. In an age when the majority of young white male colonists were obsessed with cutting trees, digging up hillsides in search of gold, and building towns on previously undisturbed lands, Seth recognized the wilderness itself held an intrinsic value that went far beyond the resources it could offer a growing nation.

Among the tall pine trees, with the cries of wild wolves echoing in the woods and mighty grizzly bears stalking the salmon-rich rivers, Seth found a timeless beauty and power. He was aware that the ever-hungry beast of westward expansion was swallowing up endless tracts of once-pristine wilderness. Wildlife and wild places were not so much being tamed as they were being utterly destroyed. Seth felt a deep urgency not to let that happen to the area he loved.

By 1870, Seth had left Agnes's home and built a life for himself at the age of twenty-one. He was a successful auctioneer and was becoming a respected figure in his local community. At this point, his dream of going into politics and becoming a leader in his community started to materialize.

Montana, at the time, was not yet a state; it would only become one in 1889. However, it was a US territory, complete with its own territorial legislature and a territorial senate. Seth, a Republican, had his sights set on being elected to the legislature and ran for it in 1870. While his bid proved to be unsuccessful, he ran for the territorial senate the following year, and this time, he achieved his goal. He was elected.

One of Seth's duties around this time was to ride on the local Helena fire engine. Firefighting in the 1870s was very different from what we know today; firefighters were almost always volunteers, and they carried their fire engines around by hand or drove them around by a team of horses. When wooden buildings caught on fire, they were slow-burning—in sharp contrast with the fires of today, where homes are outfitted with gas and electricity—and most of Seth's work likely consisted of salvaging things from burning houses. Still, it quickly made him a hero in his community.

One of his most important contributions as a senator involved the landscape that he had grown to love during his years in Helena. That pristine wilderness was under increasing threat from the ever-encroaching, gold-hungry Americans, and Seth knew that something drastic would have to be done to conserve even a piece of the American West. In an era long before nature conservation would become a buzzword, Seth proposed a daring new idea. He wanted a huge area that stretched over Montana, Wyoming, and Idaho to be declared not simply a state park—which Yosemite, nearby, already was—but a national park. A place that would be safe from encroachment forever.

Seth's daring idea was accepted by the territorial legislature, and Montana Territory worked hard to get the proposal pushed through to the federal level. Ultimately, it was successful. In March 1872, during Seth's last year as a Montana senator, the world's very first national park was established. It was named Yellowstone National Park, and it remains the oldest national park in the world, protecting over 3,000 square miles of wilderness, nearly 400 animal species, and the famous geyser Old Faithful.

If it wasn't for Seth Bullock, we might not have a Yellowstone today. In fact, considering how instrumental Yellowstone has been in the conservation of some of America's most critically endangered species, some of the continent's most amazing animals might have gone extinct without the park. These include icons like the grizzly bear, gray wolf, pika, and Canada lynx. These animals have Seth Bullock, at least in part, to thank for their existence. Without his vision of preserving the area he explored as a young man, they might have been hunted to extinction.

\* \* \* \*

Although Seth's stint in the Montana Territorial Senate ended in 1872, his interest in politics and community leadership was far from over. Instead of waning, his interest grew. While he still enjoyed trading and making business deals, the now twenty-three-year-old Seth was very interested in being a leader in his community—a real leader, one with integrity and firmness, very unlike how his corrupt father had been.

It was easy, then, for Seth to be elected as the county sheriff in 1873. As the sheriff of Lewis and Clark County, Seth was given the unenviable task of establishing law and order in the Wild West. The county was only eight years old at the time, and while Helena had been fairly civilized, Seth now found himself governing a scattering of mining towns that were filled with the wildest and most lawless characters the West could offer.

Faced with such a daunting task, many Old West sheriffs became unspeakably violent. Long before the term "police brutality" was ever coined, these sheriffs sometimes acted with wanton violence, abusing their power and killing, imprisoning, and even torturing with abandon. Seth Bullock was determined not to be one of those sheriffs. He'd tasted enough violence at the hard fist of his father, and he knew that there had to be a better way.

Still, Seth had a keen eye for justice and a willingness to do whatever was necessary to ensure what he considered to be fair treatment in the eyes of the sometimes-brutal Western law. It was inevitable that Seth would come to blows with some criminal or another. That criminal turned out to be a dangerous character named Clell Watson.

In the Old West, horse theft was considered to be one of the most serious crimes that a man could commit. In a time when raping a Native American woman carried little penalty, stealing horses could get you hanged. While the injustice is obvious to the modern reader, it is true that horses were essential to businesses and to survival in the West, making them extremely valuable. The law decreed that horse thieves had to be prosecuted, and Seth was determined to follow the law to the letter.

So, when Seth came upon Watson stealing a horse, he was quick to make his presence known. Watson briskly drew his firearm, and despite his aversion to unnecessary violence, Seth had no scruples about defending himself and carrying out what he perceived to be his duty. Gunfire was exchanged, and blood was drawn. Seth Bullock was wounded for the first time in action. However, he succeeded in his mission. Clell Watson was arrested and sentenced to hanging.

The hanging would take place publicly, as most executions of the time did, but it turned out that Watson was quite popular among the local population. They swarmed around the scaffold, ready to do violence and rescue their thieving companion. The noose was already around Watson's neck, but the executioner's courage deserted him. He abandoned his prisoner and fled, but before Watson could go free, Seth leaped into action. Even though he was wounded, Seth seized a shotgun and chased off the mob, then pulled the lever himself. Clell Watson dropped through the trapdoor to his death. No members of the mob were injured, but they had heard the message from Seth loud and clear: he was not going to allow anyone to stand in the way of the United States law. Seth Bullock was going to uphold everything that he stood for, even if it meant putting himself in life-threatening danger.

\* \* \* \*

Seth Bullock's stint as the sheriff of Lewis and Clark County would continue until 1875. In 1874, the handsome young sheriff married Martha Eccles, a woman he had been in love with for years. Martha had fallen in love with a lost boy; now, she was married to a tall, strong sheriff with a thick mustache and steely eyes.

Shortly after Seth and Martha were married, history was once again in the making 500 miles away in the Black Hills of South Dakota.

The Lakota were still arguing against the squatters and trespassers mining on their land, but theirs was a losing battle. The United States government was far more concerned with the gold that these illegal miners were discovering than they were with the cultural significance that the Black Hills had for the waning Lakota tribe. Thus, a blind eye was turned as miners continued to push farther and farther into the Black Hills, looking for gold.

While many miners would find themselves as penniless after their efforts as before them, there were a few that struck lucky. One such was John B. Pearson. A desperate miner like all the others, Pearson was scrambling through a deep gulch in the hills, its cliffs sheer and littered with dead trees. Through the thick tangles of dead branches, he could hear the quick hiss of a fast-running stream at the bottom.

It was a beautiful stream, pure and cold like all the others. But unlike all the others, this one's floor flashed with real gold.

It was 1875, and by this point, around 800 miners were squatting on Lakota land in the Black Hills. When word got around of the gold that Pearson had found, these miners didn't waste any time flocking to the ravine, which was quickly dubbed Deadwood Gulch. Tents sprang up overnight like mushrooms; in a matter of weeks, the wilderness had become a mining camp, filled with rowdy men hungry for gold.

The disorganized array of tents and shanties multiplied as more and more gold was drawn from the stream. It became obvious that there was a real opportunity here, and the more gold there was, the more men came. They started to live permanently in the gulch, and it wasn't long before men did as men will: they began to drink, gamble, steal, seek after prostitutes, and kill one another over seemingly trivial arguments.

By 1876, Deadwood had become a mining camp, and it was the most notorious camp in all the West. There were almost no families here, just a great restless mass of wild men. Some say that a murder was committed every single day of the first year of Deadwood's existence; another shocking statistic is that nine out of every ten women living in Deadwood was a prostitute.

One of the men who played a key role in making Deadwood so dangerous was an Iowan-born businessman by the name of Ellis Albert Swearengen. He would eventually go by a name that became an outlaw legend: Al Swearengen. While he appeared to be an educated, sophisticated, and cultured man at first glance, the truth was that Al was one of the most dangerous men in the West.

Born just a few weeks before Seth, Al grew up and worked in Iowa, but he quickly saw a business opportunity in the booming West. In the spring of 1876, Deadwood was undoubtedly the place to be. Its hills were rich with gold, but it wasn't gold that Al was after. Gold was hard to find. But gold miners were a dime a dozen; they swarmed through the gulch, filling it with their tents and shanties, and Al knew that there was money to be made off them.

At the time, Deadwood had a ramshackle saloon and not much else. In fact, there wasn't even a hardware store. Hundreds of men were crammed into the miserable gulch with no way of distracting themselves from the hardships of frontier life. Al decided that there was money to be made in entertaining them.

Just seven days after his arrival in Deadwood with his wife, Nettie, Al's first business opportunity was up and running. He had started a dance hall in Deadwood, and it proved to be unbelievably popular. Soon, Al expanded the dance hall into a tiny saloon named the Cricket Saloon. Here, he provided men with as much beer as they could drink and as many women as they could paw at.

Al's own woman led an absolutely miserable life. Al treated her like property, which was not unusual for the time, but he also abused her physically. Nettie was being bruised and battered just like any of the hapless prostitutes that were trapped in Al's service at the Cricket. And with a town swarming with restless young men whose morals had been degraded by the hardships of the frontier, the prostitutes' lives were nothing less than miserable.

And this was only the beginning for Al Swearengen. He would grow more and more bold, his establishment more and more seedy and violent, over the next three months. After all, there was no one around to stop him.

Deadwood was about as lawless as it is possible to be. But not for long.

A new sheriff was coming to town.

# Chapter 3 – Deadwood

*Illustration II: Deadwood*

Although Seth would later become known as the man who tamed Deadwood, when he first traveled to the booming town, he wasn't going as a lawman.

While Seth had spent several years working hard in leadership positions, establishing Yellowstone National Park and helping to tame the corner of the Wild West dubbed Lewis and Clark County, he was by no means neglecting his other major strength: his keen business acumen. Having established himself as a trader and an auctioneer in Helena, Seth was always looking out for other ways to develop his business and become even more of an entrepreneur. One man who was instrumental in his business career was Solomon "Sol" Star.

Sol and Seth had a lot in common. For one thing, Sol, too, had grown up almost without parents. Five years Seth's elder, Sol was born just before the Christmas of 1840 in Bavaria. At the time, this state in the south of Germany was an independent kingdom, an absolute monarchy torn apart by revolutions in the changing political climate of the 19$^{th}$ century. Sol's mother and father realized that their son didn't have a future there. When he was only ten years old, he was sent on the long voyage to the United States of America to live with his maternal uncle, Joseph Friedlander.

Joseph lived in Ohio and worked as a merchant, running a busy store. Young Sol, robbed of his family and everything he held dear, possibly also struggling with a language barrier, was nonetheless quick to pick up on the trade. He had a keen sense of business and was quickly intrigued by his uncle's ideas. It wasn't long before the young Bavarian immigrant became an important member of his community.

He moved west to Montana in 1865 at the age of twenty-five to start up a store of his own. Even though the journey was more than a thousand miles, and Sol was starting up in an entirely foreign state, he threw himself into the task with great fervor. By 1872, Sol had become involved in politics as well. President Ulysses S. Grant appointed him to the Land Office of Montana that year. It was the same year that Seth was serving on the territorial legislature.

Since Helena was the territorial capital of Montana, Seth and Sol inevitably would meet and work together, and the two young men quickly struck up something more than just a business relationship. Since they shared so many interests and even elements of their childhood, it wasn't long before Seth and Sol were firm friends. Their strong leadership capabilities and their good business sense made them a formidable pair.

Somewhere around 1873, soon after Seth pulled the lever on Clell Watson and had established himself as the county sheriff, Seth and Sol decided to enter into business together. With booming mining towns and growing ranches all around them, they were quick to settle on a lucrative opportunity: they'd build a hardware store. Everyone in the area needed hardware for something or another, and soon, Seth and Sol were running a successful little store.

But as Seth's tenure as the sheriff of Lewis and Clark County drew to a close, the two men threw themselves into their business, and they began to realize that even better opportunities lay much farther afield. In particular, South Dakota was absolutely thriving. Now that gold had been found in the Black Hills, men were pouring into the territory at an amazing rate, and boom towns were springing up all over the once-perfect wilderness. There was no Yellowstone National Park for South Dakota; there was just a constant invasion of people.

And the town that was the most lucrative of all was Deadwood.

Like Al Swearengen, though, Seth and Sol were both uninterested in mining for gold. Instead, they recognized that thousands of people in Deadwood were eventually going to realize that they needed more than just mining tools, alcohol, and prostitutes. They would begin to build houses, and they would eventually come to need all ordinary equipment and household items that Seth and Sol had been selling in Helena for years.

For Seth, it was a bittersweet moment when he and his friend decided to seek their fortune in Deadwood with a new store. His marriage to Martha was important to him, and they had just had their first child, a little girl called Margaret. He had striven to be the father to her that George never was to him. But now, it meant moving to Deadwood and forging a better future for all of them.

Perhaps the Wild West really could be tamed; perhaps Martha and Margaret could come and join him soon.

With a heart heavy yet excited for the future, Seth set off on the long trail to Deadwood. Today, the 500 miles between Helena and Deadwood can be covered in eight hours by car, but in the summer of 1876, the only way that Seth and Sol could travel between the two towns, laden as they were with their wares, was by ox wagon. It was a long, slow journey, and they rumbled on through the summer heat and the many dangers that stalked the West—from angry Native Americans robbed of their homes to plain old highwaymen looking for their next victims.

On the first day of August 1876, Seth Bullock and Sol Star reached Deadwood, exhausted from the trail. Neither of them could possibly know that they would forever shape the character and future of the wild mining camp. Still, despite the long journey that lay behind them, Seth and Sol wasted absolutely no time in getting down to business.

Deadwood was, at the time, filled with young single men who had come to the West with romantic ideas and a thirst for gold, and their mining camp certainly reflected their priorities. There were plenty of pans for panning gold in the stream, plenty of women, and plenty of booze. However, the supply of basic hygiene products was pitiful. Most of these men were living in tents; they probably hadn't had a bath (except for dipping their feet into the stream) in months, and they smelt like it. Worst of all, even though flushing toilets had become common in more civilized areas around the 1850s, there were none of these to be had in Deadwood. Even a latrine was considered a luxury. Most men were hankering simply for a chamber pot.

Luckily for the men and for their business, Seth and Sol had come prepared with a whole wagonload of chamber pots. Still, they hadn't brought enough to sell one to every desperate Deadwood resident. Instead, they auctioned the chamber pots off to the highest bidder, raking in cash on their very first night in

Deadwood. It may not have been a glamorous start to their new business venture, but it was definitely a promising one.

The duo, however, would soon learn that they weren't in Montana anymore. Deadwood was a whole new world, a place whose reality lived up to the West's notorious reputation. The very day after Seth and Sol arrived, an appalling murder took place in Deadwood's No. 10 Saloon. The murderer would come perilously close to getting off scot-free, and although Seth didn't know it yet, this killing would be the start of the most illustrious part of his career as a lawman.

\* \* \* \*

James Butler "Wild Bill" Hickok might have been born in Illinois, but he would become a true legend of the Wild West.

Wild Bill grew up simply as James, and he spent most of his early life farming peacefully, but he always had a penchant for firearms. His skill as a gunslinger was tested early on when he moved to Kansas in 1855 to claim a homestead and start his own farm. The years of 1855 and 1856 were a terrible time in Kansas Territory. With tensions over the issue of slavery erupting all over the United States, new territories like Kansas were deeply divided over whether they would be a slave or free state. Many pushed to uphold slavery, seeing dollar signs as they considered the potential of the already-lucrative West being tamed by unpaid labor. Others believed in abolition and wanted the new territories to be free. Kansas became a center for conflict over this issue, with pioneers turning on one another. Although it would be another six years before the American Civil War officially began, the period known as "Bleeding Kansas" was a gruesome foretaste of the slaughter to come.

James Hickok was only eighteen years old at the time, but he did what thousands of other young men in Kansas did. He took up his gun, and he fought for what he believed in: freedom for all men.

He emerged from Bleeding Kansas not as James Butler but as Bill, taking his father's name now that he felt like a man. He had garnered a reputation as being a terrifyingly accurate marksman and a fearless gunfighter, and it was a reputation that would only grow in the years to come. He served as a constable in Kansas for a time before relocating to Nebraska, where he chose a quieter life for a short while, becoming a stockman at Rock Creek Station.

If Bill was hoping to find peace and tranquility at Rock Creek, his hopes were dashed. As he went about his work tending animals, his neighbor, David McCanles, decided that young Bill was a target. He started to mock him, giving him the derogatory nickname of "Duck Bill." This may have been rooted in his suspicions that his mistress was cheating on him with Bill. This suspicion was not groundless, as Bill was indeed sleeping with David McCanles's mistress.

Bill appears to have taken McCanles's mocking with good humor, or at least without violence. All that changed on July 12th, 1861. With the Civil War in its infancy, conflict was erupting in the East. It had not yet affected Nebraska, but blood was nonetheless shed at Rock Creek Station on that dark day.

David McCanles came looking for trouble. Accompanied by two older men and his son, then a preteen boy, McCanles swaggered up to the station manager and started arguing with him about payment for a piece of land. His real target sat inside the station behind a curtain, minding his own business but ever alert—and, as always, armed. Bleeding Kansas had taught Bill to always be ready for a fight.

Finally, McCanles announced to the station manager what his real intent had been in coming to the station. He demanded that the station manager step aside and allow him to assault Bill, calling him "Duck Bill" as usual.

Behind the curtain, Bill heard every word.

"There'll be one less [of you] if you try that," he said, with rather more profanity than is recorded here.

David McCanles considered Bill's words to be an empty threat and very quickly found out that they weren't. He rushed at the curtain, ready to pluck it aside and kill Bill, but he never got the chance. Through the curtain, Bill fired off a shot that echoed across Nebraska and into the annals of history. The bullet punched into McCanles's chest, and he stumbled out of the station, white-faced and dying.

His poor little son, only twelve years old, was appalled at the sight of his bleeding father. He ran to catch him as he collapsed, just in time for McCanles to breathe his last.

Outraged that their leader was dead, the other two men who had accompanied McCanles charged upon Bill with their weapons drawn. They started firing, and soon, the station was filled with the blast and whine of bullets.

When the shooting stopped, one of McCanles's two companions was dead. The other had been wounded by Bill and ran out of the station, after which Bill's allies, coming to help after hearing the sound of gunfire, killed him.

It wasn't long before the newspapers were filled with the exploits of the great gunslinger, calling him the name that would go down in history: "Wild Bill" Hickok. And while some of the accounts of Wild Bill's exploits were most certainly exaggerated, it is absolutely true that he was one of the best gunslingers the West had ever known.

Despite his nickname of "wild," Bill generally kept to the right side of the law. During the American Civil War, he fought with the Union Army, first as a scout and then later—possibly—as a spy in the Confederacy. His stint in the Union Army is veiled in secrecy, lending credence to the theory that he worked as a spy.

After the Civil War, Bill was still not tired of fighting. In fact, just months after the war ended, he was a part of a gunfight so classically Old Western that it almost doesn't feel real.

Bill was in Springfield, Missouri, at the time, drifting as he waited for the war to end and undoubtedly up to no good. He'd had a falling out with one of his friends, Davis Tutt, as both young men had fallen in love with the same woman. Things were only made worse between Bill and Davis when Bill lost a poker game to Davis and failed to pay his debt. Davis pinched Bill's treasured pocket watch and then proudly strutted around the Springfield town square wearing it.

This angered Bill, who was now twenty-eight years old. He warned Davis repeatedly to stop wearing the watch, which Davis completely ignored. Why would he listen to Bill? He had won the watch fairly in a poker game, and it was his property.

Bill didn't see it that way. And, back in 1865, there was only one sure way to settle this argument: a duel to the death.

The duel took place in the town square, and just the description of the event fills one's mind with Ennio Morricone's iconic music, the theme from the 1966 film *The Good, The Bad and the Ugly*. The people in the square parted to make way for the two gunslingers, and total silence fell as Wild Bill and Davis faced one another about seventy-five feet apart.

Accounts vary on exactly what happened next. Both men were armed. Both men drew their weapons. The accounts agree that Wild Bill was quicker on the draw. Some say he shot first; others say that he stood, pistol in hand, waiting for Davis to fire. Davis's shot missed completely, and before he could shoot again, Wild Bill raised his gun. As one of the witnesses said, "Bill never shoots at the same man twice." Davis died with Wild Bill's bullet in his heart. Wild Bill was tried for manslaughter, but for better or worse, the authorities at the time reasoned that it had been a fair fight, and they let him go.

In general, despite his murder of a man over a pocket watch, Wild Bill was seen as an astute lawman and a pillar of strength in the Wild West. He became the sheriff in Hays City, Kansas, and served there for many years to tame the outlaws of the region. His status as a legendary gunman and uncompromising sheriff spread all over the West, and his name became synonymous with the old gunslingers of the American West.

It all came crashing down for Wild Bill in 1871. He was raiding a saloon in Hays City on suspicion of illegal activity taking place there (as it generally did in most saloons), and as he and his deputy took on the saloon owner and his cronies, bullets were flying, smoke filled the air, and utter chaos broke loose. For the first and final time, Wild Bill lost his head in a gunfight. He fired at the nearest man, killing him the way he always did, with one or two quick shots to the chest.

When the smoke cleared, it turned out that the dead man was no outlaw. It was Mike Williams, Wild Bill's trusted deputy.

That was Wild Bill's final gunfight. He never drew his weapon in anger again, unable to forget his accidental killing of an innocent friend. With no other skills, Wild Bill turned to target shooting, traveling around for a few years with Buffalo Bill Cody in his famous Wild West show. He entertained the crowds with his great feats of marksmanship.

Even though Wild Bill shot only at targets for the cheers of the crowd, even that wouldn't last for long. Glaucoma stole his legendary eyesight, robbing him of the one great skill he'd ever had. By 1876, Wild Bill was almost blind. Despite the fact that he was not yet forty years old, Wild Bill was a has-been—a down-and-out, destitute relic of a once-legendary lawman.

He came to Deadwood in desperation, hoping to find some way to survive there, and he fell back on poker for his existence. Everything had been taken from Wild Bill. He had no career, no eyesight, and no real skills. All he had was desperation and the sad knowledge that, at the age of thirty-nine, his glory days were behind him.

Still, Wild Bill might have had some kind of a future if it hadn't been brutally taken from him in a senseless act of appalling violence. In fact, despite his destitution and sad prospects, Wild Bill had just gotten married to Agnes Thatcher Lake. Agnes was a force to be reckoned with in and of herself, as she ran her own circus and also performed in it as a tightrope walker, lion tamer, and horse rider. After several chance encounters throughout the years, Agnes and Wild Bill were married on March 7th, 1876. After a two-week honeymoon in Cincinnati, Ohio, during which the two appeared to be thoroughly in love, Wild Bill left for South Dakota.

And he never returned.

Although Wild Bill had ostensibly gone to South Dakota to seek a fortune, there is little evidence of his mining activities. Instead, Wild Bill had become nothing but a gambler, trying to scrape together enough money to be reunited with his wife by playing poker.

On the morning of August 2nd, 1876 (a morning when many Deadwood men were awakening to their glorious new chamber pots from Seth Bullock and Sol Star), Wild Bill was heading to the No. 10 Saloon in Deadwood as he usually did. He sat down with his back to the door, a seat he typically avoided, to play a poker match with some other local gamblers.

He was looking down at his hand, noting that he had two black aces and two black eights. This hand is known to this day as the "dead man's hand" because of what happened next.

The door of the saloon swung open. No one took any notice of the armed young cowboy who walked into the saloon. It was Deadwood, after all; literally everyone was armed. Everyone continued to mind their own cards and beer as the young man walked up to Wild Bill, drew his pistol, and shot the gunslinger in the back of the head.

Wild Bill was dead before his head hit the poker table, splattering blood over the game. Chaos broke loose in the saloon, but the shooter, Jack McCall, was not particularly concerned. He walked right out of the saloon and left. Agnes was made a widow not even six months after she'd become a wife.

\* \* \* \*

Wild Bill had lived through so many dazzling exploits and gained such a great reputation as a warrior and lawman, yet his death was absolutely senseless and brutal. However, it was more than just a terribly tragic end to Wild Bill's life. It was a horrifying example of how lawless Deadwood had become, that someone could simply walk up and shoot an ex-sheriff and national legend in the back of the head, then walk right out again.

McCall was detained shortly after the shooting of Wild Bill. As Seth and Sol were finding their feet in the new town, Deadwood was setting up an impromptu camp court. Somehow, despite the fact that McCall had murdered Wild Bill in front of many witnesses, he was found not guilty and was allowed to walk free. Such was the extent of the lawlessness that held Deadwood in its carnal grip.

Ultimately, however, McCall's acquittal proved as a wake-up call for South Dakota authorities. Believing that he was invincible after his acquittal, McCall, who had shot Bill due to a perceived insult the day before the shooting, started to brag all around the territory that he had courageously taken on and killed the famous Wild Bill Hickok. It did not seem to occur to McCall that his act had been one of unbelievable cowardice and cruelty. All he'd really done was to walk up to an unarmed, destitute old gambler and take his life from behind at point-blank range.

McCall's boasting finally got the attention of the authorities, and he was recaptured more than six months after the murder in March 1877. This time, he was tried in front of a real court, which obviously found him guilty. McCall was hanged. His foolish act had brought about the premature and violent ending of not one life but two.

\* \* \* \*

Seth Bullock must have been appalled to hear of the killing of Wild Bill. While Seth was no edgy gunslinger like Wild Bill, as Seth's adherence to the law was far more rigid (it is difficult to imagine him killing a poker player over a pocket watch), he must have nonetheless felt a connection to Wild Bill since they had both been sheriffs. And it must also have been sobering to realize how easily one could lose their life in Deadwood.

To make matters even worse, one month after McCall was finally hanged for his crimes, Al Swearengen decided to expand his booming business. He had more sketchy business deals than we will probably ever know about, and most of them involved prostitution in some way or another. The vast majority of the women of Deadwood were working for Al Swearengen, forced to bed one reckless miner after the other. Al didn't care about the poor girls suffering in his Cricket Saloon. All he wanted was to make money, and he was making piles of it as a pimp.

On April 7th, 1877, Al opened the biggest front yet for his prostitution ring: the Gem Variety Theater. On the outside, the Gem appeared to be just that, a rare jewel of culture in the Wild West. There was beautiful wallpaper, a dance floor, and entertainment that appeared fairly civilized at first glance. But that was just the literal front of the theater building. Behind it, prostitutes were waiting, propositioning men from behind the bar because they had no other choice. The penalty for refusing to obey Al's orders was physical punishment.

Between the McCall debacle and the Gem Variety Theater, crime spiked wildly in Deadwood, and the authorities realized that enough was enough. What Deadwood really needed was a sheriff— a stern-eyed, iron-fisted lawman. The once-lovely wilderness of the Black Hills was now marred by the truly untamed portion of the

Wild West, that of the animal savagery existing in the hearts of men. Someone needed to scare that right out of them. Someone who wouldn't get sucked into corruption. Someone who wouldn't place a single toe on the wrong side of the law.

Someone like Seth Bullock.

At the time, Sol and Seth had progressed from running a general and hardware store out of a tent to purchasing an actual lot on the corner of Deadwood's main street. At first, they could only build a false front for their shop, but as the months went on, Seth and Sol were beginning to prove that it was possible to make good money in the West without resorting to illegal activities. The Star and Bullock Hardware Store was booming, and it grew into a building that attracted plenty of customers every day.

Seth was working hard at his business, but he was also acutely aware that there was no way he could bring Martha and Margaret to Deadwood, not with the likes of Al Swearengen controlling the town. So, when Governor John Pennington, who was in charge of Dakota Territory, approached him, asking if he would serve temporarily as Deadwood's appointed sheriff, Seth eagerly agreed. It was March, shortly after Jack McCall's trial.

Interestingly enough, Seth would never be elected as the sheriff of Deadwood. That honor belonged to Democrat John J. Manning, who was elected in November 1877 and would serve two two-year terms, both times defeating Seth Bullock in the election. Seth only served as the sheriff of Lawrence County (which included Deadwood) for a matter of months. But a few months was enough for Seth to whip the wild town into shape.

As the sheriff of Deadwood and already one of its most prominent residents, Seth held a considerable amount of power. His decisive action during his gunfight with Clell Watson had already proven him to be a formidable fighter, yet in the nine months that Seth served as the sheriff of Deadwood, he never killed anyone in a gunfight.

Somehow, Seth Bullock tamed the town of Deadwood without any of the frontier justice that characterized the careers of many Western lawmen of his era. While executions undoubtedly would have taken place—Seth would have been raised to consider these as a form of justice—there were no gruesome gun battles during which outlaws were shot and killed, no ugly murders or duels simply to make an example out of a criminal or to make a spectacle out of Seth's gunslinger skills. He held power just like his father, George, had; but unlike George, who thought nothing of brutally beating an innocent child, Seth was aware of the weight of responsibility that this power gave him. And despite his lack of brutality, Seth tamed Deadwood in nine months.

He made several of Deadwood's more respectable citizens into sheriff's deputies, and he worked with them to systematically uproot the crime that had grown so deep into the very identity of the town.

The one nemesis that Seth never conquered, unfortunately, was Al Swearengen. Despite numerous confrontations over the years, Al somehow clung to the Gem Variety Theater and continued to run it as a brothel for the ever-eager string of customers with which the gold mines provided him. The fact that Seth Bullock never put a stop to the Gem's operations was a terrible tragedy for the prostitutes working in it. Many of them had been practically kidnapped from their homes, as they had been desperate women from the overpopulated East, attracted to Deadwood by advertisements Al placed in newspapers promising lucrative job opportunities as "waitresses" and "actresses." The women would then find themselves trapped in prostitution, and while there is little evidence to suggest that they were actual sex slaves, they certainly didn't have many other options besides staying and working at the Gem. There was a reason why Seth had not yet brought Martha and Margaret to Deadwood. It was a dangerous place for women, even more so outside the Gem than within it, and there were no opportunities for women to find respectable work. Many of them had spent their last penny getting to Deadwood. They had no choice but to stay at the Gem, and for as long as they stayed, they would be beaten for any perceived transgression. These bruised, beaten, hollow-eyed girls waited in vain for Seth to save them. It can be assumed that this was not for lack of trying, but whether he didn't have enough power or resources, or for whatever other reason, Seth never did get Al Swearengen to leave town.

Nonetheless, except for the den of vice that the Gem had become, by the time John J. Manning was sworn in as the county sheriff, Deadwood had changed. It was now safe enough that Seth Bullock could have his wife and little girl finally reunite with him in South Dakota. They came to join him in his now-booming business with Sol, and they were able to walk the streets fearlessly thanks to Seth's efforts in reforming the town.

As for Al Swearengen, he might have evaded Seth, but he eventually got what was coming to him. The Gem Variety Theater burned down twice in 1879, yet this was no major setback for Al; there was so much money to be made in his cruel line of work that he just built bigger and better theaters after each fire. Some estimates of the Gem's profits run as high as $10,000 a night—a huge sum even by modern standards, let alone in the 19th century.

Ultimately, the Gem burned down again in 1899, and Al finally got out of Deadwood. He returned to the East for a time before moving to Denver, Colorado, in 1904. It was in the streets there that he was struck and killed with a blunt object. His twin brother, Lemuel, had been shot in a similar manner a short while before; it is suspected that Al had always been the target of a hit from one of the many, many people he had harmed.

# Chapter 4 – The Bullock Hotel

*Illustration III: The Bullock Hotel today*

By 1881, although Seth was no longer the sheriff of Deadwood and the most famous part of his life was over, he was certainly by no means done living. In fact, Seth was really just getting started.

His famous stint as the sheriff of Deadwood had never failed to distract him from his business and family life. The Star and Bullock Hardware Store was thriving in a two-story wooden building on the corner of Main and Wall Street, Deadwood. He was still happily married to Martha, and they were building themselves a good life in the once-wild mining camp that was now rapidly turning into the biggest city in Lawrence County, South Dakota. In fact, Martha had borne Seth two more surviving children: a little girl, Florence, and a little boy, Stanley.

Seth's career as a lawman was also by no means stagnant. While he no longer carried the title of sheriff, he was made a deputy in Medora, North Dakota.

However, it was his business that would truly expand during the 1880s and 1890s. By 1881, Seth and Sol were ready to take the next step. They pooled their resources and purchased an enormous ranch together on the confluence of the Belle Fourche River and a nearby creek. The acres upon acres of beautiful arable land were soon put to use raising cattle and thoroughbred horses. To feed his livestock, Seth decided to plant a crop that was well known back East: alfalfa. This high-protein roughage crop has become the staple of livestock feeds across the world today, but Seth was the first to ever plant it in South Dakota. Today, the state produces several million tons of alfalfa every year.

While Seth was enjoying tending his ranch, his political career was far from over. Soon, he would meet a man who would become one of his dearest friends and also one of the most powerful influences on his life and career.

\* \* \* \*

Theodore Roosevelt was a broken man in 1884.

Thirteen years Seth's junior, Theodore, who hated being called Teddy, hadn't had an easy childhood. Asthma and other health issues had made his childhood a nightmare, and it was only when he discovered how much physical activity and fitness improved his symptoms that he was finally rid of terrifying nightmares of suffocating in his sleep. The same year that Seth came to Deadwood, Theodore went to Harvard and later lost his beloved father in 1878.

Despite these struggles, Theodore's career was promising in every way by 1884. He was thirty years old and had already proven himself an excellent writer with numerous published books; his capability as a strategist was evident, he had been elected to the New York State Assembly, and he was married to Alice Hathaway Lee.

On Valentine's Day, 1884, everything fell apart for Theodore. His first child had just been born two days earlier. The pregnancy and childbirth had proved too much for his treasured Alice, who died from kidney failure; on the very same day, Theodore's last surviving parent, his mother Mittie, also passed away in the same house.

Theodore's world was torn instantly to pieces. He is quoted as having said that his life had fallen apart. While he was still active politically in New York, Theodore had to find solace somewhere. He remembered an 1883 hunting trip during which he had visited South Dakota. Something about the harsh beauty of the Black Hills had captivated him, and he thought he could find peace and healing somewhere under that wide blue sky.

Theodore invested in a ranch near Medora and moved there, hoping to turn it into a business opportunity. The ranch would ultimately not succeed, but it did turn Theodore into a roping, range-riding cowboy over the next two years. And it introduced him to one of his closest friends and a man for whom he had endless respect.

At the time, Seth, who was a deputy in the area, was hot on the trail of yet another criminal. With more than a decade's experience as a Wild West lawman, he had become a force to be reckoned with, the veteran of many a tense stand-off and violent arrest. He was riding across the hills seeking a horse thief known only as Crazy Steve.

Theodore, who had been interested in community leadership in Medora since his arrival, was also hunting for the same horse thief. He spent weeks chasing after Crazy Steve, sleeping on the ground and riding all day, and he was a scruffy figure when he spotted an intimidating figure approaching him.

Seth was the picture of a hard-eyed sheriff. His six-foot height was topped by gray eyes that, in the words of his grandson, could stare down a mad bull. When he met Theodore, however, he was as courteous as ever, and Theodore was instantly inspired by the man. They went searching for Crazy Steve together, cementing a friendship that would last for the rest of their lives, even after Theodore sold his ranch in 1886.

\* \* \* \*

When he wasn't chasing after horse thieves with interesting nicknames, Seth was expanding his business. A golden opportunity came to him in 1890—nine years after purchasing the Star and Bullock Ranch Company.

At the time, railroads were spreading out across the West like spiderwebs, linking the many boom towns together and enabling trade to build them into real cities instead of mining camps. By then, the land had been neatly parceled out and sold, so the railway companies had no choice but to buy large tracts of lands on which to lay their tracks. They were interested in laying a railroad to Minnesela, South Dakota, a town very close to the S&B Ranch Company, and a nearby speculator quoted them a truly exorbitant amount of money to buy enough land for it.

Seth and Sol, the partners-in-crime that they were (figuratively—by all accounts, their business was always above board), immediately pounced on this opportunity. They offered the Fremont, Elkhorn, and Missouri Valley Railroad forty acres of land at no charge at all but with one caveat: instead of building the station in Minnesela, the railroad company was asked to build it on the ranch itself, about five miles from the town.

Given the prospect of free land, the railroad company immediately accepted. The station was built near the Belle Fourche River, and Seth started offering free land to anyone who would start a business near the station. Within months, Minnesela had waned in importance, and buildings were springing up on this part of Seth's ranch. It wasn't long before the town of Belle Fourche had sprung up like a colony of mushrooms almost overnight, and fueled by Seth's and Sol's astute business sense, it constantly grew in size and importance. Soon, it became the county seat and one of the largest railheads in the entire United States.

Seth, Martha, the two girls, and little Stanley were still living in Deadwood at this time, and the Star and Bullock Hardware Store remained an integral part of their livelihood. Even after a devastating fire swept through Deadwood in 1879, burning down hundreds of buildings (including the Gem Variety Theater, although it was rapidly rebuilt), the Star and Bullock store survived and continued to thrive.

It was not so lucky in 1894. A blazing inferno swept once again through the town, and this time, the Star and Bullock store was not spared from the wrath of the blaze. It burned to the ground aside from a small brick storeroom.

Sol and Seth decided that the time for a mere hardware store was over. Deadwood was a very different town than the mining camp they had entered eighteen years before. It was no longer a place where gold miners went; now, it was a bustling city, filled with commerce and even tourism, and Seth decided it was high time that a reputable counterpart to the Gem Variety Theater was built. Instead of rebuilding their hardware store, they were going to build a hotel.

It took two years and many, many blocks of pink and white sandstone, but by 1896, the Bullock Hotel was complete—and it was a marvel. With three floors filled with opulent luxuries, the Bullock Hotel was a place of genteel culture, a world away from the raunchy world of the Gem. It boasted a grand lobby, a vast dining room, and even a sample room for use by the many salesmen who came to Deadwood—and all that only on the ground floor. The other two floors contained sixty-three luxurious rooms kitted out with oak dressers and brass bedsteads, en-suite bathrooms, and even a balcony and library. The whole thing was decorated in an Italian-Victorian style that would have befitted a hotel in the tamer reaches of the East. For the Wild West, the Bullock Hotel was a rare jewel.

In fact, to this day, guests can enjoy beautiful décor and endless luxuries at the very same Bullock Hotel, still located on the corner of Main and Wall Street in the city of Deadwood. While many of its amenities have obviously been upgraded, the Bullock Hotel still retains its historic charm.

Arguably, while Seth is better known for his exploits as a county sheriff, the Bullock Hotel was his real passion. He was an elegant host and enjoyed serving his guests. It was the apple of his eye, his pride and joy.

\* \* \* \*

In 1898, still licking its wounds after the American Civil War less than forty years earlier, the now-reunited United States' mettle would be tested in its first international conflict since the Civil War.

Cuba, the tiny island to the south of the US, had been embroiled in a bloody revolutionary war since 1895. Cuba was still a Spanish colony at the time, and the Spanish were subjecting native Cubans (many of them of mixed-race heritage) to appalling oppression. The United States quietly supported the Cuban rebels, but it had not yet actually joined the war.

All that changed on February 15th, 1898. The USS *Maine* had been lying quietly at anchor in Havana Harbor when it suddenly and violently exploded during the night, killing hundreds of men. A perfect storm of yellow journalism and long-standing tensions between the Old World and the United States resulted in a bitter conflict that would become known as the Spanish-American War.

Theodore's political career had by then taken off in a big way. He had become the New York City police commissioner in 1894, and in 1897, he was appointed the assistant secretary of the US Navy.

However, it was not as the assistant secretary of the Navy that Theodore would serve in the Spanish-American War. Theodore wanted to fight with his boots on the ground. He promptly resigned from his position and put together a volunteer cavalry regiment that would make him famous: the 1st United States Volunteer Cavalry, better known as Roosevelt's Rough Riders.

Seth never saw active duty, but he had maintained his friendship with Theodore, and he was quick to volunteer. While he wasn't part of the Rough Riders themselves, he joined another US volunteer cavalry regiment and traveled all the way down to Louisiana for training, earning the rank of captain of Troop A during training.

The war, however, did not last long enough to benefit from Seth's leadership. Although the Spanish American-War was officially ended on December 10th, 1898, the last battle had been fought on July 17th. The war lasted less than three months, and Seth returned home to Deadwood.

In 1899, Theodore's political career had nearly reached its zenith. The vice president at the time, Garret Hobart, died unexpectedly of heart failure. Although Theodore was reluctant to take the position, he was eventually made vice president of the United States under President William McKinley. This fateful choice would catapult him into the most powerful position in the country just two years later. When President McKinley was assassinated at a convention in September 1901, Theodore, the scruffy, unshaven cowboy that Seth had met in South Dakota, became the president of the United States of America.

For America, Theodore's presidency meant, among many other things, an increased emphasis on conservation. Part of South Dakota's Black Hills—Seth's home for twenty-five years—had been made a reserve, and Theodore considered that there was no one better than Seth to become the forest supervisor of it. He always maintained his deep respect for Seth, even though Seth was just a lowly businessman and sheriff. Nonetheless, Theodore called him an example of a true frontiersman.

This became more obvious than ever in 1905. Theodore had served for four years as the US president simply because he had been in the right position at the right time; in 1904, however, he was elected president in his own right. The inauguration took place in 1905, and Seth was deeply proud of his friend. He ordered fifty cowboys to get ready for Theodore's inaugural parade. They were a testimony to the influence that Dakota's wilderness had had on Theodore, and they were a spectacular sight as they rode down the street with silver on their hand-tooled saddles and their six-shooters flashing in their holsters, led by Seth Bullock and his steely-eyed stare.

Considering that Seth had tamed Deadwood, it was little surprise that Theodore made him a US marshal the same year that he was inaugurated. Seth would serve in his treasured home of South Dakota until 1914.

Although Seth was sixty-five years old by this time and had led a very long and busy life, this by no means meant retirement for the aging sheriff. When the First World War broke out, Theodore, who was no longer president but rather a Nobel Peace Prize laureate for his role in mediating the end of the Russo-Japanese War, appointed eighteen officers to raise a volunteer regiment to assist on the French front in 1917. Unsurprisingly, one of these officers was Seth Bullock. He threw himself into the task, but it was all in vain. President Woodrow Wilson never approved the volunteer regiments, and they were disbanded before the end of the war.

For both Seth and Theodore, this was the beginning of the end.

Sol Star, who had been Seth's staunch friend since the Helena days (nearly forty years), was growing old. He had never married; Seth was the closest thing to family that he had. He lived on the S&B Ranch Company while Seth lived in Deadwood, and they remained good friends. Still, no friendship between mortals can last forever. Sol died in October 1917 at home on the ranch he loved. Seth gave him a funeral in Deadwood, which was, according to some accounts, "fit for a president." Sol had been one of the most influential citizens that Deadwood ever had.

Theodore was still young in comparison; by January 1919, he was only sixty years old and still as healthy as a horse, at least to all appearances. Tragically, his death would be unexpected. He was feeling a little unwell on the evening of January 5th, 1919, but he went to bed as usual. However, he would never rise again. He suffered a pulmonary embolism—a blood clot that affects the lungs—and died that evening.

His death was an awful blow to Seth. Having lost both Sol and Theodore, Seth grieved deeply and intensely. All he could think of was dedicating a monument to Theodore, displaying the deep mutual respect that the two men had held for one another. Helped by some fellow Black Hills residents, Seth erected a monument facing a nearby mountain, which was renamed Mt. Roosevelt. It was unveiled on the Fourth of July, 1919.

After a lifetime of chasing crooks and taming the Wild West, it wasn't a bullet that ultimately ended Seth's life. Unlike Wild Bill, he didn't die from a bullet to the brain. Instead, he passed away peacefully at home in the town he had helped to tame. Belle Fourche might have been the town he built, but Deadwood would always be his home, and he died there from colon cancer on September 23rd, 1919.

# Conclusion

The Wild West is undoubtedly one of the most fascinating periods in the history of the United States of America. From the illustrious cowboy to the snaggle-toothed outlaw to the steely-eyed lawman, it is peopled with characters who loom larger than life. Romanticized though it may be, it was a brutal time for many, a testimony to the extent of human depravity and an example of the violence of which mankind is capable.

Yet among all of these hard characters and frontier lawmen, Seth Bullock stands out not for his sternness, nor for his marksmanship skills, nor for any kind of legendary exploits or brutality. He stands out for traits that were undervalued in the Old West yet shine in the modern day: his honesty, integrity, intense loyalty to his friends and family, and the capability of using a difficult childhood not as a fuel for a life of crime but as a springboard to greater things.

In the time of the Wild West, Seth Bullock had succeeded in taming the one thing that most Western men—notably those who so willingly patronized Al Swearengen's Gem Variety Theater— never managed to rope or break. These men captured wild horses and bucked them till they broke, yet they never succeeded in taming themselves.

But Seth Bullock was a man in complete command of himself. And it was his ability to control his own desires, his own fears, and his own flaws that made him the man who tamed Deadwood.

More than one hundred years after the death of Seth Bullock, Deadwood has become a thriving city. Its colorful history attracts tourists from all over the world, with many of them staying at the Bullock Hotel. And perhaps Seth, even in death, couldn't quite bring himself to let go of the town that made him who he was. Some say that if one of the servers stands idle for just a few minutes too long in the Bullock Hotel, the ghost of Seth Bullock walks the halls once again, ready to ensure that justice will always be done.

# Part 5: Davy Crockett

*A Captivating Guide to the American Folk Hero Who Fought in the War of 1812 and the Texas Revolution*

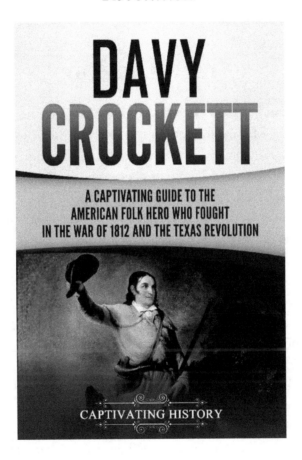

# Introduction

If, as historian Thomas Carlyle said, the history of the world is but the biography of great men, then it is also true that the story of the great men is a parable of their times, places, and generational aspirations. The life of Davy Crockett, one of the most cherished and remembered American frontiersmen, is an accurate representation of the United States as it stretched westward to become one of the largest nations in the world.

Yet David Crockett was not a mythical character but a very real person. Such was his mark in the process of westward expansion that, among hundreds of other frontiersmen, only he got the informal title of "King of the Wild Frontier" for posterity. The frontiersmen were a special class of rambling men, explorers, naturalists, hunters, and pioneers who formed the vanguard in the territories beyond the Mississippi. As such, they were the eyes and ears of a nation that was craving more territory, excited by the promise of a safe route to the Pacific. But America was not discovered by the Europeans. When the British and French arrived, the native peoples had been living on the continent for centuries. So, the westward expansion was also inevitably the story of the struggle between whites and Native Americans.

Davy Crockett represented the best of that generation because, although he took part in the wars against the Native Americans, when he was a congressman in Washington, he vehemently opposed the land dispossession and injustices against the Native Americans. Hence a long political rivalry arose between the ill-tempered President Andrew Jackson and the silver-tongued adventurer. Crockett did not earn a place in Congress for his noble birth or political patronage. In fact, he was one of the first examples of a genuine man of humble extraction reaching such a high political position. Crockett had spent his childhood with a family burdened by debt and had to work before reaching adolescence to help his father pay it off. His success as a politician was helped in no small measure by his extraordinary eloquence, which made him famous, and the tales of his incredible adventures in the wild that circulated in his lifetime. During a good part of his existence, he made a living as a bear hunter in the Tennessee forests, selling the fur, oil, and meat of the animals. We can say with certainty that Davy Crockett was a tough, hardened, and skilled man, with a deep understanding of the natural world.

When he was alive, books about his adventures, unauthorized biographies, almanacs, and even plays—think of them as the equivalent of the great movie premieres of our times—were produced lavishly, in some cases with such crazy stories that Crockett himself was compelled to write his own books to correct the inaccuracies. Crockett also wrote because, although he was far from being a literary genius or a great naturalist, he was moved by a spirit of openness to new experiences and new conquests. The fame of this simple American "kid" from Tennessee became even greater decades after his death, to the point of Crockett becoming an undeclared national hero and a symbol of the struggle for freedom. Crockett, of course, owed his greatest boost to fame to the Alamo, an old mission built by the Spanish, where one of the most iconic battles was fought in the Texas War of Independence. Crockett's death among the Alamo's defenders, to whom United States history assigned a special status as martyrs of liberty, elevated him to unsuspected heights. More than one hundred years after his death, he was a superstar and a model for children, who watched his adventures on television. In a way, Crockett was perhaps the first superhero in the history of the United States, although this happened many years after his death in the war against Mexico.

This does not mean that his life was not riddled with controversy or that his true achievements do not continue to be the subject of discussion between historians and laymen. Davy Crockett was a celebrity in life, but he was far from being acknowledged as a national hero. He had many enemies, critics, and detractors who, from the moment he entered politics, tried to ruin and discredit him. People from his homeland of Tennessee came to consider him a traitor because he sided with the Native Americans on delicate issues. Many malicious newspapers accused him of being a compulsive gambler and criticized his drinking escapades. Other questions are raised after reading any "Life" of Crockett: Did he defend the Native Americans for reasons of humanitarianism or just to make life difficult for his political opponents? What was he doing in Texas? Did he go with a political nose in search of power, to rebuild his life, or to help the cause of independence? Did he really die as a hero in the Alamo?

What is undeniable is that Davy Crockett was always faithful to his convictions, as he was guided by a deep commitment to justice, and above all, he was someone who always did what he thought was right, even running to aid his strongest political enemy, President Andrew Jackson, when someone tried to assassinate him. And that philosophy of life—doing the right thing no matter what— is much more than can be said of many others of his generation. That is why David Crockett is one of the great national symbols of the United States of America.

# Chapter 1 – The Frontiersman

"Like many of them, I stood no chance to become great in any other way than by accident."

—Davy Crockett

David Crockett was not born in a privileged home. His arrival in this world was on August 17th, 1786, in Tennessee, when the region was still part of North Carolina. He was the fifth of nine children. His father, the son of an Irish couple, was John Wesley Crockett, a veteran of the American Revolution who fought at the Battle of Kings Mountain. After that, he had managed to acquire a piece of land to build a humble log cabin for his family. But beyond that, he hadn't accomplished much more in life except living in debt. Since he was very poor, young David and his brothers grew up without an education, spending most of their lives in the wilderness, where life was hard and every man had to hunt. When Mr. Crockett found someone as poor as he was to start a business in partnership, he invested his few savings in a grist mill, but a sudden flood wiped away his plans to earn a steady income. Years later, Davy wrote about that misfortune in his memoirs, the first of many that would haunt his family: "I remember the water rose so high that it got up into the house we lived in, and my father moved us out of it to keep us from being drowned. I was now about seven or eight years old, and have a pretty distinct recollection of everything that was going on."

After the flood, the senior Crockett moved his family to Jefferson County, where, in 1796, he built a log tavern, which he used to offer lodging and food for travelers between Virginia and Tennessee. The cabin survived until the Civil War, during which it was used as a hospital, and later on, it became a hospice for smallpox patients. Davy's father's tavern "was on a small scale, as he was poor; and the principal accommodations which he kept were for the wagoners who traveled the road." At the same time, Mr. Crockett taught Davy how to shoot a rifle to become a skilled hunter and thus contribute to help put food on the table. Davy's first rifle was called "Betsy," and this firearm is still kept in a museum to this day.

Mr. Crockett's fifth son spent his early years away from school and working for the family, at a time when children were expected to help their parents. He also spent many hours exploring the forests. In the tavern, his first informal school, as these were places where travelers gathered to tell stories, the boy must have heard tales about distant lands that aroused his curiosity. When his father finally sent him to the local school, his stay was short, lasting exactly four days.

In the first week, Davy was the victim of the school's bully—a boy much taller and older than he—and being a self-sufficient person from a young age, he decided to put things right. He waited for the older kid on the road, hidden in the bushes, and when the boy passed by, he jumped like a tiger and beat him up. "I scratched his face all to a flitter jig and soon made him cry for quarters in god earnest." Since he feared the teacher's punishment, or possibly the bully's revenge, Davy decided to stay away from the classroom. Of course, he did not tell this to his parents. What he did was leave home in the morning with his brothers, and before reaching the school, he would sneak out into the woods to explore. He stayed there until it was time to go home. That was how things worked until the principal wrote a letter to his father asking why Davy had stopped going to class. The scolding was so severe that the young man, barely thirteen, decided to run away from home and live on his own.

For the next three years, Davy wandered from town to town, performing several jobs as a hired hand. Finally, at the age of sixteen, he decided he had had enough and returned home. His parents hardly recognized him.

* * *

"Though he was poor, he was an honest man," wrote David Crockett about his old man in his autobiography. David's humble background and the fact that his father spent his life chased by debtors, as well as the constant changes of residence, left a deep mark on his personality. Always wandering from place to place in search of a definite home and never settling permanently in a single place, Davy would always be in search of greener pastures in the pursuance of a fortune that never came. When he was a congressman, he always had the less fortunate in mind. At the start of the westward expansion from the initial colonies on the Atlantic, people who lived bordering the Native American country did so with a feeling of inferiority. They were second-class Americans compared to the urban classes of the East Coast cities. Thus, when Davy became famous, he was truly a "man of the people."

But perhaps money was not the biggest problem for the adolescent Crockett, who felt that he was unlucky in love and he had the idea that he was going to stay alone for the rest of his life. During a hunting expedition, he arrived at the home of a German family, where he spent the night. There he met a girl who seemed to him "as ugly as a stone fence." When she realized that she would not have a chance, she assured his guest that there were plenty of fish in the sea waiting for a good man and promised that she would introduce him to the most beautiful woman his eyes had ever seen if he only attended the "reaping," or harvest celebration. Since it was an opportunity to socialize, drink, tell adventures, and listen to other exaggerated tales, all activities that he enjoyed, Davy agreed. There he met a girl named Polly, whom he liked immediately.

Davy offered his employer, an old Quaker who was his neighbor, a deal, where he would work for six months in exchange for a horse, the first he would ever own and something he saw as necessary to woo the beautiful Polly. However, Polly's mother was not thrilled with the idea of giving her daughter's hand to a nineteen-year-old adventurer who didn't have a penny in his pocket. The girl's father viewed Davy with more sympathy, but the young man knew that without Polly's mother's consent, things would be complicated. One night, Davy was hunting a wolf in a part of the forest that he didn't know, which was very uninhabited, and he lost his way. He was thinking about how he would return home when he suddenly saw "a little woman streaking it along the woods like all wrath." Intrigued, he ran to catch up, determined not to lose sight of her. When he grabbed her, he was surprised to see that it was Polly, who had also gotten lost looking for her father's horses. "She looked sweeter than sugar," wrote Davy, "and by this time I loved her almost well enough to eat her."

Tired of the mother's disdain, Davy asked Polly whether she would agree to go with him if he went to her house with two horses. The young woman nodded. On his way back home, Davy went to see a justice of the peace to get a marriage license. On the fixed day, he rode to the girl's house escorted by a group of relatives, as was the custom in those days. Outside Polly's family's property, he asked Polly if she would marry him and showed her the extra horse. Polly said yes, and they were about to ride off together, but at the last moment, the tearful father stopped Davy and asked him to please have the wedding at his house. Crockett, who had nothing against the old man, told him that he would if Polly's mother asked him too and apologized for the cold shoulder she had given him. The wedding was then held at the girl's house.

The couple was in love, but they were both poor. Davy rented a farm, which had two cows and some calves that Polly's parents had given them as a dowry. Polly also had a sewing wheel, and "she was good at that, and at almost anything else that a woman could do." Despite the fact that the two worked hard, with the arrival of two children, Davy knew that he would have to do something else if he did not want them to starve. The couple left the rental property and settled in Lincoln County near Elk River, an area that was just beginning to become populated. It was there that Davy began to stand out as a hunter. Dissatisfied with the declining population of bears, they moved back to Franklin County, most likely to Polly's chagrin since she saw that nothing of what her husband began bore fruit and since she also had to endure his constant absences. Davy was a restless soul, and apparently, he did not do much for the physical improvement of his house. His passion was in the great outdoors. In the words of Michael Wallis, his most important modern biographer, "Hunting always proved to be Crockett's salvation, sanctuary, and escape."

For a long time, David lived like a wandering soul, taking his family from one place to another. In every new site that he encountered, he explored, hunted bears with his pack of wild dogs, and sold meat, fur, and fat. When the population of these animals began to decline and new colonists began to push the border farther east, he took his belongings and went in search of more deserted lands, as if he was engaged in an endless search for the right place. Many others like him formed a slow exodus to the west, poor men and their families, burdened with debt, looking for a new beginning. "The frontier was moving on, and David, at the age of twenty-five, wanted to move right along with it," writes Wallis. "As was always his way, he had a desire to know what waited for him on the other side of every river and mountain he encountered. His curiosity and restlessness never wavered."

In 1898, pastor and historian John Cabot Abbott, who also wrote the biographies of Napoleon Bonaparte and Frederick the Great, published his biography of David Crockett and described with great detail this part of his life as a frontiersman.

He loved to wander in busy idleness all the day, with fishing-rod and rifle; and he would often return at night with a very ample supply of game. He would then lounge about his hut, tanning deer skins for moccasins and breeches, performing other little jobs, and entirely neglecting all endeavors to improve his farm, or to add to the appearance or comfort of the miserable shanty which he called his home. In hunting, his skill became very remarkable, and few, even of the best marksmen, could throw the bullet with more unerring aim.

As a skilled hunter and trapper, he traveled around the Mississippi Valley as a fur trader and became acquainted with the Native Americans and their way of life. Perhaps he was curious about these inhabitants and made friends among them, but he was not the only one—a tide of people and speculators penetrating the indigenous country came behind him, and it would not be too long before conflicts exploded.

# Chapter 2 – The Militiaman

At the beginning of the 1810s, the conflict between the Native Americans and the white population reached a boiling point as the Anglo-American settlers began to cross the Mississippi to take lands where several native peoples lived. With the number of white settlers and traveling traders rising, a Shawnee leader called Tecumseh and his brother, Lalawethika, better known as the Prophet, began a movement to repel the settlers in the Northwest Territory (modern-day Ohio, Indiana, Illinois, Michigan, Wisconsin, and the northeastern part of Minnesota). The idea was to establish a large confederation that would unite all the Native Americans.

Tecumseh is an important figure in the history of indigenous resistance in America. The occurrence of a series of devastating earthquakes in the central United States just a month after a disgruntled Tecumseh, in the absence of indigenous unity, said he would return home to "stomp the ground," convinced many that the Great Spirit was with him and that the time had come to push the whites out of their ancestors' lands. "Your blood is white! You do not believe the Great Spirit sent me. You shall believe it. I will leave directly and go straight to Detroit. When I get there, I will stamp my foot on the ground and shake down every house," Tecumseh had said. Between December 1811 and February 1812, four earthquakes of apocalyptic magnitude, the most intense recorded to date in the history of the region, shook the Mississippi Valley, causing devastation and death. They were felt from the Great Lakes to Florida, which was then under Spanish control, an area greater than three million square kilometers (approximately one million square miles). The effects were so awe-inspiring that the Mississippi River ran backward for a few hours.

The Creek War was a consequence of Tecumseh's call, the inexorable expansion of the United States, internal disagreements between the Creeks that led to a civil war between the Creek factions, and the interference of European powers (namely, Spain, France, and Great Britain), which were interested in supporting the Native Americans to stop the advancement of the United States. When a group of Creeks was ambushed by 180 militiamen in the forest while they were having a noonday meal by the river in July of 1813, the Creeks' radical wing considered it to be a declaration of war. Although they won that first battle, they sought further revenge when they attacked Fort Mims a few weeks later, located in modern Alabama, and massacred 250 defenders and other Native American allies, including civilians, women, and children. The massacre was so abhorrent—the accounts talk of unspeakable cruelty and sadism—that upon hearing the news, the white population became greatly incensed. An American fighter who arrived at the fort after the massacre described the horrific scene he stumbled upon: "Indians, negroes, white men, women and children lay in one promiscuous ruin. All were scalped, and the females of every age were butchered in a manner which neither decency nor language will permit me to describe. The main building was burned to ashes, which were filled with bones. The plains and woods were covered with dead bodies."

Davy heard about the carnage and felt compelled to go. "When I heard of the mischief which was done at the fort, I instantly felt like going, and I had none of the dread of dying that I expected to feel." But Polly was not so convinced. The Crocketts were living in a region where they had no friends or family, and to Polly, the prospect of becoming a widow with three children seemed terrifying. Even so, Davy gathered volunteers and announced that he would go to defend his land and their families. Polly cried a little and then went back to work. "I took a parting farewell of my wife and my little boys, mounted on my horse and set sail to join my company." At the forefront of Tennessee's 5,000 troops was General Andrew Jackson, with whom Davy would cross paths for the first time and whom in a few years would become the seventh president of the United States.

Several days into their journey into the Mississippi Territory, Davy had his first participation in the war. Two men were required to go into the Creek territory on a scouting mission. Since Davy was one of the best shooters, he was chosen to go, and he brought a small band with him. The team crossed the Tennessee River into a hostile region. They advanced thirty miles and found several houses and farms of frightened settlers. The inhabitants knew that if they were seen with the scouts, the Creeks would kill them all. When Davy and his group received reliable reports that the Creeks were marching toward their camp, they made the dangerous journey back under cover of darkness. As they passed through the region, they noticed that everyone had fled and abandoned their homes. When they arrived at the camp, an uninterested colonel dismissed David without uttering a word. Crockett was furious. After all the risks he had taken, to be simply pushed aside like this! When another man in the military, Major John H. Gibson, returned and reported the same thing, the colonel went on alert and mobilized the troops. This, wrote David, "convinced me, clearly, of one of the hateful ways of the world. When I made my report, it wasn't believed, because I was no officer; I was no great man, but just a poor soldier. But when the same thing was reported by Major Gibson why, then, it was all as true as preaching."

Although David spent most of the campaign as a scout and hunter, getting fresh meat for his companions when winter interrupted the supply line, he was involved in some incidents that, despite his belief in the need for war, left a deep mark on his heart. During the attack on the village of Tallushatchee, he wrote:

> We shot them like dogs; and then set the house on fire, and burned it up with the forty-six warriors in it. I recollect seeing a boy who was shot down near the house. His arm and thigh were broken, and he was so near the burning house that the grease was stewing out of him. In this situation he was still trying to crawl along; but not a murmur escaped him, though he was only about twelve years old. So sullen is the Indian, when his dander is up, that he had sooner die than make a noise, or ask for quarters.

Davy returned home in time for Christmas to see Polly, his two boys, and a newborn baby girl, but he left them again in January. In the Creek War, future President Andrew Jackson nearly died at the hands of a Native American warrior who had him under his ax when he was saved at the last minute by a Cherokee Indian and ally named Gulkalaski, later renamed Tsunu'lahun'ski. Later, Gulkalaski would regret saving Jackson's life. The Battle of Horseshoe Bend was a devastating defeat for the Native Americans, and with that defeat, the war came to an end, resulting in the loss of 23 million acres of Creek territory, which became the property of the United States as spoils of war. This brought not only the Creek nation to an end but also many other peoples, and the dream of a great Native American federation west of the Mississippi was lost. Crockett returned home to Polly, but if he had hoped to rebuild his family and enjoy the bliss of domestic life, a bitter surprise awaited him.

In 1815, Polly fell seriously ill, and after a few miserable days for the family, she expired in her bed. Crockett was left a widower with three children, one of them a girl who was just a few months old. Feeling like the most miserable man in the world and unsure of what to do with three children, Davy asked his brother and sister-in-law to live with him to lend a hand. However, the presence of these relatives was not the same as genuine maternal care, and David soon realized that he needed to build a new family. That same year, he met Elizabeth Patton, a neighbor who was a war widow and who had been left alone with a daughter and a son. Davy reflected, "I began to think that, as we were both in the same situation, it might be that we could do something for each other." He married Elizabeth soon after.

Historian Michael Wallis recounts a strange occurrence in the ceremony that shows that even in the most solemn of occasions, David´s life was never lacking in adventure and color. When the bride was walking toward the altar, a pig busted through the chapel door, provoking much excitement, laughter, and probably some faintings among the women. The groom kicked the pig out of the chapel, shouting, "Old hook, from now on, I'll do the grunting around here." Crockett perhaps never killed a bear with a single blow of his knife, but he sure could kick a pig out of a church.

# Chapter 3 – The Congressman

"Two years ago the inhabitants of this district of which Memphis is the capital sent to the House of Representatives in Congress an individual named David Crockett, who had received no education, could read only with difficulty, had no property, no fixed dwelling, but spent his time hunting, selling his game for a living, and spending his whole life in the woods. "

—Alexis de Tocqueville

"I would sooner be honestly and politically damned, than hypocritically immortalized."

—Davy Crockett

Davy Crockett's political career began in 1821 when he was elected to occupy a seat in the Tennessee General Assembly, his first major public assignment. It was there that he began to demonstrate his skills as a speaker. Six years later, he successfully ran for a seat in the US House of Representatives, where he showed his independent spirit and generosity. At least for the time being, his life as an adventurer and hunter in the woods gave way to another, more civic activity.

After successfully campaigning for a place in the House of Representatives, Crockett sat down to have several portraits of him made, the only images we have of the man since photography did not exist yet. A recently discovered charcoal portrait shows him as a respectable white man in his late twenties or early thirties, with a dark frock coat and a high collar, long sideburns, prominent nose, thin eyebrows, and a plump face. His expression is that of curiosity. However, Crockett's iconography (seven portraits were made in his life) does not fully capture the personality of the hunter, explorer, politician, and hero of Texas of the stories and anecdotes passed down throughout the years. In the paintings, even those made in his lifetime, Crockett looks serious and solemn. His biographers and the contemporary accounts that have survived give a different idea. Crockett was apparently a kind and good-natured person, a wisecracker, and a likable character with a great sense of humor. He always had a fun anecdote ready for any occasion. Generous and simple, even in his days as a congressman, Crockett was always ready to offer what little he had, as he had no attachment to comforts and privileges. He could make a crowd laugh, and his remarks were so ingenious that many people went to the deliberations of Congress to see Davy in action. "It mattered not that Crockett was ignorant of the important questions discussed, and that it was beyond his power to comprehend many of the important measures likely to come before Congress," wrote Edward S. Ellis in a biography he wrote a few years after Davy´s death. "The people felt he was one of them. They took personal pride in his skill with the rifle, and his inimitable powers as a humorist and funny storyteller."

Crockett first served as a representative between 1827 and 1829. In the last year, his old acquaintance Andrew Jackson became president of the United States. During his three terms in Washington, Davy lived in a boarding house in the city and became a recognizable and even an off-the-wall figure in the nation's capital.

Despite his innate generosity, Crockett was not wasteful with public resources. On the contrary, from the little that we know about his interventions, Crockett showed a tendency to limit the power of the government, was against putting more resources in its hands, and refused to use federal money for "charitable works." In a famous incident, Congress proposed to give a pension to the widow of a veteran of the War of 1812. But the man had not died in battle; instead, he had lived many years after the end of the war. Crockett was against that endowment. He asked his fellow congressmen to read the constitution and see how it did not say that Congress could give taxpayer money for charity. "We have the right, as individuals, to give away as much of our own money as we please in charity; but as members of Congress we have no right so to appropriate a dollar of the public money." He added that there were thousands of widows in the country about whom nothing was known. However, this does not mean that David had a cold heart. Immediately afterward, he offered to pay a week of his own salary to the widow, despite the fact that he was "the poorest man on this floor," and he invited all the other congressmen to do the same. In the end, a higher amount than the one originally proposed was collected for the widow.

The frontiersman-become-congressman knew firsthand about the hardships of the common people, those who didn't have the luxuries of Washington, DC. On one occasion, he observed, "I am, sir, but a farmer, destitute of those advantages of education which others possess. I thank heaven I know their worth from having experienced the want of them. The rich require but little legislation. We should at least occasionally legislate for the poor!"

Davy demonstrated that he had an independent spirit and that his commitment to what was right was above his loyalty to President Jackson. "During my two first sessions in Congress, Mr. Adams was president, and I worked along with what was called the Jackson party pretty well," he explained. "I was re-elected to Congress in 1829, by an overwhelming majority; and soon after the commencement of this second term, I saw, or thought I did, that it was expected of me that I would bow to the name of Andrew Jackson, and follow him in all his motions, and windings, and turnings, even at the expense of my conscience and judgment. Such a thing was new to me, and a total stranger to my principles."

His final break with the president was on the occasion of the infamous Indian Removal Act, where Davy gambled his political future. The whole affair possibly contributed to his fatigue with politics.

### The Trail of Tears

In his second annual presidential message to Congress in 1830, Andrew Jackson said with satisfaction, "It gives me pleasure to announce to Congress that the benevolent policy of the Government, steadily pursued for nearly thirty years, in relation to the removal of the Indians beyond the white settlements is approaching to a happy consummation." Seven months earlier, Congress had passed, with just three votes of difference, the Indian Removal Act, whereby the Native American tribes still living east of the Mississippi were to renounce all their lands and be relocated to another territory. The law assigned funds and powers to the United States government for the forced removal of the Cherokee and other Native American groups if they objected. The law had been hotly debated during the months of April and May in the Senate and later in the House of Representatives. Davy Crockett opposed it with all of his might.

Although the exodus of tribes to the west of the Mississippi, an operation as aggressive and destructive as those applied to the vanquished in the ancient wars of extermination, is today remembered as one of the darkest incidents of the young American nation, various justifications were offered at the time, mainly the development of agriculture caused an urgent need to incorporate more land. President Jackson also foresaw the need to separate the Native Americans from the white population because he knew that there would be infinite conflicts, and finally, there was the question of interference from other countries. At a time when the final borders of the United States had not yet been defined (the entire west belonged to Mexico), Spain and France made secret alliances with the tribes to make war on the US. All of these justifications, in one way or another, were a part of Manifest Destiny, the philosophy that saw westward expansion as a divine mandate for moral progress and the expansion of Christianity and civilization at the hands of God's people: the United States.

In a letter sent to the official US interpreter at the Choctaw Agency, John Pitchlynn, in 1830, the president, who had referred to the tribes as barbarians with "savage habits," asked him to communicate to the Native Americans:

> Their happiness, peace & prosperity depends upon their removal beyond the jurisdiction of the laws of the State of Mississippi. These things have been [often times] explained to them fully and I forbear to repeat them; but request that you make known to them that Congress to enable them to remove & comfortably to arrange themselves at their new homes has made liberal appropriations. It was a measure I had much at heart & sought to effect because I was satisfied that the Indians could not possibly live under the laws of the States. If now they shall refuse to accept the liberal terms offered, they only must be liable for whatever evils & difficulties may arise. I feel conscious of having done my duty to my red children and if any failure of my good intention arises, it will be attributable to their want of duty to themselves, not to me.

But in the end, it was just Jackson's nonsensical way to dress up what they were doing. The reality was simple and crude: the tribes did not want to give up their lands, and the act was a humiliating dispossession, no matter how much the president tried to embellish it with good intentions.

Many congressmen strongly opposed the law. Crockett had experienced firsthand the rigors of warring against the Indians, as he had participated in the attack on Tallushatchee, but he understood that beneath all that talk was a strong nation acting unkindly against weaker ones. He understood that if it was carried out, the Indian Removal Act would be remembered as one of the most shameful events in the history of the nation. Congressman Crockett was one of the few whites who dared to openly oppose the presidential initiative, and he was the only one from Tennessee to do so. According to the Congressional Register of Debates, Crockett said that he knew many of the Chickasaw tribe because they lived near his district and that he would not consent to move them against their will to an unknown land where the United States had no property. He also said that he knew that the Cherokees would rather die than leave their home, and he repeated their words: "No, we will take death here at our homes. Let them come and tomahawk us here at home: we are willing to die."

In doing so, Crockett became not only Jackson's enemy but also one to the Tennessee voters, who craved more Native American territory to turn into farmland. Crockett preferred to follow the dictates of his conscience. "I opposed it from the purest motives in the world," he wrote in his autobiography. "Several of my colleagues told me how I was ruining myself. They said this was a favourite measure of the president, and I ought to go for it. I told them I believed it was a wicked, unjust measure, and that I should go against it, let the cost to myself be what it might; that I was willing to go with General Jackson in every thing that I believed was honest and right. I voted against this Indian bill, and my conscience yet tells me that I gave a good honest vote, and one that I believe will not make me ashamed in the day of judgment."

The strongly enforced Indian Removal Act is one of the most controversial acts not only in Andrew Jackson´s presidency but in the history of the United States, to the degree that some commentators have called it genocide. It set a sad precedent for what would be the rest of the expansion toward the Pacific, marked by the idea that the Americans were the chosen people who were called to possess all of North America. When the Indian Removal Act was carried out, the tribes were, for the most part, brought against their will into the current state of Oklahoma.

The exodus that took place at the point of bayonets is known as the Trail of Tears. The Native Americans suffered unspeakable hardships and left many dead on the journey. Hundreds died from starvation and from exposure to the elements. "My heart bleeds when I reflect on his cruelty to the poor Indians. I never expected it of him [Jackson]," lamented Crockett. Tsunu'lahun'ski, the Cherokee veteran of the Creek War who had saved Jackson's life, said, "If I had known that Jackson would drive us from our homes, I would have killed him at Horseshoe." To date, many Native Americans refuse to touch twenty-dollar bills, as it has the portrait of Andrew Jackson on it.

Crockett's brave stance earned him the recognition of the Native American nations. Cherokee Chief John Ross wrote him a letter in which he said that Davy´s vote in Congress had "and will produce for you among the friends of humanity & justice a just respect and admiration." In turn, Crockett was always proud to say that he did not obey any master or political party. "Look at my neck, and you will not find there a necklace with the engraving: [this is] MY DOG - ANDREW JACKSON," he wrote shortly after winning his first reelection as a congressman.

Still, that was perhaps the beginning of the end of his political career. Opposing Jackson, who was just beginning his eight-year stay in office, was not a clever move, much less in Tennessee. "Jackson was ill-tempered, a fierce hater, unbending, dictatorial and vindictive," writes Mel Ayton, an author of American history and true crime books. His opponents placed many traps for Crockett, like scheduling a tour of Tennessee for him, where he would have to explain to many angry voters why he had sided with the Cherokee. The press also destroyed him, accusing him of being a player, a charlatan, a trickster, and a drunk. Another newspaper made fun of the stories told about him regarding his adventures in the woods. For his part, Jackson commented on Davy Crockett's reelection campaign, saying, "I trust, for the honor of the state, your Congressional District will not disgrace themselves longer by sending that profligate man Crockett back to Congress."

Frustrated by the multitude of attacks, especially the lies of his adversary in the congressional reelection campaign, a 34-year-old lawyer named William Fitzgerald, Crockett publicly threatened to beat him up if he insulted him again. When the two men met at a public event in Tennessee, Fitzgerald took the stand and placed an object on the table covered with a cloth. When Fitzgerald began slandering Crockett as he stared at him, Davy got up and ran to his opponent, ready to pulverize him. It was a naive act and his biggest political mistake. Fast as lightning, Fitzgerald pulled out a pistol that was hidden under the cloth and aimed it at Crockett's chest, warning him that if he took another step, it would be his end. Confounded by the unexpected action, David froze and returned to his seat, stunned.

Crockett said goodbye to politics as only he could. "You may all go to hell; I will go to Texas," he told his constituents at the end of his last term in 1835, for he had decided that exploring and crossing new borders was more fun than living in a boarding house near the Capitol. And he was only on his way to becoming a legend.

# Chapter 4 – The Celebrity

"Him an' his jokes travelled all through the land
  an' his speeches made him friends to beat the band,
  his politickin' was their favorite brand
  an' everyone wanted to shake his hand."
—*The Ballad of Davy Crockett,* 1955

It is a characteristic of free-spirited people, like Davy Crockett, to have a rebellious and indomitable side that is not always well regarded by society. After passing through Congress, Crockett sold his property and rented a piece of forest, where he set out to build a cabin, sow the land, and plant fruit trees. But Elizabeth, his second wife, could not cope anymore with the "bad" behavior of her husband, which the newspapers called vices. So, they may not have been all an invention of the press. The famous hunter and frontiersman constantly abandoned his family to go on expeditions, and he had a problem with drinking—something that was common in this period in America. His wife left him, and suddenly, David found himself without a political career or a marriage. Throughout the year of 1832, he lived alone in his cabin and passed the days hunting bears, while the exaggerated tales of his exploits continued to grow. The newspapers, aware that their readers wanted more frontier adventures, did not shy away from delivering and even inventing more wild tales.

In 1831, a play by James Kirke Paulding, called *The Lion of the West*, featured a man named Colonel Nimrod Wildfire, who was a caricature of Crockett. Although the play did not bear his name, people recognized that it was a tribute to the hunter. An assistant recalled how, when the play was about to begin, Crockett appeared at the entrance and was escorted by the manager to the first row, where they had a seat reserved for him. The audience erupted in applause. When the curtain was lifted, and the actor appeared with his raccoon cap, impersonating the royal frontiersman in the front row, David rose again from his seat and bowed toward the audience.

The play's character imitated Davy's colorful way of speaking. It is difficult to know whether Crockett actually said many of the things that are attributed to him or if they were taken from plays, fake news, and almanacs. But one of Crockett's most esteemed phrases is undeniably authentic: "Be always sure you are right, then go ahead." However, the context in which this maxim first appears is not romantic or heroic by today's standards: the frontiersman scribbled it on a contract for the sale of a black slave named Adaline, for the sum of $300, whom he was forced to sell to pay his eternal debt. It is worth mentioning that Crockett, like many other families of Tennessee, didn't own many slaves, and there was even an anti-slavery sentiment in the region. According to the 1820 census, there was only one slave in the Crockett household.

At a popular level, however, the common people made Crockett's alleged exploits reach mythical proportions. It was said that he was going to jump and ride the tail of Halley's Comet, which appeared on the horizon in 1835. Davy himself, with his strong personality, his exploits, and autobiographical books, the first of which was published in 1834, fueled Crockett-mania.

A note in Boston's *Daily Evening Transcript*, after Crockett's visit to Washington, reported a fantastic incident, which serves as proof that the newspapers of the time not only indulged in many poetic licenses but also of the mythical character of Crockett, who was a kind of prototype of America's superhero. The *Daily*

*Evening Transcript* says that during Crockett's first visit to the country's capital in 1828, a caravan of wild animals was in an exhibition in the city. Large crowds were gaping before the beasts, and the famous frontiersman was there too. "The house was very much crowded," Crockett says in this highly fictionalized account.

> The first thing I noticed was two wildcats in a cage. Some acquaintances asked me if they were like the wildcats in the backwoods, and as I was looking at them, one turned over and died. The keeper ran up and threw some water on it. Said hi, stranger you are wasting time. My looks kill them things, and you had better hire me to go out there or I will kill every varmint you've got.

In addition to his very real adventures in the woods, Davy allowed and exploited these fairy tales and the tendency of the people to mythologize him, a trend that continued after his death until he became a kind of demi-god, a cycle that is studied today by anthropologists interested in myth formation in North America. Davy Crockett's real and fictional feats were exploited by the Whig Party, one of the two great political parties in the first half of the 19th century in the United States. His extraordinary tales deal with the themes of the self-made American man and the myth of the almost supernatural but still mortal hero, who finds his death through a treacherous act or is unnaturally slain.

Not that Crockett was alien to adventures or heroic deeds, even before his participation in the Battle of the Alamo. In 1835, when President Jackson was leaving a funeral in the Capitol building, an unemployed painter approached him and said, "I'll be damned if I don't do it," drew his gun, and shot the president. The man had a terrible aim. Jackson, an old soldier, tried to defend himself with his stick. The unemployed painter pulled a second pistol from his clothes and shot the 67-year-old president again, only to fail a second time. "I know where this came from," shouted Jackson, thinking that the Whigs had sent the madman to kill him. Davy was close to Jackson and ran, along with Navy Lieutenant Thomas Gedney, to seize the would-be assassin and then rushed the president to a carriage. The unemployed painter spent the rest of his life in a mental asylum.

When Crockett had enough of this mythification, he decided to disappear and escape from hell, like Orpheus, although it was not the real underworld that Crockett escaped from but rather Washington politics and the Mississippi Valley. In search of new frontiers, Crockett said goodbye to his constituents in his inimitable style. "Since you have chosen to elect a man with a timber toe to succeed me, you may all go to hell and I will go to Texas." In this way, the legendary frontiersman prepared to cross a new border, this time that of his own country.

# Chapter 5 – Gone to Texas: The Freedom Fighter

"Do not be uneasy about me, I am with my friends."

—Davy Crockett's last known letter, January 1836

For a time, it was common to see these three letters roughly drawn with a knife on the doors of Tennessee houses: GTT. The initials meant that the aforementioned had taken his few belongings and left for Texas in search of a new beginning. Like many other people who had lost everything or were fleeing the law, Davy Crockett, with a finished political career, a broken family, an absent wife, and with no place to call home, fulfilled his promise of going to Texas and Mexico instead of staying in a country where his adversaries made everything increasingly difficult. Texas was offering more than 4,000 acres to each person who came to colonize it. Davy's intention was to explore that piece of northern Mexico and try to make "a fortune" for his family. Along with a small group of people, including his nephew, his brother-in-law, and a neighbor, he made the long trip from Tennessee to Texas under the ghostly light of Halley's Comet, which, in those months, was visible at night. When he crossed the Red River, he was effectively saying goodbye to the United States and entering another country. "I do believe Santa Anna's kingdom [Mexico] will be a paradise compared with this [the United States under Jackson]."

In January 1836, he wrote to his daughter, saying, "I must say as to what I have seen of Texas it is the garden spot of the world the best land and best prospect for health I ever saw is here and I do believe it is a fortune to any man to come here." Crockett was enthusiastic, and according to the people who saw him, he was almost euphoric with the new life that awaited him since he was certain that he would finally get some good land. "I have no doubt that it is the richest country in the world," he wrote in a letter, without using commas or other punctuation marks. "Good land and plenty of timber and the best springs and good millstreams good range clear water it is in the pass where the buffalo passes from north to south twice a year and bees and honey plenty."

Davy was about to turn fifty. Although in our day, fifty is considered to be relatively young, in the early 19$^{th}$ century, a man of that age was already in his golden years. So, when Davy Crockett participated in the Battle of the Alamo, he was officially an elderly person, far from the images that are known of him as a young man in his twenties, full of vitality, with a raccoon cap on his head, knocking down ten Mexican soldiers with a single blow. All in all, despite being in his sixth decade of life, Davy remained in very good shape thanks to the active life he had led. Wars, hunting, and scouting had hardened him. Politics was apparently the only thing that had left him exhausted.

### Mexican *Tejas*

The Americans called it Texas, but its official name was the "New Kingdom of Philippines, Province of Tejas." It was a part of Mexico, although the name "New Kingdom of Philippines" was already in disuse, and the Mexican government simply called it *Tejas*. For centuries, the territory had been largely uninhabited by Europeans. At the beginning of the 19$^{th}$ century, the total population did not exceed 3,500 Mexicans, who lived in the towns of San Antonio de Béxar (modern San Antonio) and Bahía del Espíritu Santo (modern Goliad). Since Mexico's independence in

1810, the government had been concerned with this unoccupied and yet so promising part of the country.

In 1820, the Mexican government had begun an active colonization policy for Texas to check the Apache incursions. The government gave away the land and granted tax exemptions and the free import of necessary items for the new colony. They were such exceptional conditions that US Secretary of State Henry Clay could not help but exclaim, "Mexicans must have little interest in keeping Texas, since they are giving it away!" However, hardly anyone in Mexico wanted to move north because Texas was the region of the Apache, the Comanche, Cherokee, and other relentless warrior tribes.

One of the persons who took the offer was an American named Moses Austin, who began to organize the transfer of 300 families to the region. Old Austin died before taking the road, and it fell upon his son, Stephen Austin, to take the Old Three Hundred on that journey. Stephen appeared in the city of San Antonio in August 1821 before the governor of Texas, Antonio Martínez, who gave him permission to explore the land and find a suitable place to establish a colony. Accompanied by some Native American friends and guides, Austin made his way to the Gulf Coast and built a settlement. In 1826, he presided over 1,800 people, of whom about a quarter were black slaves.

The newcomers had a clear sense of identity. Compared to the Mexicans who lived in Texas, the Anglos were more educated, they were better off economically, and they were Protestants with a capitalistic spirit and highly driven by their personal freedoms. This was of paramount importance to unite them around a common cause. In 1830, the so-called *Texians*, the Anglo settlers, tripled the Mexican *Tejanos*. Many Americans from the Mississippi area, who were affected by the agricultural crisis and fleeing from debtors, began arriving en masse with their slaves. The problem was that Mexico had abolished slavery in 1830 by order of the first president of African ancestry in the Americas, Vicente Guerrero. Although President Guerrero temporarily exempted Texas from the law, the news shook the settlers since almost all of them had slaves. Andrew Jackson offered Mexico five million dollars in exchange for Texas. The proposal could not have come at a worse time for the alarmed Mexican authorities, though, as they were watching the territory slip from their hands. Many lands north of the Nueces River were sold to speculators in New York, although they were occupied by Mexicans and Native Americans.

In 1835, a major change occurred in Mexico that fueled the cause of independence in Texas. In that year, a new constitution put an end to federalism and inaugurated a centralist system, under which states lost their power, thus creating what is known to historians as the Central Republic of Mexico. Under the new regime, the authority resided in the country's capital, limits were placed on who could vote, and sovereign states were abrogated and replaced with departments. Meanwhile, *Tejas* had become Texas—the Anglo population had grown to 35,000 people. Most of them had entered illegally, but there was no denying the fact that the de facto language in the province was English and that the Hispanic population was being expelled across the Nueces River.

In September 1835, when the new Central Republic came into effect, the Texas settlers disavowed the Mexican government. Up to this point, their intention was apparently to rebel against the centralist regime and return to the Mexican Republic once federalism was restored. Austin was officially in command of the movement, but he had no military experience. Within weeks, most of his men deserted and returned to their fields. A personal friend of President Jackson, Sam Houston, arrived in Texas and took the command from Austin, leading 300 men from New Orleans and Mississippi. Throughout the United States, Houston presented Texas as the promised land where everyone could get rich as long as they brought a rifle to help. In December, the pro-independence rebels seized the Alamo fort—an old Franciscan mission built by the Spanish—which was guarded by a party of malnourished Mexican guards, who had arrived in San Antonio tied by their necks in order to prevent them from fleeing. By March 1836, there was not a single Mexican soldier left in Texas.

The President of Mexico, Antonio López de Santa Anna, went berserk when he heard the news. In February 1836, he marched north with 6,000 men to subdue the Texas rebels. On February 23$^{rd}$, the Mexican troops arrived at the Alamo. Davy Crockett was inside.

### How Did Crockett Arrive at the Alamo?

How in the world did Davy Crockett end up inside a fort surrounded by Santa Anna's army? For this, we have to go back a few months, when he crossed the Red River into the Mexican province of Texas, where tensions with the federal government of Mexico were about to erupt. David spent his first days making stops at different farms, where people lodged him. He hunted and explored, looking for a place to settle. He spent the winter looking for buffalo and other game. On one occasion, when he did not return in time to celebrate Christmas with his guests, the family feared the worst, and word spread that Davy Crockett had died at the hands of the Native Americans. Several newspapers reported his passing, but as always, the mythical man defeated death and reappeared with the best of spirits to move on. As he made his way south, word spread that the famous frontiersman, the one who could shoot the moon and kill a bear with a single stab, was entering Austin´s land. Crockett's fame as an adventurer and uncanny explorer was greater than as a politician. Rumors that he was going to join the cause of Texas independence were received by the colonists as if Achilles *redivivus* had come to fight Santa Anna.

Crockett arrived in excellent spirits at Nacogdoches in January 1836 with other men who had joined his caravan, attracted by the promise of cheap lands and the opportunity to make a fortune. Crockett was welcomed with enthusiasm, and they offered him a banquet. He received adoration from the people when he uttered his famous phrase where he said that he had left hell to go to what must logically be the kingdom of heaven: "I was, for some years, a member of Congress. In my last canvass, I told the people of my district that if they saw fit to reelect me, I would serve them as faithfully as I had done before. But, if not, they might go to hell and I would go to Texas. I was beaten, gentlemen, and here I am."

Several revolutionaries were concentrated in Nacogdoches, the oldest town in Texas, where the Spaniards had built a mission in 1716. In this town, Crockett understood that if he aspired to receive land and to have a position in the government of the new republic, he would have to sign an oath of allegiance to the government of the, until then hypothetical, Republic of Texas, and more importantly, he would have to take the offer to serve as a mercenary for the rebels. From Nacogdoches, he went to the town of San Augustine, where he wrote his famous last letter to his daughter.

> I have taken the oath of the Government and have enrolled my name as a volunteer for six months and will set out for the Rio Grand in a few days with the volunteers from the United States...all volunteers is entitled to a vote for a member of the convention or to be voted for and I have but little doubt of being elected a member to form a constitution for this province.

On January 16th, 1836, Crockett joined a band of armed men led by a certain Captain William Harrison. Although Davy was a common foot soldier, he was the center of attention. The mythical Davy Crockett was walking among them! On his way south, he took the opportunity to demonstrate his hunting skills to get food for the soldiers, as he had done in his youth during the Creek War, until they arrived at Sam Houston's headquarters in Washington-on-the-Brazos. From there, Davy left for San Antonio. Along the way, he stopped at John Swisher's farm, who left an invaluable description of Crockett's physical appearance: "I judged him to be about forty years old. He was stout and muscular, about six feet in height, and weighing 180 to 200 pounds. He was of a florid complexion, with intelligent gray eyes. He had small side whiskers, inclining to sandy. He was fond of talking and had an ease and grace about him."

In February, after several days of enjoying the hospitality of the Swisher family, Crockett headed to San Antonio de Béxar. There, he appeared in the plaza and spoke in what already seemed to be a full-fledged political campaign: "Fellow citizens, I am among you. I have come to your country, though not I hope, through any selfish motive whatever. I have come to aid you all that I can in your noble cause." From there, he marched to the Alamo with a dozen men. The men at the Alamo, who were ecstatic at seeing Crockett, demanded a speech from the legendary man. His presence was felt as if the savior himself had descended from the clouds, especially at the news that Santa Anna was approaching the fort with his dragoons, as everyone was now expecting a merciless fight. But Crockett was the man who could shoot and hit the moon—the Alamo was in good hands.

### The Battle of the Alamo

When Santa Anna's army arrived in the vicinity of San Antonio, there were between 180 and 250 fighters and several frightened citizens inside the Alamo. Santa Anna first sent a white-flagged messenger to offer the defenders a chance to surrender, but before he arrived, William Travis, who was in charge of the fort, shot him. This act angered the Mexicans, who then planted a red flag, meaning they would take no prisoners. Santa Anna subjected the fort to an incessant rain of cannon fire and artillery, gaining ground every day. However, according to some eyewitnesses from San Antonio, "Santa Anna left the East side of the Alamo unprotected, waiting for the *Texians* to leave in peace and save the Mexican army from a costly victory." According to other testimonies, Crockett and his men fought under the flag of Mexico, with the date "1824" stamped on it, which is the year of the signing of the Mexican Constitution. The image of a homogeneous group of Anglo defenders fighting against Mexicans is also fiction, as evidenced by numerous testimonies compiled by historian Timothy Matovina, the director of the Institute for Latino Studies at the University of Notre Dame, Indiana. Both inside and outside the Alamo, many Hispanics fought alongside the Anglo defenders.

On March 5th, the Mexican Army paused the attack, possibly as a psychological tactic, as the defenders of the fort were caught asleep in the early hours of the 6th. After a fierce battle, lasting an hour and a half, the clash ended in furious hand-to-hand combat, a moment that has passed into the history of Texas as one of its most heroic episodes. For many years, it was believed that Crockett and his men from Tennessee died defending one of the fortress walls until the end. "Here, am I, Colonel, assign us to some place, and I and my Tennessee boys will defend it all right," Crockett allegedly said, according to a version of the conflict published in 1911. Travis assigned him and his band the duty of protecting the low wall and stockade on the south side of the fort, where they died in a desperate fight. The embellished stories that followed Davy like a shadow reported that dozens of dead Mexican soldiers were found around his pierced body. However, no one ever recovered Crockett's body.

The appearance in the mid-20th century of a lost diary by a Mexican captain named José Enrique de la Peña, who fought at the Alamo with Santa Anna, put to rest all the glorious descriptions of Davy Crockett´s last moments. According to de la Peña's testimony, Crockett did not die inside the Alamo. He and a small group fought to the end until they were captured and brought alive to Santa Anna. The diary's discovery produced a wave of outrage and skepticism, with allegations that the document was a forgery. But José de la Peña left not only a description of Crockett's ultimate fate that other sources have since confirmed but also a beautiful portrait of the man in his last moments.

> Some seven men had survived the general carnage and, under the protection of general Castrillón, they were brought before Santa Anna. Among them was one of great stature well proportioned with regular features, in whose face there was the imprint of adversity but in whom one also noticed a degree of resignation and nobility that did

him honor. He was the naturalist David Crockett, well known in North America for his unusual adventures, who had undertaken to explore the country and who, finding himself in Béjar [San Antonio] at the very moment of surprise, had taken refuge in the Alamo fearing that his status as a foreigner might not be respected. Santa Anna answered Castrillón's intervention in Crockett´s behalf with a gesture of indignation and, addressing himself to...the troops closest to him, ordered his execution.

De la Peña expresses horror and shame at what happened next. According to his testimony, the commanders were outraged at this order and did not support it, hoping that Santa Anna would cool down once the fury of the moment had passed. But the president's personal guard, wanting to win his favor, slaughtered the prisoners with their swords right on the spot. Davy thus crossed a final and definitive frontier, one from which there would be no return. "I turned away horrified in order not to witness such a barbarous scene," wrote de la Peña. He notes one last act of Crockett´s nobility, saying, "Though tortured before they were killed, these unfortunates died without complaining and without humiliating themselves before their torturers."

The revelation that Davy did not die at the Alamo should not have come as a surprise. The scene matches Edward Ellis's description in his biography published in 1884, though Ellis adds that Crockett resisted.

> At last only six of the garrison were left alive. They were surrounded by General Castrillon and his soldiers. The officer shouted to them to surrender, promising that their lives should be spared. In the little group of Spartans were Davy Crockett and Travis, so exhausted they were scarcely able to stand. Crockett stood in an angle of the fort, the barrel of his shattered rifle in his right hand, while the massive Bowie in his left was dripping with blood. His face was crimson from a gash in his forehead, and nearly a score of Mexicans were stretched around him, either dead or

dying from his fearful blows. There were a few brave and humane officers, and among them were General Castrillon and Burdillon. They spoke sympathizingly to Crockett and Travis, and with several other officers walked to where the scowling Santa Anna stood and asked that the surrender of the few survivors might be received. The reply was an order that all should be shot. Seeing his treachery, the enraged Crockett roused himself, and swinging his Bowie aloft, made a furious rush for the Mexican Nana Sahib. The intrepid Tennessean was riddled with bullets before he could pass half the intervening distance.

In the end, it doesn't matter if the hero died inside or outside the Alamo, shooting his rifle or with his hands tied, or even how many Mexicans he killed. The fact is that Davy Crockett shared the fate of his companions and that he was ready to give up his life for a cause that he considered to be just. After the unfortunate incident, all of the Alamo's dead were stripped of their clothes, cut to pieces, and piled on top of each other. Then they were incinerated, a particularly humiliating fate for the deceased at the time. The ashes of the defenders remained there for more than a year until a party arrived to put them inside a chest in March 1837, after which they buried them in a nearby site, which has not been found to this day.

# Chapter 6 – The Myth

"Davy Crockett could run faster than any man in Tennessee. He could stare down a streak of lightning without blinking. He could pull a rainbow out of the sky. He had the surest rifle and the ugliest dog anywhere."

—20th-century popular book about Davy Crockett

When he was alive, fame embraced Davy Crockett. After his death, it grew to unsuspected heights. Davy Crockett's first almanacs—a type of yearbook that was very popular until the mid-20th century that was directed primarily at peasants with information on harvests, the phases of the moon, and other meteorological phenomena—appeared in Nashville in 1835 and 1836, which was during Crockett's lifetime. They continued to appear for years afterward. In addition to the usual information, Davy Crockett´s almanacs told anecdotes of his life, to which the American public had become addicted. Almost all of them bordered on exaggerations and myths. Some of them may have been reworkings of stories that the frontiersman himself told his friends. He allegedly fought a cougar and won. Another story said that, on one occasion, he sighted a wild stallion on the prairie. When he was within a few steps of the horse, it came snorting at him, but Crockett jumped and mounted it. The horse started to run like lightning and ran for three days, with its rider holding its mane, until they came to a "Mad River." There, the horse ran under a tree, trying to brush Crockett off its back, but the brave man leaped over the tree, and the horse finally stopped, allowing Crockett to get off.

In other tales, Davy is like a character of ancient myths, making huge leaps that transported him over long distances and even among the planets. His popularity was revived in the 1950s with a Disney movie that introduced an almost forgotten Crockett to a generation that had never heard of him, especially children, with a refurbished image, juvenile looks, and his classic raccoon cap. He was the king of the wild frontier, a man who fixed the crack in the Liberty Bell and fixed up the government. Reacting to his incredible surge in popularity, *Harper's Magazine* retorted in a cynical editorial that Crockett was never "a king of anything except maybe the Tennessee Tall Tales and Bourbon Samplers Association."

For Texans, he is an untouchable figure; for baby boomers, a beloved figure of their childhood; for his country, a brave and honest congressman; and for the Native American nations, an honorable enemy and later a compassionate human being. Crockett was, after all, a man who always acted chivalrously, sometimes perhaps a little too idealistic. He was a man with strong convictions that had been ingrained in a life lived on the border, not only a physical border but a social one as well. His temperament made him face adversaries—natural and human— bigger and more powerful than he: the border, wild beasts, the president of the USA, a foreign army. Davy Crockett always took the challenges that were presented to him with a resolution worthy of admiration, with a heart that didn't know hypocrisy.

His death in the Battle of the Alamo got him a ticket to the pantheon of heroes, but Davy would probably be the first one to frown upon that idea. "Most men are remembered as they died, and not as they lived," he wrote in 1834. "We gaze with admiration upon the glories of the setting sun, yet scarcely bestow a passing glance upon its noonday splendor. I know not whether, in the eyes of the world, a brilliant death is not preferred to an obscure life of rectitude." And in the case of Davy Crockett, it will always be his life and the ideals that he defended when he was alive that will grant him a place among the great men of America.

# Part 6: Annie Oakley

*A Captivating Guide to an American Sharpshooter Who Later Became a Wild West Folk Hero*

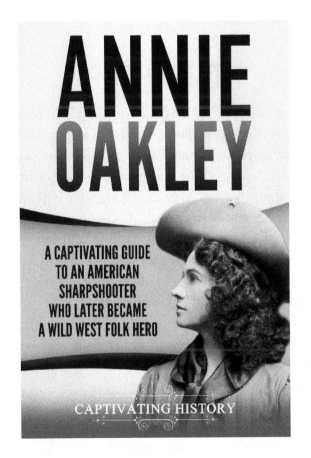

# Introduction

How could Annie Oakley, a woman of barely 110 pounds, beat so many of the greatest sharpshooters with her skill and talent?

The name is probably familiar to most readers, but not many know about her early life or her great love for her husband, who was also a sharpshooter. We are taking you back more than a century to meet one of the greatest American folklore heroines who ever existed. Annie Oakley dazzled and awed millions of people during her career and met some of the most memorable people of her time, including Thomas Edison, Sitting Bull, Prince Edward, and the queen of England herself.

Annie Oakley is just one of the many impressive legends of the Wild West, and her journey took her from the small town of Greenville in Darke County, Ohio, to some of the biggest stages in America and Europe.

Embark on that journey with Annie Oakley, from her humble beginnings to the glory and fame she achieved as one of the greatest sharpshooters of the Wild West, where legends of cowboys and sharpshooters abounded as one of the greatest nations of today was being forged.

# Chapter 1 –Phoebe Ann Moses: Early Life of Miss Sharpshooter

Before Annie Oakley became known as "Little Miss Sure Shot" and one of the greatest Wild West heroes, she was known by her birth name: Phoebe Ann Moses.

Phoebe Ann Moses was born on August 13ᵗʰ, 1860, around two miles northwest of Woodland, now known as the small unincorporated community of Willowdell in Darke County, Ohio. The county got its name after William Darke, who was an officer in the American Revolutionary War. Darke County was peaceful farmland, and it had been mostly inhabited by Native Americans until they lost the Battle of Fallen Timbers to General "Mad" Anthony Wayne in 1794. After the battle, settlers started flocking in. The battle was symbolically named, as the area of Darke County was covered in lush, thick virgin forests that seemed to have no end; at least, that was the case before the battle against the confederation of Native American tribes took place. Once the battle was won, the settlers cleared the forest and started cultivating corn.

Annie's father, Jacob Moses, fought in the War of 1812, which was a conflict between the United States and the United Kingdom, although both sides had assistance, mainly from the Native Americans. The war ended in February 1815 after a peace treaty. A little over thirty years later, in 1848, Annie's parents, Susan Wise and Jacob Moses, would get married. Annie's mother was eighteen, while Jacob was close to turning fifty.

Around 1855, the Moses family decided to take a chance and moved west to Darke County, Ohio, where they rented a farm. At this point, the family consisted of Susan, Jacob, and their five young daughters (Mary Jane, Lydia, Elizabeth, Sarah Ellen, and Catherine). Jacob Moses also brought along his Kentucky rifle, which can only be described as an extension of his own body, as he was rather skillful in hunting and shooting. Jacob Moses, who was an athletic man despite being in his late fifties, was ready for a life of hard work in a new settlement.

When the family first arrived in Darke County, it was rather rural, as it had no railway service or even a general store. The Moses family lived in a cabin along the borders of the state of Indiana, five miles east of North Star. Jacob built the family cabin out of timber, and Annie would be born there only five years later.

Annie was Susan and Jacob's sixth child out of the nine they had together. Besides her five sisters, who were mentioned above, the Moses family would later grow to include John and Hulda. Susan and Jacob had more children, but they did not survive past infancy.

Susan Wise was the one who decided to name her baby Phoebe Ann; however, Phoebe's sisters started calling her Annie, so her given name didn't stick for long. Annie was a small girl with dark hair and bright blue eyes. She was strong for her size and had a direct gaze that caught people's attention.

While Annie had many sisters to play and spend time with, she wasn't that interested in playing with them. Instead of dressing up dolls, Annie enjoyed tagging along with her father, who frequently hunted and set traps in the woods to provide food for his big family. The little curious Annie enjoyed learning more about hunting and trapping from her father, who unknowingly prepared his young daughter to take over his role as the family's caretaker. Annie's only surviving brother was one year younger, which might be why her father decided to teach Annie what he knew about hunting, weapons, and trapping. Still, even though her brother John was a year younger, he also tagged along with his father and sister when their father went hunting, as well as when they worked around the farm. They built fences, butchered cows, collected and cultivated apples, beans, and corn, and gathered berries and nuts from the forest. Even though Annie assisted her father with his work around the farm, she found marksmanship the most interesting of all. Annie was fascinated with guns and hunting from an early age. Her father taught her the ways of the forest surrounding their rough cabin, teaching her how to make traps out of cornstalk and track rabbits, which she would bring home as family dinner. Annie was a true tomboy and a rather vivacious little girl.

When she was only six years old, Annie's father died, and the family faced hard times. Jacob Moses got hypothermia in 1865 during a blizzard, after which he became an invalid, struggling to provide for his family due to his illness. He died from pneumonia in 1866, leaving Susan widowed and alone with their eight children. Annie's life and carefree childhood would change from that point on.

After her father died, Annie couldn't attend school regularly, although she would later go back to school in her later childhood and adulthood. The family was also forced to move to a smaller home in Darke County. However, her interest in guns, hunting, and marksmanship didn't die with her father. Annie became rather skillful at trapping before the age of seven, and she would be the one to bring meat to the table and feed her family.

Annie was only eight years old the first time she tried to shoot a gun, and she didn't just "try"—she excelled. It was her first move toward becoming one of the best shooters the Wild West ever saw.

As she recalled later, she used her father's old muzzle-loading rifle for her first kill shot. Since her father was dead, his Kentucky rifle hung above the fireplace. Annie was not allowed to take the rifle, even though her father had taught her the basics of shooting before his death. Despite the rule imposed by her mother, Annie took the rifle regardless. She managed to shoot a squirrel off the fence of her family's backyard by steadying the gun on the porch rails, and her mother preserved the meat. That was only the beginning of Annie's contribution to her family. Even though Annie used the rifle to help feed her poor family, her mother was utterly upset with seeing one of her youngest children, a girl at that, using a firearm.

One of the historians who wrote about the history of Darke County, Frazer Wilson, claims that Annie's brother was angry that his sister had a chance to shoot a rifle. Wilson writes that her brother John was so agitated that he decided to double the load for his gun. He handed the gun to Annie afterward, believing that the kick would be so strong that it would discourage her from shooting a gun ever again. However, it seems that marksmanship was in Annie's blood. John wanted to use his hat as a target, and he tossed the hat up in the air. According to Frazer Wilson, Annie's shot was so smooth and quick that it promptly made a clean hole in her brother's hat. It was not a common thing for a girl to shoot a gun, and a girl so talented in marksmanship was an even rarer thing to see in that period.

By the age of eight, Annie was hunting and trapping, not only to place food on the family's table but also to sell. She sold the game in Greenville to people such as shopkeepers G. Anthony and Charles Katzenberger. The game she sold would then be resold and shipped to hotels in Cincinnati and other cities. Her mother insisted that Annie go back to school and stop using a rifle, as she was scared of having one of her youngest children, a girl at that, shooting guns with no real supervision. Still, Annie remained a fruitful provider in her family.

In 1867, Annie's sister, Mary Jane, died of tuberculosis, and her widowed mother had to sell their family cow named "Pink" to pay for the medical and funeral bills. Soon afterward, since food was scarce and Susan was only earning $1.25 per week, she gave her youngest daughter, Hulda, to the wealthy Bartholomew family, who watched over Hulda for a short period of time until Susan could get back on her feet.

In 1870, Annie and her sister, Sarah Ellen, were sent to the Darke County Infirmary, as the family was struggling to survive. In the spring of the same year, Annie was sent to a local farmer, where she was supposed to get an education and help with their infant son, for which she was supposed to be compensated 50 cents per week. The payment turned out to be nothing more than a false promise, as the family essentially made Annie a slave. She was expected to do all the hard work around the farm for free, and she did not receive any kind of education. Annie spoke about her experience working on that farm later in life, saying she was "a prisoner" and the family were "wolves." She describes the farmer as a "wolf in sheep's clothing," but she never revealed their true names.

Annie's work on the farm would have been exhausting even if she was a man, as she had to get up before everyone, milk the cows, skim the milk, make breakfast, wash the dishes, work around the garden and farm, feed the farm animals, put the farmer's baby to sleep, pump the water for the cattle, pick wild berries, and make dinner. Annie recalled that her mother sent her letters, telling her to come back home, but they wouldn't let her. They wrote letters back to her mother, saying she was happy and content.

Annie also recalled that she was physically abused, mentioning scars on her back, probably from whippings, although she never revealed the extent to which she was abused during her time on that farm. She did disclose that the farmer's wife threw her out barefoot in the snow after she had accidentally fallen asleep during her work. Annie would have died from cold if the farmer hadn't let her back into the house. In 1872, Annie decided she was done with the "wolves" and ran away.

A kindly man paid her train fare, and she returned to the infirmary and discovered there was a new superintendent in charge, Samuel Crawford Edington, who lived there with his wife Nancy and their children. Unlike the former superintendent, who had sent Annie right into a den of wolves, Edington and his wife made friends with Annie and treated her as their child. Annie later said later that Nancy was a friend of her mother's, which might have been why the Edington family accepted Annie as one of their own.

Annie was invited to live and sleep in the living quarters of the infirmary, and the couple taught her embroidery, sewing, and the art of decorating. They also paid Annie for her efforts, as Annie sewed orphans' uniforms, dresses, and quilts. She even learned how to make lovely cuffs and collars that made the dark uniforms seem brighter. Annie became close to the Edington children, with whom she attended school. The family placed their faith and trust in Annie, and although she was only a young girl, Samuel Edington put her in charge of the infirmary's dairy. The infirmary had twelve cows, and she would milk all of them, then proceed to collect the cream, out of which she made butter. Soon, Annie got a raise and started to save some money.

Annie spent around three years with the Edingtons, and when she was about fifteen years old, she decided to return home to her mother. At the time, her mother had already remarried and was building a house near the crossroads at North Star. On her return, Annie decided to stop by the store that belonged to the Katzenberger brothers, where she used to sell the game she hunted and trapped. She offered to bring game to the Katzenberger brothers, who would then sell it to hotels, in return for compensation that would help her earn a living and escape poverty. The Katzenbergers accepted her offer, and Annie would spend the rest of her life making a living with her marksmanship and trapping skills.

Annie made a great business deal and had major plans for her future. Despite the hardships she had endured, including her father's and sister's death and the experiences with the "wolves," Annie stood proud and was determined to make her dreams come true.

# Chapter 2 – The Huntress of the North Star

Annie decided to escape poverty by relying on what she did best—shooting, trapping, and hunting. Unlike many hunters, who preferred shooting their game when their target was still, Annie always shot moving targets. She wrote in her autobiography that it is only fair to give the animal you are hunting a fair chance to escape or dodge the shot. Her shot, however, couldn't be dodged. Annie appeared to be born to hold a gun in her hand, and whatever the target was, she would shoot right through it. Her aim was flawless, and her hand was steady, so even when the game was in motion, she could make a kill shot, which made her an exceptional hunter.

However, this took practice, and in the beginning, she was determined to improve her hunting skills as much as she could. She started hunting small game, such as rabbits and quail, and learned where the game would hide. In her autobiography, Annie talked about how easy it was for her to track game and make exceptional shots, which made her business with the Katzenberger brothers flourish. Annie said, "Nothing more simple, I assure you. But I'll tell you what. You must have your mind, and nerve, and everything in harmony. Don't look at your gun, simply follow the object with the end of it, as if the tip of the barrel was the point of your finger."

Like her father before her, Annie's gun was an extension of her body. Annie was the happiest girl in the world when she smelled the scent of burnt gunpowder, and she was at her most natural when she was alone in the wilderness and on the hunt. She hunted all her game fairly, allowing the animals to be on the move and giving her targets a chance to escape the destiny that would be served by her steady hand. The way Annie hunted, with the game on the move, made her an even better shooter, as she had to learn how to be quick with her trigger finger and her eye.

The Katzenberger brothers grew fond of Annie. It is no real surprise why. Besides delivering an abundance of game to the brothers, Annie was also very likable, although perhaps a bit odd. They decided to send Annie a special gift, and on one Christmas, Annie was given two boxes of percussion caps, one can of DuPont Eagle ducking black powder, and five pounds of shot. The powder she received was of the highest quality on the market, and Annie was so enchanted with her new gift that she couldn't bring herself to open the can for days. Soon afterward, Annie received another gift, a gift that would change her marksmanship game for the better. This present was a Parker Brothers 16-gauge breech-loading hammer with one hundred brass shells. Other girls would be thrilled to get a new dress or a piece of jewelry, but Annie's perfect present was a shotgun that showcased the power of innovation in the world of firearms. Breech-loading guns appeared in the United States around the late 1870s, and they were far more efficient than the previous generation of muzzle-loading rifles, which could fail a shooter if the powder got wet. Shooters also didn't have to bring a powder horn and a ramrod with them, making shooting and hunting more efficient. Now, Annie could just load the gun shells with powder before hunting and simply insert them in the barrel while she was out looking for game.

Not only was Annie's new gun more convenient to use, but it also allowed her to hunt more game. She started sending game in batches of six or a dozen to the Katzenberger store, from where it would be sent to hotels and restaurants from Greenville to Cincinnati and the surrounding area. There is a legend that the restaurant and hotel guests preferred the game shot by Annie, as she would make a kill shot through the head. However, as is the case with many other Wild West figures, there is no way to confirm if this was true or only a folk story.

At the time, there were no limitations when it came to the number of wild animals that could be hunted, as the preservation of wildlife wasn't of great concern to the settlers in the United States. That meant a successful hunter could hunt as much as he or she wanted, allowing them to make a substantial amount of money in the process. If one truly worked at it, hunters could make a higher yearly profit than a miner, lumberjack, or an average farmer. Still, a huntress was a rare thing, which was why Annie came across as an odd girl to many, although everyone was fascinated by her marksmanship skills. She was well known in all of North Star and the wider area by the time she was sixteen.

*Annie Oakley by Baker's Art Gallery, c. 1880.*

Working as a market hunter, Annie paid off her mother's mortgage in less than a year. Annie was a determined and hard-working girl, and she was proud of herself for being self-sufficient. Annie was so proud of her earning power that she used to say with great pleasure that ever since she was ten years old, she didn't have a dollar that she hadn't earned herself.

Before Annie was in her late teens, she had won so many shooting contests that she was banned from entering any more. She had also shot so much game that she was embarrassed to see her total kill number in the Katzenberger's books once limitations were brought about to regulate hunters and the number of animals they could kill in a season.

Everyone in North Star and Darke County knew Annie by her reputation. However, her life was about to change yet again, this time right on the doorstep of early adulthood.

# Chapter 3 – Annie and the Star Shooters of the West

Annie must have been an odd sight to see back in the day. She wore long stockings made of yarn, boots with copper toes, a short dress with knickerbockers, and mittens with a stitched-in trigger finger. Annie compensated for her oddities with her marksmanship skills and hunting talent. However, Annie wasn't the only exceptional shooter that America talked about.

The name of Captain Adam H. Bogardus appears in the annals of leading sharpshooters in 1869, which was the year when Bogardus became famous for shooting a hundred pigeons without missing a single target. The same year, Bogardus made a bet with Mr. R. M. Patchen that he could shoot and kill 500 pigeons in 645 minutes. Not only did Bogardus succeed in shooting all 500 pigeons, but he also managed to do so in 528 minutes. By the time Annie was fifteen, Bogardus had become the national trap shooter champion after defeating Ira Paine. After becoming a champion in the United States, Bogardus traveled to England, where he challenged anyone who wanted to compete against him in shooting. He won eighteen matches, which brought him distinction as a world trap shooter champion.

In the 1870s and 1880s, there were plenty of champion shooters, and the number of exhibition shooters was increasing as well. Bogardus was only one such champion, with William Frank "Doc" Carver being his greatest rival. One day in 1878, Doc dressed up, wearing a velvet shirt and a large sombrero with his pants tucked in his long boots. He made his way to Deerfoot Park in New York City with an ambitious plan—he was going to shoot and break 5,500 glass balls in 500 minutes with his Winchester rifle, a shooting stunt that had never been done with a rifle. Doc's assistant tossed the glass balls, which were filled with white feathers, and as they were thrown into the air, Doc would shoot each one. Some park visitors left Deerfoot Park, as the noise of the gun being fired was too loud and frequent, but many stayed to watch the show, which started at 11 o'clock sharp.

Whenever Doc would empty one gun, another freshly loaded and oiled gun would be handed to him, and the used gun would be placed in a barrel of water so it could cool down. The sulfur, broken glass, smoke, dirty water, and feathers made Doc's eyes become inflamed, and it got to the point that he had to pause and place a handkerchief filled with ice on his eyes to get some relief. Once he felt he couldn't go on any longer, he found out that he only had eighteen minutes left to shoot one hundred feather-filled glass balls. He made it to his goal with ten minutes to spare. Even though he succeeded, Doc spent the most painful night of his life in his bed with his eyes aching so much that he said he would never do such a thing again.

Exhibition shooting was a rather competitive sport, and shooters were always trying to outperform one another. Annie wasn't the first woman to join this sport, which was considered to be more appropriate for men. John Ruth's wife also enjoyed partaking in shooting shows with her husband in Deerfoot Park. Mrs. Ruth would use a mirror and shoot with her back turned to the target, and she would also shoot glass balls her husband tossed—her aim was incredible, as she rarely missed. John Ruth wasn't a bad shooter either. However, none of them were nearly as famous as Captain Bogardus or Doc Walker.

Exhibition shooters had performed with circuses and other traveling shows since the early 1800s, but it reached its peak in the 1880s. It became so popular that even a twelve-year-old girl claimed to be the champion of the world, holding a $500 bet that she could shoot and break 1,000 glass balls in 50 minutes.

One of the famous exhibition shooters that used to perform with theatrical troops and organized shows was Frank E. Butler. Butler arrived in America as an Irish immigrant. He was below average in height for a man, but he was attractive and had a good sense of humor. Butler liked to tell stories to make people laugh, and he worked on any job he could get upon arriving in the United States. Before he became an exhibition shooter, Butler trained dogs for a theatrical troop. He wasn't brilliant in this endeavor, but better times were ahead, as Butler decided to start practicing shooting. He trained himself by shooting at a target bent backward while holding a mirror. Butler found a partner in Baughman, and they performed with a poodle they called George in various New York City theaters in 1875. Around 1881, Butler and Baughman decided to join the Sells Brothers Circus. The Sells brothers—Allen, Peter, Lewis, and Ephraim—were the head of one of the leading entertainment attractions. They had over ten years of experience in the industry and billed their entertainment business as "The Biggest Amusement Enterprise on Earth." Joining the Sells brothers was a good choice for the pair, as Butler and Baughman performed in numerous acts and shows all across the United States, which gave them a regular income.

When they were welcomed to the Sells brothers' business, Baughman and Butler were told to pack their bags and leave the hotel in Cincinnati where they were staying and come to Columbus, Ohio, where the new season for the circus was about to start at the end of April 1881.

In the hotel where they were staying, Butler was asked by one of the farmers who frequented the hotel about what he could do with his gun and if he could shoot a little, offering a hundred dollar bet if he could beat a local legend. What Butler didn't know was that he would be competing against Annie Oakley. Butler accepted the challenge, which required him to travel from Cincinnati to Greenville. Since the journey to Greenville wasn't too long and since he needed the money, Butler decided to go before leaving for Columbus with his partner. Butler most likely thought it would be easy money, as he thought he could outshoot any shooter except for the likes of Bogardus and Doc.

After reaching Greenville, Butler had to make his way to a little town known as North Star. He still didn't know who his opponent was. The townsfolk would only tell him that he would measure his skill against their local sharpshooter.

*Frank E. Butler, Courtesy by the Annie Oakley Center at Garst Museum*

Once he arrived at North Star, Frank Butler was presented with his opponent, and he couldn't have been more surprised to see a slim, short girl, wearing a short linsey dress and knickerbockers, as she readied herself to shoot the moving targets prepared for the occasion.

Butler often spoke about his first encounter with Annie, doing so on at least three different occasions in 1903 and twice in 1924. Butler told reporters that nothing could have prepared him for the surprise he encountered in North Star. He was caught off guard, describing the outcome as Annie's first big match and his first defeat. On that day, Annie shot twenty-three birds, while Butler killed twenty-one.

At the time, Annie was in her early twenties, and she was quite a sight to behold, with her long dark hair and piercing blue eyes. After the match was over, Frank invited Annie to see his act that he performed with his poodle George. Annie accepted his invitation and was thrilled with Butler's poodle. Frank showed her some of his acts, such as shooting an apple placed on the poodle's head. The poodle would sit still, which allowed Butler to shoot the apple easily, making it burst into pieces.

When Annie came to see the act, Butler picked up a piece of the apple he shot and placed it by Annie's boot. This is how the romance between the shooting pair commenced. Annie was shy and reluctant when it came to courting, and even if she had any suitors other than Frank Butler, she never talked about them. George was somewhat an intermediary in their romantic relationship. Even though she was already twenty-one, to Frank, Annie seemed like a little girl, while to Annie, Frank must have seemed like a worldly man.

When Frank left for Columbus to join the Sells Brothers Circus, they kept in touch. Frank would send her greetings and presents in the name of George, his poodle.

Frank was a man of many talents, and one of these talents was writing poetry. He frequently sent letters to Annie, one of which included the poem that was inspired by his love for Annie. Frank called the poem "Little Raindrops."

There's a charming little girl
She's many miles from here
She's a loving little fairy
You'd fall in love to see her
Her presence would remind you
Of an angel in the skies,
And you bet I love this little girl
With the raindrops in her eyes.

Frank was married before he arrived in the United States, having two children with his first wife. Their marriage took a wrong turn, although Frank was a good man who never drank, gambled, or had problems with the law.

Things get a little muddy when it comes to the date of Frank and Annie's marriage. Not even their closest relatives knew the exact date. It is believed the pair married on June 20th, 1882, in Ontario, Canada. This book places the initial meeting of Frank and Annie in 1881, but some scholars place the famous shooting contest as taking place in 1875. If this is true, their marriage would have taken place in 1876. It is possible the contradictory dates have to do with Butler's divorce from his first wife, which was finalized in 1876. Whatever the case may be, they married a year after they met, meaning Annie was either sixteen or twenty-two when she married Frank. If she was sixteen, it is also possible that the couple decided to keep the exact date of their wedding a secret, as Annie left Darke Country before the wedding, which wasn't proper behavior for an unmarried girl back then.

According to some sources, after their marriage, Frank sent Annie to a Catholic school in Erie, Pennsylvania. While Frank traveled with the Sells Brothers Circus, Annie stayed there and received additional education. However, it is not known for sure if this actually happened. If it did, Frank completed the contract he had with the Sells brothers and found himself a new partner, John Graham, while Annie finished up her schooling.

It is known that Graham's mother was the head of a boarding school in Erie, and it has been recorded that Butler was a visitor there at the time when Annie was residing in Erie. It is suggested that Annie might have stayed with Graham's mother at the time, as the story of Annie attending a Catholic school is not confirmed by any written records.

Graham and Butler created quite a name for themselves while touring the United States, calling themselves "America's all rifle team and champion shot" and awing people who attended their shows with shooting stunts. The pair shot apples off each other's heads, and Butler also shot targets bent backward while holding a rifle upside down between his knees.

In 1882, while Graham and Butler were performing in Ohio, the name Annie Oakley wasn't on everyone's lips, but that was about to change. Soon after, Annie left Erie and joined her husband, and soon, all of America knew the name of Annie Oakley.

# Chapter 4 – The Birth of Annie Oakley

Soon after leaving Erie, Phoebe Ann Moses would become known as Annie Oakley, one of America's most treasured folklore heroes.

Annie left Erie either at the end of 1882 or the beginning of 1883 to join her husband. Even when Annie joined Butler, who was working with Graham at the time, she didn't join the duo as a shooter. According to Annie's autobiography, she would never have become a part of Butler's act if Graham hadn't become ill before one of their shooting shows. Since he was left without a partner and had an audience waiting to be amused with some exhibition target shooting, Butler asked Annie to hold objects that he would then shoot.

Annie agreed, and she became a part of the show, but she did not shoot until one particular day. Butler used to amuse his audience by missing a couple of his targets on purpose at the beginning of a show. That way, he could stun his audience once he started shooting targets without missing. One day while Annie was assisting him, Butler kept missing his targets to the point where the audience started to disapprove. According to Butler, who later spoke about the event, a man from the audience stood up and demanded Butler to let the girl, Annie, shoot the target instead, as he had missed the target over a dozen times.

Annie obliged and took the gun. She had never practiced on the targets Butler used for the show, but she still managed to hit the target on her second try. The audience was thrilled and cheered for Annie to continue. She never missed a single target from that point on. As Butler recalled, he tried to resume his act and take the gun back from Annie, but he was howled down and had to let Annie finish the act. Butler knew better than to let Annie go back into the shadows, so he suggested she become a regular part of the act. Annie would become the star of the show, even though Butler's name preceded hers in the show's announcement. The two never competed against each other from that point on. As Frank Butler liked to say, Annie outclassed him in what he did best, which was shooting targets and putting on a show for his audience.

Imaged by Heritage Auctions, HA.com

*Annie Oakley and Frank Butler*

Frank Butler decided to teach Annie everything he knew about sharpshooting show business and allowed her to have the spotlight. As mentioned above, Annie wasn't the only girl competing for fame in the world of sharpshooting, as there was a great number of women who performed for audiences as sharpshooters. Tillie Russell and Lillian Smith were just some of many women seeking to become famous, but unlike those shooters, who wore revealing outfits or bragged about their sharp eye and mistake-free shooting, Annie was a modest girl no taller than five feet and of small build. She appeared as a child to any viewer in the audience, which made her shooting act even more amazing. Annie also dressed modestly, wearing a black dress with cuffed sleeves and a white collar. Her looks and her attitude made her even more appealing to the audience, as she always wore a wide smile on her face, which was framed with her long dark hair.

Phoebe Ann Moses was a true definition of a rising star, and her stage name of "Annie Oakley" seemed to carry a note of magic itself, as it was melodic and easy for the audience to remember. Annie never revealed why she picked that name. As time passed, people were curious about the origins of this unparalleled sharpshooter. While some have suggested Annie took the name "Oakley" based on the neighborhood in which she and Butler resided, others have suggested that it was the name of the man who paid her train fare when she was running away from the "wolves."

What is known is that Annie disliked her family name, Moses, insisting that her family's name was actually "Mozey." She even entered a feud with her brother when she had the name "Mozey" engraved on the headstones of her two nephews who had died.

Whatever the reason for picking her stage name, Annie created a brand and was easily recognizable as one of the top sharpshooting performers of her time. However, very little is known about the first year of Annie and Butler working together. It is presumed they mostly performed in the Great Lakes region and the Midwest during 1883.

Working alongside Butler involved a lot of traveling, which wasn't unusual for performers and even famous actors at the time. Annie and Frank Butler mostly depended on trains, boardinghouses, and cheap hotels to save some money. As Annie said on one occasion, saving money on traveling meant that she could afford pretty hair ribbons, nice new gloves, and other things she would wear to look neat and pretty for the show. She never relied on her sexuality to earn money and attract more spectators. She looked like a plain but interesting and attractive woman, who could rely on her charming smile and her undisputed sharpshooting skills to win over the audience.

Frank was the perfect partner for Annie, as he loved and cherished her for who she was. He never took credit for her skill, saying that he couldn't have taught her to shoot since she could outshoot him even before she became a performer. He said the only thing he did for Annie's career was to get her a position as his partner.

As Annie's popularity grew, Frank allowed her to have the entire show to herself, and he settled into the role of manager. Frank made sure to manage Annie's bookings, talk to theater managers, check the train schedules, count and keep their earnings, and place ads in newspapers to advertise Annie's sharpshooting shows.

Annie was more than happy with how Frank managed her bookings and their finances, on one occasion saying that she had whatever she owned due to Frank's "careful management." Annie and Frank were still poor when they started doing shows together. When Annie was just starting out as the main star of the show, they had enough money to buy her a pretty hat after a week's work.

Soon, they were tired of counting every penny they earned, as they were constantly going through financial struggles, so the pair decided to join the Sells Brothers, who offered them a contract for forty weeks. With the Sells Brothers Circus, Annie and Frank wouldn't have to worry about traveling fares and paychecks, as they would get fair compensation for their performance and could save up some money while performing a couple of times a day.

However, before Annie Oakley and Frank Butler joined the Sells brothers, Annie performed in the Olympic Theater in St. Paul, Minnesota. It was a show that would become known as one of the most memorable moments in the life and work of Annie Oakley, as it was when she became known as "Little Sure Shot."

# Chapter 5 – Miss "Little Sure Shot" and Chief Sitting Bull

Back in March of 1884, Annie was still struggling to get the recognition she thought she deserved. Frank and Annie wanted to get all the bookings they could during that winter, so they accepted a job to join a traveling show known as the Arlington and Fields Combination.

Annie grew up in poverty, and she was driven to achieve financial stability and enjoy the fruits of her labor and efforts. Annie competed in shooting matches during the day and performed in the evenings. She was too busy to notice what was going on in St. Paul the week the traveling show arrived in that town.

What Annie didn't know at the time when she and Frank arrived in St. Paul was that one of the most infamous prisoners of the Territory of Dakota was in town as well. Chief Sitting Bull of the Hunkpapa Lakota was visiting St. Paul. He was blamed for the death of Lieutenant Colonel George Armstrong Custer in the Battle of the Little Bighorn, which took place eight years before.

While Sitting Bull did not directly partake in the fighting, he was an easy scapegoat, as he was the leader of the rebels who defeated Custer. The American forces were brutally defeated in this battle, which stands as one of the most significant actions of the Great Sioux War. For that reason, Chief Sitting Bull was hated amongst the people of St. Paul, as well as many other places. In March 1884, Chief Sitting Bull, who, after surrendering to authorities in 1881, lived at the Standing Rock Agency near Fort Yates, arrived in St. Paul with Indian Agent James McLaughlin.

Agent McLaughlin had brought Sitting Bull and his nephew One Bull to tour various parts of the country. In St. Paul, they visited schools, a cigar factory, where Sitting Bull rolled a cigar and then smoked it, and a millinery, where they were greeted by forty women who worked there.

*Sioux Chief Sitting Bull, 1885. The United States Library of Congress Prints and Photographs Division*

The women from the millinery decorated the Sioux chief's hair with ribbons, which made Sitting Bull appear far less ferocious to the locals of St. Paul. Although many feared Sitting Bull and even resented him for his conflicts with the US Army, there was something admirable about the chief. He always looked people in the eye while talking to them, and he always spoke clearly and deliberately.

At night, after taking a tour around the town, Sitting Bull went to the theater. On the first night of his visit, the chief enjoyed "Muldoon's Picnic" at the Grand Opera House, and the next night, he laughed at the Rex Reed show. On the third evening, Chief Sitting Bull was taken to see the Arlington and Fields Combination show at the Olympic Theater.

At the time, Arlington and Fields Combination advertised their shows as the greatest congregation of talent ever to arrive at St. Paul. The chief enjoyed the acrobatics show, the singing of Miss Allie Jackson, and watched the afterpiece called "St. Patrick's Day in the Evening." A part of the show included Annie Oakley's shooting exhibition.

Frank assisted Annie as she shot cigarettes off his lips, corks off bottles with unearthly precision, and blew out the flames of candles with bullets flying by. Chief Sitting Bull observed Annie's act in awe. He was so fascinated by the petite girl with long dark hair, blue eyes, and steady hand and eye that he decided to meet Annie Oakley in person.

*Annie Oakley, Underwood Archives*

The same night after the show, as well as days afterward, Chief Sitting Bull sent his messengers to Annie, asking to meet her in person. Annie and Frank were staying at the hotel in St. Paul, and Annie's mind was only set on work and money. Since she competed in shooting matches during the day, she didn't have time to meet Chief Sitting Bull. But the chief didn't give up. He kept sending his messengers in hopes of meeting Annie.

The chief must have eventually realized that Annie cared more about earning money and that she couldn't spare the time to meet him because of her busy working schedule, as he decided to send her sixty-five dollars along with a message saying he would like to have a photograph of her as a memory of her talent and unique and charming appearance.

Annie was so amused by the chief's decisiveness to meet her that she decided to accept the invitation. She returned the message, agreeing to meet the chief and also returning the money he had sent. After meeting Annie Oakley in person, Sitting Bull was so taken with her that he wanted to adopt her, giving her the name "Watanya Cicilla," which translates to "Little Sure Shot." Thus, Annie symbolically became a daughter of a chieftain, which came with certain privileges that Oakley liked to brag about. Annie liked to talk about how she was entitled to have five ponies, an endless number of cattle, other presents in livestock, and a wigwam.

Frank made the business decision to utilize the story of the adoption as an advertisement for Annie's show. Frank made a publication in the *New York Clipper*, advertising Annie through the prism of Sitting Bull's fascination. As proof of the chief's admiration, Annie had the original moccasins the chief wore, a feather from his hair, and a photograph of him, which was given to her as a present.

What Annie might not have noticed was that the chief might have had a romantic interest in her, even though most believe his interest was more fatherly in nature.

With this move, Annie became known as "the greatest of the greatest" and the main star of "the best shooting show ever seen," as advertised by Frank and promoted through the famous Chief Sitting Bull.

The legend of Annie Oakley, Little Miss Sure Shot, was born. However, it would take some time until Annie became a major star in the world of Wild West entertainment.

# Chapter 6 – A Faithful Trip to New Orleans: Buffalo Bill's Wild West Show

Frank and Annie worked on a variety of shows for the Sells Brothers Circus. However, they didn't make enough money to live solely off their shooting acts in the circus, so Annie and Frank participated in a comic act as well. In addition, Annie rode a side-saddle for the Rose Garland entrée. If anything, the Sells brothers knew how to make a show and attract a crowd.

They arrived in New Orleans with fifty wild animals, which included a pair of hippopotamuses, a grown giraffe, and an arsenal of wild beasts, birds, and even an aquarium of amphibious sea creatures. The circus also introduced Chemah, a Chinese dwarf, who was advertised as the tiniest man on earth. Annie and Frank were certainly earning their dime with the contract they had with the Sells brothers.

Although the pair performed for thousands of people across 187 cities in 18 states, the name of Annie Oakley and Frank Butler barely made it to the newspapers. An elephant named Emperor, which was a part of the Sells Brothers Circus, received more fame at the time than the sharpshooting duo.

In late 1884, during the World Industrial and Cotton Centennial Exposition, all of New Orleans was decorated with flowers, as the city was celebrating a hundred years since America started to export cotton. Exhibitions were set up, and every country brought its own variety of plants, with Texas alone bringing over 21,000 different specimens. The Sells Brothers wanted to cash in on the crowds arriving in New Orleans. That day, there were over 25,000 people on the streets, all renting rooms in hotels and all looking for something to do as they waited for the exhibition to open.

The Sells Brothers Circus had a fair number of visitors, but the number wasn't as high as the brothers would have liked, as it was constantly raining. The Sells brothers had planned to stay in New Orleans for the exhibition opening, but the stubborn and persistent rain changed their minds. After only two weeks, the brothers decided to close and head home.

Annie and Frank still had a contract with the Sells brothers, and they renewed their contract for the next season. The next season, though, wouldn't start until April. Even though there was an increase in salary, the sharpshooting duo was left without a job in December 1884 while staying in New Orleans, Louisiana. They had four months before the start of their new contract, which meant they had to find a way to make some money until the next circus season started.

Frank started to look for work and bookings for their show. As he often used to do, Frank listed an advertisement in a trade publication known as the *Clipper*, hoping to hear from a prominent employer.

Frank was a keen reader of newspapers, and only several days after publishing the advertisement, he stumbled upon an ad that caught his interest. It read, "Mr. E. W. Woodcott, Buffalo Bill's Wild West show—an original American amusement enterprise."

Woodcott was the general manager for Buffalo Bill's Wild West show, which contained a great number of shooting acts and horse racing. To Frank, the fact Buffalo Bill's show was arriving in

New Orleans was a sign that he and Annie should stay in New Orleans and try to score a shooting act. The prominent William Frederick Cody, better known as Buffalo Bill, arrived in New Orleans on December 8th, 1884, and the Sells Brothers Circus left the city only several days later, on December 13th.

*Buffalo Bill's Wild West show poster*

Before the Sells Brothers Circus departed, Buffalo Bill paid for a ticket to see one of their shows. On that occasion, he asked to meet Annie Oakley and Frank Butler. The pair saw this as the perfect opportunity to ask for a job at his Wild West show; however, they were turned down by Buffalo Bill, who said the show already had more than enough shooting acts.

Recalling this event in her autobiography, Annie said that her vanity was wounded, but she saw consolation in the fact that one of the shooters performing for the Wild West show was the famous Captain Adam Bogardus. Bogardus performed with his sons, Peter, Henry, Edward, and Eugene, and he was also a part-owner of Buffalo Bill's Wild West show.

For Annie and Frank, Buffalo Bill's refusal meant they had no further business in New Orleans, and not wanting to spend their winter in idleness, they packed their bags and headed north, performing in a variety of shows. Buffalo Bill's show moved on without them, opening acts in New Orleans that winter of 1884.

Buffalo Bill had a tough season that year, and his troubles began with the transportation of equipment and animals for the show. The steamship that was transporting the show collided with a steamboat on the Mississippi River, and the show's equipment sank. The losses included guns, ammunition, wagons, camp equipment, and animals. The losses were so great that Bogardus decided to head to Cincinnati to try and find the owner of the steamboat and recoup the damages done to their equipment and the steamer.

The weather wasn't in their favor either, as it was constantly raining, and Cody had to postpone the start of the season in New Orleans more than several times. In March 1885, Bogardus was so fed up with their bad luck that he announced he was going back home and was taking his sons with him. Bogardus planned to enroll his sons back in school. This was yet another blow to Buffalo Bill, as he had now lost the greatest stars of his shooting acts, Bogardus and his four sons.

However, one man's misfortune is often another man's luck. Annie and Frank saw a new opportunity once they heard of Bogardus's departure. Annie immediately wrote to Cody, asking for a place in the show for Frank and herself. However, Annie wanted a fairly high salary, and Buffalo Bill was already in debt for an estimated $60,000 due to the horrible winter the show had in New Orleans. Cody responded to Annie, claiming that her payment demands were rather steep. He was also worried that such a small woman wasn't fit to take over the act that had been previously led by Bogardus and his sons. Each of Bogardus's rifles weighed at least ten pounds, and Cody didn't think a woman of barely 110 pounds could carry, shoot, and use these guns day after day.

Buffalo Bill shared his concerns with Annie, suggesting that she wouldn't be able to withstand the recoil from these guns. Annie Oakley's confidence was so great that she wasn't ready to back down, but she asked for a thirty-day trial during which she could prove her ability to perform. If she wasn't up to the task, Annie promised to leave the show as soon as the trial expired. Cody agreed, and Annie and Frank planned to meet up with the show in Louisville, Kentucky, where the show was supposed to open in the last week of April.

Before Annie and Frank headed to Louisville, Annie wanted to practice her shooting stunts in the same manner as Bogardus and Doc Carver. Annie decided to use three 16-gauge Parker shotguns to shoot 5,000 glass balls in a single day. However, Annie was up for the challenge, as she shot 4,772 glass balls in nine hours, finishing the endurance test by shooting an additional 984 glass balls. She announced this shooting feat as her personal record. Annie was determined to make a name for herself and join Buffalo Bill's Wild West show.

Many historians wonder why Oakley and Butler wanted to join the Wild West show so badly, especially since the show was already in debt and had suffered a difficult year, losing property, money, and the star of their shooting exhibitions, Bogardus. However, it was more than obvious that Annie was growing tired of variety shows, as there were too many shooters to compete with. It was becoming difficult to make a living and save money with so many sharpshooters constantly raising the bar. Moreover, by 1884, there were so many shooting acts that Annie lost her edge as being a woman shooter. Frank heard of at least twenty women doing the same thing, some of which used tricks to make the audience believe their hand was as steady as Annie's was.

Annie and Frank had never heard of a female shooter using a shotgun, though, so they decided to grab the opportunity and use it the best they could. Annie Oakley was ready to join Buffalo Bill's Wild West show, which was known at the time as the greatest outdoor show in America.

# Chapter 7 – "The Greatest Entertainment Show in American History"

It wasn't vanity that drove Buffalo's Bill Wild West show to be known as the greatest entertainment show in American history. William F. Cody, a.k.a. Buffalo Bill, became a legend after working thirteen years in show business. He made sure that everyone in America and Europe had heard of his show. The successful combination of rodeo drama skits, which promoted and romanticized the way of life in the Wild West, and marksmanship shows and shooting exhibitions made his show incredibly popular. However, they weren't the only things that attracted people enough to pay fifty cents. People also came to see the legendary folk hero Buffalo Bill himself, who was just as charming and awing in his appearance as he was in his reputation. Cody was a heavy-drinking man, but he was still friendly and approachable. He had a long dark goatee and long dark hair, and he had a talent for putting on a show.

A cowboy band would play at the opening of the Wild West shows, and Buffalo Bill would introduce himself alongside Native American horse riders, who shouted and chanted while the bells on their horses' necks jangled as they sprinted around the stage. Cowboys and Mexican vaqueros would join Cody and the Native American riders on the stage, and Cody would give them a sign by shouting out. Once the riders were given the sign, they would start letting out war whoops, and their colorful feathers swirled in a dizzying display, intertwining paths with the Mexican vaqueros and cowboys. Shots would be fired into the air as the riders shouted and circled the stage. This kind of opening fired the audience up, setting a high level of energy right from the get-go.

When Annie and Frank arrived in Kentucky, where the Wild West show would open for the season, Cody was nowhere to be found. The duo was told that Buffalo Bill was out parading the streets with other members of the troop. Annie and Frank decided to unload their guns, bags, and other equipment so Annie could get some practice in before Cody returned to the camp.

Frank and Annie brought a big load of guns into the arena. They noticed that a man was sitting there, who barely even acknowledged their presence. Annie picked up her shotgun and started to shot clay pigeons in the arena.

The man who was observing Annie's practice didn't look like a part of the Wild West show, as he wore fancy clothes and carried a slim ornate cane, but as soon as Annie finished shooting, he got up without hesitation to tell her how impressed he was with her marksmanship skills.

As it turned out, the man was the business manager of the Wild West show, Nate Salsbury. Salsbury decided to hire Annie and neglect the thirty-day trial period without even consulting Cody, remarking that a woman with Annie's skill, shooting targets with a shotgun, was a novelty in shooting shows.

*Annie Oakley in a Buffalo Bill's Wild West show poster*

Annie wrote in her autobiography that Salsbury ordered posters to advertise Annie's act, as well as woodcarving of her, which cost him around $7,000. Annie found this odd, as she knew that someone who hadn't firmly established themselves in the industry shouldn't be advertised in such a vigorous way. Annie was later told that Salsbury talked about her with Cody, using only words of praise to describe her and calling her a "real daisy." According to Salsbury, Annie Oakley was an exceptional talent, and she would give the Wild West show an opportunity to offer a novelty to amusement-hungry audiences across America.

Soon, Annie and Frank met up with Cody. Buffalo Bill started to call Annie Oakley "Annie Missi," which was a nickname that soon stuck, although only people who were close to her could call her by that name. The name "Missi" was a clever combination of "Mississippi" and "Missy." Annie would call Cody "the Colonel." Later on, Annie described Cody as the kindest man with the biggest heart, a man who was loyal, simple, and trustworthy. Annie said in her autobiography that the Colonel had honest relationships with everyone he encountered and that he was the most trusting man she had ever met.

Annie and Frank were welcomed to the Buffalo Bill's Wild West show family. It was the first time Annie faced the real Wild West and met real cowboys. The show consisted of cowboys, Native American riders, who mostly hailed from the Sioux, and Mexican vaqueros; Annie was the first white woman to join the largest and greatest Wild West show in America. She would soon become one of the most popular Wild West characters, even though she had never been a part of that world and never concealed the fact that she came from Ohio.

Annie secured herself a solo act for Buffalo Bill's Wild West show, where she would remain for the next seventeen years.

# Chapter 8 – Annie Oakley as the Heart of the Wild West Show

Annie Oakley was finally at the point where she could say that people knew her name, and it was all thanks to her skills, talent, her husband's management, and her determination to get herself an act in Buffalo Bill's Wild West show.

Her act was simple but charming. It only lasted about ten minutes, but ten minutes was more than enough time to enchant the audience and become the heart of the Wild West show.

Annie would enter the stage, waving to the audience and sending kisses. She looked like an innocent, charming girl. She wore a short skirt that fell below her knees and a shirt that was loose around her waist so she could use her full motion potential. She even used a skill she had learned years back at the Darke County Infirmary and sewed flowers and ribbons on her skirts. Even though she stood out with her looks and appearance from the rest of the Wild West show, Annie still wore a wide-edged sombrero with a six-pointed star attached to it, showcasing her attachment to the show.

People who worked with Annie told stories about how she was a neat woman that took great care and pride in her outfits and the way she dressed. She always wanted everything to be perfect, so her clothes had to be sewn to perfection as well.

At the beginning of her act, Annie ran to the center of the shooting arena, where she would meet Frank, who stood there without the introduction Annie Oakley would receive as the star of the show. Annie then unveiled a table with weapons, while Frank prepared to assist her in the act.

After picking up a shotgun, Annie would shoot at the clay pigeons Frank threw in the air. He raised the excitement and difficulty of Annie's challenge by adding more pigeons to his pitches. Annie would hit all of the targets. Even if she happened to miss the first time, she always got it the second time.

Annie was swift and fast, shooting with a steady arm and a steady eye. However, she wasn't only quick; she could also use both hands to shoot since she was ambidextrous. She would take two guns and shoot at the targets simultaneously, putting on a real show for the excited crowd.

Moving around the arena and shooting from almost any imaginable position and angle, Annie showed that a woman could be as equally agile and athletic as men. She would take a glass ball and throw it herself, shooting it on the first try in a blink of an eye.

One of the audience's most favorite acts was Annie's shooting stunt that used a mirror or a polished kitchen knife. She used the mirror to observe the target behind her back and shot the gun over her shoulder. Another popular stunt involved Annie's swiftness, as well as her athletic and marksmanship skills. Annie would lay her shotgun on the ground and stand ten feet away in the opposite direction. Frank, who was standing opposite Annie and the gun, would throw a clay pigeon in the air, and Annie would run toward the shotgun and shoot the clay pigeon before it touched the ground.

Annie's most difficult and challenging task was performed at the end of her act. It included eleven glass balls, five shotguns, and a single rifle. Annie had only ten seconds to shoot eleven balls while switching between the rifle and five shotguns. This exhibition was described by the press as "the cleverest number." At the end of her ten-minute show, Annie Oakley would run across the stage, sending kisses to the audience yet again. Just before she left the stage, she would make a little kick.

Annie wasn't only a sharpshooter—she was also a performer. She knew how to engage the audience and make them laugh. If she missed the target, she would stomp her feet as if she was upset, giving off the impression of a little girl throwing a tantrum, which was enough to charm the audience.

Comedy was an important part of Annie Oakley's show. On one occasion, Annie kept missing her targets, clay pigeons in this case, so she acted all upset and took Frank's hat. She threw it in the air and then shot straight through it on the first try.

*Annie Oakley shooting over her shoulder in the famous mirror stunt*

At times when she missed her targets, she amused her audience by laying her shotgun on the ground and walking around it, as superstitious shooters walk around their guns and rifles to change their luck. Annie wasn't superstitious at all, though; she was just doing it to amuse the audience. After walking around her shotgun for some time, Annie would pick it up, and Frank would start throwing clay pigeons again, with Annie hitting all the targets.

Annie's shooting skills and her comedic performance brought her fame. Her name became more popular across America every day. Annie was excellent at what she did, and it must have been an incredible sight to watch her shoot targets and perform stunts.

Annie was so swift, and her aim was so good that many implied that she somehow cheated when it came to her shooting stunts. Cheating in shooting shows wasn't a rare occurrence. Many sharpshooters cheated, as they focused more on amusing and awing the audience than on practicing their shooting. It also didn't help that Annie was living in a man's world, as many most likely wondered how a woman could be that good.

However, Annie and Frank knew the ways of the entertainment business. Frank knew that Annie was talented enough not to miss her targets, but when she made it look easy, people questioned the authenticity of her marksmanship. The two agreed that Annie should occasionally miss a target or two, which would prove that she was not a cheater since she didn't hit every target flawlessly.

In many ways, Annie was the heart of the Wild West show. Not only did the audience adore her, but Cody himself and the rest of the troop also respected Annie's feelings and her straightforward persona.

Annie never liked to be called a champion of sharpshooting, as she feared she might become associated with fakes and immoral shooters. Regardless, she cared much for her reputation. When the troop became intoxicated or had inappropriate company around, she would ask them to avoid her. The troop respected her wishes, and they also avoided cursing, smoking, and drinking in front of her. Annie never smoked, heavily drank, or cursed, although she did enjoy an occasional beer. However, she would never pay for one herself; Annie only drank if someone offered her a cold one.

# Chapter 9 – Rivalry, Royals, and Rifles

During her long career at Buffalo Bill's Wild West show, Annie met new friends and reencountered old ones while also finding foes and rivals.

Sitting Bull joined Buffalo Bill's Wild West show soon after Annie Oakley did. Even though legend implies the chief agreed to join the show because Annie Oakley was a part of the troop, Sitting Bull was actually convinced to sign up because he was promised a fair salary, bonuses, and exclusive right to sell his autographed photos to admirers.

John Burke, who was the chief promoter for Buffalo Bill's Wild West show, was happy Sitting Bull would become a part of the show. Burke had tried to convince Sitting Bull to join the show on several occasions but with no success. Although Sitting Bull didn't join because Annie was a part of the troop, he was, nonetheless, thrilled to see her as one of the show's performers. Although Annie Oakley and Sitting Bull had a prior relationship, with Sitting Bull symbolically adopting Annie as his daughter, Burke never utilized their acquaintance and the story of Annie's adoption to advertise their acts. The two actually never shared the stage, as they performed in individual acts.

Annie Oakley became a respected and loved character on stage, as well as backstage, but a particular rivalry was brought center stage a year later in 1886. Young Lillian Smith, whose fame somewhat didn't outlive her the way it has with Annie Oakley, was only fifteen years old when she signed a contract with Buffalo Bill. Lillian Smith had been shooting since the age of seven, and she was eleven years younger than Annie. Even though the two female sharpshooters weren't advertised as rivals, the audience surely judged them by this invented rivalry.

Annie Oakley still stood proudly and put all her energy into her acts, although she chipped six years off her real age once Lillian joined the Wild West show. Lillian, as a promising fifteen-year-old shooter, was advertised by Buffalo Bill as the "Californian huntress." She was poised to become the next rising star of sharpshooting.

785 BROADWAY, N. Y.

*Lillian Frances Smith, Heritage Auctions*

Lillian and Annie were what could be called radical opposites, although the two were nearly equal when it came to their sharpshooting skills. Most likely because Lillian was younger than Annie Oakley, she was full of confidence and liked to brag. Annie recalled hearing Lillian say upon her arrival that "Annie Oakley was done for." Lillian would wear flashy clothes, which was very different from Annie's neat and simple skirts. Annie Oakley was also modest when it came to her achievements, as she always refused to be called a champion. The two even used different weapons for their shooting exhibitions, with Lillian favoring a rifle and Annie a shotgun.

One thing was certain—Annie Oakley wasn't the only girl in the troop, and the audience loved fantasizing about the rivalry between the two female performers. Even though Annie didn't seem to care much about the alleged rivalry and the fact that Lillian often boasted about her skill and how she could beat Annie at any time, the tension between the two still rose, hitting its peak a year later.

In 1887, Buffalo Bill's Wild West show headed to London, England, where Queen Victoria, Prince Edward, and the royal family were supposed to attend the show. Shooting matches were also organized at Wimbledon, and both Annie Oakley and Lillian Smith planned to show off their shooting skills at the event.

By the time the Wild West show arrived in London, Annie's name was already famous, which meant the queen didn't miss a chance to praise Annie Oakley for her talent and reputation, as well as to shake her hand. Lillian Smith was neglected in a way and remained in the shadow of Annie, although she was welcomed appropriately by the royals.

The British press mostly covered the story about Annie meeting the queen, sharing the news that Queen Victoria had only words of praise for Annie Oakley. However, the American press seemed to have liked the idea of having a top sharpshooter such as Annie being in the shadow of a younger shooter, Lillian Smith. American newspapers reported that Lillian was welcomed with praises while Annie Oakley remained on the sidelines.

While Lillian was given all the publicity that she could have asked for, which was helped by the support of Buffalo Bill, the publicity stunt failed once Annie and Lillian competed at Wimbledon. Even before the match, some Americans suggested that Lillian wasn't a match for Annie's skill and that the young shooter was a trickster. However, for Colonel Cody, having Lillian as a part of the troop was a huge win for the Wild West show. Thus, Cody refused to comment on the news that favored Lillian and bashed Annie's importance. Annie still respected Cody even though he didn't stand up for her.

However, the truth about the skill of both sharpshooters emerged several days after the ricochet of offenses on Annie's reputation. Lillian performed poorly at Wimbledon, destroying her chance to show that she was better than Annie. Annie, on the other hand, showcased her skill in all its glory, proving that she was the actual champion of sharpshooting, even though she never favored that title. Annie Oakley was so brilliant in her performance at Wimbledon that Prince Edward himself left his seat to shake hands with the sharpshooting legend.

Despite this, Buffalo Bill still favored young Lillian Smith. It was probably due to this that Annie decided to leave Buffalo Bill's Wild West show.

However, the story of Annie Oakley isn't over yet.

# Chapter 10 – The Aftermath and Well-deserved Glory

Annie Oakley and Frank Butler left Buffalo Bill's Wild West show in 1888, after which Annie joined a rivaling Wild West show. She also joined the theater and got back to performing on stage, even acting in a play called *Deadwood Dick*. In between, Annie Oakley participated in shooting matches across Philadelphia. Idleness just wasn't an option for Annie and Frank, so they kept doing what they did best.

Annie Oakley wasn't away from Buffalo Bill and his crew for long, as she decided to return once Lillian Smith left the show in 1889. Lillian later reinvented herself at an older age, performing as an "Indian princess"; however, she was never immortalized in folklore the way Annie Oakley has been.

Annie returned to Buffalo Bill's show just in time to take off for a tour in Europe, which commenced with the Paris Exposition. The Eiffel Tower was a novelty at the time, as it had just been built, and France was celebrating its centennial anniversary of the French Revolution. The exposition was visited by roughly thirty-two million people from around the world. Annie's performance was so brilliant that the president of France told her she could join the French Army for a commission. At the same time, the king of

Senegal offered Annie Oakley $100,000 to help him get rid of the tigers plaguing his country. Annie refused these offers. Annie also met Thomas Edison and asked him if he would be able to make an electric gun. Edison told Annie he would consider her idea, and Annie refused offers that she received from the President of France and the King of Senegal.

The tour in Paris lasted for six months, and after that, the Wild West show embarked on a three-year tour around Europe. Buffalo Bill's troop returned to America in October 1892 to find that the United States Census Bureau had declared an end to the American frontier since settlements were now widespread.

During the Wild West show tour in Europe in 1890, Annie Oakley visited Berlin. The last German Kaiser, Friedrich Wilhelm II, was in attendance. The Kaiser was a great admirer of Annie Oakley and had already viewed a few of her shows. As an exhibition shooter, Annie used to include all sorts of stunts in her act, and one of these stunts included asking for a volunteer who would agree to become a part of a rather dangerous act.

Annie asked if anyone from the audience wanted to volunteer to hold a cigarette in his mouth while Annie attempted to shoot the ashes clean off. No one would ever volunteer, so Frank would join Annie on the stage for the stunt. However, it was different at the Berlin show, as there was a volunteer—the German Kaiser himself.

Annie had no other options, knowing that she could not refuse one of the most powerful men in the world, so she invited him to join her on stage. The Kaiser's life was in Annie's hands as she raised her rifle. The Kaiser lit a cigarette, placed it in his mouth, and waited for Annie's shot. Annie pulled the trigger and shot the ashes right off the Kaiser's cigarette without any problem.

After performing in many successful tours, Annie Oakley was rather famous, and her every word was carefully monitored by the media and public. Her interviews could be found in practically every newspaper, and everyone wanted to meet her.

In May 1893, Annie and the rest of the troop joined the Chicago Columbia Exposition, which celebrated the 400th anniversary of Columbus arriving in the Americas. This year was the best for the Wild West show by far, as around six million people visited the show during the exposition. The show made about one million dollars that season.

The same year, Frank and Annie bought a new home in Nutley, New Jersey, where they moved in after the season ended. During the summer of 1894, Annie joined the Wild West show in Brooklyn, where they were able to perform at night for the first time since the show now owned a massive array of electric lights. In the fall of the same year, Annie Oakley traveled to meet Thomas Edison, who wanted to test a kinetoscope, a harbinger of the motion picture camera. Thomas Edison wanted to see if the kinetoscope could capture the smoke from Annie's gun, which it did. In October, the Wild West show ended its season to Cody's dissatisfaction, as the show didn't earn much. Colonel Cody blamed the cost of running electric lights and the ongoing economic depression for the lack of profit that year.

The next year, in 1895, Cody had a plan to earn enough to make up for the lack of profit from the last season, so the Wild West show embarked on another tour across America, visiting 131 cities. According to Annie's estimates, she fired around 40,000 bullets in a year.

In 1900, Annie performed for the first time with the Wild West show in Greenville, her hometown. The townspeople presented her with a commemorative silver cup, which Annie stated was the dearest award she had ever received. The next year, in 1901, just as the season with the show was ending, Frank and Annie ended up in a train accident. A show train carrying Buffalo Bill's troop was hit by a fast southbound train. The accident occurred near Lexington, and the collision derailed Annie Oakley's private car, which was attached to the train. At the time, the newspapers didn't write about Annie being injured. However, Frank had to take her to the hospital, where she was diagnosed with internal injuries, and her left side was temporarily paralyzed. The doctor thought that Annie would never shoot again.

The train accident left many people injured, and 110 horses owned by Buffalo Bill ended up either dead or had to be put down due to injuries. Two of the horses that died had been given to Buffalo Bill by the queen of England as a present. Supposedly, Buffalo Bill cried once he discovered his horses had died.

Annie decided that she couldn't travel with the show any longer. She quit the next year, and Frank accepted a job as a representative for the Union Metallic Cartridge Company.

Annie returned to the stage in 1902, starring in *The Western Girl*, which was another success for her. However, the next year, despite her success, the name of Annie Oakley was intentionally stained by journalist William Randolph Hearst. Hearst published sensational and popular stories, and he wrote that Annie Oakley was in prison for stealing a pair of pants from "a negro" to buy cocaine and soothe her drug addiction. The news was read from coast to coast, and although it was untrue, everyone was talking about the scandal.

Annie cherished her reputation, so she decided to file fifty-five lawsuits to get to the bottom of the false news and make things right. The legal battle would last until 1910, with Oakley traveling to various courts across the country to testify. In the meantime, Hearst wanted to smear Oakley's reputation even further and hired a private detective, sending him to Greenville to dig up dirt on America's favorite sharpshooter.

There was nothing to be found, of course, as Annie was an honorable girl who didn't use drugs or imbibe alcohol. She won fifty-four out of the fifty-five lawsuits and collected around $27,500. The entire amount was spent on court expenses.

During her career as a sharpshooter, Annie never missed a chance to pay a visit to her mother. In August 1908, Annie found out that her mother had died, and she immediately returned to Ohio.

Two years later, in 1910, Annie paid a visit to Buffalo Bill's Wild West show, and Colonel Cody asked her to return. Annie declined and joined a rivaling show called Young Buffalo Wild West in 1911. She performed with the show for two years and traveled across the country, even though she was already fifty years old. In 1913, Annie decided that her career as a performer had come to an end and quit performing in shows.

Frank and Annie moved into a waterfront cottage in Maryland, near Cambridge. In the meantime, Colonel Cody's show went bankrupt, and the Wild West show memorabilia was sold by creditors.

In the summer of 1915, Annie and Frank decide to visit Cody, whose health was declining. The pair then decided to spend a winter in Pinehurst, North Carolina. Annie decided to give lessons to girls who wanted to learn how to shoot. It is believed that throughout her life, Annie taught over 15,000 women how to handle a gun. Sadly, Cody never got better. He died in 1917, and although Annie couldn't attend his funeral, she wrote a eulogy for him that ran in all the newspapers across America. She described Cody as the kindest and most lovable man she had ever met.

The same year, the United States entered the First World War, and Annie telegraphed the war secretary to offer her services in recruiting a regiment of female shooters to help America win the war. She never got a reply, and the regiment was never compiled. Instead, Annie organized shooting demonstrations to raise money at army camps across the country.

The next year, the Allies won the war, and Annie joined the celebration. Four years later, in 1922, Annie joined a charity event on Long Island to help collect money for wounded soldiers. Although she was already sixty-two years old, Annie could still shoot like the legend she had been all her life. However, this was one of the last times she would shoot a firearm.

*Annie Oakley, 1922. New York World-Telegram & Sun Collection*

That November, Annie had a car accident, and she injured her hip and ankle. She would wear a leg brace for the rest of her life. After the accident, Annie stopped shooting for good. In 1924, Frank and Annie moved to Dayton, Ohio. In 1926, Oakley's health began to decline sharply, and Frank and Annie decided to move to Greenville, where Annie died on November 3rd, 1926, only months after moving back. Frank and Annie had been married for fifty years. According to some sources, his love for Annie was so great that he stopped eating and died of starvation eighteen days after Annie passed.

The story of one of America's greatest sharpshooters ended where it had started, in Darke County, with a man who adored her since the day they met.

Less than ten years after her death, the first story about Annie Oakley's life emerged on the big screens. The movie was followed by a musical in 1946 called *Annie Get Your Gun*, with lyrics and music by Irving Berlin. The Broadway show was later made into a film and a TV show, and the musical has been revived numerous times since its initial run.

# Conclusion

The American frontier gave birth to dazzling shooting shows and romanticized life in the Wild West. In such a world, there was hardly any place for a woman. However, Annie Oakley managed to make a name for herself and became nothing less than one of the most famous figures on the sharpshooting scene. Although she was not born on the frontier, Annie became a legend herself, and she is immortalized even a century later as one of the best female shooters the world has ever seen.

During her fifty-year-long career, Annie dazzled and awed various audiences around Europe and America and became a symbol of the Wild West. Not only did she win the hearts of people with her shooting skill and talent, but she also stole attention with her unique appearance and flawless sense for performance and comedy.

Due to her steady hand and steady eye, Annie Oakley will most likely always be remembered as one of the greatest, and perhaps unsuspected, folklore heroines of the Wild West.

# Part 7: Jesse James

*A Captivating Guide to a Wild West Outlaw Who Robbed Trains, Banks, and Stagecoaches across the Midwestern United States*

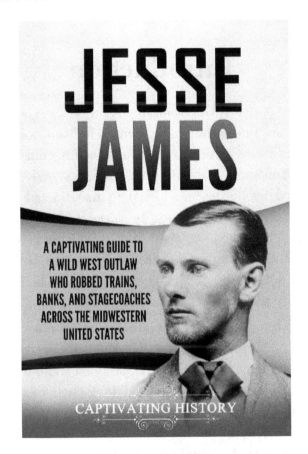

# Introduction

In the minds of many Americans, the name of Jesse James and the Wild West are practically synonymous. The bank robberies, with bullets flying from one side to the other of a dusty little town of the American frontier; the daring train robberies, with locomotives being chased by horses and forced to make a halt only to be boarded by gentlemanly bandits; the spectacular escapes of horse riders camouflaged by long coats, firing two revolvers, one in each hand. All of these are episodes that correspond to the life of Jesse James, that notable son of Missouri. In this sense, he is a vital and representative part of American history and life.

Jesse James was a robber, a murderer, and a notorious outlaw, who carried as many weapons as he could. He could shoot with both hands while he held the reins of his horse in his teeth. He was an extremely popular man in his day, a phenomenon that he readily accepted because he was a person who craved attention. He supposedly gave part of his booty to the poor, although no evidence of this can be found except in folklore.

Frontiersmen like James, who has been regarded as a monster, a vigilante, a modern Robin Hood, and as the last rebel of the Civil War, have a special appeal in the American imagination. Had he been born a century later, we would probably know him with a different name, perhaps as one of the FBI's Most Wanted; his face would possibly appear on television next to the word "terrorist" because he chose targets with political statements in mind.

It is true that he was in it for the money, but the robberies of banks, trains, and other institutions had a political edge, and his deeds attracted the sympathy of many locals, who resented the domination of big business. The newspapers, especially in the editorials of his friend John Newman Edwards, glorified his deeds for a political purpose. To some, Jesse James was the voice of those who had been defeated in the Civil War, the necessary symbol of resistance and nonconformity, and the face of the "Lost Cause," which embodied the anger of the South. Journalist John Newman Edwards essentially created a Robin Hood out of a merciless robber.

Even in our time, when there is more information than in the days when Jesse James's adventures were spread by word of mouth, many still see him as more than a bandit. Perhaps the fascination with him derives from the fact that he was a bank and train robber. But he is also seen as a romantic figure from the Wild West, as someone who rebelled against larger, overwhelming forces, forces that still makes us feel insignificant and expendable today. Jesse challenged them all and scoffed at them while doing so.

There is, without a doubt, more than one way to see Jesse James. We just have to remember the words of late historian William A. Settle: "Badman or Robin Hood, take your choice! Whichever form of the legend you please, both are based in fact."

# Chapter 1 – A Boy Named Jesse

"We called him outlaw, and he was, but Fate made him so."

—John Newman Edwards

Jesse James was born in 1847 to a family on the American frontier. His parents were named Robert Sallee James and Zerelda. They were originally a couple from Kentucky who moved to Clay County, Missouri, five years before Jesse's birth. His father was a Baptist minister and a part of the so-called Second Great Awakening, a Protestant revival that swept the United States in the mid-1800s. His mother, Zerelda, was a tall, opinionated, and dominating woman. The couple met at a religious gathering and got married when she was only seventeen years old. They soon moved to the small town of Kearney in Clay County, Missouri, where they settled with the help of relatives. Jesse's father founded the Baptist temples of New Hope and Providence there.

The couple's first child was named Frank, who was followed by another boy named Robert, who died at a young age. Jesse Woodson James came next. Although he was too young to be fully aware of what he was seeing, in his early years, he must have witnessed his father fervently preaching from the pulpit of his small Baptist temple or seen members of his congregation experience states of fervor, piety, and even mass hysteria at camp meetings.

On one occasion, Jesse's father baptized sixty-four people in the river in a single day, without leaving the water once. This seems like an unlikely background for one of the most legendary bandits in the United States. The abilities of Robert James as a preacher must have been extraordinary, for, in a short time, he managed to convert the small log cabin that he inherited into a respectable temple, and he vastly increased the number of the faithful who attended his sermons.

Camp meetings were a religious phenomenon suited to the rural setting of frontier towns. Since the population density was low, this meant there were fewer churches, and people traveled long distances to have religious experiences at these meetings, which could last from four to seven days. The people sang hymns and listened to itinerant preachers of austere morals. In those places, some of the great religious hymns that persist to this day were created, in some cases spontaneously.

In 1847, the year Jesse was born, the war between Mexico and the United States came to an end. As a result of the conflict, the northern part of Mexico was absorbed by the United States as spoils of war. This fact had consequences for the James family. Just a year after the peace agreement, in which California became part of the American Union, the first reports of gold began to arrive. A real fever exploded amongst the Americans to go and get some of those riches. People heard the news of huge finds, of tales that one could find more gold than the fruit of a whole year's labor on a farm in a single day. Pastor James, even though his priority was to save souls, could not avoid temptation and left in 1851 for the West, although he also supposedly wanted to preach to the prospectors.

Four-year-old Jesse held onto his father's leg, begging him not to leave. Perhaps this was a presage for Zerelda, who knew that day that she would never see her husband again. However, the pastor expected to get rich and return with enough money for his family. Sadly, Zerelda's premonition would come true. Instead of seeing her man return laden with gold, Zerelda opened the door to strange, grave-faced men, who broke the news that her husband had died of cholera in the Wild West. Jesse's father had not survived more than one month in California.

For the family, this was the beginning of great difficulties, especially since, according to the legislation of the time, the widow did not automatically inherit the farm. The creditors threw themselves on her, expecting to collect the debt by auctioning off her properties. The three small children went to live with relatives. After a while, in 1852, Zerelda married again to a man named Benjamin Simms. This marriage was not lucky either, as the man also died, leaving Zerelda widowed a second time. Remembered as a tall, strong-willed woman who was resistant to adversity, Zerelda was unwilling to see her three young children—Frank, James, and baby Susan—starve to death. She married a third time, this time to a man younger than her. His name was Dr. Reuben Samuels, and Zerelda managed to convince him to give up medicine and dedicate himself to farm work. The small property finally began to flourish again. The family hired temporary workers, but the farm prospered thanks to the work of seven black slaves that they owned. Jesse and his brother James attended school when they could, but they spent most of their time working on the farm, riding horses, and learning to shoot a gun.

According to a writer of the time, young Jesse had a face as smooth and as innocent as the face of a schoolgirl, with piercing blue eyes and a delicate figure. He and his brother Frank had everything to live a good life. Their lives in rural Missouri were pleasant and tranquil, but that was about to change.

## The Civil War

After swallowing half of Mexico, the United States almost doubled in size, but indigestion followed soon after. The 1850s were marked by division over the issue of slavery. Both Missouri and the adjacent territories of Kansas and Nebraska were being settled by people who were both for and against slavery. The topic divided families and neighbors.

Tempers grew hot, and violence arose between both sides, first verbal, then physical. The region became a red-hot war zone. Many locals formed guerrilla bands to attack anti-slavery towns in neighboring Kansas. Missouri was flooded with spies, guerrillas, and militias who were for and against secession. These armed men not only fought among themselves, but they also harassed and killed civilians.

In 1861, the Civil War began in the United States, whose fire was fueled by the social division around slavery. The issue disunited Missourians too. Although the state remained loyal to the Union, many families wanted to belong to the South, so they formed resistance groups called bushwhackers. In 1861, eighteen-year-old Frank James, Jesse's older brother, went to fight with the Missouri State Guard. Jesse was fifteen and still too young to fight with the State Guard or the bushwhackers, who had no formal connection with the Confederate Army but were still doing their best to create chaos among the Union ranks.

Jesse's mother had a clear pro-slavery stance. The abolitionists detested her because she was very vocal about her sympathies for the Southern cause and because of her strong and determined personality that agitated many People. Zerelda and Dr. Samuels also had a financial motive. The operation of their farm depended on the slaves. Besides, many slaveholders had formed strong bonds with their slaves, which they considered to be almost as strong as family ties. Of course, they could not understand that in order for the bond to be genuine, it had to be accepted by both sides.

Zerelda railed against the Union, and she served as a spy for the rebels and fed the guerrillas, of which her eldest son Frank was a militant. The guerrillas robbed civilians and killed their war prisoners. One day in June 1863, a party of armed men belonging to the Union arrived at the farm of Dr. Samuels and his wife, Zerelda. They entered violently, demanding the woman tell them the whereabouts of William Quantrill, who was the leader of the guerilla forces in Missouri.

Sixteen-year-old Jesse James was plowing with his stepfather when the gunmen broke in. They violently dragged Dr. Samuels to a tree on the property. After pulling out a rope, they hung the doctor from one of the branches until he was almost dead. They brought him down, and after reviving him, they demanded that he reveal Quantrill's whereabouts, but the doctor swore that he did not know. Unconvinced by the answer, they hung him again, while others dragged young Jesse through the tobacco fields and whipped him with a rope before forcing him to watch his stepfather being hanged. They also pointed a gun at his mother, who was pregnant at the time. The men threatened to kill the doctor if his wife did not say what she knew. "What I know, I will die knowing" was the answer that Zerelda's grandson recorded in his memoirs, which he wrote when Zerelda was still living. Then Zerelda asked the men what they intended to do with her husband. "We're going to kill him and let the hogs eat him," they told her. Zerelda then heard several gunshots.

Zerelda thought she had become a widow again, but the men had only taken Dr. Samuels away. Under brutal pressure, he finally revealed what the soldiers wanted to know. It was that or lose his life. The mistreated Jesse went to his mother and showed her the stripes on his back. Zerelda wept at the sight of the bruises, but her son told her she shouldn't cry. "Ma, don't you cry. I'll not stand this again." He then expressed his resolution to join Quantrill and his guerrilla. "But they have stolen all the horses, and you have no money," said his mother. In the spring of 1864, Jesse parted with the guerrilla in a unit led by one of Quantrill's men, "Bloody" Bill Anderson, who was one of the fiercest men in one of the bloodiest wars on the continent.

\* \* \*

Being part of "Bloody" Bill Anderson's gang surely had a crushing effect on an angry and hurt young man like Jesse. William

Anderson, a man that looked like a pirate, had also seen his father mistreated and murdered by a judge. "Bloody" Bill Anderson killed his father's assassin and became a fugitive, storming the roads. Two of his sisters died while under arrest, and Bill vowed revenge. His methods were inhuman. He never took prisoners, and he let his men mutilate and behead their victims to such an extent that many historians consider him a psychopathic and sadistic murderer. The adolescent Jesse James participated in the massacres, and the guerrillas also looted towns, stole liquor, and executed unarmed Union soldiers. Sometimes they even scalped them—such was the brutality of the war on the frontier. Jesse also learned how to ride a horse, as well as how to use both hands to shoot while controlling his mount by holding the reins with his teeth. He also earned the nickname "Dingus" among his fellow guerrillas, supposedly because that was what he furiously yelled when he accidentally blew off a piece of his finger from his left hand.

On July 10th, 1864, the guerrillas raided the city of Platte City, Missouri. Jesse was among the forty men who entered the city. The town surrendered without a fight, and the men defending it took the oath to serve the Confederacy. Two days later, the *New York Times* reported, "All of the arms were brought out and turned over to the raiders. With scarcely an exception, they were welcomed with open arms; a rebel flag was hoisted; the women of the place, old and young, immediately set to work making rebel flags as emblems for their horses and badges to be worn in their hats." This was not a famous battle of the Civil War or a heinous date remembering a massacre, but according to some sources, it was here in Platte City, on this date, that sixteen-year-old Jesse James had his most famous picture taken. The image shows the young teenager in a typical bushwhacker shirt, looking like a juvenile pirate, with a long revolver in his hand.

## The Carnage of Centralia

In September of that year, pro-Confederate fighters looted the small town of Centralia, burned the railroad station, and then brutally executed twenty-four Union soldiers who had just arrived on the train. The soldiers were young, unprepared, and unarmed. The guerrillas pulled them off the wagons, stripped them naked to keep their uniforms as disguises, then shot them point-blank one by one. The guerrillas proceeded to mutilate the bodies and scalp some of them. It was one of the bloodiest acts of the Civil War, and Jesse was part of it. Some horrified civilians protested only to get killed too. According to Frank James, Jesse killed his first man here, a man named Major Johnston. It would be the first in a long list.

Seeking to punish the guilty, a task force led by Major Andrew B. E. Johnston went with 150 men after them. But the decision was catastrophic. A small detachment of guerrillas ambushed them at the top of a hill. The enemy approached them from all sides and massacred every man. Some of them begged for mercy only to be tortured until death. Then, completely mad with the smell of blood, the bushwhackers beheaded every soldier that lay on the hill. When the Union troops arrived at the site, they were beyond words at the sight of the mutilated bodies. Scattered decapitated heads greeted the incoming soldiers with horrified expressions, and some heads even had their own private parts stuck in their mouths. One can only wonder what doing and seeing this did to the psyche of the young Missourian. Certainly, a normal life was out of the question for any of the men from that day on.

# Chapter 2 – Back Home

"Proscribed, hunted, shot, driven away from among his people, a price put upon his head—what else could the man do, with such a nature, except what he did do? He had to live. It was his country. The graves of his kindred were there. He refused to be banished from his birthright, and when he was hunted, he turned savagely about and hunted his hunters."

–John N. Edwards

In 1865, with the triumph of the Union, the Civil War came to an end. More than 600,000 people perished, but in many places like Missouri, no one believed that the war was really over. The resentment and violence did not end overnight. Although the Confederate Army surrendered, many bushwhackers were still active in the field, wishing for revenge. For the United States, it would be the beginning of a long road to reconciliation, and it would not be an easy one.

Jesse had escaped to Texas with seventy other bushwhackers. When he learned that the defeated Southern soldiers were allowed to return to their homes and farms, he went back to Missouri in June of that year. In July, his brother Frank voluntarily surrendered to the Union. Their mother, Zerelda, had been arrested during that difficult period in which the animosity between factions was still red-hot. When Jesse James's gang arrived in Missouri and found out about General Robert E. Lee's surrender, they said it was surely a Yankee lie. Along the way, they committed atrocities disguised as Union soldiers. They looted towns, and James even cold-bloodedly murdered the Kingsville postmaster.

However, the truth is that they were debating between giving up, accepting the offer to return home in peace, or continuing to terrorize and fight. More and more rebels were embracing the amnesty and taking the oath of allegiance to the Union, swearing that they would not commit acts of rebellion so they could go back to their families. But many of them were also penniless, their property mortgaged.

As Jesse and other men approached Lexington, a squad of cavalrymen opened fire on them. The order of events in this unfortunate event is unclear. According to one version, the men approached in peace, waving a white flag, and the Union soldiers fired when they saw them because they knew they were former guerrillas. According to a witness that recalled the scene twenty years later, the Union soldiers had only approached the gang to escort them, but the guerrillas' nerves wavered, causing some to flee. This led an inexperienced soldier to open fire amid the confusion. James himself later narrated that he was going to Lexington to take the amnesty. Whatever it was, the moment was decisive for the genesis of the bandit.

In the skirmish, a projectile penetrated Jesse's chest and became lodged in his lung. While he was being pursued by two men on horseback, he turned to kill one of the horses and barely escaped into the woods, where he lay by the water all night. The next day, a farmer found him and dragged him to his house.

Jesse could barely walk, but with the help of one of his former comrades, he managed to reach a hotel room, where they took the oath of allegiance to the Union and surrendered. But the danger of death had not passed, as the bullet was still in his lung. Jesse made it to Nebraska, where his mother had moved. He was so close to death that Zerelda would put her ear to his chest just to see if his heart was still beating. The remainder of his convalescence was spent at his uncle John Mimms's home in the village of Harlem, where his cousin Zerelda (who was named after his mother) nursed him. The cousins fell in love. "Ma, I am going to marry Zee," he told Zerelda when he recovered. Jesse got baptized and joined the Baptist church. But holiness and marriage weren't really in his plans.

### The Clay County Savings Bank

The bullet stayed in Jesse's lung his entire life, but the ex-combatant recovered. As soon as he was healed, he joined a new group of former guerrillas. But the raison d'être of the bushwhackers had vanished. As in many other wars in other countries, peace did not come without difficulties. The most pressing question was what would happen to the hordes of armed, angry young men like Frank and Jesse. All they knew was how to shoot a gun, fight, and lead desperate lives. The brothers would not accept defeat and go back to the simple farming life.

Jesse joined Archie Clement's gang—a pro-Confederate ex-guerrilla remembered for his cruelty—with the idea of robbing banks. Banks weren't simply the places where people saved their money. Many saw them as Northern instruments of control, as places that mortgaged the properties of farmers who could not pay their interest. In other words, they were instruments of oppression. The Clay County Bank, which was located where many ex-guerrillas like Jesse James lived, was probably the first daylight bank robbery in the United States, a scene that would become common in the years to come.

February 13th, 1866, seemed like a normal day inside the Clay County Savings Bank. At two o'clock in the afternoon, the main teller, a man named Bird, was working when two men approached the counter, put a ten-dollar bill on the desk, and asked him to change it for them. Bird's son approached to assist the strangers when he realized they had guns. One of them jumped over the counter, threatened the young man, and ordered him to go to the vault and put the money inside a cotton sack. The young Bird began to fill the sack with bags of gold coins, while another bandit threatened his father with a revolver.

When the cashier's son finished, Mr. Bird was taken inside the vault. The two bandits left the bank to meet the rest of the gang. In a few seconds, they had managed to seize almost $60,000—nearly a million dollars in today's money. At that moment, Bird appeared, as the thieves had forgotten to close the door to the vault. The exasperated cashier began to shout that the bank had been robbed. A dozen outlaws fled down the street, firing their pistols into the air, while a party was organized to follow them. Within days, posters were hung on the street, offering a reward. It has not been possible to establish with absolute certainty that Frank and Jesse James were among the dozen men who galloped down the street, shooting at the bewildered inhabitants of Liberty. However, it is a fact that they belonged to the former men of "Bloody" Bill Anderson, who had been captured and executed by the commander of the Union, Samuel P. Cox, in 1864.

At the end of 1866, the gang entered another bank in Lexington, Missouri. They approached the teller, who managed to close the vault just in time, and the bandits left the town empty-handed. They had much greater luck in the spectacular December robbery in Richmond, Missouri. The clan gathered outside the Hughes & Mason Bank, but the neighbors became suspicious when two of the strangers stepped inside while the others waited outside. The inhabitants of Richmond approached the building, and after noticing that the men were hostile, they unleashed a shower of bullets on the bandits, who escaped after taking the money. The outlaws shot at the people as they tried to leave the town, killing the mayor of Richmond. They headed for the Crooked River, but a party of fifteen men was on their heels, firing their guns. So, Jesse and his band turned and shot their horses. They finally split up and escaped. In the following weeks, the indignant people of Richmond lynched several people that looked suspicious to them. After all, at a time when there were no insurance or bank bailouts, they knew that the thugs had taken their savings for good.

### Jesse James Becomes (In)Famous

Jesse James's gang began to set their sights beyond Missouri. Knowing that the alerted residents of their home state might be prepared to confront them in the event of another robbery, they decided to strike the next blow in Kentucky. There, they met an even more surprising reaction. In March 1868, brothers Frank and Jesse left the small town's hotel with at least five other bank robbers, after having planned the details of the job and buying horses and weapons in Russellville. One of them pretended to be a cattle buyer and went to check the bank before the big day. When the hour came, two other men did the usual trick. One entered the building, went to the counter, and asked the teller to change a bill for him. After losing his patience, the outlaw planted the mouth of his revolver on the head of the cashier, Nimrod Long, who ran bravely to the back door and began calling for help.

Several armed people rushed to defend the bank where their modest savings were deposited. Many came, some with buckets of water, as they thought the building was on fire. The James brothers and their henchmen fled with more than $12,000. The bank owner decided to hire a detective to hunt down the fugitives. Several of the robbers fell into the hands of the law. The James brothers, possibly feeling they should keep a low profile for a while, disappeared for a few months. Historians have speculated what became of Jesse for most of 1868 and 1869. Some believe that he was in New York, and others place him in California as a cowboy, working on his uncle's farm.

Jesse returned in a brutal way before the end of 1869 to launch his first solo robbery, accompanied by his brother Frank. At noon on December 7th, 1869, he got off his horse and headed inside the Daviess County Savings Association in Gallatin, Missouri, while his older brother waited outside. He headed to the back of the bank, where the teller was writing at his desk. The bandit repeated the trick: he produced a $100 note and asked it to be changed. As the cashier examined the paper to determine its value, Jesse pulled a huge revolver from his clothes and pronounced the death sentence of the terrified clerk. "Cox, this is my revenge." Then he shot him point-blank. Jesse was sure he had killed Major Samuel P. Cox, who was responsible for the death of "Bloody" Bill Anderson, whom Jesse considered a brother. Behind him, a lawyer, who had his office on the bank's premises, panicked and ran toward the exit. Reacting quickly, the bandit shot him twice. Before escaping, Jesse grabbed a suitcase from the bank.

The brothers had just left the bank when they heard the first shots behind them. The neighbors were ready to strike back. Jesse's horse jerked, and he fell from his saddle. He was dragged for several feet until he released his boot from the stirrup. When an alarmed Frank spotted him on the ground, he turned around and hoisted him onto his mount. They fled together, with the inhabitants of Daviess almost on their heels. When the brothers found Honey Creek and knew their tracks had been lost, and they opened the briefcase. There was not a dollar there—just worthless papers. But for Jesse, it had been a successful journey because he had killed Samuel P. Cox. He would be greatly surprised later when he found out that Cox was still alive and that the poor teller had been the owner and sole employee of the bank.

The news spread like wildfire. Jesse James started to become a well-known figure, feared by some, considered to be a brave and exciting fellow to others—thus began his curious transformation into a kind of folk hero. Anecdotes about his misdeeds when he stole people's savings circulated by word of mouth. In 1871, after convincing the cashier of the bank in Croydon, Iowa, to give him all the money in the safe, the fleeing gang approached a political rally that was taking place in the yard of the local Methodist church, where a politician was giving a speech to the community.

According to some testimonies, Jesse interrupted the attorney, Henry Clay Dean, and said that he needed to say something important. The speaker, a little impatient, asked him what it was. "Well, sir," said Jesse, "I reckon it's important enough. The fact is, Mr. Dean, some fellows have been over to the bank and tied up the cashier, and if you all ain't too busy you might ride over and untie him. I've got to be going." By the time the people reached the door of Ocobock Brothers Bank, the band was far from Croydon.

The gang members weren't always the same, especially since several months passed between the robberies. Some were arrested, others were killed, and some took advantage of the amnesty that the government offered them. Jesse established himself as the natural leader of the gang, which included the core members of Frank and the Younger brothers—Cole, Jim, John, and Bob.

# Chapter 3 – An Unlikely Ally

One might think the notorious outlaw savored his misdeeds because Jesse wrote elegant letters about his robberies to newspapers, in which some of them he claimed his innocence. After the unfortunate incident in Gallatin, where he confused and murdered the cashier, he wrote a letter to a Kansas City newspaper addressed to the governor, declaring to be guiltless and saying that he was certain that if he appeared in public, he would not have a fair trial. "I well know if I was to submit to an arrest, that I would be mobbed and hanged without a trial."

Although Jesse was a good reader, those well-written letters he sent to newspapers were not completely the product of his own mind. They were most certainly heavily edited or even wholly written by a helping hand, an unlikely ally, the aforementioned newspaper editor named John Newman Edwards, a former Confederate major and journalist with whom the highwayman befriended around this time.

John N. Edwards was born in Virginia, and he was eight years older than Jesse. He was a composer, but he had also worked as a printer and had been in the Civil War on the side of the Confederacy. He later settled in Missouri, where he became a newspaper editor and an advocate for the so-called "Lost Cause."

Edwards had a strange fascination about Jesse, one that bordered on enthusiasm and adoration. In Jesse, Edwards saw a symbol of the unconformity of the defeated. He also saw the opportunity to have a symbol for the South, an anti-hero. With this new symbol, Edwards hoped to achieve what the Confederates had not been able to accomplish with arms: to keep the rebellion alive. Therefore, Edwards served as a sort of PR man to the James brothers and their gang. "They come and go as silently as the leaves fall," he wrote. "They never boast. They have many names and many disguises. They speak low, are polite, deferential and accommodating. They do not kill save in stubborn self-defense. They have nothing in common with a murderer. They hate the highwayman and the coward. They are outlaws, but they are not criminals, no matter what prejudiced public opinion may declare."

Through his editorials, Edwards presented James as a good man who was simply rebelling against the big capitalists who had the working families of the South under their thumbs. Jesse James and his gang were waging war against the greed of the North, which was represented by the banks. "Fate made him so," Edwards wrote. He reported that Jesse wouldn't take money from ex-Confederate soldiers, nor from honest, working men. While some newspapers wrote about the robberies with disgust and outrageous adjectives, Edwards penned his articles as if he were reviewing an entertaining Wild West film. For example, when Jesse and his brother stormed the box office of the Industrial Exposition in Kansas City, Edwards wrote in the *Kansas City Times*, "It was a deed so high-handed, so diabolically daring and so utterly in contempt of fear that we are bound to admire go and revere its perpetrators for the very enormity of their outlawry." Thus, Jesse was, in Edwards's eyes, a working-class hero, a maverick rebel who enjoyed making the powerful mad. "With them, booty is but the second thought; the wild drama of the adventure first."

In the rural South, the bankers and the railroads were especially hated. The bankers confiscated the land of the peasants when they defaulted on their payments, and the railroads seized rich land for nothing to lay tracks. On top of everything, the government had raised taxes to finance the construction of more railroads. Knowing that a man from the South was kicking the giants—someone who, like them, had grown up on a farm—delighted ordinary people, even if they did not receive a part of the loot. Through his editorials, Edwards cultivated this image to perfection. "The war made them desperate guerrillas...they were men who could not be bullied who were too intrepid to be tyrannized...They were hunted, and they were human. They replied to proscription by defiance, ambushment by ambushment, musket shot by pistol shot, night attack by counter-attack, charge by counter-charge, and so will they do, desperately and with splendid heroism, until the end."

Jesse was self-conscious about his public image, and he liked to cultivate it. On one occasion, for example, during a coach robbery, Jesse announced that he would inspect the hands of all passengers. If anyone had hard and callused hands, a sign that they were working men, he would respect them and leave their items alone. According to him, he also refrained from robbing ex-Confederate soldiers. On another occasion, when he was leaving a bank, he left a letter with a description of the events and a blank line for the cashier to fill in with the total amount stolen by the gang. The letter was possibly written by Edwards. Someone with Jesse's precarious formal education could hardly have written, "We are not thieves, we are bold robbers. I am proud of the name, for Alexander the Great was a bold robber, and Julius Caesar, and Napoleon Bonaparte."

In 1877, Edwards published his controversial book, *Noted guerrillas, Or, The warfare of the Border*, where he recounted the lives of former Confederates turned bandits as if they were heroes. The book justified the misdeeds of people like Quantrill, Bill Anderson, and, of course, brothers Frank and Jesse, about whom he said, "Since 1865 it has been pretty much one eternal ambush for these two men, one unbroken and eternal hunt twelve years long...By some intelligent people they are regarded as myths; by others as in league with the devil. They are neither, but they are uncommon men. Neither touches whiskey. Neither travels twice the same road."

But how much of the brothers' activity was motivated by greed, and how much was political spectacle? Although they never put their activism or supposed chivalry above monetary interest, the truth is that Jesse James became aware of his public persona and used it to promote the "Lost Cause." After yet another bank break-in but before making himself scarce, he shot into the air, shouting hurrahs for former Confederate generals.

### A "Mobile Bank"

So, while Edwards was dedicated to turning Jesse into a mythical figure, a kind of lovable anti-hero, Jesse was busy diversifying his criminal activities. With each new job, Jesse and his brother became more ambitious and confident, thanks to the support of the people. If only he could find banks far enough from the town's main street so as not to be seen and hunted by neighbors, a bank far from lawmen. It would be even better if that bank went away after they robbed it and to walk off with more than the meager savings of villagers. As incredible as it may seem, there were vaults with those characteristics, a vault that was more profitable, safer for the gang, and certainly more exciting: trains.

During those years, there had been an expansion in the construction of railways. For many in the South and frontier towns, the trains were a symbol of the economic and political dominance of the North and corporations affiliated to the Republican Party. Taxes had been increased for their construction. Besides, rail lines transported much larger riches than what modest banks could hold in their safes. In 1848, gold had been discovered in California, and large shipments were carried from the West to safe vaults on the East Coast. Besides, as T. J. Stiles wrote, "all year long, physical stocks of money moved toward New York, to return in the fall to the spawning grounds in the countryside. And it all went by rail." In other words, trains were the ideal victims.

The robbery of the Chicago, Rock Island and Pacific Railroad in July 1873 was spectacular; it produced headlines across the country, and the size of the felony left more than one commentator speechless. Although railroad robberies had occurred before, this was the first armed occupation of a train at the hands of a hostile party. The site was carefully chosen. The gang decided to strike a section of the track where the tracks curved, meaning the train had to reduce its speed. It was far from any town and near a bridge; it was the ideal place to attack and disappear in less than fifteen minutes. The band waited in hiding, about fifty feet from the track. When they heard the sound of the locomotive, they bent the rails out of place with a cord. The engine driver watched the intrusion and desperately tried to stop the vehicle without success. The train passed over the wrecked track, and the locomotive toppled over, although the rest of the train was unharmed. The assailants opened fire on any window where a face appeared.

One of the assailants boarded the second wagon, where the transcontinental express shipment and some gold was supposedly stored. Jesse approached the company employee guarding the shipment and took off his mask. Later, witnesses reported, "The man who seemed to be the leader...light hair, blue eyes, heavy sandy whiskers, broad shoulders and a straight, tolerably short nose, a little turned up; a tolerably high, broad forehead, intelligent looking, looked like a tolerably well educated man and did not look like a working man." That was, without a doubt, the legendary Jesse James. He demanded the man to open the safe or else. Meanwhile, in the passenger cars, other bandits walked through the corridors, looking at the terrified faces of the gentlemen and hearing the sobs of the women. "We're none of your petty thieves; we're bold robbers," they said, with their guns in the air. "We're robbing the rich for the poor. We don't want to hurt you; we're going through the express car." They wore masks like the Ku-Klux Klan. Both their speech and the masks were clear political statements. Other sources claim that the men actually robbed the passengers, probably after they learned there was no gold in the safe. With their task done, the men climbed onto their horses and fled with less than $3,000 and no gold, far less than they expected. The next day, they would learn from the newspapers that the gold shipment they had hoped to steal had been shipped the night before.

It was the first train robbery west of the Mississippi, and it basically amounted to a military occupation of the vehicle. Suddenly, James became a national figure; some saw him as a dangerous thug, while others realized he was an improbable hero that capitalized on "Missouri's rage against the railroads." If anything, the nation was flabbergasted. The event made headlines across the United States. A $5,000 reward was offered by the railroad company, but the "gentlemanly" robbers escaped unharmed. To hunt them down, the company hired the Pinkerton National Detective Agency of Chicago. The agency had been founded in 1850 by a Scottish spy named Allan Pinkerton. Pinkerton proved his credentials when he discovered a plot to assassinate President Abraham Lincoln. When the famous agency was hired in 1874 to hunt down the James and Younger brothers, its founder would take that mission as a personal matter.

# Chapter 4 – Northfield: A Watershed

"They wouldn't let me stay at home, so what else can I do?"

—Jesse James, on his life as a bandit after the Civil War

The brothers disappeared in the months that followed the famous train robbery. They were fed and protected by locals who thought they were still championing the cause of the South. During these months, Jesse's admirer, journalist John Newman Edwards, perfected Jesse's larger than life figure and turned him into almost a hero.

In April 1874, Jesse married his long-time girlfriend and first cousin Zee James after ten years of romance. The ceremony was at the house of Zee's sister, and her uncle, a Methodist minister, presided. The wedding was almost perfect, except for a cop alarm in the middle of the ceremony. All the guests ran for cover, and after realizing the cops weren't actually there, the wedding resumed. Edwards ran a humorous editorial: "CAPTURED! The Celebrated Jesse W. James Taken at Last. His Captor a Woman, Young, Accomplished, and Beautiful." The couple apparently honeymooned in Texas at the beaches of Galveston, where Jesse might have been spotted by a reporter of the *St. Louis Dispatch*, as he claimed to have seen the famous outlaw. Always with work in mind, Jesse apparently robbed a few stagecoaches during the honeymoon. However, as with many other things about Jesse, it's sometimes hard to tell fact from legend.

A year later, the couple saw the birth of their first son, Jesse Edward. There would be no peace for their marriage, as Pinkerton continued to hunt Jesse, his most coveted prey, in inept and dirty ways. A few months after the wedding, the detectives of the agency, called the Pinkertons, thought they could hunt him down at his house, and to that end, they surrounded Dr. Samuels's farm. During the night, they decided to set fire to the building with an artifact, which they threw through the window. This item was an "iron ball surrounded by kerosene-soaked cotton." Unfortunately, the device ended up in the family's chimney, where it exploded. The metal fragments killed Jesse's half-brother, a son of Samuels, and shattered his mother's arm. The agents panicked and escaped. The press was sympathetic to the brothers and attacked the Pinkertons mercilessly. Indignant over the events that had transpired, Jesse made a vow to go after the main detective and take revenge. According to Jesse himself, he found Allan Pinkerton in Chicago and had many chances to kill him, but he ended up going back to Missouri with his thirst for vengeance unquenched. "I had a dozen chances to kill him when he didn't know it. It wouldn't do me no good if I couldn't tell him about it before he died. I want him to know who did it."

### A Disaster in Northfield

Despite the pleas of his wife, Jesse continued his career as a bandit with even more determination. In July 1876, he robbed another train, where a traveling minister made passengers sing religious hymns while the bandits stripped them of their watches, chains, and money; it must have been a very surrealistic scene indeed. "If you see the Pinkertons, tell them to come and get us," they shouted before they left the train.

It seemed that a life of thievery would continue without end for the brothers, especially since they were in the public's favor. Jesse James was a myth among the common folk. Although he had a few setbacks—attacking targets that, in the end, did not reward him with the amounts he expected—he had robbed banks, trains, and coaches with impunity and had escaped from bullets and ruthless detectives. And Jesse had played these games while feeling like a celebrity—one of Jesse's victims even thanked him for distinguishing them with the honor of being assaulted by the famous robber himself. On top of everything, Jesse could read his exploits in the papers as if they were an adventure novel by Karl May. But attitudes were changing, and in the unimportant town of Northfield, the tables started to turn against the gang. It seemed as if Jesse's immense reserves of luck had been depleted.

Northfield was a peaceful and orderly farming community with a single bank, where the savings of the hard-working mill town of 2,000 inhabitants were kept. Jesse expected to secure one of the biggest heists of his career, close to $75,000. It was September 1876, and the money from the freshly harvested crops would be in the vault. Not everyone in the gang agreed. Some were beginning to yearn for a quiet life with their girlfriends, who would hopefully become their wives, and to dedicate themselves to raising cattle.

Perhaps the comrades of the James brothers agreed to this one last job before reforming their lives. The plan took several weeks to materialize. The band traveled to Minnesota separately, meeting in agreed-upon towns, spending days in hotels, drinking and playing poker, and then moving on. Closer to Northfield, they bought horses and trained them to learn not to fear the noise of gunfire. Meanwhile, the bandits began making separate peaceful raids into Northfield, wearing their long coats, with their guns hidden under their linen dusters. They studied escape routes, searched for hiding places, and talked to the inhabitants, pretending to be ranchers interested in purchasing a piece of land. Come the day, they would be stationed in three different places: three on the edge of the town, two outside First National Bank, and three would commit the robbery. In case of trouble, the three men guarding outside Northfield would gallop in and fire their pistols to scare people off. After the break-in, they would meet in the town of Rochester, where they would separate again and return to the safety of Missouri. Nothing could go wrong.

At two o'clock in the afternoon, Jesse and two accomplices approached the bank. They dismounted to have breakfast peacefully—ham and four eggs each—at J. G. Jeft's Restaurant, where they chatted with the owner like any other patron. They immediately went to the bank, while the other group, consisting of two bandits, took up their positions in front of the building. When Jesse and the other man stepped inside, the accomplices locked the door and stood guard. But after this point, the plan began to fall apart.

The owner of the town's hardware store tried to enter the bank to do some business, but one of the bandits stopped him and told him to go away. A few steps away, a young medical student named Henry Wheeler, who was in the town on vacation, witnessed this suspicious interaction and ran to the bank, but he stopped at the sight of a huge revolver between his eyes.

Undaunted, he ran back to get a gun and climbed to the upper floor of a building, from where he began shooting at the robbers. In the meantime, the store owner ran through the street, screaming, "Get your guns, they're robbing the bank!" The two outlaws started to fire their pistols in the air to intimidate the people, but it looked as if the entire town had been waiting for such an occasion to use their guns. After all, it was hunting season. The inhabitants of Northfield rushed for their arms and began to pull their triggers at First National Bank, while the two desperate bandits awaited the help of those on the outskirts of town. Sure enough, when they heard the gunfire, they hastily rode from their positions to help their comrades get out of there. The church bells rang. Even the girls from the nearby Carleton College each took an ax, ready to put up a fight if necessary. Some inhabitants threw stones. The men of Jesse's band started to drop dead or fell from the injuries they sustained under the heavy fire.

But what was happening inside the bank? The men inside were meeting their own nightmare, as they had been obstructed with fierce resistance. After they drew their revolvers from under their clothes and demanded to see the vault, the cashier tried to trap one robber inside. The teller had run from his chair and closed the heavy door, but he failed and was punished for his actions. Still resisting, the brave bank employee refused to open the safe, falsely claiming that it had a time lock. He held firm to this, even though he had a gun on his temple and a superficial cut in his throat. Another clerk, surnamed Bunker, ran to the rear exit and into the alley. One of the bandits shot him but missed hitting his vital organs. The young man reached the street, screaming for help, while Jesse and his two companions heard their desperate partners urging them out. "Better get out, boys, they're killing us!" Furious, Jesse James ran over to the cashier, who was lying helplessly on the floor. He must have thought it was all over, that the men had given up. Sadly, it was over for him as well, for Jesse shot him in the head.

Outside, Jesse saw that the street had become a battleground. The bandits were shooting from behind some wooden boxes, but they were being battered by the people of Northfield. One of the gang members, Stiles, lay dead. Frank had been hit in the leg, and the elbow of one of the Younger brothers had been shattered by a gunshot. The bank robbers fled toward the river, through streets littered with broken window glass, as they dodged the bullets. Cole Younger bravely returned to pick up his brother, who was lying on the ground, and he galloped after his cronies, who were heading toward the Cannon River. But it had not ended. The bold inhabitants of Northfield rushed to their horses to pursue the gang and, hopefully, bring it to an end once and for all. In their haste to flee, the six surviving members forgot to cut the telegraph lines, and soon the entire region was alerted, unleashing the most intense manhunt ever known in the state and even the country. And the gang had only taken $26.60 from the bank. The following days would be the most challenging for Jesse James and his men, as they were wounded and unable to seek refuge.

### A Narrow Escape

Battered, wounded, and with two partners dead, the gang wandered the countryside for days, mostly on foot, under cold, eternal rain. Jesse wanted to leave the wounded because of the blood trail they were leaving and the fact they were slowing the others down. Jesse knew that by carrying the wounded with them, they had a higher risk of being captured by the great manhunt that had been organized after the Northfield fiasco. It was probably for this reason that a bitter argument broke out among the members of the band. In the end, they decided to separate and form two groups. Jesse and Frank stuck together, while the rest went the other way. This proved to be a stroke of luck for the James brothers. When the Younger brothers and their posse stopped at a farm to ask for lodging, they were recognized by the farmer's son, who rode eight miles to Madelia to inform the inhabitants that the famous outlaws were at his house.

After an intense shooting, in which one of the bank robbers was killed, the Younger brothers were captured and arrested. They were practically dead themselves. One of them had eleven gunshot wounds in his body. In the meantime, Jesse and Frank James were desperately crossing hostile territory, heading for Dakota. They avoided any human being, stole food from the fields to survive, and made it through the harsh autumn weather. But they survived. "In every way," one of their pursuers later remembered, "they were masters of the situation. Their bravery and their endurance on horseback for days and nights, wounded and almost starving, and without sleep, are without parallel in the history of crime." They made it to Kentucky and then to Texas, where they crossed the border to spend some months in Mexico. This time in their lives is mysterious, as little is known, meaning legend is interwoven with history.

### In Old Mexico

In a town near Matamoros, on the border between the US and Mexico, the town's holiday was being celebrated. There was a very crowded dance when two dirty, bearded Americans suddenly entered, dusty after several days of riding. The reigning happy mood seemed to infect them, and they decided to participate in the festivity and asked a couple of Mexican girls to dance.

Amused, the young women accepted the invitation, trying not to laugh as they turned their faces away so as not to smell the unpleasant odor of the strangers and avoided their clumsy dance steps. Little by little, the girls' giggles grew louder until the whole party erupted into a torrent of laughter at the sight of the inept dancers. Infuriated, one of the Americans punched one of the unkind Mexicans, while his partner drew his pistol to kill another. There was then a devilish confusion that the strangers took advantage of to flee, leaving five dead and several wounded on the dance floor. Jesse and Frank James, the legendary American gunmen, had staged the first of a long series of bloody episodes in Mexico.

Toward the beginning of 1877, the brothers appeared in the north of the state of Chihuahua, near a mining town. They had settled in a ranch and won the confidence of the people. One morning in May, six packs of mules passed by, carrying seventy-five kilos of silver bars each, guarded by a detachment of eighteen men with pistols. Jesse, Frank, and three criminals who had joined them asked the muleteers to let them accompany them since the route to Chihuahua was infested with hostile Native Americans. The chief of the muleteers agreed, thinking that the journey would be safer if his group was more numerous.

On the fifth day, the caravan, exhausted from fatigue, fell asleep. Only two remained on guard. The James brothers and their gang treacherously murdered them silently. Then they disarmed the rest of the muleteers and tied them to some trees.

In Piedras Negras, Coahuila, they were assaulted by a band of Mexican bandits. In the resulting shooting, Jesse suffered a wound to his arm. The James brothers then rode to Monclova, where they met a former bandit who had once worked with them in William C. Quantrill's gang. This former gang member had become a respectable businessman, and he was married to a Mexican woman. To celebrate their reunion, the old marauder threw a party at his house.

Between drinks, Jesse noticed that a lieutenant in the Mexican Army was staring at him. He discussed the matter with his brother, but Frank did not care. Soon after that, Jesse saw that his concerns were not unfounded. Peering out a window, he saw a group of soldiers surrounding the house. Suddenly, the besiegers slammed down the doors, and the officer ordered the James brothers to surrender.

"Let the women out first, and we'll fix it," Jesse suggested. The lieutenant accepted. He ordered the women to leave and announced, "There is no possibility of escape. Surrender your guns." But the James brothers fired back. They jumped out of a window, and under cover of darkness, they managed to escape back to Texas, where, according to legend, they served as vigilantes and liquidated a Mexican bandit named Bustendo, who was ravaging the region.

# Chapter 5 – A Man Named "Howard"

"They continued the war after the war ended; such, at first, was their declared purpose, and, in a measure, so executed. But as time passed on the war, even to them, was a thing of the past, but having imbued their natures in crime, they became the outlaws they now are."

—*Kansas City Times*, July 27th, 1881

Like a wounded beast, Jesse James remained out of the public eye for two years after Northfield, hoping that as time went by, the pressure would lessen and possibly erase the memory of his last failure, which had almost cost him his life and had effectively marked the end of his band. For years, Jesse lived incognito with his family, near Nashville, under another name: John Davis Howard. In 1878, his wife had twins, but they died shortly after birth. Although he posed as an honest farmer, whose passion seemed to be only horses and playing cards in his spare time, Jesse was constantly on the alert. One of his horses was saddled all the time; he carried revolvers and slept with a gun under his pillow. In contrast, his more refined brother Frank, who also lived incognito, seemed to be enjoying his new life. He made friends with his neighbors, attended church, and met up with his acquaintances to talk about Shakespeare. Frank even befriended the Nashville cops, while thirty-two-year-old Jesse languished and died of boredom.

Apparently, his career was over, but he was still restless. Legend says that during his last months as a "family man," he visited Las Vegas and met Billy the Kid. Supposedly, the two famous outlaws discussed the possibility of joining forces. However, according to Jesse's biographer T. J. Stiles, this is "a very questionable account.". In 1879, Jesse finally gathered people to form a new gang. But there was an important difference. This was no brotherly band made of ex-guerrillas and idealist fighters. The recruits were much younger, greedier, and harder to handle. Among them was a new pair of brothers, Robert (better known as Bob) and Charles (better known as Charley) Ford. But at least they decided to follow Jesse into this new chapter of his life, one that would be very short. Jesse stopped a train in Glendale, Missouri, and robbed the passengers with these words to the train messenger: "I didn't get your name, but mine is Jesse James." He was back, and he wanted everybody to know it.

However, things had changed. There was no sympathy in any newspaper after the robbery. There was no symbolism other than money-hungry bandits looking to score. There weren't even large amounts of money or gold in the wagons, which was a symbol of the new times when the country's banking system was consolidating—it was no longer necessary to physically transport bills and coins. The Civil War was beginning to become a distant memory in the minds of many people in and around Missouri, and there was no longer the same ardor for the "Lost Cause." Now James's assaults were no longer seen as those of an avenger against the greedy capitalists of the North but as the misdeeds of a dangerous criminal, one who was driving investment away from Missouri, thereby condemning its inhabitants to live in "the Outlaw's Paradise," as a newspaper of Chicago called it. The Democratic nominee in the 1880 campaign for governor, Thomas T. Crittenden, had personally battled guerrillas during the war. He based his campaign by promising the capture of Jesse James, and he even got the railroad companies to offer a reward of $10,000 for the outlaw, dead or alive, plus $10,000 for Frank James and lesser amounts for each one of his henchmen. Several bounty hunters claimed to have killed Jesse James, and many newspapers printed the news about his death, only to later retract it.

Jesse James, possibly the most wanted man alive at the moment, was guilty of overconfidence. Undaunted, he continued to plan new blows. Since they did not know what he looked like, he taunted his pursuers by approaching them in the street and then sending them notes telling them how and where he had seen them. He constantly changed his address, moving from Kentucky to Kansas, and then back to Missouri, where he settled in the town of St. Joseph, committing petty crimes: a coach of passengers, a store, a solitary horseman, and the payroll of a crew of workers, where, for one last time, Jesse showed his legendary Robin-Hood persona. When they robbed the month's payroll of an engineering crowd in Alabama, the bandit returned the money that belonged to the chief of the crew. "The robber inquired if the money was government money or my own money," the man later recalled. "I told them it was mine, meaning that it would form a part of my salary. The robber told me, he did not want it, neither did they take my watch. They said, they only wanted government money."

A year before his death, Jesse carried out his last big hit, one that wiped out what little popularity he had left. During a new train robbery, Jesse unintentionally killed the driver. He had been shooting at the roof of the wagons to intimidate the passengers, but a bullet hit the driver, who, it was learned later, had also been in charge of the train that took the Pinkertons to his farm the night his mother lost her arm and his half-brother died. Witnesses to the robbery agreed that the driver's death had been accidental, but the newspapers were quick to say that the bandit had murdered him in revenge. The search for Jesse James intensified on all fronts, and the pressure mounted. That his head had a price of $10,000, which was offered by the railroad companies, his old enemy, made Jesse furious, but at the same time, he was pleased to be back in the spotlight. He decided to try it one more time, not knowing it would be his last. Or maybe he did know. For the night of September 7th, 1881, Jesse James acted as if he knew it would be the last time.

After stopping the train by piling rocks on the track, Jesse's men boarded the cars, with their guns in the air, and began to strip the terrified passengers of their belongings. But Jesse seemed more eager to be remembered than to get money. When one of the drivers gave him a 50-cent coin, saying it was all he had, Jesse returned it with an extra dollar and said, "This is the principal and interest on your money." When a woman fainted, he wet her face with his handkerchief and gave her a dollar too. He quoted the Bible several times and said that since they were already wicked, they might as well be good at it. He shook hands with some passengers and introduced himself, saying, "Hello, my name is Jesse James." To the engineer, he handed two dollars and told him, "You're a good one; take this and spend it with the boys." Then, he said goodbye to the passengers before leaving the train and claiming prophetically, "This is the last time you will ever see Jesse James."

### Death

"Well it was Robert Ford,

that dirty little coward.

I wonder now how he feels,

for he ate of Jesse's bread

and he slept in Jesse's bed,

and he laid poor Jesse in his grave."

—*Jesse James*, author unknown

In the end, Governor Crittenden's plan worked. He believed Jesse's gang was now more about money and less about politics and revenge, so the temptation of an easy win could be the means of winning over one of the younger members of the gang. Ironically, it was the Ford brothers, whom Jesse trusted the most, who fell for the easy win and especially for the fame they would gain by bringing about the demise of a great legend. Bob Ford, who was only twenty at the time, contacted the authorities in Kansas City to speak with Crittenden.

Meanwhile, Jesse told the brothers he had a new job, and to plan the details, they moved into Jesse's house in St. Joseph. The robbery would take place on April 4th, 1882, in Platte City, Missouri. Bob and Charley were getting more and more nervous living in the house of the bandit they planned to kill. Jesse was quick with the gun, and any mistake would only spell a horrible death for the Fords. They would have to surprise him while he was unarmed, an impossible situation. But the opportunity came on the morning of April 3rd, after breakfast.

According to the Ford brothers, Jesse's wife was in the kitchen, the children were playing outside, and the notorious outlaw went to a painting on the wall to straighten or dust it off. Unusually for him, he took off his guns for a moment to climb onto a chair and move the painting. He placed his revolvers on a bed. Why he took his guns off has intrigued historians. It was unusual for him to lay down his guard for even a second, much less in the company of other men who could betray him. "He was so watchful that no man could get the drop on him," as his killer would go on to say later. Perhaps Jesse trusted the Ford brothers, or maybe he was trying to show them that he still trusted them so they would become easy targets after the next robbery. We can only speculate.

Bob Ford, who was standing behind Jesse, knew this was his chance. Approaching from behind, he drew his revolver and made a little click as he hammered his gun. Jesse began to turn around to see what was going on. Then Bob shot him in the head, and the most famous American bandit of all time fell to the floor, bleeding badly from his head. He was dying. His wife heard the gunshot from the kitchen and ran to see the scene. Crying, Zee desperately tried to stop the bleeding, but it was too late. Jesse died in her arms.

The brothers ran in fear, shocked by the magnitude of what they had done. From the modest house, they rushed to the telegraph office to send a statement to Governor Crittenden: I HAVE KILLED JESSE JAMES.

The news spread like burning powder. Within minutes, the James home in St. Joseph was packed with onlookers who had heard the incredible news. Here lay the man who had lived among them under a false name, the man they now knew was none other than Jesse James. Zee, his tearful wife, revealed his identity to the lawmen. His beard was dyed black, and he was less skinny than in his youth, but he was indeed the famous wanted man. This was confirmed more than a century later with a DNA test when his remains were exhumed in 1995, but well into the 20th century, many impersonators stepped forward, claiming to be Jesse James.

Frank James heard the sad news, but he did not attend the funeral for fear of arrest. For most of Missouri, it was good news. Months later, Frank turned himself in to Governor Crittenden, and he was accompanied by his friend, the journalist John Newman Edwards, who negotiated fair treatment with the authorities.

In a mock trial, Jesse James's murderers were sentenced to death by hanging, only to be pardoned by the governor, who then gave them a part of the reward. But history did not treat Bob Ford, the man who hoped to be a hero for killing Jesse James, well. After the bandit's death, the Ford brothers had to go into hiding because they feared being attacked by the public. Soon after, a song appeared about the adventures of the famous outlaw. Its author is unknown, as well as the year of its appearance in oral tradition. Popular lore glorified Jesse, turning him into a sort of Robin Hood, and repudiated his murderer. "Jesse was a man, a friend to the poor, he couldn't see a brother suffer pain, and with his brother Frank he robbed the Springfield bank, and he stopped the Glendale train." The song was performed in the streets, sometimes with different lyrics, according to the taste and creativity of the interpreter, and it was a quick success. Above all, it contributed to the glorification of Jesse James, who had spent more than half his life as an outlaw. It was his revenge on those who had done him wrong.

# Conclusion

For a long time, the murderer of Jesse James toured the country reenacting his deed in a popular play, which he always ended with the words "And this is how I killed Jesse James." But after a while, the novelty wore off. Most people, although they recognized that the death of the bank robber had been for the common good, saw Bob as a traitor and a viper. The truth is that Bob and Charley never slept soundly again, and life became intolerable for them. Charley committed suicide two years later, highly depressed after suffering from tuberculosis. Bob, who worked in circuses and Wild West shows, was shot down by a man hoping to be remembered for having shot the man who shot Jesse James. And then Bob Ford's name was forgotten, while the name of his victim, Jesse James, became legendary. Newspapers contacted all the living people who had known the most famous bank robber in the country, and they began to build upon the legend with the sometimes-fanciful material that people contributed. A large number of dime novels and books appeared about Jesse James's life as an outlaw. His brother Frank lived an honorable and quiet life for many years until his death in 1915. He died at the age of seventy-two.

People continued to visit the house where the rebel had died, as well as the farm where Frank and Jesse grew up. There, a mother in financial hardship received tourists and charged them a small fee for the tour, plus a little extra if the visitors wanted to take a souvenir, such as a sliver from the fence or a pebble from the ground. The visitors saw the places where Jesse and Frank had played, worked, slept, and been nursed by their mother, who never made apologies for her sons. "No mother ever had better sons," she used to say. This was the same woman who wrote a powerful epitaph for Jesse, who, sure enough, had been a ruthless, merciless executioner but also a symptom of social unrest. He was a so-called "social bandit," who represented the voice of the voiceless. He rests forever in Mount Olivet Cemetery, Missouri, under this epitaph:

In Loving Remembrance of My Beloved Son, Jesse W. James.

Died April 3, 1882.

Aged 34 Years, 6 Months, 28 Days.

Murdered by a Traitor and a Coward whose Name is Not Worthy to Appear Here.

# Part 8: Geronimo

*A Captivating Guide to One of the Most Well-Known Native Americans Who Was a Leader of the Apache Tribe and a Prominent Figure of the Wild West*

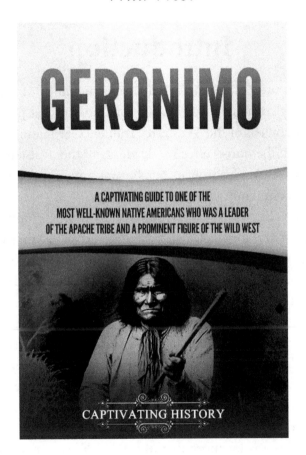

# Introduction

His name was Geronimo. And any mention of that name immediately conjures up images of the last gasp of Native American control of the Western Frontier. Geronimo, to be sure, was one of the most effective leaders in the resistance against America's westward advance, but he was much more than just a good field commander for the Apaches.

For even after the West was supposedly won, Geronimo proved more than ready to adapt. And when the Apache Wars came to a close, he was able to rebrand himself as an icon of Western Americana. In many instances, he actually got paid by the very ones who thought they had vanquished him, as Geronimo became a kind of celebrity, participating in Wild West shows in which he basically acted out what was his life—or at least what was perceived to be his life. But in reality, the real Geronimo was much more than an accomplished horseman riding the range. He was more than a marauder raiding hapless settlers. And he was more than a skilled marksman, medicine man, and shaman.

Geronimo was far more than the Wild West caricature that he was later made out to be; he was a real flesh and blood man who had real emotions, real hopes, and real dreams. He had a wife—actually wives—of his own, and he had children whom he dearly loved. For most, "family man" probably doesn't come to mind when gazing at the old black and white photos of Geronimo's grim visage, but he was a deeply dedicated husband and father.

As harsh and cruel as he was known to be on the battlefield, he could be just as kind and gentle when he was away from it. In this text, you will get the full picture of Geronimo: the good, the bad, and the downright incredible.

# Chapter 1 – The Days of His Youth

Although his birth year is not known for certain, it is believed to have been around 1829. He was a part of the Bedonkohe band of the Chiricahua tribe, which was a part of the larger Apache group, and his grandfather had been a chief. Growing up, Geronimo lived a relatively carefree life as a child, playing and roaming about his ancestral lands. As he neared adolescence, however, it became incumbent upon him to prove his worth as a man. For it was at this time that he entered into what was known as his "novice" period.

This was the point in time in which it was ingrained upon a young man from the Apache tribe to prove that they could hold their own. This meant learning how to hunt, fight, and ride a horse just like any other member of the tribe. It was during the course of this quest for manhood that Geronimo's father, Taslishim, introduced him to a tribal elder who instructed him how to build his own "sacred bow and arrows."

This was a rite of passage that enabled Geronimo to begin life as a full-fledged member of the tribe who could hunt wild game on his own. Along with hunting, he was also shown how to adapt to the harsh environment of the Apache homeland, which at that time stretched across the desert sands of the southwestern United States.

These lessons included endurance training, in which Geronimo would learn to survive without water and even improve his breathing.

To improve his breathing, he would be sent on long runs across the desert terrain during which he would purposefully keep his mouth closed so that he would be forced to inhale and exhale nasally, rather than orally. This was a technique that had been refined by the Apache for generations in order to teach adherents how to build up their lung capacity. In order to perfect the method, Geronimo himself would later recall how he would bite down on rocks he had placed in his mouth so that he was left with no choice but to inhale through his nasal passages.

Geronimo is thought to have been around ten years old when he was engrossed in these rigorous exercises, and by Apache standards, he was very successful in his efforts to transition from a young boy to a man. However, Geronimo wouldn't have long to celebrate this rite of passage before the abrupt death of his father, Taslishim.

With the death of his father, young Geronimo was officially considered the head of his household. Nevertheless, he still had to complete his training. With his father out of the picture, this important form of mentorship most likely fell upon the able shoulders of an uncle or a similar relative.

Under this tutelage, Geronimo further perfected his hunting skills, as well as his ability to ride a horse. Buffalo, deer, and pronghorn antelope were some of the real prizes during these forays out on the range, but turkeys and rabbits were acceptable fare as well. The hunt for turkeys, in particular, was a real sight to behold. It involved a band of Apache flushing out the birds and then relentlessly chasing them until the animals simply became too exhausted and gave up.

In the years after his father's passing, Geronimo became quite skilled at hunting all manner of wildlife. But the final trial that Geronimo needed to pass was not one that involved animals; instead, it involved people. The capstone experience of his Apache training would not rest on how well he hunted turkey and buffalo but rather how well he would perform in raiding settlements.

Although the Apache were skilled hunters and knew how to live off the land, a mainstay of their existence involved the launching of raiding parties against their rivals. Geronimo was seventeen years old when he went on his first raid. A special shaman accompanied Geronimo and the other initiates for their first raid and served as counsel during the course of the exercise.

Beforehand, he gave the young men special ceremonial clothing to wear, such as a special jacket and hat that were said to "protect men in battle." Along with this protective gear, the shaman also gave them prudent advice as to what they should expect during the raid. This was a make-or-break moment for Geronimo and his peers because if they proved to be ineffective during the raid, or, even worse, if they displayed cowardice, they would have the stigma of their failure follow them for the rest of their lives.

Those that displayed true courage and cunning, however, would be welcomed in as a full-fledged member of the tribe. Knowing the stakes, Geronimo carefully prepared for his first raid, making sure to follow every piece of advice that the shaman gave. Fortunately for Geronimo, he passed his test with flying colors. He was considered to have performed admirably during the course of the raid and therefore was made a full-fledged member of the tribe.

Geronimo would later recall just how proud he felt on this occasion. He would reflect, "I was very happy, for I could go wherever I wanted and do whatever I liked." As a full-fledged member of the tribe, Geronimo had the freedom to be his own man. He was a free agent on the Apache range, and very soon, he would become a free agent of his own destiny.

# Chapter 2 – Geronimo Comes into His Own

With his ascendency as a full member of the tribe assured, Geronimo was now able to take his official place as an Apache. This meant that he would marry and start a family of his own. The woman he chose hailed from the Nednhi tribe, and she was known by the name of Alope. Not much else is known about Alope, but she must have been greatly loved by her family since Geronimo paid them a large dowry in the form of numerous horses. These animals were most likely stolen from ranches in northern Mexico during subsequent Apache raids launched in the area.

After paying this dowry, Geronimo took Alope to be his wife. There was no wedding ceremony; instead, he simply set up his semi-nomadic dwelling, known as a wickiup, and invited Alope inside. This mobile home on the range already held all of Geronimo's hunting gear, such as knives, spears, and arrows. Alope did her best to spruce up their new place by adding beaded decorations and "wall paintings."

Geronimo was fond of his wife but always kept any mention of her fairly brief. He would later recall, "She was a good wife, but she was never strong. We followed the traditions of our fathers and were happy. Three children came to us—children that played, loitered, and worked as I had done." By this time, Geronimo was the head of a growing family, and his own personal renown was growing as well.

Geronimo had become an acknowledged veteran in the field, and in the dangerous world in which he lived, all of his finely honed skills would be necessary for the survival of himself, his family, and his tribe. By the time he was in his early twenties, Geronimo had taken part in several armed conflicts, primarily in Mexico. In the fall of 1846, in particular, Geronimo took part in a massive conflict with Mexican forces that involved around 175 Apaches.

The year 1846 was a pivotal one, as a war broke out between the United States and Mexico that very year due to a disagreement over the Mexico/Texas border. The war would end in 1848, with the Americans victorious and Mexico defeated. As a result of the American victory, Mexico was forced to sign the Treaty of Guadalupe Hidalgo, which ceded much of what today comprises the American Southwest to the United States.

After the end of the Mexican-American War, an exhausted Mexico, weary of fighting, developed a policy of appeasement when it came to the Apache by installing "feeding stations" at the edge of Apache territory. These were designated areas where food and supplies were left for the Apaches to pick up of their own accord. This was done in order to prevent them from conducting further raids in Mexican territory.

As long as they gave the Apache these handouts, it kept them from going on the warpath to take things by force. And for a while, the situation remained one of relative peace, and an official peace agreement between local Apache and Mexican authorities was entered into on June 24th, 1850. But a short time later, the Mexicans began to withdraw the feeding stations, and soon after, the Apache raids resumed.

This resurgent conflict would touch Geronimo far closer to home than he could have ever imagined, for it was in 1851 that disaster would strike. Geronimo and a small band of Apache warriors had left their wives and children camped out on the outskirts of Mexico while they went into a nearby town to trade. While he was gone, a Mexican militia stumbled upon Geronimo's camp and slaughtered the inhabitants.

A distraught Geronimo returned to find that his wife, his children, and even his mother had all been killed. Along with their deaths, he found that all of his supplies, arms, and food had been confiscated as well. This was certainly a black day for Geronimo, and he would remember it for the rest of his life. As Geronimo himself would later recall, "I had lost all. I was never again contented in our quiet home. True, I could visit my father's grave, but I had vowed vengeance upon the Mexican troopers who had wronged me, and whenever I came near his grave or saw anything to remind me of former happy days my heart would ache for revenge against Mexico."

Geronimo wanted to seek out immediate revenge, but when his comrades advised him that such a move would be futile, as they were outnumbered and in Mexican territory, Geronimo was finally convinced to withdraw. Upon returning to Apache lands, Geronimo attended a council of war and made sure that reprisal against Mexico was a top priority. At this time, Geronimo's chief was a man named Mangas Coloradas.

Mangas Coloradas had managed to unify his tribe with another local chapter by marrying his daughter to a chief named Cochise. It was to Cochise that Mangas sent Geronimo in order to cobble together enough braves from the allied tribes to stage a retaliatory strike. This group of assembled warriors set up camp near the town of Arispe on the Mexican border.

It wasn't long before Mexican officials were informed of the group's arrival. Initially, it wasn't clear what Geronimo and his band were there for. This wasn't the first time the Apache had come to this Mexican town since it was a major hub of commerce in the region. As such, the Mexicans didn't know whether they had come to do battle or to do business. In order to get to the bottom of the situation, the Mexicans sent a small scouting party to inquire as to what the Apaches were up to.

These Apache warriors were not interested in answering questions, however, and instead attacked the approaching Mexicans. This unlucky envoy was overwhelmed, and every last man was killed. It was after the scouting party failed to return that the local garrison realized that they had a real problem on their hands. In order to face the threat that was camped just outside of town, they quickly mobilized a militia that could take on the waiting Apache.

Knowing that the real battle was growing near, the Apache began to feverishly prepare for their main assault on the town. This engagement occurred at around ten o'clock the next morning. As the fighting commenced, there was no doubt who was in charge of the Apaches. Geronimo would later recall, "I was no chief and never had been, but because I had been more deeply wronged than the others, this honor was conferred upon me, and I resolved to prove worthy of the trust."

His warriors were assembled in what Geronimo called a "hollow circle." They remained in this position until the Mexican militia approached. Then, as soon as the Mexican troops were within a few hundred yards, the Apache opened fire on them. Just as the Mexicans began to fire their weapons, the Apache charged, attempting to overwhelm the enemy with their ferocity.

But the opposition was equally fierce, and soon, Apache warriors were falling down left and right. Geronimo himself came dangerously close to being killed at one point when the Mexicans closed in around him. By using the cunning maneuverability tactics he had learned in his many years of training, he was able to evade his attackers.

Upon regaining his footing on more stable ground, Geronimo then turned the tables on his pursuers. At one point, he managed to grab a slain Mexican's sword and used it to hack into a couple of nearby Mexicans. It was the ferocity of Geronimo and his band that ended up winning the day.

It is believed that this conflict occurred sometime around 1851, although the date cannot be known for certain. Whatever the case may be, from that day forward, Geronimo was seen as a leader and a man of distinction.

# Chapter 3 – Geronimo Continues His Quest

It was a stunning victory that Geronimo had achieved against the Mexican forces, but he wasn't through yet. After this initial strike against Mexican power in the region, Geronimo took his band of followers even deeper into enemy territory and had them hole up in the Sierra de Antunez Mountains.

It was while they were in the Sierra de Antunez range that Geronimo found a new target on which to launch an assault—a sleepy little Mexican village at the foot of the mountains. Although this band of marauders probably thought that the village was easy pickings, as soon as they stepped out from the mountains, they found a fully armed Mexican militia waiting for them.

A firefight then ensued, with the Mexicans and Apaches becoming embroiled in a bloody and protracted battle, as the Apaches attempted to gain a foothold and the Mexicans struggled to push them out. During the course of the carnage, there were numerous instances in which Geronimo almost lost his life. But in the end, Geronimo escaped unscathed, and realizing that this battle was a lost cause, he managed to lead his men out of the fray and back up the mountains. Although it was the able leadership of

Geronimo that allowed for this escape to be possible, many of his men openly accused him of both cowardice and incompetence.

To be sure, the raid was indeed a failure, and to make matters worse, the braves had left their families vulnerable and undefended back at their camp. This was something that the Mexicans had anticipated, and in the continuous cycle of carnage between the Native Americans and Mexicans, civilians were very much fair game when it came to reprisals. Geronimo, realizing the vulnerability of those they had left behind, rushed back to the encampment just in time to fend off a Mexican militia.

When the Mexicans fled, Geronimo and his men were able to pursue them from a distance. The Mexicans eventually led them right to their own base in the mountains. Geronimo, the master strategist, always looking for an opportunity, had his men assemble nearby and prepared to strike. At first, they tried to shoot the Mexicans out of their hideout, but it soon turned into a melee. And it slowly became clear that the Apaches were running out of ammo.

Geronimo, knowing that this battle had to be won—and won quickly—signaled for the braves to descend to take the Mexicans out at close range. Geronimo led the assault, and he almost met his end when he lost his footing in a "pool of blood" and fell down on the ground. Seeing the prone Geronimo, a Mexican rushed over and struck him in the back of his skull with the end of his rifle. Geronimo was nearly knocked out from the blow.

The Mexican was in the process of finishing the Apache commander off when one of Geronimo's fellow braves managed to save the day by charging forward and engaging his attacker. Geronimo was gathered up by other comrades who had been alerted to his plight, and they carried him off the battlefield so that he could recover. Even though Geronimo was taken out of the fight, his men continued the engagement and managed to achieve a total victory against the Mexicans.

Geronimo would have been pleased if he had been awake, but as it were, he was completely out of it at the time, sleeping some distance away. There was no time for a nap, however, and his men quickly brought him back to reality by splashing water in his face. Once he regained consciousness, they bandaged the wounded warrior up, and the whole group headed back to the camp.

It would take a while for Geronimo to heal from the wounds he had received, and with their commander out of commission, his band of loyal Apache would just have to hold their fire. Geronimo would wait it out until 1861 before he once again struck out against the Mexicans. Geronimo's next assault would occur while he and his group traversed through the Sierra Madre range, which runs through northern Mexico. Here, they came upon a convoy that included a bunch of mules, donkeys, and other beasts of burden, which were loaded with food and ammo.

For a band of marauders like Geronimo and his Apache, this was just too much to resist. Perched from on high, Geronimo signaled his men to charge down on the travelers as they made their way through the mountain pass. Taken by surprise, the frightened Mexicans took one look at the Apaches charging at them and took off, leaving all of their supplies behind.

The Apaches were more than happy to let them depart as long as they could grab their belongings. But it seems that what goes around comes around because Geronimo and his Apache were likewise waylaid by a group of Mexicans shortly thereafter. According to Geronimo's own later recollection, "It was at daybreak and we were just finishing our breakfast. We had no idea that we had been pursued or that our enemies were near until they opened fire."

As the Mexicans opened up on the Apaches, Geronimo himself would have a bullet graze across his "left eye," causing him to reel backward and fall to the ground. It was a minor wound, but Geronimo's enemies apparently took him for dead, for as they chased off the rest of the Apache, they left him there lying in his own blood. It took Geronimo a few minutes to recover his senses, but he finally managed to rouse himself and escape into the wilderness.

Some of the Mexican troops saw his mad dash and began to shoot at the fleeing figure of Geronimo. According to his account, he just "kept running, dodging, and fighting" until he managed to get out of range of his assailants. He suffered another minor "flesh wound" in his side during the melee, but he otherwise managed to escape without mortal injury. As was the custom, Geronimo had previously instructed all of his warriors to return to a preordained location in case they became scattered.

And sure enough, a few days later, Geronimo and several others arrived at the Santa Bita Mountains, where they discussed what they should do next. They didn't have long to lick their wounds before their enemies struck them once again. A Mexican militia managed to catch Geronimo and his men off guard, and the Apaches were forced to run for their lives and leave all of their supplies and ammunition behind.

However, that's not all they left behind because, as Geronimo would later recall, "Many women and children and a few warriors were killed, and four women were captured." Geronimo would then relate how he later received word that some of the women taken prisoner were actually taken back to Mexico to be used as forced labor.

This tale has a happy ending, though. According to Geronimo, the women managed to escape those who held them, and they found their way back to the tribe. These women displayed the steely-eyed determination that the Apache were known for. And it was this fighting spirit that Geronimo very much wished to channel in his continued quest for revenge.

# Chapter 4 – The Apaches Go on the Warpath

Not a lot is known about how Geronimo spent the next few years of his life, but before the decade was through, he had married two other women—Chee-Hash-Kish and Nana-Tha-Thtith. The Apaches, at this time, practiced polygamy, and as long as a man could support them, he was free to marry as many wives as he wished. It was with Chee-Hash-Kish that Geronimo would have a son named Chappo and a daughter named Dohn-say. Nana-Tha-Thtith, meanwhile, would give Geronimo a third child, whose name was not recorded. Sadly, both Nana-Tha-Thtith and her child would be killed in subsequent engagements with the Mexicans in 1861.

That same year, President Abraham Lincoln would be sworn into office, and the United States found itself in absolute turmoil. Due to tensions over slavery between the free North and slave-holding South, by the time Lincoln began his term, several states had already left the Union. Geronimo and his fellow Apaches in the American Southwest were fairly far removed from the fray, but as the war began to heat up, even they would be affected.

It was only a short time before volunteers began to travel from California, passing through Apache lands to join the Union fight against the Confederate strongholds in the Southeast. The war also impacted traditional routes that led west, which had previously circumvented Apache territory. Unable to go around Apache lands because of the fighting between the Union and the Confederacy, those wishing to head out west were forced to push right through Apache territory.

All of these things combined would inevitably lead to confrontation and conflict, as the newcomers stumbled right into the Apache. It was along the aptly named "Apache Pass" that most of these confrontations would take place. Apache Pass is situated inside a mountainous region of Arizona. At the time, the Apache steward of this region was the powerful chief with whom Geronimo himself had direct dealings, a man named Cochise.

Chief Cochise had entered into various agreements with the United States in the past in regards to traffic through Apache territory. In 1858, in fact, he had crafted an agreement in which he granted safe passage to the US Postal Service and other shipping companies when they had to deliver letters and packages to California. But once the Civil War began in 1861, the situation had become incredibly tense.

The first major conflict between the Americans and the Apaches erupted in the spring of 1861 when the stepson of a local American man by the name of John Ward was abducted by the Apache. Ward aired his grievances to the nearby military installation of Fort Buchanan. The burden of recovering the child then fell onto the shoulders of Second Lieutenant George Nicholas Bascom.

Bascom left the base with a search party comprised of 54 troops to scour Apache Pass for any sign of the boy. They set up camp in the region right as Chief Cochise happened onto the scene. It must be noted that Cochise knew nothing of the kidnapping at the time and that he had no reason to believe that his previously good relations with the US Army had soured.

As such, when he was called over to pay a visit to Lieutenant Bascom's tent, he thought nothing of it. But he was quickly double-crossed. As soon as he stepped into the tent, he was told he would be held hostage until the kidnapped child was returned. Cochise, not willing to be made into anyone's pawn, had an ace—or in his case a knife—up his sleeve, and he was able to slice his way out of the tent.

Running on pure adrenaline, Cochise fled through the hole he had torn through the tent's fabric and took off as fast as his feet could carry him. But unfortunately for Cochise, he was not alone that day; his wife and children had been in attendance with him as well. And although Cochise managed to escape, they could not. His family members would become bargaining chips for the US Army, and they were held as hostages for further negotiations with the Apache.

Despite the duplicitousness with which he had been dealt, Cochise, who was just as good of a peacemaker as he was at making war, attempted to broker an agreement with the Americans the following day. He arrived near the camp with a small entourage of Apache and raised the white flag as a sign that he wished to enter into negotiations with them. Some American troops and an interpreter came out and entered into dialogue with Cochise.

In the discussion, Concise insisted that he was not involved with the missing child's disappearance. But the Americans didn't want to hear it, and they made it clear that the chief's family members would not be returned until he had located the child and brought him back. In the midst of this turmoil, a representative from the US side of the discussion later decided to head over to Cochise's camp to see if he could negotiate matters directly with the chief himself. This proved to be a bad move because as soon as he arrived, the Apaches seized him and made him a hostage. In this cycle of never-ending drama, this man was then held for the ransom of Cochise's own family, which were, in turn, being held for the return of the missing boy.

The very next day, Geronimo, fresh from the warpath in Mexico, arrived on this troubling scene. However, it was about to get even more troubling because Cochise, seeking to gain even more leverage with the Americans, decided that he was going to obtain more hostages to negotiate with. It was in these efforts that he had Geronimo and several Apache lay in wait for unwary travelers that they could waylay along Apache Pass.

It was in this manner that they took a group of people from a wagon train that had the misfortune of passing through. With his new hostages secure, Cochise went back to the US military encampment and demanded a trade of his hostages for his family. But it was a no-go. Bascom was only interested in retrieving the missing boy and steadfastly refused to take part in any further negotiations until the child was produced.

Frustrated, on February 8th, 1861, Cochise directed Geronimo and his men to attempt another kidnapping at Apache Pass, but this new group of travelers, who had been apparently alerted to the danger they faced, put up a ferocious fight. During the ensuing battle, American troops arrived on the scene. The Apaches were not prepared for this stiff resistance and had to make a hasty retreat.

Before leaving, however, they killed their remaining hostages, leaving their discarded corpses behind. In response to this outrage, the American troops summarily executed two of Cochise's nephews and his brother, who had been under their care. It was now clear that the negotiations were over and that an all-out war between the Apache and the American forces stationed in the area was about to begin.

# Chapter 5 – The Greatest Wrong

The early 1860s proved to be a pivotal time for the Apache in general and Geronimo in particular. While Chief Cochise was caught up in continued conflicts and intrigue with the US Army, Geronimo was on the warpath in Chihuahua, located in northern Mexico. It was during one of these exchanges that Geronimo sustained some pretty serious injuries. He had just barely recovered from his wounds when he was forced to flee from Mexico to Arizona.

Mexican militias were in hot pursuit of Geronimo and his men, though, and they sought to wreak vengeance upon Geronimo's camp. The day of reckoning came when the militia observed the main group of warriors leaving the encampment. Wishing to attack when the camp was at its most vulnerable, the militiamen laid siege to those who remained behind. Many lives were lost in this skirmish, but Geronimo himself managed to escape.

At the very same time that this was going on, Cochise and Mangas Coloradas, Cochise's father-in-law, put together a sizeable contingent of Apache in preparations for a major showdown. This group headed for the settlement of Pinos Altos, New Mexico. The assault began during the early morning hours of September 27th,

1861. The Apache spread out and surrounded the town from all sides.

But the siege would be much more difficult than any of the Apache realized. The main trouble came from Confederate troops that were holed up in the town. The Apaches at this point had mostly dealt with Union soldiers, but as the Civil War heated up, some Confederates were beginning to spill over into this region as well. The Confederate troops in Pinos Altos ended up putting up a fierce fight, and most troubling for the Apaches was the use of their cannons.

As soon as the cannonballs began to fly, the Apaches were forced to give up their assault. These Confederate soldiers were under the leadership of Lieutenant Colonel John R. Baylor, who, after the battle, put together an additional unit of soldiers commanded by Captain Sherod Hunter. Union troops, meanwhile, were surging in from the west to take on this Confederate menace.

In order for these reinforcements to arrive, they had to go through Apache Pass. This set the stage for another confrontation between Cochise and the Americans in the summer of 1862. The conflict occurred when Cochise and his group, who were roaming the high parts of the pass, came across a band of some 140 Union troops camped down below. Cochise had nothing but vengeance on his mind this day, and without warning, he had his men open up on the troops below.

The Union soldiers were so unprepared for the assault that they immediately raised a white flag to sue for mercy. Seeing this sign of submission, Cochise ordered the Apache to hold their fire, and he traversed down to the encampment in order to speak with the leaders of the Union contingent. The Union officer proceeded to make nice with Cochise, giving him gifts of "tobacco and pemmican." This was the standard sort of bribe that was made for those wishing to make their way through Apache Pass. Initially, the Union officer thought that the appeasement had worked, but after Cochise departed, he found that while he was distracted with these overtures for peace, three of his men "had been shot, lanced, and stripped."

The Apaches, who had slipped into the camp to commit these atrocities, had already made their way back up to higher ground and were openly "mocking" the Union troops down below, as they were unable to do anything about it. Nevertheless, Cochise eventually allowed the troops to pass.

For the Apache, the most important aspect of the whole encounter was the intelligence that had been gathered. Cochise was able to rightfully estimate that this large influx of reinforcements meant that a great offensive was shaping up. Wishing to be prepared, he contacted Mangas Coloradas to forge an alliance. They were also able to join forces with Chief Victorio of the Warm Springs band, Chief Delgadito of the Copper Mines band, and the Apache warriors Juh and Nana. He also consulted Geronimo, who, while not a chief, was a strong leader and who was always more than ready to go on the warpath.

These plans would be disrupted in early January 1863 when Mangas Coloradas was double-crossed in a most terrible way. Mangas had tried to open up negotiations with US troops after sustaining an injury, but upon his approach, he was instead seized and made a prisoner of war. Mangas Coloradas was then brought to nearby Fort McLane, where he was placed under tight security.

Mangas Coloradas's security would be compromised, though, not from Apaches arriving to rescue him but rather from orders that came from within, as his security detail was openly encouraged by their commanding officer, American Brigadier General Joseph Rodman West, to mistreat Mangas. He told them, "Men, that old murderer has got away from every soldier command and has left a trail of blood for 500 miles on the old stage line. I want him dead or alive tomorrow morning. Do you understand? I want him dead."

Tipped off that their commanding officer would prefer the chief to be killed, his guards sought to actively agitate Magnas Coloradas. They wanted to provoke him enough so that he would lash out so they could say that they killed him in self-defense. And this is precisely what occurred on January 18th, 1863.

The chief, who was over six and a half foot tall, had been given a blanket that barely covered his body, and so, his feet kept finding their way out of the thin sheet he clung to. It was when the guards caught one of his feet sticking out that they decided to have a little "fun" with the chief by taking the tips of their bayonets, heating them up in the fire, and then burning the sleeping chief's exposed feet with the hot metal. Mangas attempted to ignore this indignity, but the guards wouldn't quit. And after he was poked with the hot bayonet several times, the chief got up and shouted, "I am no child to be played with!"

This obviously played right into his tormentors' hands, and they used his agitated stance as a reason to attack him. As soon as the chief got up, one of them shot him in the chest. Another soldier, hearing the commotion from outside, ran into the tent and finished Mangas off by shooting him right through the forehead. The indignities faced by Mangas Coloradas had sadly only just begun because after being given these mortal wounds, he was then scalped before being decapitated.

The grisly trophy of the chief's head was cooked over a fire, the flesh taken off, and the skull preserved. The skull was then sent off to a phrenologist in New York and was said to have been taken to the Smithsonian, although modern attempts to locate the skull have come up empty. When this event came to the knowledge of Geronimo, he was obviously enraged, to say the least. He would later refer to this episode as being, "Perhaps the greatest wrong ever done to the Indians."

With Mangas Coloradas gone, Geronimo had to consolidate his forces and head over to Apache Pass to consult with Cochise. As he watched and waited, he saw his first chance for retaliation on March 22nd, 1863. Through their various means of reconnaissance, the Apache had discovered an army installation underway in nearby Pinos Altos.

Geronimo led a raid that allowed the Apache to steal some sixty horses from the US troops. The US military was caught completely off-guard, and they were virtually unable to mount any kind of pursuit. Geronimo had become an expert at conducting lighting raids. This kind of hit-and-run guerrilla warfare was where he really excelled, but little did he know that he was about to bring the full fury of the US Army right down on top of him.

# Chapter 6 – Geronimo the Renegade

While Geronimo began exacting vengeance on US troops through multiple raids, the Civil War was winding down. And by the war's end in 1865, the US was no longer distracted by the insurrection of the Confederacy and was therefore able to focus all of its attention on the Apache attacks in America's West. The end of the war also meant a fresh influx of settlers heading from the now peaceful East in order to try their luck in the Wild West.

In order to get a handle on all the raids the Apache leveled against the newcomers, the federal government commissioned a new army base smack dab in the middle of the notoriously treacherous Apache Pass. It was this strong, reinforced presence that led Chief Cochise to once again seek negotiations with the United States. These overtures led to a meeting between Cochise and US General Oliver Howard on October 20th, 1870.

It was from this meeting that a plan was crafted to allow Cochise and his Apache to peacefully lay down their arms in exchange for agreeing to be relocated to a specially prepared reservation in the Canada Alamosa region of New Mexico. According to the agreement, the tribe would be provided with regular foodstuffs and other supplies to help them settle the land. At first, the deal seemed decent enough, and Cochise was ready to sign off on it. But at the last minute, the US mediators altered the bargain and changed the location of the reservation to a much less attractive piece of real estate nestled in the dry desert sands of Mescalero, in southern New Mexico.

Cochise, not wanting to accept the degraded proposition, backed out of the deal. He came back to the bargaining table in 1872, however, to see if decent terms could still be met. Geronimo was in attendance at this meeting. The talks went better than either Cochise or Geronimo could have imagined, with the US allowing the Apache to remain as stewards of Apache Pass.

This put a big burden on Cochise's shoulders because it was up to him to ensure that all those traveling through his land were not harmed by any member of his tribe. In other words, he was now the designated peacekeeper who had to make sure that no further hostile actions erupted. Cochise was quite happy with the deal, but no matter how good the terms may have been, Geronimo maintained his stiff upper lip.

As one eyewitness to the signing of the treaty, a certain Lieutenant Sladen related, "His [Geronimo's] sensual, cruel, crafty face, as well as his dissatisfied manner had prejudiced me against him from the start." Nevertheless, the peace deal between the US and the Apache had been achieved. But the funny thing is, although this ended the Apache raids on Americans, Geronimo was more than happy to continue launching raids against the Mexicans! As Geronimo would later explain, he viewed the deal as being between the United States, meaning it had no bearing on any actions committed by Apache in northern Mexico. Cochise was against these activities, but Geronimo was able to act of his own accord, and he sent bands of Apache who were loyal to him south of the Rio Grande on a regular basis. In one of these raids, Geronimo and his men came back with a prisoner, a little boy from Mexico whom they had kidnapped.

Geronimo was holding the child in the hopes that he could get a hefty ransom from the family he had stolen him from. But before Geronimo could attempt to trade the boy for precious goods, his deeds came to light, and authorities immediately demanded that he return the boy to his family. United States officials alerted Cochise as to what had occurred, and Cochise then placed pressure on Geronimo to take the child back to his rightful home.

Geronimo, forced to cave in to the demands, allowed the boy to be picked up by US officials, who then brought the young one back to his grateful parents in Mexico. Nevertheless, even with the boy's return, Geronimo continued to attack Mexicans. But after the American government was petitioned by Mexico to do something to stop these incursions, the Apache were finally told that enough was enough.

This caused Cochise to finally rein in Geronimo. However, after being told that the violent raids into Mexico from those situated at Apache Pass had to stop, Geronimo decided to take his business elsewhere. And taking whoever would come with him, he decided to leave Apache Pass altogether and strike out on his own.

# Chapter 7 – Resigned to His Fate

Chief Cochise had tried his best to keep the peace, but with Geronimo and his band essentially becoming renegades, he had reached his limit of control. It was in the midst of all this duress that Cochise was found to have stomach cancer. The disease would only worsen, and he passed away on June 8th, 1874. Upon his passing, his son, Taza, would take up the mantle of his father. Geronimo, at this point, was on the run from Mexican militias but had reemerged among the Apache.

The death of Cochise certainly created a time of uncertainty. And soon, this uncertainty would become downright precarious. The trouble began innocuously enough when some local Apaches got drunk and, in their intoxicated state, decided they needed more liquor. It's not so much the fact that they wanted more alcohol that was the problem but the way that they went about getting it.

They raided a local ranch, stole their supply of whiskey, and killed the ranchers in the process. This one event managed to bring the full wrath of the American settler community down on the Apache. Under pressure from the public, in 1876, the federal government determined that the Apache would be moved farther away from American settlements in order to protect its citizens from future raids.

Geronimo and his band of Apache began raiding again by the end of the year, but this time he wasn't raiding in Mexico. Instead, he decided to tear a warpath through Arizona. This, of course, would make Geronimo the number one enemy of the United States. Geronimo and his followers had established an enclave along the borderlands between Arizona and New Mexico, and from there, they rode around, robbing and killing American settlers of the Southwest with impunity.

However, he wouldn't be able to get away with it forever, and soon a group of well-trained troops, aided by Native American scouting patrols, discovered Geronimo's camp. Geronimo was startled awake one fine morning in January of 1877 to find his base surrounded by US troops. Geronimo and his warriors sought cover, but the bullets were whizzing by on all sides.

Nevertheless, with a ferocious charge and guns blazing, Geronimo and his men managed to fight their way out. Geronimo and his people were now in desperate need of a safe haven. They found their place of refuge among the Apache of the nearby Ojo Caliente Reservation. This group of Apache, based out of Hot Springs, New Mexico, was under the guidance of Apache Chief Victorio.

Although Victorio had been warned against taking in the fugitive, he allowed Geronimo and his men to stay. Victorio remarked at the time, "These people are not bothering us." Nevertheless, it wouldn't be long before Geronimo's presence would indeed begin to bother Victorio and his Apache, as the US Army soon came calling.

On April 21ˢᵗ, 1877, a military contingent, led by an Indian affairs agent named John Clum, came looking for Geronimo. Geronimo faced the summons head-on, confronting Clum with several Apaches backing him up. Clum arrived with what appeared to be a small band of "Apache police," Apaches who had been conscripted to work as hired muscle for the department of Indian Affairs.

Geronimo thought he had nothing to fear when he saw the ragtag band standing before him. So, when Clum cautioned him, "No harm will come to you if you listen with good ears," Geronimo, only seeing a small, disorganized force, was downright haughty in his response. He shouted, "Speak with discretion, and no harm will come to you!"

Clum stood firm and declared his intention to take Geronimo back to the reservation in San Carlos so that he could answer for "breaking his promises of peace." Staring at Clum and the few officers standing around him, Geronimo couldn't believe what he was hearing. Incensed, he shouted back, "We are not going to San Carlos with you, and unless you are very careful, you and your Apache police will not go back to San Carlos either. Your bodies will stay here at Ojo Caliente to make feed for coyotes!"

However, Clum knew exactly what he was doing and who he was dealing with. Unbeknownst to Geronimo, he had already been surrounded by several Apache officers, who were hiding just out of sight in a commissary building. They were lying in wait for the cue to strike. That cue was Clum slightly tugging on the brim of his hat. And as soon as the hiding Apache police force saw this, they all jumped up and ran out of the commissary, with all of them training their guns on Geronimo.

If Geronimo or one of his associates so much as moved a muscle, Geronimo most certainly would have been killed. However, Geronimo hesitated and only considered using his gun. In the end, even Geronimo had to accept defeat, and he allowed Clum to take his weapon away from him. The two were then able to sit and have a somewhat civil conversation.

Still, when Clum alluded to the fact that Geronimo would be in chains when being transported as a prisoner, Geronimo found his sense of rage once again and brought out a dagger. One of the Apache police officers was able to snatch it out of his hand in time, and a defeated Geronimo was finally resigned to his fate.

# Chapter 8 – The Revolving Door of the Reservation

It was on May 20th, 1877, that a shackled Geronimo was hauled off to a reservation in San Carlos, Arizona. He wasn't allowed to roam free on the reservation; instead, he was immediately placed inside the San Carlos jail. Geronimo would stay inside this prison cell for the next several weeks. It's interesting to note that although Geronimo was being held in this manner, no charges had been brought against him. He was essentially being kept under wraps as an enemy combatant until further notice.

That further notice came several weeks later when Geronimo was abruptly released from bondage and permitted to walk the reservation just like any other Apache. Clum, meanwhile, had taken a leave of absence in order to go back east and get married. But he didn't go alone; he took a "troupe of twenty-two" Apache with him, including Cochise's heir, Chief Taza.

He took his guests all the way to Washington, DC, where Clum gave them a tour of the nation's capital. However, these festivities were abruptly curtailed when Taza suddenly perished from pneumonia on September 26th, 1877. As soon as the Apache back home heard of the death of their chief, the leadership was immediately passed to Taza's brother, Naiche.

Chief Naiche did his best to step up to the plate, but he was much less experienced than his older brother Taza, and the void left by his passing was obvious. This was the confusing and conflicted state of affairs at the San Carlos Reservation that Geronimo became a part of. Even though Geronimo was never a chief, he was by far the most experienced Apache leader on the reservation. And it wasn't long before many of the Apache began looking to him for leadership.

This was actually encouraged by the US officials in charge of the reservation, as they saw Geronimo as a bulwark of stability that just might be able to keep the chaos at bay. But as much as Geronimo's handlers wanted him to keep the status quo on the reservation, it wasn't long before Geronimo himself would grow restless. This restlessness would become rather apparent on August 1ˢᵗ, 1878, when Geronimo hosted a so-called "tiswin drunk."

Tiswin was an alcoholic beverage the Apache typically brewed from corn, and they used the drink in all types of ceremonies. A tiswin drunk was a special social gathering in which everyone partook of a rather strong brew of tiswin. It is said that as the night wore on, a very drunk Geronimo got into a fight with one of his nephews and proceeded to humiliate him in front of the entire tribe.

It's not exactly clear what brought on this conflict, but the results would prove fatal since the scolded young man ended up taking his own life. Once he sobered up, Geronimo must have felt pretty bad about what had transpired, so bad that he abruptly gathered his family and took off. Riding clear off the reservation, he ended up back at his old stomping grounds of Janos, in northern Mexico.

Here, Geronimo met up with some fellow Apaches that he knew from previous expeditions. At the time, these particular Apaches were trying to negotiate with the Mexican government. The Mexicans had requested that the Apache move farther down the Rio Grande near the town of Ojinaga, but this was not at all palatable to this group of Apache. As such, it wasn't long until this group of warriors began conducting fresh raids on local Mexicans.

After Geronimo's arrival on the scene, the first of these excursions occurred on September 26th, 1878. For it was on this day that the group participated in a raid just to the south of Casas Grandes, waylaying a convoy of unlucky Mexicans as they traveled through a region called "Chocolate Pass." Men, women, and children were indiscriminately slaughtered by these vengeful Apache. However, the raiding would not last for very long, ultimately coming to an end on November 12th, 1878.

On that day, one of the main contingents of Apache that Geronimo had partnered with became the victims of deceit. Mexican officials had lured them out of hiding so that they could talk, trade, and drink. After the Mexicans were sure that the Apaches were good and drunk, Mexican troops came in and "wiped out two-thirds of the group." While this was transpiring, another batch of Mexican troops managed to ambush Geronimo's camp in the region of Sonora.

Geronimo would later recall the scene. "I do not know how they were able to find our camp, but they were shooting at us before we knew they were near. We were in the timber. We kept behind rocks and trees until we came within ten yards of their line, then we stood up and both sides shot until all the Mexicans were killed. We lost twelve warriors in this battle."

According to Geronimo's account, his group barely managed to fight the Mexicans off. In such a weakened state, and with reinforcements most certainly on the way, Geronimo had no choice but to head back north to the borderlands, where he and his followers could hide in the wilderness. In the meantime, Geronimo and his men continued to launch sporadic raids from their new hiding places.

This period of banditry would begin to wind down in late November 1879 when representatives from the San Carlos Reservation tracked Geronimo down, not to fight but to offer him a lasting peace. After all of the bloodshed that had been wrought, it's safe to say that such tidings came as a surprise, and Geronimo probably would have viewed them with suspicion if it wasn't for the fact that men he trusted, such as "subchief Gordo," were among the representatives. This familiarity made the proposal at least seem believable. Nevertheless, it took several days of talks to convince Geronimo to accept the offer. Geronimo finally agreed, and on January 7$^{th}$, 1880, he stepped right through, what for him was fast becoming, the revolving door of the San Carlos Reservation.

In many ways, it's rather incredible that Geronimo, a known renegade, was allowed to return to the San Carlos Reservation. No one's quite sure how many people Geronimo may have killed during his raids. On the subject, he himself once remarked, "I have killed many Mexicans; I do not know how many, for frequently I did not count them. Some of them were not worth counting."

So, by his own admission, Geronimo had killed countless people, yet he was allowed to waltz back into the reservation, no questions asked. As much as the reservation system has been criticized, it's rather amazing how lenient the US officials were with Geronimo. Unlike Mangas Coloradas, who had faced a far worse fate, it seems that when it came to Geronimo, those in charge were willing to let bygones be bygones.

Nevertheless, San Carlos was not at all to Geronimo's liking, and it wasn't long before he was considering making a break for it once again. As Geronimo later described it, "We were treated very badly by the agents here also, and that made us want to leave. We were given rations but not all that we should have had, not all that belonged to us." In the meantime, by the time 1881 rolled around, another event would create great upheaval on the reservation.

The discord centered around an Apache medicine man called Nocadelklinny, who many Apache hailed as a divine mystic. Nocadelklinny gained a large following, which soon turned into an all-out insurrection against US authority on the reservation. In order to quickly defuse the situation, US officials sought to have Nocadelklinny brought into custody.

It was due to these efforts that, on August 30th, 1881, "two troops of cavalry and a company of Indian scouts" converged onto the scene to apprehend Nocadelklinny. In the process of securing the medicine man, the Apache scouts suddenly mutinied and joined up with Nocadelklinny's forces. This led to a pitched battle in which Nocadelklinny was killed. In the aftermath, many of Nocadelklinny's followers actually joined up with Geronimo.

For his part, Geronimo welcomed these disaffected warriors, but at the same time, he also realized that he would soon have the full force of the American government on his heels. Knowing that he couldn't remain where he was, Geronimo led the group off the reservation and back to the Mexican borderlands, which had provided refuge to him for much of his life.

Since Geronimo holed up in the Sierra Madre Mountains, just south of the border, the US soldiers were initially unable to follow. This was due to Mexican laws that, quite naturally, prohibited US troop movement across the Mexican border. But due to an agreement forged in the summer of 1882, called the "hot pursuit agreement," US soldiers were eventually given special permission to cross the border if they were pursuing Apaches.

After several engagements, Geronimo and his followers finally set up camp in Casas Grandes. Here, rather than raiding, Geronimo and his company actually began to engage in trading. But the item that was most often bartered would prove to be the Apaches' undoing. They would go into town to retrieve a particularly strong brew of alcohol called mezcal. Geronimo would later recall, "We began to trade, and the Mexicans gave us mescal [mezcal]. Soon nearly all the Indians were drunk. While they were drunk, two companies of Mexican troops, from another town attacked us, killed twenty Indians, and captured many more. We fled in all directions."

It was shortly after this episode that US General George Crook was able to intercept Geronimo and what was left of his followers. Knowing that he was beaten, Geronimo entered into negotiations with General Crook. In the end, Geronimo was once again compelled to make his return to the San Carlos Reservation. Geronimo and his band agreed to go back to the reservation, and as before, all seemed to be forgiven.

# Chapter 9 – Retired from the Range

During his first few years back at San Carlos, Geronimo tried to live by the rules of the reservation and become a peaceful resident. He even tried his luck as a farmer, planting what he could in the arid soil of the reservation. But no matter how hard he tried to adapt, Geronimo could not get used to the sedentary life of living in one spot. And he soon began to consider going off the reservation once again.

The whole reservation had been growing increasingly restless in the meantime over the rules and regulations they were being made to follow. Particularly distressing to the Apache was the fact that they had been forbidden their occasional "tiswin drunk," in which they consumed large amounts of alcohol, and they were also told not to beat their wives. All of this sounds completely absurd by modern standards, but excessive drinking and being able to "punish" their wives with physical violence were a part of Apache culture at the time. And the mere fact that outsiders would attempt to tell them how to live their lives was met with great animosity. In May of 1885, the Apache held a kind of protest by holding a massive "tiswin drunk" ceremony. Geronimo was, of course, one of the main rabble-rousers during the whole ordeal.

The next day, Geronimo and his allies went to the camp of a certain Lieutenant Britton Davis to air their grievances. Geronimo and several others were said to have been visibly intoxicated at the time. The soberest among them was a chief by the name of Loco, who served as the main mouthpiece of the group. Davis tried to tell the Apache that it was for their own good that certain changes to their customs were being made.

One of the tribal elders, an Apache called Nana, took umbrage to Davis's words, shouting to an interpreter, "Tell the Nantan Enchau [Nantan Enchau was a nickname given to Davis which, roughly translated, meant "stout chief"] that he can't advise me how to treat my women. He is only a boy. I killed men before he was born."

Shortly thereafter, another Apache named Chihuahua, who disagreed with the prohibition on alcohol, openly challenged Davis, proclaiming, "We all drank tiswin last night, all of us in the tent and outside. What are you going to do about it? Are you going to put us all in jail? You have no jail big enough even if you could put us all in jail."

Lieutenant Davis must have realized that the frustrated Apache had a point. The US Army was attempting to curtail the behavior of the Apache, but they didn't have enough resources on the reservation to enforce the arbitrary rules that they had set. Geronimo, taking note of this impotence, was now ready to make another break for it. And on May 17th, he gathered together some 144 Apache and left the reservation.

Geronimo led his entourage to his old stomping grounds of the Sierra Madre Mountains in northern Mexico. Here, Geronimo once again led lighting raids against local settlements and passersby while always staying one step ahead of his pursuers. On August 7th, however, Geronimo was nearly captured when a group of Apache scouts was sent into the region to look for him.

Geronimo's encampment was caught off guard, and Geronimo found himself under heavy fire and was forced to flee. What was left of his followers then regrouped and joined back up with

Geronimo. He and his men would then go on an odyssey, traveling throughout several regions in northern Mexico and the southeastern United States. By September, some 5,000 US troops were in hot pursuit. However, Geronimo managed to masterfully elude his pursuers, crisscrossing into Arizona and then back into northern Mexico.

But by 1886, Geronimo was just about out of gas, and he began moving toward negotiations with US officials once more. In March of that year, Geronimo began to meet with General George Crook to discuss terms. This event was actually documented by a photographer who was in attendance, giving us one of the few early glimpses of what Geronimo was like in the flesh.

Geronimo often appeared angry in these early photos, and during this particular exchange, he most certainly was. He had just been informed by Crook that he would accept nothing but his "unconditional surrender." And if Geronimo did not surrender according to these terms, he and his band would be hunted down to the last man. At first, Geronimo seemed like he was going to cave to the pressure and surrender, but by March 31$^{st}$, he got his second wind, and after gathering a core group of people around him, he snuck off early in the morning before Crook would even realize he was gone.

Crook, who was very wary of dealing with Geronimo, would ultimately be replaced by General Nelson Miles on April 11$^{th}$, 1886. It would be General Miles who would put an end to Geronimo's freedom once and for all, but not before Geronimo and his men led a reign of terror all over the Southwest. One of the most appalling of these episodes—and the most well documented—occurred on April 27$^{th}$, 1886.

For it was on this day that Geronimo raided an Arizona ranch near the Santa Cruz River, leaving a traumatic memory on the rancher that would scar him for life. The man's name was Artisan Peck, and he was busy herding his cattle when Geronimo and his warriors descended upon his homestead. They confronted and killed the man's wife, as well as his infant child, before taking

Artisan's ten-year-old niece as a prisoner. They then went outside and ambushed Peck. Artisan Peck was badly beaten and was even stripped naked. For reasons only known to Geronimo, he allowed Peck to live. Beaten, bloody, robbed of everything—even the shirt on his back—Peck wandered back home where he was greeted by the grisly sight of his slain wife and child. Peck would later testify that it was indeed Geronimo who led the rampage on his home.

Geronimo would first enter into talks with General Miles in late August through his lieutenant, a man named Charles Gatewood. Even though Miles wasn't present for this first meeting, Geronimo was sure to pump Gatewood with plenty of questions in regard to General Crook's successor. This preliminary meeting with Gatewood would then produce another meeting in which Geronimo would meet with General Miles directly.

These efforts would bear fruit in the form of Geronimo's surrender on September 4th. Public sentiment in Arizona against Geronimo, in the meantime, was so bad that Miles knew that he had to quickly remove Geronimo from the region. Since Geronimo had admittedly killed so many people during his forays, it's pretty understandable that the loved ones of those who were slain might want to see him tried in a court of law.

But instead of being presented in a courtroom in Arizona, he was quietly shipped off to Fort Sam Houston in San Antonio, Texas. Here, he was held as a prisoner of war for several weeks before being relocated to Pensacola, Florida. Despite past depredations, General Miles had promised Geronimo that the "slate had been wiped clean." Geronimo and his warriors arrived in Pensacola at Fort Pickens on October 25th, 1886.

By then, Geronimo's fame had preceded him, and as soon as his train arrived at the station, huge multitudes of curious onlookers wishing to get a glimpse of the notorious renegades. Once Geronimo and his fifteen fellow Apache were ushered past the crowds, they were brought to what would be their temporary home at the fort.

They were divided up between two rooms that had wooden bunks available for each man to sleep on. They were also given new clothes to wear: military-styled "brown canvas suits," along with army boots, socks, and underclothing. For food, they were given regular rations, and while at the fort, they were made to earn their keep by clearing brush out of the courtyard a few hours a day.

Geronimo would stay at Fort Pickens until he was transferred to Mount Vernon Barracks in Alabama in May of 1888. Here, Geronimo was reunited with many of the other Apache he had been separated from since his last "breakout" from the reservation. Many were happy to see him, but others seemed to harbor a grudge against him, blaming him for their current plight.

Geronimo was given his own "two-room log cabin" right in the middle of the camp. This position seemed to signify that Geronimo was an Apache of importance, whether all of the other Apache agreed to this distinction or not. Geronimo, along with his people, were put to a wide variety of tasks to keep themselves busy. At one point, Geronimo was even taught how to write his name and make "walking sticks."

Already a celebrity, the old Apache warrior would then spend time making wooden walking sticks with his name carved into them as a kind of autograph. He sold these for a dollar a piece to the enthusiastic "tourists" who came by the community. Geronimo would stay in Alabama until 1894, when he was moved to what would be his final place of residence, Fort Sill, Oklahoma.

Geronimo was well respected at this fort for his obedience and hard work in whatever task was requested of him. His only real trouble came in 1898 due to a gross misunderstanding of someone who had tattled on him. The Spanish-American War had just kicked off over in Cuba, and many Apache had enlisted, but Geronimo, who was by then well into his seventies, was, of course, considered too old to fight.

One evening, a young woman overheard Geronimo joking with some friends about how easy it would be to "make a break for it" with everyone off fighting the war. These few idle words set off the rumor that Geronimo was planning on leading a new revolt.

Taking the matter quite seriously, the US officials in charge brought Geronimo in for questioning. Geronimo immediately denied that he had any such intentions and expressed shock and indignation that anyone suspected him of plotting such a thing. Nevertheless, he was placed under close watch for the next few weeks until the fears and suspicions died down.

After this episode, Geronimo would live out the rest of his days in relative peace. At times, he was even allowed to leave the reservation for special occasions, such as when he took part in special events highlighting Native American culture. Geronimo also participated in the so-called Wild West Shows, which were very popular at the time. They were the brainchild of William F. Cody, better known as Buffalo Bill.

Here, in these theatrical renditions of what life was like in the West, it must have been with some sad irony that Geronimo acted out what it was like to be a free Apache riding the range, as he was still considered a prisoner of the US government. But Geronimo was a celebrity all the same, and his fame would lead him to even take part in the 1904 World's Fair. Perhaps the most spectacular event that Geronimo would take part in, though, was when he participated in the inaugural procession of Teddy Roosevelt in 1905. Geronimo, flanked by various Native American chieftains, proudly rode out before the crowds. It was a much humbler Geronimo who had an audience with the new president after the parade was over. With tears in his eyes, Geronimo asked Teddy to "take the ropes from the hands" of the Native Americans. "The ropes have been on my hands for many years and we want to go back to our home in Arizona."

To this emotional display, Teddy answered bluntly, "When you lived in Arizona you had a bad heart and killed many of my people. I cannot grant the request you make for yet a while. We will have to wait and see how you act." And wait and see they did, with nothing coming from the conversation, at least in regards to Geronimo, for his life would ultimately come to a close in the spring of 1909.

He was riding on a horse at the reservation when he fell and injured himself. The accident occurred in a fairly isolated spot, and it took some time for anyone to find him. Being exposed to the cold for so long did not bode well for Geronimo, and it led to him passing away of pneumonia on February 17th, 1909.

# Conclusion

Geronimo was a man who survived by his wits. He faced much hardship in his life, but he was able to navigate hurdles that most would find impossible. Who else could live on the run from both the United States and Mexican armies, passing back and forth from one wilderness to the other, but Geronimo?

And who else, when cornered and captured by their enemies, would have the charisma to convince them to not only spare his life but aid in rehabilitating his image? Once Geronimo had retired from the warpath, he became a kind of folk hero and celebrity, and he represented the best of Americana.

Geronimo, however, wasn't just the caricature of the Wild West that later Americans created. He was a living, breathing man with a proud Apache background. Geronimo and his Apache followers were, in many ways, the last stand against Western expansion. The Apache were known to be fierce warriors—and Geronimo was among the fiercest—so it should be no surprise that he oversaw some of the last great uprisings against the growing hegemony of the United States government. His incredible resistance would be admired by friend and foe alike.

And he has remained a symbol of endurance and tenacity for the American military long after his death. After all, no paratrooper jump would be the same without someone shouting, "Geronimo!"

Osama Bin Laden, the former leader of Al Qaeda, was also codenamed Geronimo due to his stubborn resistance to be captured. Whether you love him or hate him, Geronimo's name is one that continues to reverberate in the American psyche to this very day.

Here's another book by
Captivating History that you might like

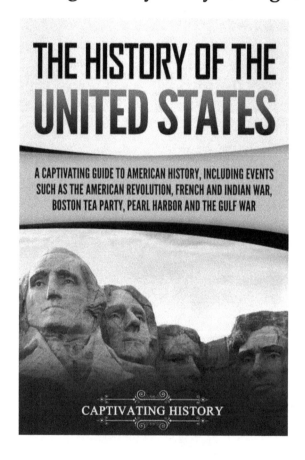

# Free Bonus from Captivating History (Available for a Limited time)

Hi History Lovers!

Now you have a chance to join our exclusive history list so you can get your first history ebook for free as well as discounts and a potential to get more history books for free! Simply visit the link below to join.

Captivatinghistory.com/ebook

Also, make sure to follow us on Facebook, Twitter and Youtube by searching for Captivating History.

# Reference

*Geronimo.* Robert M. Utley. Yale University Press, 2012.

*Geronimo: My Life.* Geronimo & S. M. Barrett (editor). Dover Publications, 1906.

Edwards, John N. *Noted guerrillas, Or, The warfare of the Border.* St. Louis Missouri: Bryan, Brand & Company, 1877.

Gardner, Mark Lee. *Shot All to Hell: Jesse James, the Northfield Raid, and the Wild West's Greatest Escape.* William Morrow, 2013.

James, Jesse. *Jesse James, My Father.* Kansas City: The Sentinel Printing Co., 1899.

Ortiz T., Manuel. "Jesse James en México". *Contenido* Magazine, March 1970, Mexico, DF.

Smith, Tom. "Jesse James in Iowa." *The Annals of Iowa* 40 (1970), 377-380.

Stiles, TJ. *Jesse James: Last Rebel of the Civil War.* Vintage, 2010.

Woog, Adam. *Jesse James.* Chelsea House Publishers, New York, 2010.

Wukovits, John F., *Jesse James.* Philadelphia: Chelsea House Publishers, 1997.

1. "Annie Oakley." lkwdpl.org Women in History. Archived from the original on July 13, 2012. Accessed in November 2020.

2. Haugen, B., *Annie Oakley: American Sharpshooter*, Capstone, 2006, p. 88.

3. "Annie Oakley." Dorchester County Public Library, Cambridge, MD. Archived from the original on February 22, 2008.
Retrieved January 20, 2007. Accessed in November 2020.

4. *"Little Sure Shot" The Saga of Annie Oakley*, Caroline Kim-Brown. 2006.

5. *The Life and Legacy of Annie Oakley, Volume Seven*, The Oklahoma Western Biographies, Glenda Riley, 2002.

6. *Annie Oakley*, Shirl Kasper, 2000.

7. *Annie Oakley of the Wild West*, Walter Havighurst, 2003.

Blackburn, Thomas. *The Ballad of Davy Crockett.* (Recorded by Fess Parker). Columbia Records, 1955.

Christensen, Carol and Thomas. *The US-Mexican War.* USA: Bay Books San

Francisco, 1998.

Crockett, David. *Life of David Crockett, the Original Humorist and Irrepressible Backwoodsman. An Autobiography.* New York: AL Burt, 1902

Ellis, Edward Sylvester. *The Life of Colonel David Crockett.* Philadelphia: Porter & Coates, 1884.

Loomis, C. Grant. "Davy Crockett Visits Boston." *The New England Quarterly*, vol. 20, no. 3, 1947, pp. 396–400.

Matovina, Timothy M. *The Alamo Remembered: Tejano Accounts and*

*Perspectives.* USA: University of Texas Press, 1995.

Wallis, Michael. *David Crockett, The Lion of the West.* New York: Norton & Company, 2011.

Williams, Amelia. "A Critical Study of the Siege of the Alamo and of the Personnel of Its Defenders: IV. Historical Problems Relating to the Alamo." *The Southwestern Historical Quarterly 37*, no. 3 (1934): 157-84.

Historic Bullock Hotel website: https://www.historicbullock.com/

Deadwood City website: http://www.deadwood.com/

---

Weiser, K. 2019, *Seth Bullock – Finest Type of Frontiersman*, Legends of America, viewed 1 February 2021, <https://www.legendsofamerica.com/we-sethbullock/>

Holtzmann, R. 2013, *Mr. Bullock Goes to Washington*, South Dakota Magazine, viewed 1 February 2021, <https://www.southdakotamagazine.com/mr-bullock-goes-to-washington>

Boardman, M. 2019, *Bullock: No Bull*, True West, viewed 1 February 2021, <https://truewestmagazine.com/seth-bullock/>

History.com Editors 2020, *Theodore Roosevelt*, A&E Television Networks, viewed 1 February 2021, <https://www.history.com/topics/us-presidents/theodore-roosevelt>

Roberts, P., *Agnes Thatcher Lake: Equestrian Rider, Circus Performer, and Wild Bill's Wife*, Wyoming Almanac, viewed 1 February 2021,

Finding Dulcinea Staff 2011, *On This Day: Wild Bill Hickok Kills Davis Tutt in a Duel*, Finding Dulcinea, viewed 1 February 2021, <http://www.findingdulcinea.com/news/on-this-day/July-August-08/On-this-Day--Wild-Bill-Hickok-Duels-Davis-Tutt.html>

Weiser, K. 2020, *Rough & Tumble Deadwood, South Dakota*, Legends of America, viewed 1 February 2021, <https://www.legendsofamerica.com/sd-deadwood/>

Carlson, G. 2014, *Roosevelt's Contemporaries: Seth Bullock*, Theodore Roosevelt Center, viewed 1 February 2021, <https://www.theodorerooseveltcenter.org/Blog/Item/Seth%20Bullock>

Deadwood, S. D. Revealed website: www.deadwood.searchroots.com

Weiser, K. 2020, *Al Swearengen & the Notorious Gem Theater*, Legends of America, viewed 1 February 2021, <https://www.legendsofamerica.com/we-gemsaloon/>

Biography.com Editors 2020, *Wild Bill Hickok Biography,* A&E Television Networks, viewed 1 February 2021, <https://www.biography.com/personality/wild-bill-hickok>

History.com Editors 2020, *Wild Bill Hickok is Murdered,* A&E Television Networks, viewed 1 February 2021, <https://www.history.com/this-day-in-history/wild-bill-hickok-is-murdered>

Weiser, K. 2019, *Solomon Star – A Natural Deadwood Leader,* Legends of America, viewed 1 February 2021, <https://www.legendsofamerica.com/sd-solstar/>

The National Parks Service website on Yellowstone National Park: https://www.nps.gov/yell/learn/historyculture/history-faqs.htm

Memmot, J. 2018, *Remembering a Rochester man's ill-fated journey to the Arctic,* Democrat & Chronicle, viewed 1 February 2021, <https://www.democratandchronicle.com/story/news/local/columnists/memmott/2018/08/01/remembering-rochester-mans-ill-fated-journey-arctic/871024002/>

Illustration II: Public Domain

https://commons.wikimedia.org/w/index.php?curid=124518

Illustration III: Photograph by Carol M. Highsmith

https://commons.wikimedia.org/wiki/File:The_Bullock_Hotel,_built_in_1886_by_Seth_Bullock,_the_Wild_West_town%27s_first_sheriff._Deadwood,_South_Dakota_LCCN2011634118.tif

*Buffalo Bill's America. Louis S. Warren, 2005.*

*Buffalo Bill and Sitting Bull: Inventing the Wild West. Bobby Bridger, 2002.*

*Buffalo Bill's Wild West: Celebrity, Memory, And Popular History. Joy S. Kasson, 2000.*

*The Lives and Legends of Buffalo Bill. Don Russell, 1960.*

Andrews, E. 2020, *9 Things You May Not Know About Billy the Kid*, A&E Television Networks, viewed February 2021 <https://www.history.com/news/9-things-you-may-not-know-about-billy-the-kid>

The Editors of the Encyclopedia Britannica 2020, *Billy the Kid*, Encyclopedia Britannica, viewed February 2021 <https://www.britannica.com/biography/Billy-the-Kid-American-outlaw>

Weiser, K. 2019, *Billy the Kid – Teenage Outlaw of the Southwest*, Legends of America, viewed February 2021 <https://www.britannica.com/biography/Billy-the-Kid-American-outlaw>

History.com Editors 2020, *Legendary outlaw Billy the Kid is born*, A&E Television Networks, viewed February 2021, <https://www.history.com/this-day-in-history/billy-the-kid-born>

Biography.com Editors 2019, *Billy the Kid*, A&E Television Networks, viewed February 2021, <https://www.biography.com/crime-figure/billy-the-kid>

Brothers, M. 2015, *About Billy the Kid* website, viewed February 2021, <http://www.aboutbillythekid.com/index.html>

O'Sullivan, N. 2013, *Scary Tales of New York: life in the Irish slums*, The Irish Times, viewed February 2021, <https://www.irishtimes.com/culture/scary-tales-of-new-york-life-in-the-irish-slums-1.1335816>

Hawksville, A. 2018, *Billy the Kid*, Black Horse Westerns, viewed February 2021, <https://bhwesterns.com/article/billy-the-kid/>

Smith, M. T., *Henry Clay Hooker*, Nevada Trivia, viewed February 2021, <https://nevadatrivia.com/nevada-history/henry-clay-hooker/>

History.com Editors 2020, *Billy the Kid Kills his First Man*, A&E Television Networks, viewed February 2021,

<https://www.history.com/this-day-in-history/billy-the-kid-kills-his-first-man>

Simkin, J. 2020, *Lincoln County War*, Spartacus Educational, viewed February 2021, <https://spartacus-educational.com/Wwlincolnwar.htm>

Weiser-Alexander, K. 2021, *John Tunstall – Murdered in the Lincoln County War*, Legends of America, viewed February 2021, <https://www.legendsofamerica.com/john-tunstall/>

Drew, Dr. D. 2013, *John Henry Tunstall – The Man Who Started the Lincoln County War*, Cowboy Country Magazine, viewed February 2021, <https://www.cowboycountrymagazine.com/2013/02/john-henry-tunstall-the-man-who-started-the-lincoln-county-war/>

Simkin, J. 2020, *Dick Brewer*, Spartacus Educational, viewed February 2021, <https://www.cowboycountrymagazine.com/2013/02/john-henry-tunstall-the-man-who-started-the-lincoln-county-war/>

Simkin, J. 2020, *Alexander McSween*, Spartacus Educational, viewed February 2021, <https://spartacus-educational.com/WwmcsweenA.htm>

Murphy, P. 2006, *Billy the Kid and the Lincoln County War: the Irish connection*, History Ireland, viewed February 2021, <https://www.historyireland.com/18th-19th-century-history/billy-the-kid-and-the-lincoln-county-war-the-irish-connection/>'

Dixon, M. N. 2017, *The Sad Fate of Huston Chapman*, Nicole Madalo Dixon, viewed February 2021, <http://nicolemaddalodixon.blogspot.com/2017/09/the-sad-fate-of-huston-chapman.html>

Illustrations:

Illustration I: https://commons.wikimedia.org/wiki/File:Billykid.jpg

Illustration II: By Unknown author - File:Джон Танстелл.jpg, Public Domain, https://commons.wikimedia.org/w/index.php?curid=46457963

Illustration III: https://commons.wikimedia.org/wiki/File:Billy_the_Kids-grave_texas.jpg

Zimmerman, B. 2016, "Native American culture of the West," Khan Academy, viewed September 2021, <https://www.khanacademy.org/humanities/us-history/precontact-and-early-colonial-era/before-contact/a/native-american-culture-of-the-west>

History.com Editors 2020, "Native American Cultures," A&E Television Networks, viewed September 2021, <https://www.history.com/topics/native-american-history/native-american-cultures#section_5>

Koch, A. 2019, "European colonization of the Americas killed 10 percent of world population and caused global cooling," The World, viewed September 2021, <https://www.pri.org/stories/2019-01-31/european-colonization-americas-killed-10-percent-world-population-and-caused>

History.com Editors 2019, "Francisco Vázquez de Coronado," A&E Television Networks, viewed September 2021, <https://www.history.com/topics/exploration/francisco-vazquez-de-coronado>

Anonymous, "Francisco Coronado," The Mariners' Museum and Park, viewed September 2021, <https://exploration.marinersmuseum.org/subject/francisco-coronado/>

Associated Press 2012, "Sir Francis Drake 'first set foot on US soil in San Francisco Bay area,'" The Guardian, viewed September 2021, <https://www.theguardian.com/world/2012/oct/21/sir-francis-drake-san-francisco-bay>

History.com Editors 2021, "Sir Francis Drake claims California for England," A&E Television Networks, viewed September 2021, <https://www.history.com/this-day-in-history/drake-claims-california-for-england>

Lawler, A. 2019, "Did Francis Drake Really Land in California?" Smithsonian Magazine, viewed September 2021, <https://www.smithsonianmag.com/history/did-francis-drake-really-land-california-180973219/>

Johnson, B. "Sir Francis Drake," Historic UK, viewed September 2021, <https://www.historic-uk.com/HistoryUK/HistoryofEngland/Sir-Francis-Drake/>

Burnett, J. 2020, "Statues of Conquistador Juan de Onate Come Down as New Mexico Wrestles With History," NPR, viewed September 2021, <https://www.npr.org/2020/07/13/890122729/statues-of-conquistador-juan-de-o-ate-come-down-as-new-mexico-wrestles-with-hist>

Weddle, R. S. 2019, "Ortiz Parrilla, Diego," Handbook of Texas, viewed September 2021, <https://www.tshaonline.org/handbook/entries/ortiz-parrilla-diego>

Weiser-Alexander, K. 2021, "Santa Fe, New Mexico – The City Different," Legends of America, viewed September 2021, <https://www.legendsofamerica.com/nm-santafe/>

The Taos Pueblo website, viewed September 2021, <https://taospueblo.com/>

James, G. 2019, "The Battle of the Twin Villages took place right outside Nocona," News Channel 6, viewed September 2021, <https://www.newschannel6now.com/2019/05/02/battle-twin-villages-took-place-right-outside-nocona/>

Chad Williams, "Twin Villages, Battle of the," THE ENCYCLOPEDIA OF OKLAHOMA HISTORY AND CULTURE, https://www.okhistory.org/publications/enc/entry.php?entry=TW005.

Anne Million, "French," THE ENCYCLOPEDIA OF OKLAHOMA HISTORY AND CULTURE, https://www.okhistory.org/publications/enc/entry.php?entry=FR020 .

The Library of Congress website for maps and historical documents: https://www.loc.gov/

"George Vancouver Charts the Pacific Coast of North America from California to Alaska." Science and Its Times: Understanding the Social Significance of Scientific Discovery. Retrieved September 08, 2021 from Encyclopedia.com: https://www.encyclopedia.com/science/encyclopedias-almanacs-transcripts-and-maps/george-vancouver-charts-pacific-coast-north-america-california-alaska

National Park Services 2019, "The Dominguez and Escalante Expedition," Dinosaur Natural Monument CO, UT, viewed September 2021, <https://www.nps.gov/dino/learn/historyculture/the-dominguez-and-escalante-expedition.htm>

History.com Editors 2021, "Lewis and Clark Expedition," A&E Television Networks, viewed September 2021, <https://www.history.com/topics/westward-expansion/lewis-and-clark>

Huban, C. J. 2017, "The Story of Chief Cuerno Verde (Green Horn)," Southern Colorado Territorial Daughters, viewed September 2021

Bagley, W. 2014, "The Astorians Discover South Pass," WyoHistory.org, viewed September 2021, <https://www.wyohistory.org/encyclopedia/astorians-south-pass-discovery>

Weiser, K. 2018, "Stephen Long's Expedition of the Great Plains," Legends of America, viewed September 2021, <https://www.legendsofamerica.com/longs-expedition/>

Jedediah Smith Society and University of the Pacific, "Biography of Jed Smith for Students," Jedediah Smith Society, viewed September 2021, <http://jedediahsmithsociety.org/home/research-information/biography-of-jed-smith-for-students/>

Govaerts, L. 2016, "Real stories behind The Revenant, Part II: Ashley's Hundred," Rogers Archaeology Lab, viewed September 2021, <https://nmnh.typepad.com/rogers_archaeology_lab/2016/03/real-stories-behind-the-revenant-part-ii-ashleys-hundred.html>

Weiser, K. 2021, "William Ashley and the Rocky Mountain Fur Company," Legends of America, viewed September 2021, <https://www.legendsofamerica.com/william-ashley/>

Andrews, E. 2018, "6 Legendary Mountain Men of the American Frontier," A&E Television Networks, viewed September 2021, <https://www.history.com/news/6-legendary-mountain-men-of-the-american-frontier>

Hill, M. 2015, "Mountain Men: History & Facts," Study.com, viewed September 2021, <https://study.com/academy/lesson/mountain-men-history-facts.html>

Ladd, K. 2011, "Three Families of the Old Three Hundred," Stephen F. Austin State University, viewed September 2021, <https://www.sfasu.edu/heritagecenter/3507.asp>

Long, C. 2019, "Old Three Hundred," Handbook of Texas, viewed September 2021, <https://www.tshaonline.org/handbook/entries/old-three-hundred>

Daniels, A. 2018, "Moses Austin's Old 300: Who, What, Why," Midland Reporter Telegram, viewed September 2021, <https://www.mrt.com/news/education/article/Moses-Austin-s-Old-300-Who-What-Why-12765420.php>

Minster, C. 2020, "Biography of Stephen F. Austin, Founding Father of Texan Independence," ThoughtCo, viewed September

2021, <https://www.thoughtco.com/biography-of-stephen-f-austin-2136243>

History.com Editors 2021, "Trail of Tears," A&E Television Networks, viewed September 2021, <https://www.history.com/topics/native-american-history/trail-of-tears>

National Park Service 2020, "What Happened on the Trail of Tears?" National Park Service, viewed September 2021, <https://www.nps.gov/trte/learn/historyculture/what-happened-on-the-trail-of-tears.htm>

Klein, C. 2019, "How Native Americans Struggled to Survive on the Trail of Tears," A&E Television Networks, viewed September 2021, <https://www.nps.gov/trte/learn/historyculture/what-happened-on-the-trail-of-tears.htm>

Anderson, W. L. and Wetmore, R. Y 2006, "Cherokee," NC Pedia, viewed September 2021, <https://www.ncpedia.org/cherokee/origins>

Handbook of Texas 2020, "Cherokee War," Handbook of Texas, viewed September 2021, <https://www.tshaonline.org/handbook/entries/cherokee-war>

History.com Editors 2019, "Manifest Destiny," A&E Television Networks, viewed September 2021, <https://www.history.com/topics/westward-expansion/manifest-destiny>

Bunbury, T. 2018, "What the Irish did for – and to – the Choctaw tribe," Irish Times, viewed September 2021, <https://www.irishtimes.com/culture/heritage/what-the-irish-did-for-and-to-the-choctaw-tribe-1.3423873>

Riggs, E. E. 1916, "The Texas Revolution," Legends of America, viewed September 2021, <https://www.legendsofamerica.com/tx-revolution/>

Weiser-Alexander, K. 2020, "David 'Davy' Crockett – Frontier Hero," Legends of America, viewed September 2021, <https://www.legendsofamerica.com/david-crockett/>

Barker, E. C. and Pohl, J. W. 2021, "Texas Revolution," Handbook of Texas, viewed September 2021, <https://www.tshaonline.org/handbook/entries/texas-revolution>

History.com Editors 2021, "Battle of the Alamo," A&E Television Networks, viewed September 2021, <https://www.history.com/topics/mexico/alamo>

Henson, M. S. 2020, "Anahuac Disturbances," Handbook of Texas, viewed September 2021, <https://www.tshaonline.org/handbook/entries/anahuac-disturbances>

Cox, M. 2018, "A Brief History of the Texas Rangers," Texas Ranger Hall of Fame and Museum, viewed September 2021, <https://www.texasranger.org/texas-ranger-museum/history/brief-history/>

History.com Editors 2019, "Mexican-American War," A&E Television Networks, viewed September 2021, <https://www.history.com/topics/mexican-american-war/mexican-american-war>

Minster, C. 2019, "The Life and Legend of David 'Davy' Crockett," ThoughtCo, viewed September 2021, <https://www.thoughtco.com/biography-of-davy-crockett-2136664>

History.com Editors 2019, "Samuel Colt," A&E Television Networks, viewed September 2021, <https://www.history.com/topics/inventions/samuel-colt>

History.com Editors 2021, "The California Gold Rush," A&E Television Networks, viewed September 2021, <https://www.history.com/topics/westward-expansion/gold-rush-of-1849>

Bell, B. B. 2014, "The Gang Slayer," True West Magazine, viewed September 2021, <https://truewestmagazine.com/the-gang-slayer-1/>

Hernandez, A. 2020, "The Reynolds Gang: Colorado Confederates and Their Buried Treasure," Denver Public Library, viewed September 2021, <https://history.denverlibrary.org/news/reynolds-gang-colorado-confederates-and-their-buried-treasure>

Eberie, J. 2015, "The Reynolds Gang," Colorado Encyclopedia, viewed September 2021, <https://coloradoencyclopedia.org/article/reynolds-gang>

History.com Editors 2021, "Gunfighter Clay Allison Killed," A&E Television Networks, viewed September 2021, <https://coloradoencyclopedia.org/article/reynolds-gang>

Weiser-Alexander, K. 2021, "New Mexico Bad Boy: Clay Allison," Legends of America, viewed September 2021, <https://www.legendsofamerica.com/we-clayallison/>

Metesh, T. L. 2021, "How Western Legend Wild Bill Hickok Died in Deadwood," Free Range American, viewed September 2021, <https://freerangeamerican.us/how-wild-bill-hickok-died/>

Biography.com Editors 2020, "Wild Bill Hickok Biography," A&E Television Networks, viewed September 2021, <https://www.biography.com/personality/wild-bill-hickok>

Kennedy, L. 2020, "5 Legendary Wild West Outlaws," A&E Television Networks, viewed September 2021, <https://www.history.com/news/famous-wild-west-outlaws-billy-the-kid-jesse-james-butch-cassidy>

Weiser-Alexander, K. 2020, "The James-Younger Gang – Terror in the Heartland," Legends of America, viewed September 2021, <https://www.legendsofamerica.com/we-jamesyoungergang/>

Biography.com Editors 2021, "Jesse James Biography," A&E Television Networks, viewed September 2021, <https://www.biography.com/crime-figure/jesse-james>

Nix, E. 2018, "7 Things You May Not Know About Jesse James," A&E Television Networks, viewed September 2021, <https://www.history.com/news/7-things-you-might-not-know-about-jesse-james>

Stanley, M. E. "Anderson, William 'Bloody Bill,'" Civil War on the Western Border, viewed September 2021, <https://civilwaronthewesternborder.org/encyclopedia/anderson-william-%E2%80%9Cbloody-bill%E2%80%9D>

Andrews, E. 2020, "9 Things You May Not Know About Billy the Kid," A&E Television Networks, viewed September 2021, <https://www.history.com/news/9-things-you-may-not-know-about-billy-the-kid>

History.com Editors 2020, "First Train Robbery in U. S. History," A&E Television Networks, viewed September 2021, <https://www.history.com/this-day-in-history/first-u-s-train-robbery>

Israel, D. K. 2010, "10 Great Train Robberies," Mental Floss, viewed September 2021, <https://www.mentalfloss.com/article/25825/10-great-train-robberies>

Weiser, K. 2019, "Belle Starr – The Bandit Queen," Legends of America, viewed September 2021, <https://www.legendsofamerica.com/we-bellestarr/>

Cogburn, B. 2011, "The Bandit Queen's Treasures," True West Magazine, viewed September 2021, <https://truewestmagazine.com/the-bandit-queens-treasures-2/>

Boissneault, L. 2017, "Murder, Marriage and the Pony Express: Ten Things You Didn't Know About Buffalo Bill," Smithsonian Magazine, viewed September 2021, <https://www.smithsonianmag.com/history/murder-marriage-and-

pony-express-10-things-you-didnt-know-about-buffalo-bill-180961736/>

King, G. 2017, "Where the Buffalo No Longer Roamed," Smithsonian Magazine, viewed September 2021, <https://www.smithsonianmag.com/history/where-the-buffalo-no-longer-roamed-3067904/>

History.com Editors 2021, "Murder Ignites Lincoln County War," A&E Television Networks, viewed September 2021, <https://www.history.com/this-day-in-history/murder-ignites-lincoln-county-war>

History.com Editors 2020, "Shootout at the O.K. Corral", A&E Television Networks, viewed September 2021, <https://www.history.com/this-day-in-history/shootout-at-the-ok-corral>

Stuart, M. 2019, "7 Strange Facts About Wyatt Earp and the Gunfight at O.K. Corral," Explore the Archive, viewed September 2021, <https://explorethearchive.com/things-you-didnt-know-about-wyatt-earp-and-the-gunfight-at-the-ok-corral>

Biography.com Editors 2021, "Doc Holliday Biography," A&E Television Networks, viewed September 2021, <https://www.biography.com/personality/doc-holliday>

Nix, E. 2018, "6 Things You Should Know About Wyatt Earp," A&E Television Networks, viewed September 2021, <https://www.history.com/news/6-things-you-should-know-about-wyatt-earp>

Weiser, K. 2019, "Seth Bullock – Finest Type of Frontiersman," Legends of America, viewed September 2021, <https://www.legendsofamerica.com/we-sethbullock/>

Illustration I:
https://commons.wikimedia.org/wiki/File:%22Life_on_the_Plains%22_LCCN2004674924.jpg

Illustration II: by Victor van Werkhooven
https://commons.wikimedia.org/wiki/File:Carte_Lewis_and_Clark_Expedition.png

Illustration III:
https://commons.wikimedia.org/wiki/File:Stephens.jpg

Illustration IV:
https://commons.wikimedia.org/wiki/File:Belle_Starr,_Fort_Smith,_Arkansas,_1886.jpg

Illustration V:
https://commons.wikimedia.org/wiki/File:SethBullock.jpg